ADVANCE PRAISE FOR

Portraits *of* Christ

"Christ is the best of subjects for our study, and Keddie and Whitla helpfully mine the unsearchable riches of Christ through forty biblical pictures of the Savior. Would you like to know Christ as your food, light, shelter, shepherd, and much more? Here is sound doctrine for heartfelt devotion in daily life."
JOEL R. BEEKE, president, Puritan Reformed Theological Seminary, Grand Rapids, Michigan

"Keddie and Whitla have given the Church a beautiful 'portrait gallery' of forty pictures of the Lord Jesus Christ framed in Scripture, mounted on clear exegesis and illuminated with application that is devotionally warm and pastorally wise. As Christ is set forth in each chapter they succeed in doing what any good portrait artist seeks to do: to allow the subject to be gazed upon and admired...."
WARREN PEEL, pastor, Trinity RP Church, Newtownabbey, Northern Ireland professor of New Testament language and literature, Reformed Theological College, Belfast, Northern Ireland

"Here is a book that is—as its title signifies—from beginning to end full of Christ. In it, we read and think of these thrillingly varied pictures of the Son of God: who he is and what he has done, is doing and will do, especially for his people...."
EDWARD DONNELLY, New Testament professor emeritus, Reformed Theological College, Belfast, Northern Ireland (from the foreword)

"This is exactly the devotional that I have been wishing someone would write....Several have tried to provide a deep, but accessible devotional guide to Christology. Whitla and Keddie have actually succeeded. This book will enrich your soul with a fuller knowledge of who

Christ is and how our Reformed tradition has so well read the entirety of Scripture to be about him."
HARRISON PERKINS, assistant minister, London City Presbyterian Church, England

"A foray into most Christian bookstores will yield a host of topical devotionals. Sadly the topic is invariably 'me'; my Bible reading, my prayer life, my relationships, and so on. In their book, *Portraits of Christ*, Keddie and Whitla have done what was so needed. They have produced a devotional book in the tradition of the Puritans that will cause us to meditate on the beauty of the person and work of Jesus Christ. It is biblical, theological, and very pastoral. It will warm the hearts of believers and kindle an ever increasing thanksgiving to the Lord for such a Savior as this."
JEFF KINGSWOOD, senior minister, Grace Presbyterian Church, Woodstock, Ontario

"...In this 'picture album' of Jesus, these two gifted preachers, who enjoyed a blessed season of pulpit partnership, use communion messages to paint on the canvas of our minds the glorious Scriptural descriptions of the Lord. I guarantee that if you begin each of these devotional chapters with prayer to have your eyes opened to see Jesus, you will end the chapter with praise as you look upon Him."
BARRY YORK, president, the Reformed Presbyterian Theological Center, Pittsburgh, Pennsylvania

"In *Portraits of Christ*, Keddie and Whitla expand our understanding of Jesus using the biblical types of Christ in a manner that is accessible and helpful for the modern reader. This is a valuable resource for those studying the doctrine of Christ or for those wanting a devotional aid that focuses on the person and work of our Savior."
KYLE E. SIMS, pastor, First Associate Reformed Presbyterian Church, Lancaster, South Carolina

Portraits *of* Christ

Portraits *of* Christ

Gordon J. Keddie
David G. Whitla

Crown & Covenant Publications
7408 Penn Avenue
Pittsburgh, Pa. 15208
crownandcovenant.com

ISBN: 978-1-943017-35-5
eBook: 978-1-943017-36-2
Library of Congress Control Number: 2020937716

Printed in the United States of America

To the
members and friends
of
Southside Reformed Presbyterian Church, Indianapolis.

2 Thessalonians 1:3:
"We are bound to thank God always for you, brethren,
as it is fitting, because your faith grows exceedingly,
and the love of every one of you all
abounds toward each other..."

Contents

Foreword

Here is a book that is—as its title signifies—from beginning to end full of Christ. In it, we read and think of these thrillingly varied pictures of the Son of God: who he is and what he has done, is doing and will do, especially for his people.

Our longing is to continue to love him intensely and increasingly, becoming ever more like him. These two authors, Gordon Keddie and David Whitla, have for themselves experienced Jesus Christ—first as their Savior on earth, then through his bringing them steadily into an eternal relationship that leads them to become like him more and more. To walk with their beloved Lord has meant, in their case, to have given their lives as pastors—first, feeding the hungry, godly members of their congregation; then, after this, reaching out with the gospel to bring salvation to those not yet converted.

Normally, the preacher of a largely converted congregation will seek to minister effectively to his people by using long, connected series of expository sermons—all from a particular book or theological theme.

This approach is solid, attractive, and enriching! Many a church member has delighted in being built up by an impressive collection of such biblical expositions.

There is, however, a different method of teaching—in some ways more attractive, more compelling: Single messages, built on single themes, and attractive to many hearers. These pictures that Christ has presented of himself show us clearly and simply who he is and what he has done. Anyone can understand their teaching—no matter what background, ability, or age. Such chapters are suitable for non-Christians—pointing them to Christ and their need of him. They are suitable also to Christians, encouraging them to grow more and more in their knowledge of the Savior and, in their joy of service, to walk with him ever constantly.

This book contains forty chapters divided evenly between the two authors. We do not know who wrote which chapter. This too fills us with delight as we find a secure, solid unanimity, though set, at the same time, against an exciting individualism. How surprising, enriching, stimulating all this is! From one God, through one Savior, to his chosen, committed people. What a variety of subjects: Life and light; sun and rain; lamb and lion; hope and truth; physician and prophet; altar and door. And so many more besides, dividing our thinking into pieces, yet holding us together.

The opening words of this lovely, challenging book point us to its ultimate Author, so faithfully obeyed by these authors: "The titles of Christ in the Bible were all given to him by himself, not by us. They are self-disclosures of Christ to his people, not clever ways that human writers 'liked to think about God.' By revealing these names and metaphors, he guides us into right thinking about himself." And the book's closing lines continue to live and call to us, leaving us with both a challenge and a comfort: "But while we live and hear the voice of Jesus calling in the gospel, the way to life is open for the repentant and believing: 'Believe on the Lord Jesus Christ, and you will be saved, you and your household' (Acts 16:31)."

Edward Donnelly
Reformed Theological College, Belfast, Northern Ireland

Preface

We all know, of course, that Jesus was not literally a shepherd, or the door of a sheepfold, any more than we are literally sheep (John 10:2, 7; Heb. 13:20; Isa. 53:6). The apostles Peter, James, and John are called pillars of the church (Gal. 2:9) and each believer is called a "temple" of the Holy Spirit (1 Cor. 6:19), but no one takes all this to mean we are literally buildings or architectural features of buildings. What might otherwise look like a silly use of language, in fact serves to broaden our understanding of Jesus, the apostles, and ourselves. Words used in unusual ways act like prisms that reveal subtler shades of meaning. Figurative language always enriches the communication of the message in a popular and down-to-earth manner that is calculated to attract people who would otherwise have little interest in the subject.

Portraits of Christ seeks to open up something of the rich variety of the figures of speech in both the Old and New Testaments that refer to Jesus. Not by any measure a complete exposition of such portraits of Jesus in the sacred text of Scripture, it does offer a window on a subject that has long suffered from a certain lack of attention.[1] This volume developed from a series of sermons on the theme of "Portraits of Christ" preached over a period of years at the monthly communion services of the Southside Reformed Presbyterian Church in Indianapolis, Indiana, by Pastor Gordon J. Keddie, now retired, and his colleague and successor, Pastor David G. Whitla, now professor of church history at the Reformed Presbyterian Theological Seminary in Pittsburgh, Pennsylvania.

It is worth noting that Scripture employs such "portraits-in-words" to build an image of Jesus in our minds that instructs us as we hasten to that day when we will see him face to face (1 Cor. 13:12). The world, meantime—in disregard of the second commandment—is full of graven and painted images, which merely present artists' imaginations of how Jesus might have looked. These are entirely fictional inventions of human minds that can only plant in our heads pictures of Jesus that God never gave us. Worse still, these lead to unbiblical notions of Christ and even to the veneration of these false images. The richness of the very Word of God, however, paints divinely inspired portraits of Christ in words that feed the soul and fill the heart. Crucially, they also have the promise of the Holy Spirit who will lead the Lord's people evermore deeply into the truth of God and the love of the crucified and risen Christ (John 16:13).

This is a vital aid in preaching the Word of God and communicating the Christian gospel. We have a world to reach with the most important message in all of human history. We should not be surprised that the Bible does not come to us as a spare listing of assorted facts and truths (even if it has, here and there, a few genealogies and some challenging theological and prophetic statements). Scripture is replete with figurative usages drawn from everyday life in Bible times. Even though we are two millennia removed from both the cultural context and the language(s) of those days, the Word of God continues to be perennially fresh as it calls our world to the Lord Jesus Christ.

Scripture is laced with figures of speech that invest its message with a verve that draws and even commands our attention. The Bible's figures of speech, types, emblems, allusions, and parables make the ancient text both immediate and alive in the way that similar figurative language gives movement, variety, and meaning to our everyday conversation. Figurative language speaks to the common man in the common language about the common experiences of life. No wonder, then, that the Bible is a great work of literature. It is, though, literature with a unique plus, for in his Word God speaks to us in the language of the soul about our relationship with him, our life now, and our destiny hereafter.

The most comprehensive study of the wider subject of figurative language in Scripture came from the pen of E. W. Bullinger in his massive reference work of 1898: *Figures of Speech Used in the Bible*.[2] This tome fills some 1,103 pages and catalogs with no fewer than 217 distinct figures of speech in Scripture together with the citation of over 8,000 Scripture verses exemplifying these various usages. It is, however, essentially a vast compendium of lists and definitions and is inevitably short on biblical exposition and practical application. Helpful to the interests of the academic grammarian, it is of marginal usefulness to the public ministry of God's ministers—and still less to the private devotion of God's people.

At the opposite pole, the Anglican Henry Law published five beautifully written and warmly devotional volumes between 1855 and 1877 in which he seeks to show how the gospel is pre-figured in the Pentateuch in the various objects, events, people, prophesies, and teachings that relate to Christ in some way.[3] Among a number of "classic" treatments on the theme of figures of speech about Christ, the most notable are *Christ All and in All* (1660) by the Puritan Ralph Robinson (1614–55),[4] and *Christ All in All* (1691) by another Puritan, Philip Henry (1631–96).[5] A more obscure work is *Horæ solitariæ: Essays on Some Remarkable Names and Titles of Jesus Christ Occurring in the Old Testament* (1776) by Ambrose Serle (1742–1812).[6] C. H. Spurgeon's *Types and Emblems* is another collection of sixteen sermons sampling some of the less-trod paths of Scripture symbolism.[7]

As has already been noted, Scripture employs figures of speech precisely because these make for lively communication. To say, for example, that the Battle of Britain was won by the Royal Air Force in 1940 after 114 days of military operations would be true enough, if rather dull; but to say, as did Winston Churchill, that "This was their finest *hour*!" can still bring tears to British eyes. Jesus uses the same figure of speech when he tells his disciples "the *hour* is coming, and now is, when the dead will hear the voice of the Son of God; and those who hear will live."[8] The hour does not refer to one literal hour in all of history, but rather to a special time or times, whether past, present, or yet future. In Jesus's usage, these are the times when people believe in him and are saved—an hour that is nothing less than the whole course of human history, particularly between the cross and the consummation.[9] Furthermore, Jesus assumes, as do writers and rhetoricians ancient and modern, that their readers and hearers will get the point. They all expect people generally to grasp the intent and application of figurative language, without first—or ever—being able to place each form within the index of finely-tuned technical definitions. Likewise, the aim of this book is not to define and categorize figures of speech as such, but rather to show both how they illumine the person and work of the Lord Jesus Christ, and how they touch our hearts and bless the lives of Christians.

We intuitively recognize when language is figurative and not literal. When for example Christ is described prophetically and metaphorically as "the fountain of living waters," we immediately grasp that he is being spoken of as the source of the also metaphorical "water of life" that flows to eternal life for believers, both now and forevermore. Jesus tells the woman at the well that, "whoever drinks of the water that I shall give him will never thirst. But the water that I shall give him will become in him a fountain of water springing up into everlasting life" (John 4:14; Rev. 21:6; compare with Zech. 13:1 and Jer. 2:13). She knows and we know that he is not attributing salvific powers to the H_2O from that well in Samaria. The word *metaphor* means literally "carry over" and simply says that the "fountain…opened for sin and for uncleanness"

(Zech. 13:1) *represents* that which Christ accomplishes in saving sinners from the corruption and penalty of sin.

Likewise, the several characterizations of Jesus as a door (John 10:9), as light (John 8:12), as the sun (Mal. 4:2), and as a vine (John 15:5), are metaphors in which representative characteristics of these well-known objects "carry over" to Jesus in various aspects of his person and work. Metaphors are so common in our verbal expressions and interactions that the word has become the catch-all term for all figures of speech, whether they are, or are not, metaphors. Figures of speech are about saying "this" is "that," by an unusual and even dramatic concourse of words and meaning.

Scripture also, most significantly, uses figures called *types*—from a Greek root meaning the mark or impression left by a blow. Milton Terry points out that types (and symbols) are "not, properly speaking, figures of speech," but are "figures of thought in which material objects are made to convey vivid spiritual conceptions to the mind."[10] Bullinger catches the distinctiveness of the type from all other figures and symbols when he says that a type is "a figure or ensample of something future and more or less prophetic, called the 'Antitype.'"[11] "A type," says Alexander Stewart, "is a prophecy expressed in symbols." He adds, "It is also an absolute promise. God alone is the author of prophecy. He also gave the promises of salvation, and confirmed them with an oath."[12] A type is, therefore, more than the descriptive device that is a figure of speech.

Terry notes that "the type is always something real, not a fictitious or ideal symbol."[13] Adam, for example, is a type of Jesus, who is the second Adam and antitype of the first Adam (Rom. 5:14). Adam is not a figurative portrait of Christ, and so, with other typical persons in Scripture, is not included in this book of word-pictures. We have, however, included certain *offices* that may be said to be typical—"prophet" (Deut. 8:15), "great high priest" (Heb. 4:14), and "king" (Ps. 2:6)—because they speak to the three-fold office of Christ that is central to the gospel.[14] Each is a prophecy of its antitype, which antitype—Jesus as prophet, priest, and king—is much greater than the original type.

In his recent work *Jesus on Every Page*, David Murray speaks of the need "to restore a sane, yet spiritually edifying typology to the Church to help Christians profit not just from Jesus's prophetic words, but from His prophetic pictures (typology). One problem is that there are so few good modern books on the subject."[15] It is our hope that this volume may in some small measure fill that lacuna. All of these studies seek to exalt the Lord Jesus Christ in his person and work. They are sent out with the prayer that the Lord will bless his Word and draw every reader more closely to himself.

Gordon J. Keddie, Indianapolis, Indiana
David G. Whitla, Pittsburgh, Pennsylvania

Jesus Is Our

Alpha & Omega

I am the Alpha and the Omega, the Beginning and the End.
—Revelation 1:8

READ REVELATION 1:4–8

The titles of Christ in the Bible were all given to him by himself, not by us. They are self-disclosures of Christ to his people, not clever ways that human writers "liked to think about God." By revealing these names and metaphors, he guides us into right thinking about himself. "I am the Alpha and the Omega" is a double metaphor, made up of the first and last letters of the Greek alphabet. The wider context is the book of Revelation, written to encourage the persecuted church by showing Christ's sovereignty over all events and his victory over all her enemies so as to cement her confidence in his power.

The first use of the title is in the immediate context of John's greeting to the seven churches in Asia (Rev. 1:4–8).[1] This begins with a *benediction* to the churches, employing a trinitarian formula, which unfolds from the Father ("Him who is and was and is to come") to the Spirit ("seven Spirits before the throne"),[2] and finally to the Son ("Jesus Christ, the faithful witness, the firstborn from the dead, ruler of the kings of the earth"). This is followed by a *doxology* to Christ focusing on his work of redemption in both past and future and an *affirmation* from Christ himself that tells us who he is and what he has done.

Jesus Is "the Alpha and the Omega"

Jesus's designation as "the Alpha and the Omega" tells us at least three things: he is sovereign, eternal, and unchangeable—all of which are divine attributes.

Jesus is sovereign.

The iconic street-map of Britain's capital is called *London A–Z*, but it includes not just places starting with those two letters, but every street in the *entire* metropolis. Alpha (A) and omega (Ω)—first and last letters of the Greek alphabet—also signify complete comprehensiveness in Jesus Christ and add up to the doctrine that he governs all of human history. He is not just Alpha *and* Omega, but Alpha *through* Omega. He is sovereign over both ends of history, and everything in between. "Nothing lies outside the scope of his sovereignty."[3] He is "the Beginning and the End…the Almighty" (v. 8). He is creator and consummator of the universe. He is supreme administrator of all the affairs of men and angels. He is Lord of the timeline of history. Several things follow:

For one thing, Jesus is not just a player in the story; he is the *omniscient storyteller*. He is its efficient cause; he is the Beginning and the End. He wasn't just there at the beginning; he began it. He won't just be there at the end; he will end it.

He is the *beginning of all*, who created all things: "All things were made through Him, and without Him nothing was made that was made" (John 1:3; compare with Col. 1:15–16).

He is the *end of all*, because he accomplishes the final victory: "Then comes the end, when He delivers the kingdom to God the Father, when He puts an end to all rule and all authority and power.

For He must reign till He has put all enemies under His feet" (1 Cor. 15:24–25).

Finally, he is the end or *goal of all history*: "He is the head of the body, the church, who is the beginning, the firstborn from the dead, that in all things He may have the preeminence" (Col. 1:18). This is the same language as our text: he began all things so that he might be the end of all things. He is, was, and is to come, "the Almighty" (Rev. 1:8). Jesus here applies Isaiah 46:9–10 to himself. Jesus is the speaker, not John, who is merely bearing witness:

> For I am God, and there is no other; I am God, and there is none like Me, declaring the end from the beginning, and from ancient times things that are not yet done, saying, "My counsel shall stand, and I will do all My pleasure."

Let us apply this. Practically, what does this truth mean for you? Is Jesus Christ the goal of your life? Do you want him to have pre-eminence above all else? Is his glory the aim in all your choices and plans? Is his smile what you seek in all your life's activities? Is Jesus more glorified on earth because of you, or less? Do you rest in the sure knowledge that he is sovereign over life's uncertainties and trials? Jesus isn't just a distant "absentee landlord" watching your life randomly unfold itself from afar: he is personally unfolding his plan for you every microsecond of your life. Is Jesus your Alpha and Omega? If so, he gave you life and he will gather you to himself when you breathe your last. Your gravestone, after all, will have two dates on it: *your* Alpha and Omega. Our only comfort can be that Jesus is sovereign over both, and that in him, Omega is not the end.

Jesus is eternal.

As the Alpha and the Omega, Jesus is the one "who is and who was and who is to come" (Rev. 1:8). This explains Jesus's relation to time.

Man strives to beat time. Time can be a good servant, but too often we become its slave. Man is limited. Finite man strives for infinitude. Man is obsessed with the "is, was, and…to come" of his existence on earth. Man in sin strives to possess Alpha and Omega in his knowledge if not in his experience. Think about it: Man desperately tries to prolong the "is" (the present) with things like wrinkle cream, Botox, medicines, supplements, and cryogenics. He hopes to cheat death.

Then there is humankind's search for the "was"—the question of origins. Whether it is heavenly bodies via the Hubble telescope or the so-called "god-particle" from the European Council for Nuclear Research (CERN) in Switzerland, man is always searching for the age of universe and where we came from.

Man's quest for the "to come" is the question of destiny. What comes after death? What is the future of the planet? The obsessions of our time are global warming, nuclear war, asteroids, and end of the world disaster movies.

But it is all in vain. Why? The answer to our search is Jesus Christ. "But you, Bethlehem Ephrathah, though you are little among the thousands of Judah, yet out of you shall come forth to Me the One to be Ruler in Israel, whose goings forth are from of old, from everlasting" (Mic. 5:2). Yes, his incarnation through Mary took place in time-and-space history in Bethlehem; but he is "from everlasting."[4] Only he is eternal, and only he can provide both the knowledge and experience of eternal life. Think about it:

He preceded all things; he that created all could not be a part of the "created all." He that is the beginning has no beginning.[5] Jesus is pre-existent: "In the beginning was the Word, and the Word was with God, and the Word was God. He was in the beginning with God" (John 1:1–2).[6] He that is the Beginning has no beginning; he that is the End has no ending himself.

Christ is not bound by the constraints of time. But you are bound by time—its constraints, waiting periods, uncertainties, and brevity. Are you facing a period of waiting—for a job, or a medical result, or for a rebellious child? What difference does it make to you that you have a friend who is Alpha and Omega and is not hampered by these limitations but has carefully planned the end from the beginning; and who takes you by the hand and says "do not worry about tomorrow" (Matt. 6:34)? The eternal Jesus offers you eternal life: "I give them eternal life, and they shall never perish; neither shall anyone snatch them out of My hand" (John 10:28). A finite physician may extend your finitude but no more: a human surgeon may be able to extend your days, but life beyond death is not his to give. No one but Christ can promise life beyond the grave eternally with a new body. Is this your hope?

Jesus is unchangeable.

Jesus Christ is "the same yesterday, today, and forever" (Heb. 13:8).[7] Alpha and Omega means he "is and...was and...is to come, the Almighty"—a title he shares with his Father (compare with Rev. 1:4).[8] This is an expansion of Exodus 3:14: "I am that I am."[9] He is Alpha and Omega and always has been. This title does not mean that the Son of God has been developing in a process throughout time. He is the great unmoved and fixed mark, the unchanged Absolute: "For I am the LORD, I do not change; therefore you are not consumed, O sons of Jacob" (Mal. 3:6). This is a comforting truth for believers. His purposes are fixed and will never end. He will keep his covenant with you. He will never change his mind nor "leave you nor forsake you" (Heb. 13:5).

Jesus Is "the Alpha and the Omega" for You

Jesus's titles instruct us as to who he is, but also inform us about his redemptive work. Alpha and Omega is a redemptive title indicating that his redemptive work is present, past, and future. Revelation 1:5–7 provide a neat summary of this, showing how his redemptive work as the Alpha and Omega "who is and who was and who is to come" is connected to you:

His redemptive work in the present.

John begins with the present exalted state of Christ in glory at the Father's right hand. He is "the faithful witness, the firstborn from the dead, and the ruler over the kings of the earth" (v. 5). The *Shorter Catechism*, Question 23, notes that "Christ, as our Redeemer, executes the offices of a prophet, of a priest, and of a king, both in his estate of humiliation and exaltation." This is exactly what John teaches us here.

"The faithful witness" addresses his prophetic work. He bears witness to himself as Savior: "If I bear witness of Myself, My witness is true, for I know where I came from and where I am going" (John 8:14). His witness is true because of "where he came from (Alpha) and where he is going (Omega)."[10] He is the eternal God who cannot lie. He bears witness to you daily in his Word.[11]

"The firstborn from the dead" speaks to his priestly work. He offered himself as a sacrifice for sin, was raised from the dead, and presently lives to intercede for you whom he will also raise. He is thus firstborn in pre-eminence and also in order as surety for those whom he will similarly raise when he comes.

The "ruler of the kings of the earth" proclaims his kingly work. He rules over you—and over those who rule over you. What encouragement to the persecuted churches! Jesus rules over nations because he is firstborn from the dead (Col. 1:18; compare with Eph. 1:22).

His redemptive work in the past.

In Revelation 1:5–6, John next calls us to consider Christ's accomplishing salvation in his state of humiliation. He has loved us, even "before the foundation of the world" (John 17:24). He loved us when we were "dead in trespasses," and he has "made us alive" (Eph. 2:4–5). He is the "author and finisher of our faith" (Heb. 12:2). And how did he prove his love? Christ "washed us from our sins in His own blood" (Rev. 1:5). This was the cost of your liberty. The word "washed" (NKJV) may be rendered "freed" (ESV, NIV). Calvary is the apex of his redemptive work. For your sins to be washed away, his blood had to be spilled by a violent death. His cry, "It is finished" assures us that the rest of his redemptive work in your experience will be accomplished as well.

Christ has "made us kings and priests to His God and Father" (v. 6). Here is the promise made to Israel, a special people to God, at Sinai in Exodus 19:6 and now applied to the Church: you are kings because you reign with Christ, the "ruler over the kings of the earth," and priests because you each have access to God through his blood.

To summarize, *Christ is the Beginning and the End of your salvation*. He is the Alpha of election and the Omega of glorification, and every step of the order of salvation in between, whether regeneration, justification, adoption or sanctification (see Phil. 1:6). No wonder John cries out in Revelation 1:6, "To Him be glory and dominion forever and ever. Amen" (compare with Ps. 110:1–2).

His redemptive work in the future.

John finally presents us with the glorious return of Christ to gather believers and condemn unbelievers. Both are redemptive acts: raising and perfecting his people in glory and finally destroying all his and their enemies. The phrase in Revelation 1:7, "Behold, He is coming with clouds," employs a common Old Testament image of God coming in splendor and power (e.g., Ezek. 1; Dan. 9).

> Then the sign of the Son of Man will appear in heaven, and then all the tribes of the earth will mourn, and they will see the Son of Man coming on the clouds of heaven with power and great glory. And He will send His angels with a great sound of a trumpet, and they will gather together His elect from the four winds, from one end of heaven to the other. (Matt. 24:30–31)

Just as God came down upon Sinai in clouds and thick darkness to give the law, so shall Christ return to judge those who break it.

Furthermore, "every eye will see him" (Rev. 1:7), for it will be as public as possible. There will be no secret raptures. "Even they who pierced Him" will see Christ coming (Rev. 1:7; citing Zech. 12:10). He is coming for his enemies too, and that means not just those who actually crucified him, but all those who have likewise scornfully rejected Jesus as their King. If you will not cry "Crown Him, Crown Him!" then you have effectively cried "Crucify Him, Crucify Him!" (see Heb. 6:6). No unbeliever will escape the notice of the omnipotent Alpha and Omega and avoid his certain and sudden appearing to judge. And what will he judge? Your sins that you love. But that is yet "to come." In the meantime, Christ sincerely offers to "wash [you] from your sins in His own blood," and so to make you "kings and priests to his God and Father" (Rev. 1:5–6). If you find yourself judged, there is no other reason but that you willfully refused his offer of forgiveness (Heb. 10:30–31).

Finally, "All the tribes of the earth will mourn because of Him" (Rev. 1:7). His enemies will melt with fear. It will be too late then. This lament will be the first note of a chorus of mourning that will last forever. Will you be among them? Mourning with the tribes or rejoicing with your conquering king, the Alpha and Omega, with whom you shall be seated on thrones as kings and priests? "Finally, there is laid up for me the crown of righteousness, which the Lord, the righteous Judge, will give to me on that Day, and not to me only but also to all who have loved His appearing" (2 Tim. 4:8). What will you wear at his appearing? Crown or curse? Will you experience coronation or condemnation (Rev. 5:9–10)?

> Then He who sat on the throne said, "Behold, I make all things new." And He said to me, "Write, for these words are true and faithful." And He said to me, "It is done! I am the Alpha and the Omega, the Beginning and the End. I will give of the fountain of the water of life freely to him who thirsts. He who overcomes shall inherit all things, and I will be his God and he shall be My son." (Rev. 21:5–7)

Jesus Is Our

Altar

We have an altar...
—Hebrews 13:10

READ HEBREWS 13:10–14

We humans have a knack of turning the best of things into the most incredible superstitions. Church buildings and other sites become "holy places" and people imagine they are blessed by making "pilgrimages" to them. There are whole industries in so-called sacred places and their associated paraphernalia, such as water from the River Jordan and the like. Even the Bible, which is the Word of God, can be treated like a lucky charm. I knew a lady who said she felt naked without a Bible in her purse, although I have no reason to believe she ever read it. It is as if the thing in itself somehow emanated a special gift of God's goodness. This is, of course, a fantasy and a mere illusion of blessing.

The same thing happened with the Old Testament sacrifices and ceremonies. What were designed to point to a yet future Savior became perverted into the very means of salvation. So also with the Old Testament law, as Charles Simeon observes: "The Jews gloried in their law, and were with great difficulty brought to renounce their reliance on it for salvation."[1] This is why the letter to the Hebrews closes by returning to the superiority of Christ and the gospel over all that preceded and foreshadowed them. The writer emphasizes that Christ is our altar and our salvation—the Savior whom we are to follow all our days.

Christ Is Our Altar

There were no altars or animal sacrifices in the worship of the New Testament church. Imagine how that impacted a Jew at a time when the Temple still functioned. Standing upon his biblical heritage, he could look at the Church and say: "There's something missing—you have no altar and no sacrifices for sin." This begs the question as to why there was a physical altar and blood sacrifices in the Old Testament in the first place.

The answer is that this was the heart of the Old Testament sacrificial system—the bridge to God and the place of acceptance and forgiveness. In the sacrificial system, no altar meant no sacrifice, and therefore no forgiveness of sin and no reconciliation to God. So where would reconciliation with God come from? What were the Christians to say to this? The writer to the Hebrews answers that there is indeed a New Testament altar. "We have" he writes, "an altar from which those who serve the tabernacle have no right to eat" (13:10–11).

The priests could not eat certain sacrifices.

To grasp what he is saying, we will first have to understand the distinction that he is drawing between Old Testament sacrifices that the priests could eat and those they could not. The priests in the Old Testament could eat certain portions of the animal sacrifices and cereal offerings (Lev. 6:16; 7:6, 15, 31; compare with 1 Cor. 9:13 and 10:18). What the priests could not eat was meat from the sin offerings where blood was taken and sprinkled either on the altar or in the Holy of Holies on the Day of Atonement (Lev. 4:11ff.; 16:14). This meat was to be burned "outside the camp," thereby establishing a symbolic removal of sin from God's people (Lev. 16:27; Heb. 13:11).

The church does have an altar.

The New Testament Church has an altar and a sacrifice of the same order—that is, a sacrifice of the kind the Old Testament priests could not eat, namely, an atonement for sin. It is not a literal altar, of course, although it is a real sacrifice—and that altar and sacrifice is Jesus. The writer already pointed out that the earthly Tabernacle altar is only a copy of the heavenly one: that Christ is the one fulfilling the offering for sin (Heb. 9:23–28). Christ is the substance of which the blood sacrifices are the foreshadowing. Accordingly, the writer to the Hebrews compares the ineffectual animal sacrifices with Jesus, who is the one and only effectual sacrifice for sin (Heb. 10:4, 10). This underscores that, in the New Testament, we have the true altar in Jesus Christ himself: "this Man, after He had offered one sacrifice for sins forever, sat down at the right hand of God" (Heb. 10:12).

Believers now partake of Christ's sacrifice.

The difference is that, unlike the Old Testament priests, New Testament believers actually partake of this once-for-all sacrifice of Christ. We do feed on him and we are made a holy priesthood of believers (1 Peter 2:5). There is more: we do something the Old Testament priests *never* did. We spiritually drink the blood of the sacrifice—the crucified Savior. Jesus explains this to us:

> "I am the living bread which came down from heaven. If anyone eats of this bread, he will live forever; and the bread that I shall give is My flesh, which I shall give for the life of the world."
>
> The Jews therefore quarreled among themselves, saying, "How can this Man give us His flesh to eat?"
>
> Then Jesus said to them, "Most assuredly, I say to you, unless you eat the flesh of the Son of Man and drink His blood, you have no life in you. Whoever eats My flesh and drinks My blood has eternal life, and I will raise him up at the last day. For My flesh is food indeed, and

> My blood is drink indeed. He who eats My flesh and drinks My blood abides in Me, and I in him." (John 6:51–56)

But how can we "eat" Jesus's flesh and "drink" Jesus's blood?

How does this happen? How do believers eat and drink the sacrifice which is Christ? Jesus already told us just a few verses earlier: "he who comes to Me shall never hunger, and he who believes in Me shall never thirst" (John 6:35). Coming to Christ is the same as believing in him—personally, as Savior and Lord. In believing in Jesus Christ, we feed upon the Savior who has saved us by his grace and to whom we are committed by faith. Paul enjoins us,

> Therefore purge out the old leaven, that you may be a new lump, since you truly are unleavened. For indeed Christ, our Passover, was sacrificed for us. Therefore let us keep the feast, not with old leaven, nor with the leaven of malice and wickedness, but with the unleavened bread of sincerity and truth. (1 Cor. 5:7–8)

Christ is your altar in constant and continuing Christian experience, Christian, because he is your life in virtue of his broken body and shed blood (Col. 3:4).

Christ Is Our Sanctification

Just as the Old Testament sin offerings were burned outside the camp, "therefore Jesus also, that he might sanctify the people with his own blood, suffered outside the gate" (Heb. 13:12; see Lev. 16:27). Why outside the camp or gate? Because this vividly demonstrates what Charles Simeon has called God's "indignation against sin"[2] and shows that apart from a real atonement for sin, there can be no salvation, only the fires of God's perfect justice. But there is a twist.

Jesus's death is outside the gate, whereas the animals died inside the Tabernacle. Now, if you were a Jew and "outside the camp," you were ceremonially unclean. You therefore needed ceremonial cleansing to come back into the camp of Israel (Lev. 16:26, 28). You see, *inside* is holy ground symbolizing acceptance with God, whereas *outside* is unholy, symbolizing separation from God. This means that Jesus dies in unholy ground—"outside the camp"—*unlike* all the Old Testament animal sacrifices. This is an astonishing reversal. What does it mean? It means at least three things.

First, it means that Jesus totally identifies with the world's sin, guilt, pollution, and alienation from God by going outside the camp, to the place that signifies estrangement from God under his righteous judgment against sin. Hence the words of a well-known hymn by C. F. Alexander:

> There is a green hill far away
>   without a city wall,
> Where the dear Lord was crucified,
>   Who died to save us all.

We may put it another way: we are by nature outside the camp and Jesus comes to us where we are in the place and condition of the need of a Savior. Jesus reaches into our life and our alienation from God.

Second, and following on from this, is the fact that Jesus actually becomes "sin for us, that we might become the righteousness of God in Him" (2 Cor. 5:21). God "made Him who knew no sin to be sin." As our substitute sin-bearer, he is able to save and sanctify us, so that what is unholy is made holy before God.

Finally, Jesus saves by grace through faith. In the Old Testament, there was no apportionment of the sin offering—no right to feed on it on account of being inside the camp (i.e., observing the law). Compare this to Paul in Philippians 3:8–9 when he testifies,

> I also count all things loss for the excellence of the knowledge of Christ Jesus my Lord, for whom I have suffered the loss of all things, and count them as rubbish, that I may gain Christ and be found in Him, not having my own righteousness, which is from the law, but that which is through faith in Christ, the righteousness which is from God by faith.

Jesus's passive obedience, dying on the cross in suffering the penalty of sin, atones for the sin of sinners and secures forgiveness. His active obedience, living a life of perfect righteousness, secures the justification of the forgiven by giving to them his unblemished righteousness in place of their very blemished unrighteousness. He was "delivered up because of our offenses, and was raised because of our justification" (Rom. 4:25). Christ, our altar, makes his people holy before his heavenly Father and ours.

Christ Is Our Life

Christ dies "outside the gate." He comes to the sinner where he *really* is—"beyond the pale" of God's offended righteousness, alienated from and unacceptable to a holy God. And he bears the penalty of sin—*our* reproach—and secures forgiveness of sin for all who trust in him. How then are we to apply this?

The answer is that as Christ united himself to our reproach and saves us by his death and resurrection, we must unite ourselves to him in his reproach (Heb. 13:13–14). Jesus's reproach is that "He [was] despised and rejected by men, a man of sorrows and acquainted with grief" (Isa. 53:3). In giving himself to the cross and its shame, he has become our life—having given us new life; and our portion—having given us himself as our companion and inheritance (Ps. 16:5). We are, in consequence, united to him in both "the power of His resurrection, and the fellowship of His sufferings" (Phil. 3:10). This has very practical implications for Christian experience.

We are called to follow Jesus.

"Therefore let us go forth to Him" (Heb. 13:13) is gloriously evocative, but what does it mean in practice? It means at least three things:

First, following Christ means *taking God's Word seriously* in daily life—thought, word, and deed. Psalm 119:57 testifies, "You are my portion, O Lord; I have said that I would keep Your words." "If you love

Me," says Jesus, "keep My commandments" (John 14:15). This also means, of course, not returning to Old Testament "weak and beggarly elements" that are now fulfilled in Jesus's person and work (Gal. 4:9). No legalisms. No ceremonies. No dietary rules. No earning salvation by performance. We do not obey God's law to be saved, but we are saved by God's grace in Christ in order to obey him freely.

This also implies being *separate from the world*: "Come out from among them and be separate, says the Lord. Do not touch what is unclean, and I will receive you" (2 Cor. 6:17). Jesus has sent you—his followers—"into the world" (John 17:18). You are, however, "not of the world, just as [Jesus is] not of the world" (v. 16). That is why he says to his heavenly Father and yours, "I do not pray that You should take them out of the world, but that You should keep them from the evil one" (v. 15). Our separation to him is spiritual, moral and ethical. We are here to be his witnesses, calling others to him.

Furthermore, following Jesus involves *a certain cost*. Jesus is perfectly honest on this point. "A disciple is not above his teacher, nor a servant above his master" (Matt. 10:24). "If anyone desires to come after Me, let him deny himself, and take up his cross, and follow Me" (Matt. 16:24). Your "cross" is not, as is popularly and erroneously assumed, the disappointments and disabilities that come in the course of almost every life—troubles with health, jobs, relationships, and the like. These are common to humankind. Rather it is the cost of being openly and consistently faithful to the Lord, which may indeed affect health, jobs, relationships, and life itself. "Bearing His reproach" means sharing the reproaches heaped on Jesus (Heb. 13:13). There is a very real "fellowship of His sufferings" (Phil. 3:10; compare to Moses in Heb. 11:26). Following Jesus is a serious business.

We are given compelling reasons for following Jesus.

Biblical faith is neither blind nor irrational. Jesus advances two cogent reasons for continuing to follow him.

Negatively, we are persuaded that "here we have no continuing city" (Heb. 13:14). We cannot be tied to Jerusalem, Rome or where we were born, where we presently live, or where we might like to retire or be buried. The truth is that as God's Kingdom comes and our life in this world goes—inexorably one day at a time—we are increasingly aware that "the form of this world is passing away" (1 Cor. 7:31).

Positively, we are looking to a different world: "we seek the one to come" (Heb. 13:14). It is "the city which has foundations," our eternal "homeland" and "heavenly country" (Heb. 11:10, 14, 16). The Christians' ultimate country is Jesus's "New Jerusalem, which comes down out of heaven"—his church and kingdom consummated in that "glory which shall be revealed" (Rev. 3:12; Rom. 8:18; 1 Peter 4:13; 5:1).

New life and heavenly glory are inextricably intertwined, for, as Paul says, "When Christ who is our life appears, then you will also appear with Him in glory" (Col. 3:4). How so? Christ is every believer's altar and sacrifice, and therefore every believer's eternal life, both on earth now and in heaven hereafter. In coming to him in faith as your Savior, "you died, and your life is hidden with Christ in God" (v. 3).

Do you know Jesus as your altar and once-for-all sacrifice? Then continue in union and communion with him, testifying with the apostle Paul, "God forbid that I should boast except in the cross of our Lord Jesus Christ, by whom the world has been crucified to me, and I to the world" (Gal. 6:14).

Jesus Is Our

Apostle

Consider the Apostle and High Priest of our confession, Christ Jesus.
—Hebrews 3:1

READ HEBREWS 3:1–6

The book of Hebrews was written to suffering Jewish converts who were contemplating a return to Judaism. The writer, therefore, points them to the superiority of Christ over the Old Testament economy. After a series of examples in which Jesus has been exalted as God's final Word to man (1:1–2), the creator of the worlds (1:2), greater than angels (1:5), the last Adam (2:5–9) and the captain of salvation (2:10–18), the writer now makes one of the boldest statements imaginable to a Hebrew ear: that Jesus of Nazareth is greater even than Moses. He backs up this remarkable contention by employing a most intriguing title for our Lord: "The apostle and High Priest of our confession, Christ Jesus" (3:1). To understand it, we need to consider the whole passage of Hebrews 3:1–6, where we find the *sender*, the *recipient*, and the apostle *himself*.

The Sender

"Consider the apostle!" the writer urges. To do so, we must first understand what this term actually means. The Greek word "apostle" (*apostolos*) is derived from the verb *apostello*, which means "to send with a commission, to send with authority, to send for a purpose."[1] So, simply put, an apostle is a "sent one." While Jesus conferred this title on his twelve disciples (see Luke 6:13), this is the only place in the Bible that it is conferred upon him, though he made it quite clear that his appointing *them* as apostles was analogous to his *own* having been sent: "Peace to you! As the Father has sent Me, I also send you" (John 20:21). Indeed, Jesus often described himself as the sent one, by using the same root verb:

* John 5:30: "I do not seek My own will but the will of the Father *who sent Me.*"
* John 5:36: "... the very works that I do bear witness of Me, that the Father *has sent Me.*"
* John 6:44: "No one can come to Me unless the Father *who sent Me* draws him..."
* John 8:18: "The Father *who sent Me* bears witness of Me."
* John 8:29: "...and *He who sent Me* is with Me." (Italics added throughout.)

This unmistakable pattern shows an intimate connection between the sent one and the sender, which means this apostle is also an *ambassador*. He *represents* the sender, and performs and proclaims whatever the sender has commanded him; thus our text tells us Jesus "was faithful to Him who appointed Him" (Heb. 3:2).

Whenever a new government comes to power, it makes *appointments* of certain individuals to certain tasks. A wise king or prime minister will select the right man for the right job, matching the nature, difficulty and scope of the task with the ability, strength, and experience of his appointee. This done, he will *send him* with all his authority to carry out his mission. In the same way, God the Father has an astounding task for his apostle: Adam has fallen and led our race into rebellion against its Maker. Who could God possibly *send* to atone for their guilt, to woo them back to trust him and live for him? Who indeed? "The apostle and High Priest of our confession, Christ Jesus;" which is really another way of saying, Jesus is our apostle *in order to be* our High Priest. He was sent by God so that he might be slain for our salvation.

Behold the love of the sender! Never wrong the Father by imagining him as an enraged deity thirsting for your damnation, forced begrudgingly to save you through his Son's appeasement. Rather, Hebrews 3:2 says that *God* is "[He] who *appointed* Him." Thus the mission on which the Father sent Jesus as apostle commends itself to your thoughtful "consideration" (v. 1), you who are the *receiver* of God's apostle.

The Receiver

If the *sender* of the apostle is God, then the *receiver* is the Church, God's people, who are given three specific titles in Hebrews 3:1–6. If you have received Jesus, God's apostle, then you are:

Holy brethren. In verse 11 of the previous chapter we are told that "He is not ashamed to call [you] brethren." In other words, God's apostle has become your Elder Brother, thereby making you "*holy* brethren," set apart to God.

Partakers of a heavenly calling. Your calling to be a Christian is "heavenly," because it originated in heaven with the sender (see 2 Tim. 1:9), and also because it is a call *to* heaven. The apostle of God has come from heaven to earth to call you from earth to heaven (see Phil. 3:14).

God's House. This is the most significant of the three titles for the receiver of God's apostle, found in verses 2–6 of our passage, and a total of 14 times in this entire chapter. If we want to "consider the apostle," then we must grasp the meaning of this important metaphor, which is so central to the argument of the passage. A "house" can refer in Scripture to a literal physical dwelling (see v. 4), but here it refers to a people or family (as in "the house of David"). In other words, the "*house* of God" means the *people* of God, the *family* of God, and the Church "whose house we are if we hold fast [our] confidence" (v. 6). This is also how Peter and Paul explain it: "You also, as living stones, are being built up a spiritual house, a holy priesthood, to offer up spiritual sacrifices acceptable to God through Jesus Christ" (1 Peter 2:5); "I write so that you may know how you ought to conduct yourself in the house of God, which is the church of the living God, the pillar and ground of the truth" (1 Tim. 3:15).

So the receiver of the apostle is the Church; the house of God, which is peopled with "holy brethren," each "partakers of a heavenly calling."

The Apostle

Now that we've identified all the components of the text (God as the *sender* of the apostle, and the *house* of God as the *receiver* of the apostle) we're in a better position to "consider the apostle" himself (Heb. 3:1). All three characters in God's great story of redemption come together in verses 1 through 4—the sender, the receiver, and the apostle:

> ...Christ Jesus, who was faithful to Him who appointed Him, as Moses also was faithful in all His house. For this One has been counted worthy of more glory than Moses, inasmuch as He who built the house has more honor than the house. For every house is built by someone, but He who built all things is God.

Clearly then, God's plan is to build a house. And as with any architect, God in the counsels of eternity drew up a plan, which is awesome in its scope (sometimes called the "Covenant of Redemption").[2] A house doesn't just appear; it must be planned, and the grander the structure, the greater the planning, cost and time to construct.

Likewise, God's house is built in two stages throughout redemptive history. In the Old Testament, it is the *house of Israel,* whom God set apart and redeemed from Pharaoh by hand of his Old Testament apostle, Moses. In the New Testament, it is the *Church*, comprising both Jews and Gentiles, whom God sets apart and redeems from Satan by the hand of his New Testament apostle Jesus Christ.

It is important to understand that there are not *two* houses, but *one only*. God's house is not divided; Israel is not "plan A" and the New Testament Church "plan B." Rather, there are two stages of God's single master plan, which the inspired writer says correspond to the two great biblical apostles, Moses and Christ. Both were sent to be "faithful over God's house," but only one is worthy of your worship (vv. 5–6 NIV). So let's join the Author as he compares them—Moses and Christ—and shows the Hebrews (and us) that however great Moses was in God's house, *our* apostle Christ is far more worthy of our consideration.

Moses, God's Old Testament apostle.

The Hebrews revered Moses greatly, and the writer, sensitive to his audience, also esteems him highly: In chapter three, he says that Moses was faithful, was glorious, was a faithful servant, and was "a testimony of those things which would be spoken afterwards" (vv. 2–3, 5). The great Old Testament apostle proved "faithful in all [God's] House" (v. 2) in at least the following roles:

Moses was a prophet with a unique relationship to God. The text cites Numbers 12:6–8: "If there is a prophet among you, I, the LORD, make Myself known to him in a vision; I speak to him in a dream. Not so with My servant Moses; He is faithful in all My house. I speak with him face to face, even plainly, and not in dark sayings" (see also Deut. 18:15–18). Moses also served God as a priest. Psalm 99:6–7: "Moses and Aaron were among His priests…they kept His testimonies and the ordinance He gave them" (see also Ex. 24:8). Moreover, Moses functioned as a kingly ruler and redeemer, as Stephen explained to the Sanhedrin in Acts 7:35 (ESV): "This Moses…God sent as both ruler and redeemer by the hand of the angel who appeared to him in the bush" (see also Deut. 33:4–5).

In sum, "Moses indeed was faithful in all His house as a servant, for a testimony of those things which would be spoken afterward" (Heb. 3:5). And exactly what "things that would be spoken afterwards" did Moses typify? The answer is, the gospel preached to the world by God's New Testament apostle, Jesus! As Paul explains to another Hebrew audience in Acts 26:22–23, "to this day I stand...saying no other things than those which the prophets *and Moses said would come*—that the Christ would suffer, that He would be the first to rise from the dead, and would proclaim light to the Jewish people and to the Gentiles" (italics added).

So Moses, God's servant, was "faithful in all God's house" in his prophetic, priestly, and king-like roles, and as such points us to Christ and the gospel.[3] He too was an "apostle"—sent by God at the burning bush to redeem God's house from slavery (Ex. 3:10). This is high praise for Moses. But for all this, he is still only a *type*: a foreshadowing of the reality. However faithful and glorious Moses's apostleship was, Jesus leaves him far behind.

Jesus, God's New Testament apostle.

If God's apostle, Jesus of Nazareth, truly is greater than God's apostle Moses, what did he do for God's house that was so great? Hebrews 3:3 explains, "For this One has been counted worthy of more glory than Moses, inasmuch as He who built the house has more honor than the house."

Jesus is the faithful house-builder. Christ was faithful too, but in a far superior way. For one thing, Jesus was faithful from the beginning, whereas Moses had put up a fight: "But [Moses] said, 'Oh, my Lord, please send someone else'" (Ex. 4:13 ESV). Contrast the reluctant apostle of the Old Testament with the willing apostle of the New, who said: "For I have come down from heaven, not to do My own will, but the will of Him who sent Me" (John 6:38; compare with Ps. 40:7–9). Furthermore, Jesus is worthy of more honor because he himself is the divine builder of the house, and "He who built the house has more honor than the house" (Heb. 3:3). Moses was merely a *servant* within the house, not its divine builder, and just to reinforce that Christ is on an altogether different level than his predecessor, he adds, "for every house is built by someone, but He who built all things is God" (v. 4). God, the great architect, "built" the universe by "His Son...through whom also He made the worlds" (Heb. 1:2); that makes Christ superior to Moses because he is the agent of both creation and redemption—God *through Christ* created the worlds; God *through Christ* redeems his people and builds a house.

Jesus is the faithful Son. If Moses bore a unique relationship to God, then Christ did infinitely more so: Hebrews 3:5–6 says, "Moses indeed was faithful in all His house as a servant...but Christ as a Son over His own house." Notice, Moses was a servant in the house; Jesus is a Son over it. Certainly, Moses had an elevated position; he was personally sent as an apostle by God, he shared a special intimacy with God, and yet for all this, was still but a mere resident of the house, like you and me.

In contrast, Jesus is the master of the house; he is the only-begotten Son who inherits the estate, and is worthy of greater honor by far, just as the heir apparent of the palace is far superior to its butler. It would fall to another servant in the house, King David, to receive from God a much clearer preview of this heir apparent in 1 Chronicles 17:11–14 (NIV):

> I will raise up your offspring to succeed you, one of your own sons, and I will establish his kingdom. He is the one who will build a house for me, and I will establish his throne forever. I will be his father, and he will be my son...I will set him over my house and my kingdom forever; his throne will be established forever.[4]

This once heir apparent is none other than the presently-ruling King, Jesus Christ our apostle.

Practical Application

We have learned from this complex passage that God is the *sender*, and the Church the *receiver* of Jesus Christ who is the *apostle* superior to Moses. But if you're tempted to view this passage as merely doctrinal and academic, bereft of any heart-warming application, remember that the writer says he included this metaphor of Christ the apostle and its comparison with Moses for your devotional attention: "consider the Apostle and High Priest of our confession, Christ Jesus!" (Heb. 3:1). There is an application.

For your meditation: Do you set aside time regularly to think about what Jesus your apostle has done for you? The Word of God exhorts you to consider the apostle; or as the NIV has it, "fix your thoughts on" him—meditate deeply upon, think carefully about, seek to better understand him. John Brown comments,

> This is a duty of radical importance to Christians. It is because we think so little, and to so little purpose, on Christ, that we know so little about Him, that we love Him so little, trust in Him so little, so often neglect our duty, are so much influenced by things "seen and temporal" and so little by "things unseen and eternal."[5]

For your witness: Is Christ the apostle of your confession? To confess is "to make a formal, public declaration;"[6] in other words, Jesus's apostleship is a truth to be proclaimed openly to the world. So if he is *your* apostle, do you tell others about him? As the Father has sent him, so he also sends you. And you possess the best news this world has ever heard: that Jesus has been commissioned to rescue men and women, boys and girls from sin, and establish a relationship with his sender. To this day, Christ is still building the house, and many must yet be added to his household, but in order for this to happen, Jesus must be the apostle of your confession. Is he?

For your self-examination: The author closes this section with a challenge for every one of us. Hebrews 3:6 reads, "whose house we are if we hold fast the confidence and the rejoicing of the hope firm to the end." In that little word "if" lies the test of your household residence. Are you holding fast the confidence and the rejoicing of the hope that Christ brings in the gospel, or are you instead holding fast to the works of the law—your own efforts? Or to put it another way, which apostle do you belong to: Christ or Moses? The Pharisees boasted: "You are

His disciple, but we are Moses' disciples" (John 9:28). Whose disciple are you? The apostle of the Old Testament, or the superior apostle of the New? May you "consider the Apostle and High Priest of our confession, *Christ Jesus*," because "the law was given through Moses, but grace and truth came through Jesus Christ" (John 1:17).

Jesus Is Our

Banner

And in that day there shall be a Root of Jesse,
who shall stand as a banner to the people.
—Isaiah 11:10

READ ISAIAH 11

Visitors to Fort McHenry in Baltimore, Maryland, will know that in the movie presentation at the Visitor Center, the US Naval Academy Choir sings the national anthem while the titles roll. As this powerful rendition rises to a crescendo, the curtain draws back on the window wall—and there is the fort with a huge "Stars and Stripes" flag flapping in the breeze. It is the most electric patriotic moment this writer ever witnessed in his many years in the USA. It is truly a goosebump special! Behind it, of course, is the historic defense of Fort McHenry against British attack in the War of 1812. Francis Scott Key's words, "our flag was still there," tells you a great deal about what the sight of that flag did for his spirits. As he stood, a prisoner, on the deck of a British warship, it stirred within him the hope of an American victory. And he was not to be disappointed.

There is something of this sentiment in our text, in its description of Jesus to be "a banner to the people." In context, Judah was threatened by the Assyrian Empire, which had already gobbled up the ten northern tribes—Israel as opposed to Judah. God's Word to his remnant people was to promise that Assyria would be destroyed and that they would be given a deliverer from the family of Jesse, the father of David. This "Root of Jesse" is the then future Messiah, who is none other than Jesus Christ. Paul shows this in his quoting this very verse in the New Testament: "And again, Isaiah says: 'There shall be a root of Jesse; and He who shall rise to reign over the Gentiles, in Him the Gentiles shall hope'" (Rom. 15:12).

Messiah's Advent

God's promise is that "in that day"—that future day of deliverance—"there shall be a Root of Jesse, who shall stand as a banner to the people" (Isa. 11:10). Notice the two closely related images here: one is the *root* (of Jesse) and the other is the *banner* (to the people). The root sprouts into a banner—and both refer to the Messiah, for he is *the* root that grows into a banner.

How is the Messiah the root of Jesse?

After all, Jesse looks more like a root, since he arrives in this world a millennium before the Messiah. The tree is the family of Jesse, the father of David. Jesse is mentioned to emphasize the humble beginnings of David's royal house. That tree would be cut back level with the ground. There will be no Davidic king ruling in Judah in "that day" when the Messiah, the new Davidic king, comes and restores David's fallen tabernacle (Amos 9:11).

How will this restoration happen? It will be by the coming of "a root from the stem of Jesse" that grows into a "branch" (Isa. 11:1). Isaiah will later prophesy that he "shall grow up before Him as a tender plant, and as a root out of dry ground. He has no form or comeliness; and when we see Him, there is no beauty that we should desire Him" (Isa. 53:2). The later prophet, Micah, connects the dots, so to speak: "But you, Bethlehem

Ephrathah, though you are little among the thousands of Judah, yet out of you shall come forth to Me the One to be Ruler in Israel, whose goings forth are from of old, from everlasting" (Mic. 5:2). This takes us in its historical outworking to Joseph and Mary and a stable in Bethlehem. Jesus says of himself, "I am the Root and the Offspring of David, the Bright and Morning Star" (Rev. 22:16). Jesus is the Root of Jesse, the new and permanent root, which can never again be cut down to the ground, but will prevail until his purposes of salvation are perfectly fulfilled.

How is the Messiah a banner to the people?

What is happening in this picture? Just this—that when all the Davidic kings were long dead and gone, and David's descendants are no more than insignificant commoners, a *root* appears and grows up into a *branch*, which then becomes a *banner*. And thus is the Messiah revealed. He is lifted up. The world sees him. This is the first reason why Jesus is called a banner. And what do banners do? On a busy street in south Edinburgh, Scotland, a strangely shaped stone is mounted on a wall in front of an old church. It is called the Bore Stone because it has a vertical hole down its center. Into this stone, in 1513, King James IV of Scotland planted his standard for the mustering of his army for war with England.[1] His banner was the great rallying point. Since time immemorial, would-be conquerors have raised their banners to muster their forces. King Charles I repeated the process in Oxford in 1642; and Bonnie Prince Charlie in Glenfinnan in 1745. These royal Stuarts all lost their kingdoms, and some their lives, but the Messiah comes "conquering and to conquer," because he—the Christ—is "King of kings and Lord of lords" (Rev. 6:2; 19:16).

Messiah's Victory

The raising of Christ as a banner has powerful implications. The prophecy that "the Gentiles shall seek Him" indicates a new state of affairs is to dawn upon the world when the Messiah comes (Isa. 11:10). And so it has been ever since.

There is a war on and God is fighting back.

As in the instances cited above, the raising of the various kings' battle flags acknowledged the existence of a state of war. In raising his banner, God is pointing to the fact that a rebellion against him is in progress. And if you think it's bad now, consider the world before Christ died and rose again and the apostles went out to preach the gospel. The nations perennially conspire against God and his Anointed (Ps. 2:2). People—even those who are outwardly numbered with God's people—will not have the Lord Jesus Christ to rule over them (Luke 19:14). And always, the "prince of this world" is "at work in in those who are disobedient" and leads "them captive to do his will" (John 14:30; Eph. 2:2; 2 Tim. 2:26 NIV). God has, however, raised his banner in the person and work of Jesus. God is fighting back.

God's Messiah is the promised Savior.

Think of the classic use of flags in battle. They are used not only to muster the forces, but also to identify and deploy them, to lead attacks, and to inspire courage. British regiments have "colors" with battle honors sewn on them. In victory, flags are waved: in defeat, they are laid on the ground. Captured, they are displayed in museums—like the "eagle" of the French 45th Regiment captured at Waterloo by Ensign Ewart in the famous charge of the Royal Scots Greys and laid up in Edinburgh Castle.

Jesus Christ, our banner, is the second Adam, who in John Henry Newman's words "to the fight and to the rescue came."[2] Compare these sentences: " 'The first man Adam became a living being.' The last Adam became a life-giving spirit" (1 Cor. 15:45; see Gen. 2:7). Jesus fights our war and defeats our enemies. In fact, the Messiah is *Christus Victor*. He has already won. He has actually won. His victory is accomplished even now. Christ our banner is first lifted up on the cross (John 3:14), and later is lifted up as judge (John 12:32; Phil. 2:9; Heb. 7:26).[3] The war goes on, but the victory is secured. Jesus is Christus Victor.

The plan of the campaign, which is the ongoing application of the victory of Christ on the cross, is laid out in Isaiah 11:10–12: Jesus comes to draw the Gentile nations to himself and to save the remnant of Israel. These two strands come together in verse 12, which proclaims: "He will set up a banner for the nations, and will assemble the outcasts of Israel, and gather together the dispersed of Judah from the four corners of the earth." Rightly understood, this is a picture of Christ and the gospel impacting human history. It is a thumbnail of what he is doing *now* in the New Testament era—from his incarnation to his second coming. But there is even more.

The Messiah is the hope of the world.

Isaiah tells us "the Gentiles shall *seek* Him" (v. 10, italics added). In this is a wonderful vista of hope that the world before Jesus's coming had never known. Why can we say this? Because, whereas in the Old Testament period the nations were comprehensively ignorant of, and opposed to, the Lord, now in the New Testament period they will come looking for the Savior. Never again would God's people be a small nation in the Middle East, plus a sprinkling of Diaspora Jews and Gentile proselytes.

Look at how God raises up Christians and churches in the most unlikely and hostile places. The Lord makes sinners all over the world hungry for something better. He convicts people of sin, and they beat a path to Jesus. He raises bright witnesses of faithfulness in dark places. Someone sees this—and asks for Jesus!

The great point is that the Lord is always on the march. It was the testimony of the converted pagan emperor Nebuchadnezzar, even in the distant reaches of Old Testament world darkness, to confess of the living God: "He does according to His will in the army of heaven and among the inhabitants of the earth" (Dan. 4:35). How much more hope is there for our world in these last days—the gospel era—when Christ our banner is lifted up calling all peoples to himself!

Messiah's Glory

The final piece of the picture is in the last clause of the verse: "His resting place shall be glorious" (Isa. 11:10). Here is the fruit secured by his advent and victory. He makes glorious the place where he is said to rest. The emphasis could not be stronger as the Hebrew text says that God's resting place *is* "glory," using the noun rather than the adjective "glorious" as in our English versions. The substance will be revealed and it is permanent. But where is this glory revealed? What is the Messiah's "resting place"?

There is glory where Christ is in his Church.

Edward J. Young notes that the Hebrew word rendered "resting place" is used in Scripture of Zion—"the place where God has settled down to rule." Zion is God's "resting place"—where the ark of the covenant rested (Ps. 132:8, 13–14). This pictures God in his church; the Shekinah in the Holy of Holies is actually, but also emblematically for all time, the glorious presence of the Lord among his people. This comes to its fruition in the Lord Jesus Christ, of whom it is declared, "the Tabernacle of God is with men" (Rev. 21:3). Christ is the glory and the beauty of the church. Christ is, says Solomon, "as beautiful as Tirzah, lovely as Jerusalem, awesome as an army with banners!" (Song 6:4). The glory of the Messiah is displayed to the world in the Church—not in the mere sticks and stones of great cathedrals, or the massive complexes of modern evangelical "worship centers" with their on-site McDonald's franchises, but in the faithful preaching of Christ, in all the means of grace, and in the witness of believers to the truth as it is in Jesus.

There is glory where Christ acts in human history.

Messiah as our banner manifests God's glory in the New Testament era. It is a richer, fuller revelation of Divine glory than ever was given before the Advent of Jesus Christ. The incarnation, the cross, the resurrection, and the ascension change everything. It is not, of course, that God was less sovereign or less involved in history before the sending of his Son into the world. It is just that "the Holy Spirit was not yet given, because Jesus was not yet glorified" (John 7:39). With the Son revealed, the light is brighter and the presence larger and fuller, because now in Jesus we have "the brightness of [God's] glory and the express image of His person" (Heb. 1:3).

There is glory in the grace of the gospel of Christ.

Christ our banner is lifted up in the gospel. He calls "all men everywhere to repent" (Acts 17:30). We are commanded to believe on the Lord Jesus Christ and assured that in doing so we "will be saved" (Acts 16:31). Jesus tells us "And I, if I am lifted up from the earth, will draw all peoples to Myself" (John 12:32). This of course, refers explicitly to the cross. It is also true, however, that in the likeness of a banner the once-for-all crucified Christ is raised before the watching world. As such, he calls people to gather to him in repentance and faith.

George Root's song of the US Civil War proclaims: "Yes we'll rally round the flag, boys, we'll rally once again, shouting the battle cry of freedom." That idea of *rallying* round the flag is implicit in the image of Jesus as our banner. It is also an invitation to embrace his victory and to enjoy his glory, from now on and forever (Phil. 4:4), and to sing with the psalmist:

Remember me with favor, LORD,
  Which You Your people show.
O come to me, draw near that I
  May Your salvation know.

That with Your chosen ones I may
  Enjoy prosperity,
And may with Your inheritance
  In You boast joyfully.
(Ps. 106A, *The Book of Psalms for Worship*)

Jesus Is Our Bronze Serpent

As Moses lifted up the serpent in the wilderness, even so must the Son of Man be lifted up, that whoever believes in Him should not perish but have eternal life. —*John 3:14–15*

READ NUMBERS 21:4–9; JOHN 3:14–15

He came by night, presumably for fear of his fellow Jews. He was a teacher of God's law, respected by the people, confident in the traditions of his fathers, and no doubt proud of the edifice of his own righteous attainments. But there was a gaping hole in his theology, right where the foundation should be. His name was Nicodemus. And Nicodemus needed to learn a lesson so basic that even Jesus spoke with surprise: "Are you the teacher of Israel, and do not know these things?" (John 3:10). His theological blind spot was that to "see the kingdom of God"—to "not perish but have everlasting life"—he had to first be "born again," and then set aside the rags of his own works-righteousness and believe in the only begotten Son of God (vv. 3, 16).

To illustrate, Jesus pointed this expert in the law to a familiar Bible story: "As Moses lifted up the serpent in the wilderness, even so must the Son of Man be lifted up, that whoever believes in Him should not perish but have eternal life" (vv. 14–15). Our Lord infallibly interprets this story of the bronze serpent in Numbers 21:4–9 as a *type*, that is, a foreshadowing of these fundamental gospel truths. This Old Testament passage teaches us about the sinfulness of sin, the misery of sin, and the cure for sin.

The Sinfulness of Sin

Israel's forty-year pilgrimage in the wilderness was approaching its end. Soon they would arrive at the Plains of Moab, where Moses would give his last instructions before the conquest of Canaan. But before this, we have another sad account of a great sin in Israel: "And the soul of the people became very discouraged on the way. And the people spoke against God and against Moses: 'Why have you brought us up out of Egypt to die in the wilderness?' " (Num. 21:4–5).

In spite of the many tokens of God's grace and patience in the wilderness, they continued to grumble against the Lord. They had grumbled about food; God had given them manna. They had grumbled about drink; God had given water from the rock. They had grumbled about enemies; God had given them victories. They had grumbled about guidance; God had given them the pillar of cloud and fire to lead them. And despite all this, now we read, "The soul of the people became very discouraged on the way" (v. 4). The Hebrew is literally "their souls grew short"—they ran out of patience, they became increasingly frustrated, they "spoke against God and against Moses" (v. 5).

The context suggests two reasons for this latest round of grumbling. The first was God's wise travel itinerary. According to Exodus 23:20–21, it was the Angel of the Lord (the pre-incarnate Christ) who was personally leading them, and the route he took them by was not always one that met with their approval. Already in Numbers 21, he had led them into a skirmish with the King of Arad in which they were victorious, and now in his wisdom, he was leading them on a detour around the land of Edom—the long way around (vv. 1–4).

The second reason they grumbled on this occasion was God's

gracious provision of food: "For there is no food and no water, and our soul loathes this worthless bread!" (v. 5). God was still miraculously sustaining this massive community daily with manna from heaven, which they thanklessly labeled "worthless bread." Their diet was admittedly unvaried, but at least they *had* a diet in the land of death. Still, this wasn't good enough for them.

The sinfulness of Israel's sin lies partly in their base self-pity and bitterness against God. Here is remarkable ingratitude for undeserved mercies. But the Apostle Paul adds to these charges the sin of testing God—and specifically, testing the pre-incarnate Son of God, the Angel of the Lord: "We must not put Christ to the test, as some of them did and were destroyed by serpents" (1 Cor. 10:9 ESV). Thus Israel commits an act of rebellion, rejecting God and the leadership of his anointed one, Moses. And when you consider that the camp had just experienced the rebellion of Korah, and witnessed God's terrifying judgment upon the conspirators, it is also an astonishingly bold and aggravated sin (Num. 16).

Jesus shares this story with Nicodemus because it illustrates well our human need. Man is a sinner—a grumbling sinner. Despite being given life by a gracious Creator, despite the undeserved provision of his needs in common grace, man continues to rebel against God and against his Anointed One, Jesus Christ (compare with Ps. 2:1–2). All sin is rebellion. The *Westminster Shorter Catechism*, Question 18, asks,

> Wherein consists the sinfulness of that estate wherein man fell? Answer: The sinfulness of that estate wherein man fell, consists in the guilt of Adam's first sin, the want of original righteousness, and the corruption of his whole nature, which is commonly called Original Sin; together with all actual transgressions which proceed from it.

Our very nature is corrupted with original sin, and that sinful nature expresses itself daily in the "actual transgressions" we also willfully commit every day. Man is not a sinner because he sins; he sins because he's a sinner by nature.[1] You and I need to fully grasp this bad news before we will ever understand the good news of the gospel. It's no good telling people "Jesus is the answer" until they know what the question is.

So in Jesus's explanation of this text, Israel's predicament is analogous to man's predicament. His relationship with God has been broken. He is estranged from God. He is in rebellion; and this rebellion of course brings terrible consequences.

The Misery of Sin

"So the Lord sent fiery serpents among the people, and they bit the people; and many of the people of Israel died" (Num. 21:6). God's judgment falls! The serpents are said to be fiery, perhaps because of their color, but more likely because of the fiery burn of the venom in the victim's wound.

The serpents' bite.

We are told three other specific things about the serpents' bite:

The serpents' bite was pervasive: "They bit the *people*"—men and women, boys and girls, the fit and the vulnerable. The plague spared no one.

The serpents' bite was lethal: "many of the people of Israel died." There are many desert-dwelling snakes, but these reptiles obviously belonged to a particularly lethal species. Snake venom is especially dangerous because it attacks multiple targets in the body at once: the cardiac and respiratory systems, or the central nervous system, leading to paralysis, coma, and death.[2]

The serpents' bite was incurable. If you're hiking alone in a wilderness area far from medical help, and you have the misfortune of being bitten by a timber rattlesnake, your situation is extremely grave. But here was a massive community out in the wilderness together, invaded by a plague of snakes and with no modern hospitals or anti-venoms. They were utterly helpless and unable to cure themselves.

The Israelites' situation is profoundly symbolic of our natural condition. The serpent is of course the biblical metaphor *par excellence* of Satan and the curse on mankind, beginning at Genesis 3:14: "So the LORD God said to the serpent: 'Because you have done this, you are cursed more than all cattle, and more than every beast of the field; on your belly you shall go, and you shall eat dust all the days of your life.' " There in the garden, the Serpent was cursed by God, and became a visual metaphor of the curse brought by sin into the world; the Serpent has inflicted a bite on man that is pervasive, lethal, and incurable.

The effects of sin.

Indeed, the term "*fiery* serpents" makes the analogy even clearer; the Hebrew word is often translated "flying serpents" or "dragons," (compare with Isa. 14:29 and 30:6). It is no coincidence that from Genesis to Revelation the same metaphor is used for the great Enemy of mankind: "Behold, a great, fiery red dragon having seven heads and ten horns, and seven diadems on his heads...the great dragon...that serpent of old, called the Devil and Satan, who deceives the whole world" (Rev. 12:3, 9). Satan the fiery serpent has bitten mankind; consequently, "All mankind by their fall lost communion with God, are under his wrath and curse, and so made liable to all miseries in this life, to death itself, and to the pains of hell forever."[3] This is exactly what we find illustrated by the fiery serpents:

* *The effects of sin are pervasive.* It affects everyone: men and women, boys and girls. Even our newborn infants are tainted with the guilt of Adam's sin (Ps. 51:5). Sin is like snake venom spreading through the body, doing horrific damage to every system, bringing acute pain, paralysis, and ultimately death.
* *The effects of sin are lethal.* God warned Adam that "in the day that you eat of [the fruit] you shall surely die" (Gen. 2:17). The serpent beguiled them and they discovered that "the wages of sin is death"—both spiritual and physical (Rom. 6:23). This is

why the Serpent is described in Hebrews 2:14 as "him who had the power of death, that is, the devil."

* *The effects of sin are incurable.* Like the Israelites, we are all under a death sentence by nature. Sin remains the defining issue of the human condition across the planet—not climate change, not the AIDS epidemic, not the sustainability of a rising global population—sin is the great calamity that has befallen us. Many have tried to cure the ailment of sin, but to no avail. Theological liberalism has *demoted* sin. Eastern monism has *mythologized* it. Postmodernism has *relativized* it. Freudian psychology has *redefined* it. But the Scriptures make clear these are all fool's errands—the Serpent's poison has no human cure. God's diagnosis remains definitive: "The heart is deceitful above all things, and desperately sick; who can understand it?" (Jer. 17:9 ESV); "Can the Ethiopian change his skin or the leopard its spots? Then may you also do good who are accustomed to do evil" (Jer. 13:23).

Lest we think we're all just helpless victims, Scripture is clear that we are willing victims, for we share the guilt of Adam's sin—"Therefore, just as through one man sin entered the world, and death through sin, and thus death spread to all men, because all sinned" (Rom. 5:12). As if that were not enough, to make matters worse, we accrue yet further guilt by our own daily sinful thoughts, words and actions, which promote the spread of the poison throughout our souls.

In short, this story teaches the biblical doctrine of "total depravity," i.e., man's sinful condition and its misery is pervasive, lethal, and incurable. And yet, how many snake-bitten human beings are utterly oblivious to the danger they're in. Is it possible that you are slowly drifting into a spiritual coma because you haven't yet come to grips with your condition? You won't seek an antidote until the reality grips you that you've been poisoned, and you won't seek it *urgently* until you realize that the poison is deadly. Thankfully, where man has failed to provide a cure, God in his wisdom and grace has done so.

The Cure for Sin

We have seen that the serpents were the agents and emblems of God's curse for sin: for God's people to be cured, they would have to be definitively dealt with. As Jesus explains to Nicodemus, in this we have a powerful Old Testament picture of the gospel. Three specific aspects of gospel redemption are foreshadowed in Numbers 21:7–9. We will consider them in the order they appear.

God expects repentance (v. 7).

"Therefore the people came to Moses, and said, 'We have sinned, for we have spoken against the Lord and against you; pray to the Lord that He take away the serpents from us.' So Moses prayed for the people." If you want to be cured of your sin, you have to start here. The cure began with the people's recognition and confession that their condition was indeed pervasive, lethal, and incurable; in other words, it began with *confession of sin*. Notice that they make no excuses, and they're very specific in their confession: "We have sinned, for we have spoken against the Lord and against you." They don't merely concede the point: "Okay then, we're sinners," but they confess "we have committed this and that specific sin!" Have *you* done that?

This confession is accompanied by crying to God through the mediator; they say to Moses, " 'pray to the Lord'...So Moses prayed for the people." They realize their relationship with God has been broken; they can only approach him through his own appointed mediator, Moses. Have *you* done this—cried out to God through Christ, his appointed Mediator?

God provides a substitute (v. 8).

Notice that God did not "take away the serpents" from them, as they had prayed. He did something even better: he provided a cure.

"The LORD said to Moses, 'Make a fiery serpent.'"[4] The word "serpent" is actually missing in the original; God says literally, "make a fiery thing!" Moses makes an emblem of the curse itself—and this is precisely what Jesus says represents him.

Christ is our fiery bronze serpent. He came in the likeness of the cursed thing to bear the curse instead: "God [sent] His own Son in the likeness of sinful flesh, on account of sin: He condemned sin in the flesh" (Rom. 8:3). So identified would he be with the cursed ones, that he would become their curse: Galatians 3:13 says, "Christ has redeemed us from the curse of the law, having become a curse for us (for it is written, 'Cursed is everyone who hangs on a tree')." Indeed, "He made Him who knew no sin to be sin for us, that we might become the righteousness of God in Him" (2 Cor. 5:21). It is not going too far to say that Jesus became our *serpent*—the righteous one who knew no sin became a cursed thing in our place.

We have seen how in the garden of Eden, the serpent was cursed by God (Gen. 3:14). But that was not the end of the story. God went on to promise, "And I will put enmity between you and the woman, and between your seed and her Seed; He shall crush your head, and you shall strike His heel" (v. 15 NIV). The curse upon the satanic Serpent would find its climax at the moment in history when Jesus, the Seed of the woman, would crush his head, in which moment the serpent would simultaneously inflict a mortal wound on the heel of his conqueror. That moment in history was when Jesus was "lifted up" on the cross. That's why Moses was to not only make a fiery serpent, but also set it on a pole. As Jesus explains, "As Moses lifted up the serpent in the wilderness, even so must the Son of Man be lifted up" (John 3:14–15). To be "lifted up" was an Aramaic euphemism for being hanged by the neck from a tree, or being nailed to one in the lingering death of crucifixion.[5] It was a shameful thing.

So Jesus is a substitute, but he is a *despised* substitute. Christ crucified is a stumbling block to many, as no doubt the bronze serpent was to many Jews (1 Cor. 1:23). After all, what kind of a Savior of the world dies the brutal death of a condemned criminal? Answer: A Savior that came to save criminals. The cross is only despised by those who have not yet confessed their own criminality before God's law. We are all rebels by nature, just like the Israelites. That's why God expects repentance, and why God provides a substitute.

God expects faith (v. 9).

The application of the cure to a dying Israelite was simple: "when he looked at the bronze serpent, he lived." The people were not to touch the bronze serpent, much less make an offering to it. God didn't set up some complex ceremony only for Levites, or some lengthy pilgrimage only for the most able-bodied, or some indulgences only for the rich, or some deep theological mystery only for the initiated few; he stuck a pole in the ground with a snake nailed to it and said: "Look upon it, believe my promise, and receive my gift of salvation!"

We have seen how pervasive the plague was; young and old alike were afflicted, so here was salvation accessible to all—even the youngest, the frailest, and those who might otherwise be excluded could avail themselves of the redemption freely offered to them. The unbelieving, skeptic Israelite might well have scoffed and asked, "what possible connection can a bronze effigy of a snake have to do with my literal snake wound?"[6] Many today likewise ask what possible connection can there be between the mangled, dead body of a Jewish prophet on a cross and, say, their foul temper, lust problem, blasphemy, or broken relationships?

It is faith that takes hold of—not the image of a crucifix—but the real Christ in his office of Savior, bearing God's curse for specific personal sins committed by specific people, so they might live.[7] Faith takes sure hold of the words of God's promise—"and it shall be that everyone who is bitten, when he looks at it, shall live"—or, as Jesus said to Nicodemus, "whoever believes in Him should not perish but have eternal life" (John 3:15). Are *you* believing in the Lord Jesus Christ? God expects faith. He says to you, "Look to Me, and be saved, all you ends of the earth! For I am God, and there is no other" (Isa. 45:22). The only prerequisite is that you have been "bitten"—that you are a sinner. If you are not a sinner, the cross will avail you nothing at all. Only those who know they have been bitten by the Serpent will venture to the foot of the cross.

Thus Nicodemus was instructed by Jesus in the rudiments of the gospel by this Old Testament story, which illustrates the *sinfulness* of sin, the *misery* of sin, and the *cure* for sin. And we do well to heed it ourselves. Like Nicodemus, you may consider yourself a "teacher of Israel." You know a thing or two about the Bible; you've read all the stories; but have the stories read you? Examine yourself carefully by this Word. Make sure you are indeed looking to Christ the bronze serpent, who became the object of the Father's curse, so that you might become the object of the Father's delight.

Jesus Is the

Captain of Our Salvation

For it was fitting for Him, for whom are all things and by whom are all things, in bringing many sons to glory, to make the captain of their salvation perfect through sufferings.—Hebrews 2:10

READ HEBREWS 2:10–18

The message of the Book of Hebrews could easily be summarized under the title, "Christ is better." The Hebrew Christians addressed by the epistle were facing persecution and so were tempted to quit and return to Judaism. The writer therefore points them to the superiority of Christ, who is described in this epistle in some of the loftiest terms in all Scripture. For example, in the opening chapters, he is shown to be God's final word to man, the One who reveals God to man most fully, because he is himself "the express image of His Person" (1:1–3). In Hebrews 1:4–14, he is the One greater than the angels; yet, he condescends to be "made a little lower" than them, becoming man (2:5–9). And then, as the second Adam, he is shown to be the representative head of a new human race,[1] the One whom God will give dominion where the first Adam failed: "you have put all things in subjection under His feet" (2:8). And so, in the rest of Hebrews chapter 2, the author explains exactly *how* Jesus, as the second Adam, rescues this new human race: he does so as the captain of our salvation (v. 10).

The Captain's Identity

"For it was fitting for Him, for whom are all things and by whom are all things, in bringing many sons to glory, to make the captain of their salvation perfect through sufferings" (v. 10). This metaphor is variously translated in the English versions, for the Greek word (*archēgos*) has a broad register of meaning. It can mean, "one who causes something to begin"; hence the ESV's rendering "founder of our salvation," or the NIV's "author of our salvation." But it also commonly means, "one who goes first on the path," a captain, leader, or pioneer.[2] The military connotation of the NKJV's "captain of salvation" comes from the several uses of the word in the Greek Old Testament (the Septuagint) that describes the heads of families as captains of armies that go ahead of their men into battle. "Captain of salvation" is thus a good translation, and it arguably captures an element that "author" and "founder" miss.

As "captain-pioneer" then, Jesus is a second Adam, the progenitor of a new race of redeemed mankind: the Church. He has led the way so that you may follow; he heads the army of the redeemed to the glory of victory; he "brings many sons to glory" by blazing the trail before them. And this trail that leads to glory is a *narrow* path: a path of suffering and cross bearing; a highway of holiness and self-denial, which inevitably leads through death, something men naturally fear (vv. 14–15). That is why Jesus is portrayed as our captain: the One who has gone before us in the battles of life and, by his cross, has secured a decisive military victory over Satan.

The Captain's Mission

The writer of Hebrews tells us that this captain of salvation is sent on a daring and dangerous mission: it will involve great hardship, epic battles, and certain death. But despite its carnage, the victory will be utterly decisive; the glory of his victory parade, unparalleled. And what is the captain's mission? Simply stated, the captain's mission is to bring many sons to glory. It was planned by God the Father ("for whom are all things, and to whom are all things"), and it will be executed by Christ in five specific assignments.[3]

The captain of salvation brings you to glory by his sufferings.

Hebrews 2:10 states, "For it was fitting for Him, for whom are all things and by whom are all things, in bringing many sons to glory, to make the captain of their salvation perfect through sufferings.". Just how is it that Christ, who is "the brightness of [God's] glory and the express image of His person" (Heb. 1:3), had to be "made perfect through sufferings"? Obviously, the writer does not mean "perfect" in the sense of *morally* perfect or imperfect; it is not that Jesus was sinful and atoned for his own sins by his sufferings. Rather, the word "perfect" means "to bring something to its goal, to complete, fulfill, accomplish."[4] The captain of your salvation had to *accomplish* certain things in order to guarantee your salvation. For instance, in John 19:28, we read of Jesus on the cross: "After this, Jesus, knowing that all things were now accomplished..." They had not been accomplished prior to this moment, but now they were. That is why, as David Dickson remarks, "How perfect soever Christ be in Himself, yet before His suffering He lacked one thing which His office towards us required: [experiential] suffering of such sorrows as his soldiers and followers are subject unto."[5]

So our captain had to suffer in order to save, but we are told that his exploits in blood on the front line are but the precursors of the glories to follow: "Ought not the Christ to have suffered these things and to enter into His glory?" (Luke 24:26). Far from a calamitous disaster on the battlefield (the death of the captain), the cross was the *master stroke* of the operation. Calvary does not declare "mission aborted" but "mission *accomplished*." It is precisely these sufferings that usher his ransomed people into glory; this truth should fill every believer's heart with joy and gratitude.

In the 1960s TV show *Mission Impossible*, each episode began with the phrase, "Your mission, should you choose to accept it..." The Christian's salvation is found in the glorious reality that Jesus willingly "chose to accept" his Father's mission of *suffering* to bring the believer to glory. The Dutch theologian Herman Witsius muses on this truth:

> For He might have been glorious as to Himself, without going to it by this way of death, and the pains of hell. [But] He looked on His own glory as the beginning and cause of ours, and whose fruit was all to redound to us. And it was the highest pitch of love, that He would not be glorious without us.[6]

Christian, does it fill you with wonder that Jesus Christ chose the nails to bring you to glory, rather than remain in glory without you?

The captain of salvation brings you to glory by sanctifying you as his brothers.

We have seen that the captain's mission is to bring you to *glory*. But heaven is a holy place—and you and I are not. To go there, you must be *sanctified* or made holy unto the Lord. And in the gospel, that is precisely what Jesus does: "Both He who sanctifies and those who are being sanctified are all of one, for which reason He is not ashamed to call them brethren" (Heb. 2:11). You are being progressively sanctified because you have been definitively sanctified by your captain.[7] It is because he has set you apart as holy that you will actually be empowered to live a holy life by his Word and Spirit: "For their sakes I sanctify Myself, that they also may be sanctified by the truth" (John 17:19). As we shall see, all of this is made possible because Jesus has united his nature to yours ("they are all of one")[8] by becoming the second Adam, the progenitor of a new human race.

But Jesus is also your brother. Jesus your pioneer has gone before you in your flesh, which is why he delights to call you his brothers.[9] On the battlefield of Agincourt, Shakespeare's Henry V memorably cries to his men, "We few, we happy few, we band of brothers. For he today that sheds his blood with me, shall be my brother."[10] So it is here; your captain is also your brother. Have *you* enlisted with the captain of salvation? Then it will show in your military discipline. You are his brothers indeed if you are being sanctified: "[Jesus said], 'Who is My mother, or My brothers?' And He looked around in a circle at those who sat about Him, and said, 'Here are My mother and My brothers! For whoever does the will of God is My brother and My sister and mother' " (Mark 3:33–35). Does this describe you? Are you being sanctified? *This* is the evidence that you are indeed enlisted with Jesus as your captain.

The captain of salvation brings you to glory by sharing your flesh and blood.

It is said that when Julius Caesar was on his campaigns in Gaul and Britain, he would march his men up to fifty miles per day with sixty-pound packs. Every evening they would dig a one-mile square trench to protect two legions of nine thousand men. They would receive only a few handfuls of grain and drink a cup of sour wine as daily rations. What is still more remarkable, Caesar himself *shared this life fully* with his soldiers; there was no special treatment to avoid the hardships of the campaigns on the part of their captain. Understandably, by these means, he won their loyalty and trust; he could relate to their adversities, and they would follow him all the more confidently to glory on the battlefield.[11] In the same way, Christ, the captain of salvation shared your life fully; he has complete solidarity with the sons he leads to glory. Hebrews 2:14 says, "Inasmuch then as the children have partaken of flesh and blood, He Himself likewise shared in the same." The children of the Father are flesh and blood, and so to identify with them, *he* must be flesh and blood too.

Jesus is unique: he is *God become flesh* to redeem you. He is a Savior that is accessible to you. In contrast, the gods of the pagans are distant, remote icons: they are Buddhas that possess "enlightenment" to strive for, but which you may never reach; they are spirits that dwell in dark places that inspire fear; they are polytheistic deities that live in inaccessible realms. But you and I "partake of flesh and blood." Therefore, we need a Savior that understands and enters fully into our life experience. And that is exactly what God has provided: "He Himself likewise shared in the same...in all things He had to be made like His brethren" (vv. 14, 17).

The captain of salvation brings you to glory
by destroying the devil and releasing you from slavery.

Our captain has an *enemy* with which to do battle. The engagement took place his entire earthly life, but the victory occurred at Calvary: "that through death He might destroy him who had the power of death, that is, the devil, and release those who through fear of death were all their lifetime subject to bondage" (vv. 14b–15).

We might well ask in what sense the devil has "the power of death"; after all, does not God alone have the sovereign prerogative to give and take life? Paul reminds us, "the wages of sin is death" (Rom. 6:23), and since death entered the world by Adam through the devil's temptation, he is called a "murderer from the beginning" (John 8:44). Thus, in every human death, the devil has a victory over Adam and his children. But in the gospel, the *second* Adam—the captain of our salvation—triumphs over death by his *own* substitutionary death, and so triumphs over the devil for himself and his children (1 Cor. 15:54–57).[12]

Until this gospel comes to us, we are like the prisoners in the concentration camps of the Second World War, who lived under constant fear of death at any moment from their devilish captors. But when General Dwight Eisenhower liberated the death camps in Europe, he came as a military captain. He destroyed those who had the power of death and liberated those poor wretches who lived under the shadow of death.

In the same way, when you were still "in Adam," you had a natural fear of dying, and worse, you had a terror of what comes *after* death: "it is appointed for men to die once, but after this the judgment" (Heb. 9:27). But God be praised, when the captain of your salvation came, he crushed the serpent's head and liberated you from this slavery (Gen. 3:15). Unlike Eisenhower, *this* captain's mission is a solo one; only he could complete this dangerous mission, which resulted in his own death. And so, as John Owen memorably put it, in the death of Christ, death itself dies,[13] so that you too may be raised imperishable.

If you are a Christian, there may remain a natural recoiling from death, but you know that death has now been "swallowed up in victory" (1 Cor. 15:54). Death now ushers you into the presence of your older brother, not your judge. Death is nothing but the end of your battle, your demobilization, and the promise of being decorated by your captain. Truly, the believers can say, "For to me, to live is Christ, and to die is gain" (Phil. 1:21).

The captain of salvation brings you to glory
by becoming your merciful High Priest.

If, as a soldier, you are injured on the battlefield and find yourself in a field hospital needing a surgeon, it does not do much good if they send you a car mechanic instead; he lacks the knowledge and experience to help you. No, you need someone who knows the anatomy and who has honed his skills. All of us need a *spiritual surgeon*; we need a *priest*: one who knows this life, who is suited perfectly to our needs. Hebrews 2:17 says Jesus is such for us: "In all things He had to be made like His brethren, that He might be a merciful and faithful High Priest." The comfort of Hebrews 2:10–18 is that your captain is also a military *chaplain*. He is perfectly suited to all your needs. This is what the apostle means when he says in verse 16: "For indeed He does not give aid to angels, but He does give aid to the seed of Abraham." Jesus took hold of the nature of the sons of Abraham, not angels. A sinless angel could not propitiate for a sinful man; only a sinless man could. According to verse 17, that is exactly what Christ did: "Therefore, in all things He had to be made like His brethren...to make propitiation for the sins of the people."

As High Priest, Jesus not only propitiates for your sins, but he intercedes for you in your trials: "For in that He Himself has suffered, being tempted, He is able to aid those who are tempted" (v. 18). Jesus has lived life in this fallen world as your pioneer. Therefore, he is able to intercede with gentleness, sympathy, and wisdom (Heb. 4:14–16).

Jesus is the captain of our salvation. But Jesus is no longer among us; he is risen, and is seated at the right hand of the throne of grace in glory. And because he is in glory, you can be sure that you will be brought to glory too, if you are united to him. The captain of salvation has gone to glory to bring many sons to glory. And so, when the good fight of faith is hard, and defeat seems almost certain, remember that his constant high priestly intercession ensures your perseverance against all odds in the battlefield below and guarantees your presence in the great victory parade above. May we each follow our captain on the path to glory, which he has tread before us.

Jesus Is Our

Chosen Stone

A living stone...chosen by God and precious.
—1 Peter 2:4

READ 1 PETER 2:4–10

Peter's first epistle was written to Christians whom he calls in the first verse "elect exiles of the Dispersion" (ESV), scattered throughout the provinces of Asia Minor. He writes to encourage them to stand firm in God's sufficient grace during a season of severe trial. Peter also drives home their Christian identity as the new Israel: they are the elect people of God; they are exiles, like Israel in a Roman Babylon; they are the dispersion—God's scattered sheep.

But to understand their own identity, they must first grasp Christ's identity, for the Christian is only what he is in Christ. Peter teaches this by a series of comparisons. Do you have the hope of triumph over death? It is because Christ triumphed over death (1 Peter 1:3). Are you suffering for God? It is because Christ suffered (vv. 6, 11). Are you holy? It is because Christ is holy (v. 16).

In the same way, Christ is described in 1 Peter 2:4–10 using the Old Testament messianic metaphor of a stone—the Greek word (*lithos*) is used five times in five consecutive verses. And as with the other comparisons Peter makes, Christ's identity as a stone has implications not only for his own people, but also for those who are not his people.

Christ the Chosen Stone

Peter says in verse 4 that Jesus is "a living stone...chosen by God and precious." God the Father has covenanted personally with God the Son and has commissioned him for a special task: that believers may be "built up [as] a spiritual house...Behold, I lay in Zion a chief cornerstone, elect..." (vv. 5–6). God chooses the chief cornerstone for the construction of God's House, the Church.

A chosen stone.

God is like a great architect with a sovereign plan to redeem a people for himself out of fallen, rebellious mankind, so they may be crafted into a spectacular temple of worshiping people. He has personally chosen the materials for building: men, women, and children from every nation, tribe, tongue, and people. He has also chosen Jesus to be the everlasting foundation upon which the Temple will be built and the master foreman who will erect the glorious edifice.

Because of this role, Jesus needs to be a special stone. So what kind of a stone is he? Citing Isaiah 28:16 and Psalm 118:22, Peter calls him the chief cornerstone. In ancient times, the chief cornerstone was the foundation stone upon which the remainder of the structure was built, but it was also the stone according to which the dwelling's dimensions and intersecting walls were aligned. The structural integrity and proportions of the building depended on the accurate placement of this foundation stone at the corner.[1] If a foundation must be solid, durable, and laid with precision on a construction site, how much more the foundation stone of the Church, carefully chosen and placed by God; for "no other foundation can anyone lay than that which is laid, which is Jesus Christ" (1 Cor. 3:11).

A chosen people.

After identifying Jesus as the chosen stone, Peter then returns to the inseparable connection between Christ and believers. If he is the chosen, living *stone* then, if you are a Christian, "you also [are] living stones," chosen by God for two purposes (1 Peter 2:5).

First, you have been chosen as the building blocks of the Church: "You also, as living stones, are being built up a spiritual house" (v. 5; compare with 1 Cor. 3:16 and Matt. 16:18). This is one of the great biblical pictures of the believer's real, organic union with Christ: together, we form one glorious edifice. Look how significant smaller pieces become when they are part of something bigger. From 1904 to 1922, countless granite boulders scattered throughout the Mourne Mountains in Ulster were gathered and piled high to build the Mourne Wall, a stone dyke twenty-five miles long, that traverses the summit of fifteen mountains. Each individual stone was just a rough piece of rubble, but when incorporated into the whole, it became a necessary component of the entire structure. So it is with your status in Christ; you were unpromising pebbles, strewn across this world, but picked up by Christ the master builder and incorporated into his architectural masterpiece. And this work is still in progress; Peter says, "You are being built." Christ is not finished with you yet. The Church in the world may not look like much now. After all, building sites often seem unpromising and messy places. But one day, the new Jerusalem will be complete and glorious (Rev. 21:2).

Second, you have been chosen as "a holy priesthood" (1 Peter 2:5). Holiness is the badge of the believer—set apart from the world and matching the holy Savior he or she professes. When our congregation added a new extension onto its original building, one important task was to match the new stones to the color and pattern of the original Bedford sandstone. If you looked at the completed new building and found here and there, amid the sandstone, several blocks of crumbly black slate, they would be unfitting and unsuitable. So it is with you as stones in God's temple. You must ask, "do I *match*?" All the stones in God's House must match the original chief cornerstone. They must be *holy* or else they will be discarded: "Nevertheless the solid foundation of God stands, having this seal: 'The Lord knows those who are His,' and, 'Let everyone who names the name of Christ depart from iniquity' " (2 Tim. 2:19).

In calling you "a priesthood of believers," Peter mixes his metaphors; he shifts from you being the stones of the temple to being the priests serving within it. You have been chosen to draw near God as a holy people, while the remainder of the world keeps its distance. Consequently, you do what priests in any temple do: you worship your God, "[offering] up spiritual sacrifices, acceptable to God through Jesus Christ" (1 Peter 2:5). After all, this is why he redeemed you in first place.

Christ the Stumbling Stone

If there is a chosen people because Christ is the chosen stone, then there is also a stumbling people because Christ is a stumbling stone.

A stumbling stone.

This stone identified as Christ was "rejected indeed by men" and "the stone which the builders rejected has become the chief cornerstone, and a stone of stumbling and a rock of offense" (vv. 4, 7). The words "chosen" and "rejected" are antonyms (opposites); what God has chosen, it is the utmost folly—indeed, wickedness—to reject. What God has placed his blessing on, let no man declare accursed. What God calls the chief cornerstone, the builders reject as worthless; they stumble over him and are cast down to destruction. The particular builders Peter has in view may be the Jews who crucified our Lord, but it can also be applied to *anyone* who rejects Christ.

A stumbling people.

Peter says of such people, "To those who are disobedient...[Christ is] a stone of stumbling and a rock of offense. They stumble, being disobedient to the word, to which they also were appointed" (vv. 7–8). Why do such people stumble?

Because they disobey. God says, "Behold, I lay in Zion a chief cornerstone." Stumbling people do behold, and then say in their hearts, "I will not believe! I will reject this chosen stone." More specifically, they are "disobedient to the word," by which God ordinarily reveals his Son (compare with 1 Peter 1:23, 25), defying his command to repent and believe the gospel (Mark 1:15).

Because they reject the only foundation stone. When Peter says the builders reject the chief cornerstone, the Greek word translated "reject" literally means "to throw out as the result of a test," "to reject on scrutiny, to reject for want of qualification."[2] Stumbling people evaluate Jesus and then pass a judgment on him, deeming him neither worthy nor adequate. The world's structural engineers appraise God's chosen stone and declare it unfit for use.

Because they imagine themselves better builders than Christ. Peter quotes Psalm 118:22 to show that those who reject Jesus are also in a certain sense builders (1 Peter 2:7). There are thus really two builders in this text: either you are being built up by Christ the builder (v. 5), or you are attempting to build your own life without reference to him. Stumbling people reject God's foundation and would rather build their houses on the sand of their own opinion, false religion, or some other human alternative.

Because Jesus is offensive to them. Jesus Christ is a "stone of stumbling" because he is "a rock of offense." Stumbling people are offended at his birth in lowly circumstances, offended at his death on a cross, offended by his teaching and offended at his exclusive claims to Lordship. The phrase "rock of offense" is *petra skandalou* in Greek—Jesus is a *scandal* to the world. Just try bringing Jesus up in polite conversation and the subject is quickly changed. Try praying in his name in a public setting and the "tolerance police" will soon object. The fact is, people often get upset at the mention of Jesus; truly, "He is despised and rejected by men…and we hid, as it were, our faces from Him; He was despised, and we did not esteem Him" (Isa. 53:3). We are disciples of an unpopular Savior.[3]

Because they are appointed to this. Why do stumbling people stumble? "They stumble…to which they also were appointed" (1 Peter 2:8). The responsibility of man for rejecting the Savior is always to be balanced with the sovereignty of God, and Peter does not see these truths as being at all incompatible. We have listed several reasons why unbelievers *willfully* stumble over Christ, but they cannot fall back on the sovereignty of God as an excuse and blame God when the responsibility is squarely laid at their door for rejecting the Savior. Ralph Robinson comments:

> God usually punisheth voluntary blindness with a penal and judiciary blindness…when men that live under the Gospel shut their own eyes, God doth ratify it by an act of His justice, and saith, "be thou blind forever." When a man hardens his own heart, God is pleased to ratify it in heaven, and saith, "let that heart never be softened."[4]

This is a deeply solemn thought. Are you one of the stumbling people Peter describes here, who disobey God's Word, reject the only foundation stone, think themselves better builders than Christ, or find Jesus offensive? Beware the hardening of your heart. You cannot read the secret will of God, or reveal the appointment of God in eternity past, or glimpse whose names are blotted out of the Lamb's Book of Life (Rev. 3:5). But you *are* personally responsible to act decisively in this brief life by "coming to Him as to a living stone," and God encourages you to do so with the promise that "he who believes on Him will by no means be put to shame" (1 Peter 2:4, 6). Will Christ be to you a *chosen* stone or a *stumbling* stone?

Christ the Precious Stone

We have seen that Christ is a chosen stone for a chosen people and a stumbling stone for a stumbling people. The pattern continues in these last verses: he is a *precious* stone for a precious people.

He is a precious stone.

Peter calls our Savior "chosen by God and precious…a chief cornerstone, elect, precious…to you who believe, He is precious" (vv. 4, 6–7). Precious stones have surpassing value and beauty and are worth exerting great effort to acquire. Whoever possesses one must be extremely rich.

Once he acquires it, he will guard it most carefully; he will not simply lock it away, but will also put it on display to admire its perfections. Jesus is precious to *God*, not only because he is chosen by God, but because he is so precious in himself (2 Peter 1:17); his value is beyond all estimation and admiration. Robinson notes, "As [Christ] is a stone of God's choosing, so He is a *choice* stone"[5]—i.e., he is set apart from *common* stones; he is in a category all of his own.

When you visit a museum and enter the hall of precious gems, you do not go to admire a slab of sandstone, or some lumps of coal, or perhaps a block of cement. And yet, many in the world view Jesus that way; he is not precious to them.

Currently, the Golden Jubilee is the largest faceted diamond in the world;[7] imagine the outrage if it were taken to an expert evaluator at Sotheby's auction house and was rudely dismissed as maybe worth a five dollar bill. What God calls precious, men call common. Jesus is "a living stone rejected by men but in the sight of God chosen and precious" (1 Peter 2:4 ESV).

If you are a Christian, search your heart; can you honestly say that Jesus is *precious* to you? Do you treasure him as the bride did Solomon, "chief among ten thousand" (Song 5:10)? Can you echo to any degree the words of Samuel Rutherford when he writes, "Oh what a fair one is Christ, what an only One, what an excellent, lovely, ravishing one is Jesus! Put the beauty of ten thousand worlds of paradises, like the garden of Eden in one; and yet it would be less to that fair and dearest well-beloved, Christ."[7]

We are a precious people.

God loves those who love his own dear Son. Those to whom Jesus is precious are precious in God's sight: "He who loves Me will be loved by My Father, and I will love him and manifest Myself to him" (John 14:21). Christ the precious stone is united to a precious *people*, set apart for himself: "You are...His own special people" (1 Peter 2:9; see Ex. 19:6). But it was not always this way. He first "called you out of darkness into His marvelous light...[you] had not obtained mercy but now have obtained mercy" (1 Peter 2:10). You were once like Israel in Hosea's day, named *Lo-Ammi* ("Not My People"), but now you are the people of God, the new Israel (v. 10; compare with Hosea 1:9 and 2:23).

What has made this dramatic transformation of your identity possible? Answer: God *rejected* his own *chosen* stone at the cross. If Christ's value is beyond human estimation—if he is God's chosen, precious stone—what could ever tempt God to part with him? How could the Father ever be prevailed upon to deliver up such a treasure as his only precious Son, whom he loves? The answer is, *you*! The transaction is powerfully described in Isaiah 43:3–4: "For I am the Lord your God, the Holy One of Israel, your Savior; I gave Egypt for your ransom, Ethiopia and Seba in your place. Since you were precious in My sight, you have been honored, and I have loved you." Egypt, Ethiopia, and Seba were the wealthiest nations of Africa and the Arabian Peninsula, rich with gold and diamond mines. All this God was willing to pay as a ransom for Israel's sin. But he has paid a far greater price still; he has given you his only Son, a chosen, precious stone. And why? "*Since you were precious in My sight*, you have been honored, and I have loved you."

Christian, do you live in the light of this? Does it make a difference in your life that though poor in the eyes of this world, you are the richest of people because you are in possession of Christ the precious stone? How many Christians live as spiritual beggars, without fully grasping that they are spiritual billionaires?

On February 16, 2004, the following news report was published:

> The Harvard-Smithsonian Center for Astrophysics [has] announced the discovery of a mass of crystallized carbon formerly known as star BPM 37093, now known as the biggest diamond in the galaxy, fifty light years away from Earth in the constellation Centaurus. The diamond is estimated to be 2,500 miles across and weighs approximately 10 billion-trillion-trillion-carats—a one, followed by 34 zeros. [The] leader of the team who discovered the gem, says "You would need a jeweler's loupe the size of the sun to grade this diamond. Bill Gates and Donald Trump together couldn't begin to afford it." When asked to estimate the value of the cosmic jewel, ... [the] CEO of Harry Winston, Inc., indicated that such a large diamond probably would depress the value of the market, stating, "Who knows? It may be a self-deflating prophecy because there is so much of it."[8]

We know this colossal cosmic precious stone is out there, but we cannot access it; it is beyond us. I wonder, do you live as if Christ the precious stone were like that? Do you feel like you cannot access him—that he is beyond you? Peter's simple advice is, "[come] to Him as to a living stone" (1 Peter 2:4). He is alive, his riches are all yours, and as with that cosmic, interstellar diamond, we may say of Christ the precious stone, "*There is so much of it!*" You do not have to construct some spiritual spacecraft to reach him; he approaches you now in his Word and invites you to come to him by faith. "And he who believes on Him will by no means be put to shame" (v. 6).

Jesus Is Our

Consolation

Waiting for the Consolation of Israel.
—Luke 2:25

READ LUKE 2:21–35

Simeon had been waiting a long time. By now he was very old, and, like so many in the evening of life, he was still looking for something to happen that would prove the defining moment of his life. But unlike those on the threshold of eternity who have no real grounds for hope, Simeon knew with absolute certainty what—or rather, Who—he was waiting for: "the Consolation of Israel" (Luke 2:25). In fact, the wait had been so long, that except for a few "just and devout" believers, most of Israel had given up waiting long ago (v. 25).

Simeon walks onto the stage of redemptive history exactly forty days after Jesus was born. According to the law, a sacrifice would be offered to release his mother from her ceremonial uncleanness after childbirth (Lev. 12:6–8), and, being a firstborn son, the baby would be formally "presented" to the Lord (Luke 2:22; Ex. 34:19–20). It was here in the temple that this old saint, heavy with years, was waiting to be consoled. But this consolation of Israel is not just an abstract feeling of comfort for Israel. Rather, it is a person: Jesus Christ is the consolation of Israel.

As with all the formal titles of the Messiah, this one is there to be mined for the treasures it yields, and to do so we will ask four questions.

Why Is Consolation Necessary?

This title of Christ has deep Old Testament roots. The prophet Isaiah, in particular, frequently spoke about the coming of the Savior in terms of the comfort and consolation he would bring to God's people Israel:

> Comfort, yes, comfort My people!"
> Says your God.
> "Speak comfort to Jerusalem, and cry out to her,
> That her warfare is ended,
> That her iniquity is pardoned.
> For she has received from the LORD's hand
> Double for all her sins…
>
> Sing, O heavens!
> Be joyful, O earth!
> And break out in singing, O mountains!
> For the LORD has comforted His people,
> And will have mercy on His afflicted…
>
> The Spirit of the Lord GOD is upon Me,
> Because the LORD has anointed Me
> To preach good tidings to the poor;
> He has sent Me to heal the brokenhearted…
> To comfort all who mourn,
> To console those who mourn in Zion. (Isa. 40:1–2; 49:13; 61:1–3)

Israel needed these words of consolation from the prophet because she had sinned against her covenant God, and as a result she faced captivity in Babylon. Her sin had reduced her to a truly miserable state, and if this was true of Israel in Isaiah's day, the same was certainly true of Israel in Simeon's day. Since their return from exile, Israel had fallen into nominal religion, dominated by powerful high-priestly families and legalistic sects. She had no messianic king on David's throne but had become the plaything of powerful neighboring empires. Little wonder, then, that many Jews were waiting for a "messianic consolation" of an entirely political and military character—the consolation and satisfaction of seeing the Roman occupier sent packing.[1] But not Simeon.

Simeon understood that the consolation the Messiah would bring his people would be experienced in spiritual, not political, terms. And so, when he holds the consolation of Israel—baby Jesus—in his arms, he says, "my eyes have seen your *salvation*" (Luke 2:30, italics added). If we are to understand this title of Christ (and apply it to ourselves) we need, like Simeon, to let the prophets drive our understanding of it: "'*Comfort*, yes, *comfort* My people!' says your God. 'Speak *comfort* to Jerusalem, and cry out to her...that *her iniquity is pardoned*; for she has received from the LORD's hand double for all her sins" (Isa. 40:1–2, italics added). This Messiah will save God's people, not from imperial Roman oppression, but from their sins. He will lead her out of her captivity to Satan and bring her the joy and consolation of redemption. *That* is the kind of consolation embodied by Jesus Christ.

If this is why Israel needed consolation, it is also surely why you and I need consolation. Like Israel, you have been born into what the *Shorter Catechism* calls "an estate of sin and misery" (Question 17). "Sin" refers to the root problem: your original guilt and personal transgression of the law of God. "Misery" refers to sin's consequences: "All mankind by their fall lost communion with God, are under His wrath and curse, and so made liable to all miseries in this life, to death itself, and to the pains of hell forever" (Question 19). You need consolation because by nature you are spiritually *disconsolate*: suffering the consequences of your sin. You may not yet be fully aware of the sheer sinfulness of your sin, but perhaps you are only too aware of the misery it has brought into your life. So naturally the pursuit of comfort and consolation becomes a life goal.

Like Israel, you need Christ as your consolation—not only to comfort you in the tragedies of life, but, far more importantly, to save you from the sin that has brought such miseries about.

How Does Christ Procure Your Consolation?

Three vital components of Christ's procurement of the believers' consolation emerge from this and other Scripture passages.

By taking your human flesh.

Luke 2:22–24 can easily be overlooked as a cluster of seemingly unimportant details, but these verses remind us that Jesus Christ was a real "male child" who indeed "opened the womb" and came into our world. His mother waited out the forty-day healing process and made her postnatal visit to the temple to be purified. But while his entry into this world was very ordinary, he was no ordinary baby. And this is something that we, like Simeon, must see with eyes of faith. While holding the baby Jesus, he declares, "my eyes have seen your salvation" (v. 30). Simeon is rightly astonished; he holds in his arms the Creator of the universe enfleshed. The early Puritan John Boys remarks,

> As Simeon saw Christ's humanity with the eyes of his body, so he saw Christ's divinity long before with the piercing eye of faith. He knew that the little babe which he lulled in his arms was the great God, whom heaven of heavens could not contain: and therefore believing in the Lord of life, he was not afraid of death, but instantly breaks forth in this sweet song.[2]

By keeping the law perfectly on your behalf.

In verse 21, Jesus receives the sign of circumcision, not because he had sins that needed to be cut off, but to identify with his covenant people, for whose sins he would be "cut off" (Isa. 53:8). It is not surprising, then, that at this moment he is given the name "Jesus" (literally, "the Lord saves"). We must see here that Jesus submits to the law right from his earliest days. This is made clear not only in the fact that "eight days were completed for the circumcision of the Child" in Luke 2:21, but in Luke's repeated emphasis of the law throughout the passage: "according to the Law of Moses...as it is written in the Law of the Lord...according to what is said in the Law of the Lord...according to the custom of the Law" (vv. 22–24, 27). Although the Son of God was the law*giver*, he submitted to the law for your sake: "But when the fullness of the time had come, God sent forth His Son, born of a woman, born under the law, to redeem those who were under the law, that we might receive the adoption as sons" (Gal. 4:4–5). This is how he will procure your consolation: by keeping the law perfectly on your behalf, which is called his "active obedience." Your efforts at perfect obedience are in vain, but his were not. What consolation it should bring you to know that you may stand before a holy God clothed in the righteousness of another.

By bearing your sins on the cross.

Jesus lived a sinless life on your behalf, without succumbing to the temptations of this fallen world, yet while suffering all of its miseries. He then died an atoning death to pay for your sins, which is called his "passive obedience." This is hinted at when old Simeon prophesies in Luke 2:35 that a sword would proverbially pierce through Mary's soul, as she would witness the crucifixion of her dearly beloved Son and Savior. You may say, "There seems little consolation in that." And yet it is there—at the foot of a Roman cross—that the consolation of Israel is most clearly seen, just as the prophet declared: "He is despised and rejected by men, a Man of sorrows and acquainted with grief...Surely He has borne our griefs and carried our sorrows...But He was wounded for our transgressions, He was bruised for our iniquities; the chastisement for our peace was upon Him, and by His stripes we are healed" (Isa. 53:3, 5).

In sum, Christ procures your consolation by the *gospel*: God the Son becomes flesh in the womb of the Virgin Mary; keeps the rigors of the law without fault in your place; and then takes not only your guilt and pollution on the cross, but bears your griefs and carries your sorrows as well (Isa. 53:4). Thus the consolation of Israel is not merely found in consoling truths or comforting words spoken *to* Israel, but it is found in a person who is the embodiment of consolation itself. This is a doctrinal truth to be both understood and admired, as Ralph Robinson explains:

> Consider it, Christ became a man of sorrow, that he might be made to you a God of all Comfort; He drank up the cup of His Father's wrath, that He might purchase for you a cup of consolation. Jesus Christ did willingly pour out His own precious blood, that He might mingle a strong cup of consolation for the reviving of thy soul. The God of consolation hath gone the most costly way infinite wisdom could devise to provide comfort for His elect.[3]

How Does Christ Convey This Consolation?

Many Christians speak knowledgeably about Christ our *consolation*, having received by faith the gift of sins forgiven, and yet they rarely enjoy the daily experience of being consoled by Christ as they ought. If Christ has procured spiritual consolation for you by his blood, how do you personally receive the consolation, not only of sins forgiven, but the *joy and comfort* of sins forgiven? To not only know that Jesus has redeemed you from your estate of sin, but to daily delight in your deliverance from the estate of misery? There are three ways Christ conveys this consolation to you.

Through the ministry of the Holy Spirit.

The first way is through the Holy Spirit. It is striking that the Holy Spirit is mentioned in Luke 2:25–27 three times in as many verses, for he plays a central role in your receiving the comforts of the gospel. While Simeon was with Christ our consolation at the beginning of his earthly life, the disciples were with him at the end of it. Just before he left them, he promised,

> I will pray the Father, and He shall give you another Comforter, that He may abide with you for ever; even the Spirit of truth...I will not leave you comfortless; I will come to you...Nevertheless I tell you the truth; it is expedient for you that I go away: for if I go not away, the Comforter will not come unto you; but if I depart, I will send him unto you. (John 14:16–18; 16:7 KJV)

When Jesus came into the world he was called your *consolation* (Greek, *paraklesis*); when he is about to go out of the world, he promises you a *Comforter* (Greek, *parakletos*). His bodily presence as the baby promises consolation through his earthly ministry; his bodily absence as the ascended King promises continued consolation by his heavenly rule, which is administered to you by his Holy Spirit. It is the Spirit who bestows the gift of saving faith and repentance unto life and who daily applies the gospel for your increasing sanctification.[4]

Through the ordinary means of grace:
the Word, sacraments, and prayer.

The second way Christ conveys consolation is through the ordinary means of grace. You receive comfort not in merely a formal, external use of these "outward and ordinary means"[5], but rather in the degree to which you meet with Christ, your consolation, *in* them. The Holy Spirit, the Comforter, must accompany them if they are to become an effectual means to convey comfort. Specifically, Christ consoles you by the reading and preaching of the Word: "For whatever things were written before were written for our learning, that we through the patience and comfort of the Scriptures might have hope" (Rom. 15:4). Christ consoles you by *prayer*, as you fetch this comfort from him by your petitions and commune with the consolation of Israel himself. Christ consoles you by your *baptism*, as you receive his mark and are visibly united to the consolation of Israel, being given a right to all the benefits of the visible Church. Christ consoles you by the *Lord's Supper*, as you commune with Christ your consolation at his table.

There is ordinarily no hope of gospel comfort without God's prescribed means of conveying it. But, once again, let us remember that these simple means are not the source of our consolation, but the channel by which Christ our consolation is conveyed to us. If Jesus is the fountain of comfort, then the means of grace are the tap by which that comfort flows to us. Do not pin your hopes of comfort on the faucet, but on the fountain of life it is connected to.

Through the fellowship of the body of Christ.

The third way Christ consoles his people is through fellowship among believers. The Lord has built a wonderful dynamic into the fabric of his Church; the consolation of her members *multiplies* through the consolation they receive from her Head. Paul explains:

> Blessed be the God and Father of our Lord Jesus Christ, the Father of mercies and God of all comfort, who comforts us in all our tribulation, that we may be able to comfort those who are in any trouble, with the comfort with which we ourselves are comforted by God. For as the sufferings of Christ abound in us, so our consolation also abounds through Christ. (2 Cor. 1:3–5; the Greek word translated "comfort" is the same word rendered "consolation" in Luke 2:25.)

God does not intend for you to go through life isolated; he expects you to comfort and encourage other believers and to be encouraged and comforted by them also. Has not one of the greatest sources of consolation in your Christian life been your Christian friends? And if Christ is *your* consolation, will you not also console others in the Church, like Barnabas, who earned the nickname, "Son of consolation" (Acts 4:36

KJV; again, same Greek word used in Luke 2:25)? Are you reflecting the Savior who has consoled you? Is your congregation known as a loving body that consoles the afflicted, encourages the weak, and builds up the brokenhearted?

Is Christ Your Consolation?

We have seen how Jesus procured consolation for his people and how you can obtain it. Now you must *avail* yourself of it. Christ is the consolation of Israel: that means the extent of his consolation is proportionate with the extent of the "Israel of God," the Church (Gal. 6:16). That is, Christ only conveys consolation to those for whom it has been procured: those Israelites indeed who, like Simeon, wait for the Lord and live by faith in him (John 1:47; Rom. 9:6).

This means that Christ is *not* a consolation to anyone outside of God's Israel. If you are not waiting on Christ, then you are in a truly disconsolate state; you are still in your "estate of sin and misery"(*Westminster Shorter Catechism* Question 17). Unlike Simeon in Luke 2:30, your eyes have not yet seen the Lord's salvation." Indeed, you are rejecting his consolation and seeking other consolations instead. The fleeting comforts of the world—its music, entertainment, hobbies, friends—while not always wrong in themselves, can quickly become avenues of escape from the real source of misery that you need to be rescued from.

But the good news is that if Christ is the only consolation of Israel, he is nevertheless a consolation offered to all those presently outside of Israel; as Simeon declared, Jesus is "Your salvation which You have prepared before the face of all peoples, a light to bring revelation to the Gentiles" (vv. 30–32). He offers himself to you—to let go of all lesser comforts and come to the fountain of all comfort. You will find the burden of your sin and misery dealt with and a perfect consolation conveyed to your soul.

Is Christ your consolation? If he is, then, like old Simeon, be consoled. Let joy mark your Christian life. Like Simeon, wait patiently upon Christ your consolation. Like Simeon, take Christ your consolation in your arms by faith. Like Simeon, do not fear your dismissal from this life. If you would confidently say, "Lord, now you are letting your servant depart in peace," you must first be able to say from personal experience, "My eyes have seen Your salvation" (vv. 29–30). Have *your* eyes seen it? Is Christ *your* consolation?

Jesus Is Our

Covenant

I will keep You and give You as a covenant to the people.
—Isaiah 42:6

READ ISAIAH 42:1–9

"The two great benefits of creation and redemption…contain a short abridgment of religion" (from the *Westminster Larger Catechism*, Answer 121).

Few summaries of the Christian faith have been more helpfully succinct than this statement of the Westminster divines. Two simple but pregnant words—creation and redemption—contain the sum of God's eternal plan for his people, and this "short abridgment of religion" is expressed beautifully in Isaiah 42:5–7.

God Created You

> Thus says God the LORD, Who created the heavens and stretched them out, Who spread forth the earth and that which comes from it, Who gives breath to the people on it, and spirit to those who walk on it. (v. 5)

The language of this verse echoes the first chapter of Genesis, where God stretched out the heavens, blessed the new burgeoning earth, and breathed into man's nostrils the breath of life so that he became a living being. God sovereignly created you. He spoke the word, and you have your being.

God Redeemed You

> To open blind eyes, to bring out prisoners from the prison, those who sit in darkness from the prison house. (v. 7)

This beautiful description of God's work of redemption in human hearts is analogous to his work of creation. Just as creation is accomplished by a divine decree (the word of the sovereign *Creator* God), so also redemption is accomplished by a divine decree (the word of the sovereign *Redeemer* God). Truly, the Christian is a "new creation" (2 Cor. 5:17; Gal. 6:15).

But, Isaiah 42:5-7, what links these two great works of creation and redemption is found in the middle in verse 6: God will redeem his people by One whom God has given "as a covenant to the people." At the heart of God's work of redemption is Jesus Christ, and at the heart of God's method of redemption is the idea of covenant, which Jesus embodies.

The Qualifications of Christ Our Covenant

But how can you have confidence that this Jesus is qualified to be your covenant Savior? To begin with, you can be confident because of *who it is that qualifies him*: "Thus says God the LORD who created the heavens…I, the LORD, have called You in righteousness" (vv. 5–6). There are many christs in the world, as Mark 13:22 says, but only this Christ speaks with all the authority of "God the LORD who created the heavens." Jesus himself was clear about this: "For I have not spoken on

My own authority; but the Father who sent Me gave Me a command, what I should say and what I should speak" (John 12:49). No wonder then that Jesus is further described in Isaiah 42 as *God's* Servant, *God's* elect one with whom he is well pleased, and *God's* Spirit-filled bringer of justice (v. 1). Jesus did not come to earth on a self-appointed errand, but was sent by your Creator to be your Redeemer. Jesus is qualified to be our covenant Savior because as ambassador of the King, he speaks with all the authority of the King himself.

Jesus is also qualified because of *what* qualifies him—God's appointment by covenant. "I, the LORD, have called You in righteousness" says verse 6. Notice how the text switches from using the third person, talking about Jesus in verses 1–4, to the second person, talking to Jesus verse 6: "I have called *you.*" In other words, we are now eavesdropping on a conversation between God the Father and his Son in the counsels of eternity, and they are using covenant-making language. In theological terms, we are witnessing the making of the covenant of redemption.[1]

An assignment is being given by the Father to the Son; a righteous plan is being conceived. The prophet Isaiah, writing in eighth century BC, records that God's Servant had been commissioned at some point in the past. The Apostle Paul, writing in the first century AD, says "[He] has saved us…according to His own purpose and grace which was given to us in Christ Jesus before time began, but has now been revealed by the appearing of our Savior Jesus Christ" (2 Tim. 1:9–10). Both inspired writers are saying the same thing: from all eternity, God had a plan to bring unworthy sinners to salvation by a Redeemer. Isaiah only knew him as "God's righteous Servant" who was yet to come, but Paul could testify that he has now been revealed in the fullness of time as "our Savior Jesus Christ."

This in essence is captured in Isaiah 42:9: "Behold, the former things have come to pass, and new things I declare; before they spring forth I tell you of them." Isaiah stands between the "former things" of the conception of the covenant plan and its future realization in

Jesus of Nazareth. And he knows what God has planned will surely be accomplished, because God not only qualifies Christ, but he also will sustain him in his redemptive work: "[I] will hold your hand; I will keep you" (v. 6). Jesus could thus say in reply to his Father, as he went to the cross: "I have finished the work which You have given Me to do" (John 17:4).

The Terms of Christ Our Covenant

So far, we have seen that God is sending his Son, a qualified Savior, on a rescue mission and has assured him of victory. Next, we enter the "briefing room" of eternity past and view the plan of action, the specific strategy and means whereby God's redemptive plan will be executed. God says to his Son, "I will give you as a covenant to the people" (Isa. 42:6; 49:8). J. I. Packer defines a covenant as follows: "A solemn agreement...that binds the parties together in permanent defined relationships, with specific promises, claims, and obligations on both sides."[2] Covenanting is a serious business. In biblical times, covenants were usually ratified by a blood sacrifice, which said, "may my blood be shed if I fail to keep the terms of this covenant." And the terms of this particular covenant referenced in Isaiah are such that bloodshed is compulsory, for it is none other than the covenant of grace:

> Man, by his fall, having made himself uncapable of life by that covenant, the Lord was pleased to make a second, commonly called the Covenant of Grace, whereby He freely offereth unto sinners life and salvation by Jesus Christ, requiring of them faith in Him, that they may be saved; and promising to give unto all those that are ordained unto eternal life His Holy Spirit, to make them willing, and able to believe. (*Westminster Confession of Faith*, 7.3)

The story of God's people in Isaiah 1–39 is the same as your story and mine: a sad catalog of repeated sin and covenant breaking. But remarkably, God intervenes and says to his beloved Son, "I will give

You as a covenant to the people." Jesus is God's undeserved gift to covenant-breaking rebels; he comes and keeps the terms of the covenant we broke and then sheds his precious blood to atone for our sins, so that you and I may be restored to a relationship with our Creator.

So the covenant of grace *is the gospel*, and Christ is its sum and substance, its beginning, center, and end. And that is why Christ is actually called the covenant itself. He is the covenant of grace personified. As E. J. Young explains, "To say that the Servant is a covenant is to say that all the blessings of the covenant are embodied in, have their root and origin in, and are dispensed by Him."[3] For an example of personification, think of James Dobson, the founder of Focus on the Family. In 2009, he stepped down from his leadership of that influential ministry. Yet even now we might say, "Jim Dobson *is* Focus on the Family," by which we mean that he is its founder, its visionary, its public face, its energy; he is identified almost synonymously with it. In a similar way, Scripture says Christ *is* the covenant: He is its founder, head, and mediator, the purchaser of its blessings, and its guarantor. Without him, there is no covenant, no blessing, no redemption, "for all the [covenant] promises of God in Him are Yes, and in Him Amen" (2 Cor. 1:20).

Now, if Christ is the covenant, then there is no salvation outside of Christ. To receive salvation is to receive Christ himself. You cannot separate the two. The covenant of grace is not a theological abstraction from Jesus's person and work; rather, "The covenant is nothing else but Christ expounded, Christ interpreted, Christ drawn out at length."[4]

Furthermore, if Christ is the covenant, then becoming a Christian is more than merely signing some decision card or a superficial subscription to a confessional standard; at its very heart is a saving relationship with Jesus Christ. If Christ is the covenant, then to be in covenant with God is to be in union with Christ, which is described by the Apostle Paul in Ephesians 5:22–33 as a marriage covenant: a daily, intimate, loving walk together with the Lord.

The Beneficiaries of Christ Our Covenant

Isaiah 42:6 goes on to announce who benefits from the covenant of grace: "I will...give you as a covenant to the people, as a light to the Gentiles." Christ did not become a covenant for himself (though of course, it ultimately brings him glory); the real beneficiaries of his work are his elect people. As we have already seen, in the covenant of redemption before time, God entered into a covenant relationship with his Son so that he might enter into a covenant relationship with you through him. Isaiah tells us that Christ is given as a covenant "*to* you," or a better translation would be, "*for* you." As *Larger Catechism*, Answer 31, says, "The Covenant of Grace was made with Christ as the second Adam, *and in Him with all the elect as His seed*" (italics added). According to the text, these elect are comprised of two groups of people. The first God mentions are "my people," i.e., the Jews. When God made his covenant of grace with Abraham, he confirmed it with his seed, who would become a great nation (Gen. 12:1–3). Later at Sinai it was formally expressed to Israel as a nation, but there was also always the promise that in Abraham's seed all nations of the world would be blessed. That is why Gentiles are also mentioned here: Christ will redeem a global Church.

Imagine a world in which the Church of Jesus Christ is confined to a tiny people group living on a small island. For centuries they alone had the Bible, only they have the means of grace, only they have the gospel. The entirety of the rest of the globe is a dark world inhabited by advanced civilizations and primitive tribes who worship demons and idols, living in wickedness, all of whom for millennia continue in their lostness to a lost eternity. The only pocket of light in this dark world is in this secluded enclave where the light of the gospel shines. This essentially describes planet earth in Isaiah's day. Only Israel had "the adoption, the glory, the covenants, the giving of the law, the service of God, and the promises" (Rom. 9:4). Although there were a few converts within the orbit of the Promised Land, the announcement by the prophets that God was sending a Light to the Gentiles was earth shaking. That is why God says to his Son, "Ask of me and I will give you the nations" (Ps. 2:7–8). That is why Jesus said to his Jewish hearers, "I lay down My life for the sheep. And other sheep I have which are not of this fold; them also I must bring…and there will be one flock and one shepherd" (John 10:15–17).

By way of application, you must ask: "Am *I* a beneficiary of the covenant of grace?" Is Christ *your* covenant? Has God made him to be a covenant for you? For as Romans 1:16 says, "The gospel of Christ… is the power of God to salvation for everyone who believes, for the Jew first and also for the Greek." Regardless of your ethnic background, have you believed on Christ?

The Benefits of Christ Our Covenant

If you have believed, then this master plan of God has been designed with you in mind as its beneficiary. As such, we come finally to the specific benefits of the covenant mentioned in Isaiah 42:7: "To open blind eyes, to bring out prisoners from the prison, those who sit in darkness from the prison house." We will now look more closely at the two specific benefits of the covenant of grace—which Christ has procured for you—mentioned in this verse.

Light for your blindness.

The "light" refers to the spiritual light of salvation from sin and its effects. In a parallel passage, this is made clear: "I will also give You as a light to the Gentiles, that You should be My salvation to the ends of the earth…I will preserve You and give You as a covenant to the people" (Isa. 49:6, 8). Sin is spiritual blindness; it is a crippling disability of the soul everyone is born with and all die with. It makes us blind to God, blind to his Word, and blind to spiritual things. As Paul explains, "The natural man does not receive the things of the Spirit of God, for they are foolishness to him; nor can he know them, because they are spiritually discerned" (1 Cor. 2:14).

Only a miracle can open blind eyes, and the only One who can perform it is the One given as a covenant to the people. Christ our covenant is the Light of the World (John 8:12; Luke 2:32). He does not just *bring* light; he declares that he *is* the light itself: "I have come as a light into the world, that whoever believes in Me should not abide in darkness" (John 12:46). How do people glimpse his light now that he is ascended? They do so by the foolishness of preaching the gospel. When the glorified Jesus met Paul on the road to Damascus in a blaze of light, he commissioned him in these terms: "I now send you to open their eyes, in order to turn them from darkness to light, and from the power of Satan to God, that they may receive forgiveness of sins" (Acts 26:17–18). If you are still blind, you must attend to such preaching of Christ our covenant, acknowledge your blindness, and cry out to Christ, "Rabbi, I want to see" (Mark 10:51 NIV).

Liberty from your prison.

The second benefit the gospel of Jesus Christ brings is liberty. God's Suffering Servant in Isaiah is often declared to be the great liberator from slavery, for instance, in Isaiah 61:1. What liberty does Christ our covenant bring to his people? It is liberty from Satan's rule; unbelievers are those Paul says have been "taken captive by [the devil] to do his will" (2 Tim. 2:26). But if Christ is your covenant, then—according to the first declaration of that covenant in Genesis 3:15—he has crushed Satan's head and set you free from his power. It is liberty from the guilt and penalty of sin. As unbelievers, "you presented your members as slaves of uncleanness" (Rom. 6:19). But if Christ is your covenant, then he has liberated you by bearing sin's penalty in the passive obedience of his death: "our old man was crucified with Him, that the body of sin might be done away with, that we should no longer be slaves of sin" (v. 6).

Liberty from the law as a means of redemption.

As unbelievers, the law broke you with its impossible demands as you tried in vain to keep it and win God's favor. Instead, it proved to be your tutor by leading you to Christ our covenant, who liberates you because he perfectly kept the law in his life of active obedience (Gal. 3:24). In short, the covenant of grace, which Christ embodies, is the great emancipation proclamation of the Church. You once "sat in darkness in the prison house," and Christ set you free (Isa. 42:7).

A helpful illustration of this gospel truth is found in the story of Operation Jericho, the 1944 low-level bombing raid by British aircraft on Amiens Prison in German-occupied France. The object of the raid was to free French Resistance prisoners, 120 of whom were to be executed the following day. On their first pass, the bombers destroyed the German barracks; on their second pass, they breached the prison walls, setting 258 prisoners free from their cells. The leader of Operation Jericho, Group Captain Pickard, was shot down and killed at the very moment he successfully completed his mission.[5]

Like those men in Amiens Prison, you were in prison, condemned to death; unlike them, you were not brave patriots, but criminals deserving death. But unbeknown to you, a plan was formed for your rescue; a covenant was established, in which Christ came as God's jail-breaker from above. He destroyed the enemy garrison and has "[brought] out prisoners from the prison, those who sit in darkness from the prison house" (v. 7). And he has done so at the cost of his own blood. For this reason, says the writer of Hebrews,

> He is the mediator of a new covenant, so that, since a death has taken place for the redemption of the transgressions that were committed under the first covenant, those who have been called may receive the promise of the eternal inheritance. For where a covenant is, there must of necessity be the death of the one who made it. (Heb. 9:15–16 NASB)

Praise be to God for his covenant grace!

Jesus Is Our

Door

I am the door…
—John 10:9

READ JOHN 10:1–30

Doors exist to keep people out and let people in. Jesus begins in the tenth chapter of John with the door of a sheepfold. The sheepfold is the church, the people of God, and in Jesus's use of this illustration he is "the shepherd of the sheep" to whom "the doorkeeper opens" (vv. 2–3). After the pattern of shepherding still prevalent in the Middle East, "the sheep follow him for they know his voice" (v. 4). Jesus is distinguishing the true shepherd(s) from the false—the latter being the Pharisees who had just excommunicated the blind man whom Jesus had healed on the Sabbath (John 9:16, 34).

However, Jesus's hearers do not, as we say, "get it." So Jesus instantly changes his tack and switches from being the shepherd in the story to being "the door of the sheep" (John 10:6–7). But how can the shepherd also become the door? The likely answer is that Jesus shifts the scene from the village sheepfold with its doorkeeper to a summer sheepfold where there is only a gap in the wall and the shepherd sleeps in the gap. He is the living door that opens to let his sheep in and closes to keep the wolves out. From this picture flow the central truths of the gospel and its application.

Jesus Is the One and Only Way to Salvation

The fact that Jesus is the Door teaches us that there is precisely one Savior and one way of salvation. Jesus's language could hardly be more clear and uncompromising: "All who ever came before Me are thieves and robbers" (v. 8). He is not of course referring to his forerunners, like Abraham, Isaac, Jacob, and David, or any of his faithful prophets. He is thinking of false prophets, false church leaders like the Pharisees and Sadducees, and false religions of all sorts. He is talking about "the broad way" that leads to destruction (Matt. 7:13).

For the narrow gate, Jesus is the Door of the *shepherds* as well as the *sheep*. He is the one Savior and through him is the one way of salvation. Those who say otherwise are robbers of lost souls. They steal heaven from sinners and seduce them for a lost eternity. This is why all the "...isms" apart from the gospel that is Christ and Him crucified are such desperate, soul-destroying outrages. Not least is the universalistic notion that all sorts of ways lead to God: We are all like people climbing up a mountain in the mist. We take our own paths and meantime cannot see (i.e., agree with) each other. But we will all arrive eventually at the sunlit mountain top and find out we were all right with God already. Jesus explodes such myths of universal salvation, for there is only one way of salvation. Jesus Christ is the Door, the only Door, and the one Door to heaven. The "men in the mist" are lost in a fog, robbed of gospel light, and condemned to the ultimate surprise of hearing the real Jesus say to them, "I never knew you" (Matt. 7:23).

Jesus's sheep will not hear the false teachers (John 10:8b).

The false teachers of this world may be influential, but they are not invincible. The vast array of alleged ways of salvation is certainly the work of the devil: "For false christs and false prophets will rise and show signs and wonders to deceive, if possible, even the elect" (Mark 13:22). These thieves and robbers certainly deceived many, "but the sheep did not hear them" (John 10:8).

One strand of the false teachers' deception is in the claim that all the religions and interpretations of Scripture absolve people from even having to hear the gospel. The argument is that the existence of so many contradictory opinions and interpretations must mean that no one of them can be true. This seems to rest on the odd notion that if the truth were only clear enough, no one would ever disbelieve it. The truth is expressed in the common proverb, "There are none so blind as those who will not see." The multiplicity of error is only a testimony to the willful denial of what is otherwise as clear as crystal. So, with the lie that truth cannot be attained, the opposite is the case: the protesters are burying their heads in the sand. All that the bewildering variety in what people believe and teach and do actually proves is the human capacity for error and the devil's capacity for deception.

There is indeed real truth amidst the contradictory clamor of human skepticism, and it is the truth as it is in Jesus (Eph. 4:21). It is there for all to see—clear, accessible, and user friendly—in the Word of God and in the Son of God. Furthermore, because Jesus is the Door, his sheep will sooner or later and forever hear his voice and follow him (John 10:16, 27). The Lord Jesus Christ will not lose a single soul of all he saves. His true sheep will recognize his voice, and he will never let them be plucked from his hand (vv. 28–29).

Believers will be saved (John 10:9ab).

Jesus argues that because he is the Door, all who believe in him will be saved, effective immediately upon coming to him in faith: "I am the door, if anyone enters by Me, he will be saved." He is the sure entrance into a new life, with forgiveness of sin and reconciliation to his Father-God and ours.

This salvation flows from the love of God from eternity to eternity. The following pasages illustrate this truth:

* "God so loved the world, that whoever believes in Him should not perish but have everlasting life" (John 3:16).
* "Nor is there salvation in any other; for there is no other name under heaven given amongst men by which we must be saved" (Acts 4:12).
* "There is one God, and one Mediator between God and men, the Man Christ Jesus, who gave himself a ransom for all..." [who believe in him savingly] (1 Tim. 2:5–6).

Coming to Christ is the one and only entrance to new life.

Believers will find pasture (John 10:9cd).

Because Jesus is the Door, those who believe in him will grow in grace. His sheep "will go in and out and will find pasture." They will operate in essential security as they live their lives from day to day, both in the church and in the world. Jesus is the constant shepherd of the sheep (Ps. 23:4–6; 30). He leads us, for as "they go out to the field in the morning," observes Matthew Henry, "they come into the fold at night; and in both the shepherd leads and feeds them." Jesus warns us that "in the world you will have tribulation"; but he assures us, his flock, to "be of good cheer, I have overcome the world" (John 16:33).

The Christian's life is not only secure in Christ, but it is expanding. George Hutcheson comments, "Such also as do thus come to God will find such satisfaction and spiritual refreshment for making them grow in grace as they shall not need to complain, or betake themselves to other comforts, for he shall 'find pasture.' "[1] This growth comes from the Lord. It does not depend simply on hearing sound sermons from solid preachers, as important as it is to be under God's means of grace.[2] Far less is it a matter of being in a church with lots of programs. It is a promise of God, whatever the circumstances.

When you hear someone complain, "I am not growing," it is so often an exercise in covering up a lack of lively discipleship or it is a complaining spirit that shifts the blame to other Christians, to the church and its leadership, and even to God. If Jesus Christ is truly the shepherd of your heart, then you will be finding *pasture*—the feeding of your soul.

Abundant Life or Certain Death?

There is a beautiful county in Wisconsin called Door County. It is a peninsula formed by Lake Michigan to the east and Green Bay to the west. It is all fruit farms, artists' colonies, and picturesque fishing villages—New England in the Midwest. But it is called Door County for a thoroughly macabre reason. At the tip of the peninsula there is an island, Washington Island, separated from the mainland by a strait that is called Death's Door because it has seen more shipwrecks than any other piece of fresh water in the world. Similarly, the world is at death's door. We are all at the door of eternity. And all who do not know Christ as their Savior are standing at the door of eternal death—the "second death"—the death that never dies (Rev. 20:14; 21:8; Mark 9:44). But Jesus is *life's* Door, and, as previously seen in Acts 4:12, the only means of salvation.

Because Jesus is the Door, he is the matter of abundant life versus certain death for every human being. Jesus expresses the issue with majestic simplicity; "The thief does not come except to steal, and to kill, and to destroy. I have come that they may have life, and that they may have it more abundantly." Philip Henry, father of Matthew, notes that Christ is a "living" Door. He adds,

> This is peculiar to him. No other door is so besides him; as he is the "living way" [Heb. 10:20], so he is the living door, the door to life and the door that has life. Other doors are dead things. Now it is true he was dead, but he is alive and lives for evermore, and thence it follows, Revelation 1:18, he has "the keys of hell and of death."[3]

Do you remember the foolish girls in Jesus's parable of the ten virgins (Matt. 25:1–13)? They had no oil in their lamps. Outwardly, they appeared to be equipped because they had lamps. They looked like believers as far as everybody else could see. They had an outward profession of faith. But inwardly they had no oil, no inward work of God's grace, and they were not in the least concerned about it. They were not saved, converted believers in Christ. So when midnight came, they looked to the real believers, who did have oil in their lamps, but they could not give them their oil (salvation). The virgins then looked to the world, but it was no longer to be found there. They were on the wrong side of the door that was now shut to them forever. They arrived too late, the door was closed, and the Lord said, "I do not know you." They had wasted a lifetime of opportunities to hear the gospel and believe in Jesus Christ from the heart.

However, there is still a Door for you. There is a way to life, and he is Jesus Christ. Jesus the Door proclaims, "The Lord has anointed Me to preach good tidings to the poor; he has sent Me to heal the broken hearted, to proclaim liberty to the captives; and the opening of the prison to those who are bound" (Isa. 61:1; Luke 4:18). Is Jesus your Door—your life, now and forevermore?

Jesus Is Our

Food

I am the living bread which came down from heaven.
If anyone eats of this bread, he will live forever; and the bread that I shall give is My flesh, which I shall give for the life of the world.—John 6:51

READ JOHN 6:22–59

Food is our physical fuel. We cannot do without it. In the world of living things, oxidation rules. We eat to live. We enjoy eating, and the Lord means us to rejoice in the food we eat. "Nothing is better for a man," says Solomon, "than that he should eat and drink, and that his soul should enjoy good in his labor. This also, I saw, was from the hand of God" (Eccl. 2:24). Elsewhere he says, "My son, eat honey because it is good, and the honeycomb which is sweet to your taste," but also adds a very practical caution against overindulgence, "Have you found honey? Eat only as much as you need, lest you be filled with it and vomit" (Prov. 24:13; 25:16).

The right balance is struck when we have in view the true purpose of all of God's gifts: "It is not good to eat much honey; so to seek one's own glory is not glory" (Prov. 25:27). Not least, we are called to depend upon the Lord for everything that sustains us from day to day by praying, as in the Lord's Prayer, "Give us this day our daily bread" (Matt. 6:11).

What is true of the body is true, in its own way, of the soul. People everywhere have a mental and spiritual diet of some kind. Sad to say, this is frequently shallow, superficial, and unhealthy. There is junk food for the soul out there, and it is far more dangerous than the hamburgers and fries that the health-minded love to hate for the simple reason that spiritual junk food can do eternal damage.

Furthermore, what you feed to your heart and mind speaks volumes about your relationship to God. Scripture tells us, "If I regard iniquity in my heart, the Lord will not hear" (Ps. 66:18). The psalmist ruefully bemoans the effect of sin on his general wellbeing: "My strength fails because of my iniquity, and my bones waste away" (Ps. 31:10). Contrast this with a heart intent on being filled with a feast of good things: "As the deer pants for the water brooks, so pants my souls for You, O God. My soul thirsts for God, for the living God" (Ps. 42:1–2).

John 6:51 is just one small slice of Jesus's discourse on the Bread of Life (vv. 22–66). It teaches that Christ, who is the Bread of Life, must be our food. This comes in the aftermath of the feeding of the five thousand (vv. 1–14). Jesus goes on to urge his hearers: "Do not labor for the food which perishes, but for the food that endures to everlasting life" (v. 27). Thus they must "believe in Him…" (v. 29).

In response, his hearers ask him for a sign, even implying that it ought to be as big, or bigger, than the manna in the Exodus (v. 31). Jesus replies with the assurance that God gives "the true bread from heaven," which is *a person who will give life to the world* (vv. 32–33). In other words, he is saying there will not be a sign, but there will be the substance—the "bread"—in a person.

The Jews clearly do not put two and two together right away, and they mumble something about desiring "this bread always" (v. 34). Jesus then answers their obvious incomprehension with the proclamation, "I am the bread of life" (v. 35). Whatever confusion had inhabited their minds to this point, it cleared up in a moment, because they grasped the messianic implications of Jesus's assertion—and they objected most loudly (vv. 41–42). Jesus drives his message home by showing how he is indeed the Bread of Life and pointedly contrasts himself with the manna in the wilderness (vv. 43–51). Jesus unpacks the metaphor of the bread in verse 51 to show that in him there is a repast provided, a response required, and a reward promised.

A Repast Provided

Jesus declares, "I am the living bread which came down from heaven…and the bread that I shall give is my flesh, which I shall give for the life of the world" (v. 51). There are four ways in particular that our Lord uses the metaphor of bread to illustrate his person and work. These add up to a redemptive repast that repeatedly restores and refreshes the soul of the believer.

Jesus is the living bread.

There is a double point to grasp here: Jesus is not only living bread but he is also life-giving bread. Remember the deliberate contrast with the miraculous manna God had given to Israel during their forty-year sojourn in the Sinai desert. Manna was dead bread, whereas Jesus is living bread. Jesus already told his hearers what this means: "As the Father has life in Himself, so He has granted the Son to have life in Himself" (John 5:26). The other significant point is that manna gave the Israelites life. That is what food is supposed to do, of course. It illustrates that Jesus is *life-giving*. Look at how Jesus progressively unfolds this truth as he interacts with his audience:

He first proposes to us all the *pathway* to new life: "Do not labor for the food which perishes, but for the food which endures to everlasting life, which the Son of Man will give you, because God the Father has set His seal on Him" (John 6:27).

He goes on to proclaim himself to be the *provider* of this new life: "I am the bread of life" (v. 48). Jesus gives himself as the Savior.

He finally points to the *promise* of new life: "This is the bread which came down from heaven—not as your fathers ate the manna, and are dead. He who eats this bread will live forever" (v. 58). Jesus is emphatic and uncompromising; he gives eternal life, both now and in the world to come.

Jesus is the heavenly bread.

The manna in the wilderness was earthly bread, even though it was miraculously given. Jesus, in contrast, "came down from heaven." He is the heavenly bread in terms of three vital aspects.

He is, first of all, "the Lamb slain from the foundation of the world" (Rev. 13:8). In an eternal decree, God—Father, Son, and Holy Spirit—determined that the Son would be the Savior of the world. God did not decree that mankind should never fall into sin, but he did decree the provision of a Redeemer to save them from their sins once entered upon. Adam as created was sinless but not incapable of falling into sin. Adam fell into sin and as fallen was thereafter incapable of not sinning, as also are all his descendants—the rest of us. It is grace in God that he purposed to save a people so that in heaven they would be incapable of sinning ever again. Our salvation, thus decreed, is not only eternal but complete. We do not merely return to the sinless state of the first Adam, but are brought to the glorified state of the second Adam.[1]

Second, the one who is "sent forth" by the Father is the divine Son enfleshed (incarnate) by being "born of a woman, born under the law" (Gal. 4:4). 1 John 4:14 says, "We have seen and testify that the Father has sent the Son as Savior of the world." And John 3:16 states, "For God so loved the world that He gave His only begotten Son, that whoever believes in Him should not perish but have everlasting life."

In the third place, he is also "the Lord from heaven" and the crucified "Lord of glory" (1 Cor. 15:47; 2:8). He is not a mere man endowed with divine qualities and notable gifts but God the Son united with our humanity (Luke 1:30–33). In the words of the Apostles' Creed, he is "Jesus Christ, His only Son, our Lord: who was conceived by the Holy Ghost, born of the virgin Mary, suffered under Pontius Pilate, was crucified, dead, and buried..." He is not to be explained away as a great man, whether preacher, prophet, or pundit. He is the "last Adam" who "became a life-giving spirit" (1 Cor. 15:45).

Jesus is gracious bread.

He is the "bread that I shall give..." Christ is in himself God's "indescribable gift"—the gift of God's love (2 Cor. 9:15; John 3:16). But he also gives himself, for he says "I lay down My life for the sheep" (John 10:15). And it all adds up to the gift of *free grace*—undeserved and unearned—wholly and unconditionally gracious. We have no right to this bread. We have no right to a second chance as so many like to say. We are not entitled to the spiritual food that he feeds to our souls. It is "by grace you have been saved through faith, and that not of yourselves; it is the gift of God" (Eph. 2:8).

Jesus is atoning bread.

You know how bread is made: grinding flour, kneading dough, baking loaves. Then eating it; it is broken, chewed, swallowed, and digested. Jesus as the living bread is also dying bread. He says of the bread he gives that it is, "My flesh, which I shall give for the life of the world." His body is broken and his blood is shed. Even his birth to Mary is humiliation. His whole ministry partakes of suffering. "The sufferings and death of Christ," writes Philip Henry, "are the food of our souls."[2]

The central point is that "without the shedding of blood there is no remission [of sin]" (Heb. 9:22; compare with Lev. 17:11). Jesus is the sacrifice for sin, the substitute for sinners, the satisfaction for justice, and the surety for salvation: "Behold! The Lamb of God" (John 1:29).

We are not saved by good works, good thoughts, or any kind of external rites and performances, "but with the precious blood of Christ, as of a lamb without blemish and without spot" (1 Peter 1:19).

Notice also that Jesus does this "for the life of the world," for "nor is there salvation in any other, for there is no other name under heaven given among men by which we must be saved" (Acts 4:12). Jesus is the living bread and alone able to secure for us the life we need in both time and eternity.

A Response Required

Although God is sovereign and salvation is the gift of grace, this gift will never be received without the response of a saving faith. There can be no consciousness of blessing without a self-conscious commitment from the heart. So when Jesus says in John 6:51, "If anyone eats of this bread..." he is requiring and inviting a response, without which there will be no participation in redemption itself. It really is a matter of eternal life or death.

Eating is the same as believing.

To eat of this bread that is Christ means exercising personal faith in the Lord Jesus Christ. This is not the physical eating of Christ as in the Roman Catholic Mass where the elements of bread and wine are erroneously and blasphemously held to be transformed into the substance of Christ's flesh and blood. Neither is it the mere ingestion of the symbols in the Lord's Supper. Rather, the Scriptures teach a spiritual ingestion of Christ by faith that looks to Jesus, receives him as offered in the gospel, trusts in him as Savior and Lord, and continues in union and communion with him by faith.

Although this is the specific purpose and promise of the sacrament, this spiritual feeding is for every moment as we wait upon the Lord. "He who comes to Me," says Jesus, "shall never hunger, and he who believes in Me shall never thirst" (John 6:35). It simply means you are called to believe on him. The same theme is set out through the prophet Isaiah, looking forward to Christ: "Ho! Everyone who thirsts, come to the waters; and you who have no money, come, buy and eat. Yes, come, buy wine and milk without money and without price" (Isa. 55:1). Jesus says of himself, "If anyone thirsts, let him come to me and drink" (John 7:37), and John reiterates God's call to repentance and faith: "This is His commandment: that we should believe on the name of His Son Jesus Christ" (1 John 3:23). Believing is eating!

Eating is for the hungry and thirsty.

Do you accept and feel your need of the Savior? Then, says Jesus, "labor...for the food that endures" (John 6:27). No one truly comes to Christ, or truly follows Christ, without an appetite for his salvation. This parallels what Jesus says about people going to the doctor: "Those who are well have no need of a physician, but those who are sick. But go and learn what this means: 'I desire mercy and not sacrifice.' For I did not come to call the righteous, but sinners, to repentance" (Matt. 9:12–13). As long as you think you do not need a Savior, you will not come to Christ. But if you are hungry you will discover that "He is also able to save to the uttermost those who come to God through Him, since He always lives to make intercession for them" (Heb. 7:25). Jesus promises that "blessed are those who hunger and thirst for righteousness, for they shall be filled" (Matt. 5:6). For what—be honest—do you hunger and thirst? Are you working for the food that endures?

There is enough for all who apply.

We have a monthly fellowship lunch in our church. People bring casseroles and desserts to share. There is the odd occasion when we wonder if there will be enough food for all who stay after the service, although we have never run out in spite of our doubts. No one is turned away hungry. So it is with Jesus: "All that the Father gives Me will come to Me, and the one who comes to Me I will by no means cast out" (John 6:37). No one will be able to say to the Lord with the slightest justification, "I came to You, and You turned me away." The words "depart from Me" are reserved for the "workers of iniquity" who never knew the Lord or were known by him (Luke 13:27; Matt. 25:11–12). The Lord says, "Come...and I will give you rest." But *you must come*. Have you? Will you? The time may be shorter than you think (Luke 13:3, 5).

A Reward Promised

"There is nothing so important" writes Charles Simeon, "as a life of faith on Christ: nothing."[3] The reason, as Jesus is teaching us, is that "if anyone eats of this bread, he will live forever" (John 6:51). Elsewhere he says, "He who believes in the Son has everlasting life; and he who does not believe the Son shall not see life, but the wrath of God abides on him" (John 3:36). Many ate manna in Israel's Sinai wanderings and they died (1 Cor. 10:5). Many eat good food all their lives, and they all die. Some eat bread in the Lord's Supper, and they do not live forever (1 Cor. 11:29–30). It is also true that some have eternal life, never ate good food, and were kept by circumstances from the Lord's Table. The real issue, of course, is whether you know Christ as your Savior. If you do, the reward is everlasting life. You will, as Jesus says, live forever. This is life from Christ, in Christ, and for Christ.

Life from Christ.

This new life is from Jesus Christ, and it is *everlasting* life. The crucified and risen Jesus came to give this life to us so that he would be "the firstborn among many brethren" (Rom. 8:29). Jesus declares, "Most assuredly, I say to you, he who hears My word and believes in Him who sent Me has everlasting life, and shall not come into judgment, but has passed from death into life" (John 5:24). For the Christian, eternal life is *now* in this life even though it is *not ye*t as to its fullness in heaven.

Life in Christ.

This new life is in Jesus Christ, and it is an *engaged* life. It is life in union and communion with Christ in an inseparable and indissoluble fellowship: "He who eats My flesh and drinks My blood abides in Me, and I in him" (John 6:55). Are you engaged with Christ—constantly in heart, soul, strength, and mind? Is he "Christ in you, the hope of glory" throughout your waking hours (Col. 1:27)?

Life for Christ.

This new life is for Jesus Christ, and it is an *expanding* life. Christ fills us into the future; we grow in grace. He satisfies; we grow in joy: "How sweet are Your words to my taste, sweeter than honey to my mouth!" (Ps. 119:103). Jesus—"the living bread which came down from heaven"—calls us in the gospel to an ever-expanding experience of his grace and his love for all eternity: "To him who overcomes I will give some of the hidden manna to eat. And I will give him a white stone, and on the stone a new name written which no one knows except him who receives it" (Rev. 2:17). Jesus is the bread without which we cannot live the life that God calls us to live—that life where the "chief end of man is to glorify God and enjoy Him forever."[4]

Jesus Is Our

Foundation

For no other foundation can anyone lay than that which is laid, which is Jesus Christ.
—1 Corinthians 3:11

READ 1 CORINTHIANS 3:1–17

Our church in Pennsylvania once had a chimney—a red-brick column that climbed up the outside of the building.[1] It looked solid enough, but one day someone leaned on it—and it swayed! Not much. But it moved. It turned out that it had no solid footing at all. For fifty years it lay on loose bricks on gravel. It was pulled down before it did anyone any damage. Likewise, during one summer holiday on the Outer Banks of North Carolina, we saw many opulent holiday homes built squarely on sand, just waiting for hurricane season. Buildings can be ever so beautiful and useful but if they have no solid foundations, it is only a matter of time before they are swept away.

You know what God's Word does with this image of the house built on sand. It is a foolish man, Jesus tells us, that builds his house on sand. It is the wise man who builds on the rock (Matt. 7:24–27). Paul applies it to the church in Corinth, where all sorts of divisions proved that they were not building on a sound foundation (1 Cor. 1:10–13; 3:3–4). The apostle directs them in our text to the foundation they desperately needed:

"For no other foundation can anyone lay than that which is laid, which is Jesus Christ" (1 Cor. 3:11). Have you ever seen a divided, fractious church grow? Have you ever found squabbling Christians to be effective disciples of Jesus? Of course not. These are built on quicksand. A solid foundation is what we need for our lives and our relationship to the Lord and his people to be effective and joyous in our discipleship.

With this in mind, let us listen to our Scripture text. It says three things: there is only *one foundation*; that foundation is *Jesus Christ*; and this addresses you with a most vital *question*, "What foundation are you building your life upon: Jesus or something, or someone, else?" This takes us to the most basic issues of the human heart and destiny both in this life and the eternity to which we all soon shall pass.

No Other Foundation

We first should ask ourselves what other foundations we build our lives upon. Paul assumes here that in life, day by day, we are laying a foundation for eternity. This is true, whether or not we accept it. He also assumes that the default position of human nature is that we are trying to please God in our own way. And he speaks here to those who believe they are Christians and want to be right with God.

The unspoken implication is that any who do not care about God, Jesus, and Scripture truth are denying the very purpose of their life. They are, so to speak, "off the map." They need the first step of coming to the Lord. They may be very active and productive in life, but they are on the wrong track from God's point of view.

Surely living a decent life will do?

Many build their lives on trying to be good according to their own light. They are decent people. They feel good about themselves. They live orderly lives. They pay their bills and help their neighbors. They cannot see God—if such a being exists, which they doubt—disapproving of them. Plenty of other people are a lot worse. They try to do their bit without claiming to be perfect. If they are able to make their mark in some notable way and generally show kindness to others, then so much the better. And, of course, much good has come to the world through such diligence and application.

Will a mixture of works and religion do?

Some, who are perhaps more consciously "religious," build on a foundation that is more of a mixture of their own goodness and a bit of church going and the assumed love and mercy of God. Luke cites the example of some converted Pharisees who were all for faith in Jesus but also said, "It is necessary to circumcise [non-Jewish converts], and to command them to keep the law of Moses" (Acts 15:5). Later on, the Apostle Paul opposes Peter to his face over the latter's effectively adding the observance of certain laws to faith as necessary for recognition as a real Christian (Gal. 2:11ff.). Christians today do not worry about keeping Old Testament dietary laws, but they do manage to invent laws of their own: habits of eating, drinking, clothing, hairstyle, devotional methods, Bible translations, and etc. The point is that they are in effect saying, Jesus Christ is not enough; Scripture alone is not enough of a rule for faith and life. So, in subtle ways, it ends up as "Jesus *plus* certain things I am expected to do" people. Charles Simeon, that great preacher of nineteenth-century England, is spot on when he says that such folk "will expect mercy at [Christ's] hands, not so much because his grace is free and all-sufficient, as because they have something in themselves, which may deserve his notice and regard."[2] They not only have done their bit; they have performed over and above the minimum.

Will any "faith" do?

Others will hold any "faith" to be as good a foundation as any other. Universalism is basically the name of that game. Whatever you believe, provided you are mostly sincere, is fine with God—no matter what Scripture says to the contrary. You are, after all, "no worse than the next man" by your chosen standard for getting to heaven (if there is a heaven). I once heard a man say with great confidence, "Isn't God in the forgiveness business, after all?" This is wonderfully convenient, because it redefines God's will in terms of what *I* have decided he wants of me. The inconvenient truth for this theory, however, is that what God actually says is that only one foundation will do, and, as we shall see, he is alone Jesus Christ and him crucified.

Why Are Other Foundations Hopeless?

There are three basic answers to why other foundations are hopeless.

Other foundations cannot support the weight of our need.

A good friend owns a cabin in the woods of Michigan. Some years back it was decided to add a second floor at one end. It looked fine in the summer sun. But the far north has a long winter with lots of snow. Guess what happened? The weight of an extra level plus several feet of snow brought the new addition crashing down.

Now ask yourself: how can the whole weight of the forgiveness of your sin conceivably be supported by your best efforts—never mind all your not-so-good efforts? Taking it a step further: how can your whole life-performance justify you before a holy God and secure your eternal salvation? If you were God, could you approve of your deeds, attitudes, motives, intentions, and thoughts? Would you be impressed by your holiness?

The fact is, "There is none righteous, no, not one" (Rom. 3:10). Not even you. This means that you—we all—need a Savior who can actually bear the weight of the sin of the world, supply us with the robe of his righteousness, and so secure eternal redemption for us (John 1:29; Isa. 61:10; Heb. 9:12).

Other foundations declare God to be a liar.

They fly in the face of God's infallible Word in that they reject what he says about our inability to commend ourselves to him. God says that "we are all like an unclean thing, and all our righteousnesses are like filthy rags" (Isa. 64:6). But we say, "Not quite all—only some," and persuade ourselves we have done enough to earn God's smile. God says, "you were dead in trespasses and sins" (Eph. 2:1). But we say, "Maybe we are only half dead?"—as if to say we are still good enough to save ourselves with maybe a little help from God. Surely our actual experience of life confirms the truth of these Scriptures, not to mention an honest evaluation of our true spiritual condition by nature?

Other foundations trample on Christ's sacrifice.

God's Word is absolutely uncompromising: Acts 4:12 declares, "Nor is there salvation in any other, for there is no other name under heaven given among men by which we must be saved." And it is "by grace you have been saved through faith, and that not of yourselves; it is the gift of God, not of works, lest anyone should boast" (Eph. 2:8–9; compare with 1 Cor. 1:20–31). Why did Paul tell the Corinthians, "I determined not to know anything among you except Jesus Christ and Him crucified" (1 Cor. 2:2)? Because there is no salvation in any other thing or person.

Jesus Christ Is the Only Foundation

The Apostle Paul defines the only foundation: "For no other foundation can anyone lay than that which is laid, which is Christ Jesus." This answers any notion that he, Paul, is the foundation. There was a faction in Corinth that was saying "I am of Paul," as if he was the true founder of the church. Paul is willing to say he is a "wise master builder" and that as part of a team he "laid the foundation" that others were building upon (1 Cor. 3:10). He is talking here about the operational side of planting the church. He came, he preached the gospel, and he worked to establish the church so he could leave it in good working order to the ministry of others. He is, however, at pains to focus on the foundation itself and not merely his role in the beginnings of the church in Corinth. That foundation is, says Paul in verse 11, none other than Christ Jesus himself. Paul did not, of course, lay the foundation that is Jesus Christ.

Who laid this foundation?

The answer to who laid this foundation is *God himself*: for "the Father has sent the Son as Savior of the world" (1 John 4:14). Furthermore, Scripture employs the language of building to describe this. Peter quotes Isaiah 28:16 to describe Jesus's appointment as the Chief Cornerstone: "Thus says the Lord God: 'Behold, I lay in Zion a stone for a foundation, a tried stone, a precious cornerstone, a sure foundation; whoever believes will not act hastily' " (compare with 1 Peter 2:6). God describes his foundation-stone Son in three ways:

Jesus Christ is a tried stone. Peter renders this "chosen" (Greek *eklekton*).[3] He had been with his people in the past. He has never failed them; for example, in the desert between Egypt and the Promised Land, the Israelites "drank of that spiritual Rock that followed them, and that Rock was Christ" (1 Cor. 10:4).

Jesus Christ is a precious Cornerstone. "To you who believe," says Peter, "He is precious" (1 Peter 2:7). The original building of this writer's old school in Scotland has a cornerstone dated 1628.[4] That stone fixed the position of all the other stones in that beautiful edifice before they were all quarried, never mind cut and installed. In the same way, Christ our foundation relates to all the stones in the church he is building, even before they are born, let alone saved.

Jesus Christ is a sure foundation. He is "the same, yesterday, today and forever" (Heb. 13:8). He is "the rock that is higher than I" (Ps. 61:2).

Yet it is precisely because Jesus is a sure foundation for those who trust in him that he is also "a stone of stumbling and a rock of offense" to those who are resolved to reject him (1 Peter 2:8). Those who would tear down that which he is building will find the effort to be to their frustration and, ultimately, their ruination.

Why did God lay this foundation?

God laid this foundation *to provide a mediator*. This mediator is able to effect the reconciliation of God and sinners by atoning for sin as the substitute for all who would be saved by his grace and so become his believing people. The Lord Jesus Christ is, writes Paul, the "one Mediator between God and man" (1 Tim. 2:5). This exclusive singularity of Jesus as the foundation of salvation is confirmed by God's gracious promise of a Savior, the covenant of grace, and the gospel of saving grace.

In Jesus Christ alone is the *promise* of a Savior (Gen. 3:15). Second Corinthians 1:20 says, "All the promises of God in Him are Yes, and in Him Amen, to the glory of God." As Edward Mote puts it, "On Christ, the solid Rock, I stand; All other ground is sinking sand."[5]

In Jesus Christ alone the *covenant of grace* is established "Now He has obtained a more excellent ministry, inasmuch as He is also mediator of a better covenant" than the ceremonies of the law of Moses (Heb. 8:6). The writer goes on to quote Jeremiah 31:31–34, in which God promises a "new covenant" will be revealed in what will be the New Testament era. This covenant of grace is progressively unfolded throughout the Old Testament from the promise that the seed of the woman would bruise the head of the serpent in Genesis 3:15, to the prediction of the second Elijah in Malachi 4:5 who prepares the way of the Lord (Jesus) as he comes into his holy temple (Mal. 3:1), and everything in between.

In Jesus Christ alone is the *gospel* of saving grace revealed. He, in his person and work, is a new foundation—a living stone—for us. The good news is therefore that,

> coming to Him as to a living stone, rejected indeed by men, but chosen by God and precious, you also, as living stones, are being built up a spiritual house, a holy priesthood, to offer up spiritual sacrifices acceptable to God through Jesus Christ. Therefore it is also contained in the Scripture,
>
> "Behold, I lay in Zion
> A chief cornerstone, elect, precious,
> And he who believes on Him will by no means be put to shame."
> (1 Peter 2:4–6)

"In this is love," says John, "not that we loved God, but that He loved us and sent His Son to be the propitiation for our sins" (1 John 4:10).

It takes Jesus to cover our sin and be, in his death and resurrection, the foundation of our new life of reconciled fellowship with his heavenly Father and ours. This is the good news of the gospel. How could we ever lay our own foundation and salvation by trying harder to be better people? Without Jesus, we are merely "condemned already" and are "strangers from the covenants of promise, having no hope and without God in the world" (John 3:18; Eph. 2:12). In him, we have a Savior who is "able to save to the uttermost those who come to God through Him" (Heb. 7:25).

What Foundation Are You Building Upon?

Are you building on your "goodness" in one way or another? Please do not. It is an illusion. Your best efforts are fatally tainted; they are "filthy rags" in God's eyes (Isa. 64:6). They simply cannot begin to approach the sinless perfection required by God's law. Anyone who is going this route has not begun to accept that he is helpless to save himself and desperately needs to admit his or her need of a Savior.

How is Jesus building his church? On "this rock," he tells Peter (Matt. 16:18). This rock is not Peter, popes, clergymen, or our best efforts; rather the rock is Jesus himself. The foundation is seen in the truth in Peter's confession of faith, "You are the Christ, the son of the living God" (v. 16). Paul knows from his own experience as a converted legalist that there is "no other foundation…than that which is laid, which is Christ Jesus" (1 Cor. 3:11; compare with Phil. 3:9ff.).

His oath, His covenant, His blood
  Support me in the whelming flood;
When all around my soul gives way,
  He then is all my hope and stay.
(Edward Mote, 1797–1874)

Jesus Is Our

Fountain

In that day a fountain shall be opened for the house of David and for the inhabitants of Jerusalem, for sin and for uncleanness.
—Zechariah 13:1

READ ZECHARIAH 13

Everybody loves fountains. They grace many city centers and gardens across the world. Natural fountains, like Old Faithful in America's Yellowstone National Park, have delighted millions of tourists over the last century or more. They are beautiful to look at, often awesome in power, and convey a grace in the tracery of their lines. Fountains are also functional. They are *de rigeur* in the design of systems of drainage ponds in modern suburbs. They look attractive, of course, but they also keep the water moving, counter stagnation, and make for healthier plant life and fish populations. Fountains are fresh and clean and transforming.

This metaphor of a fountain, as used by the prophet in Zechariah 13:1, builds on this basic idea and applies it to the still future coming Messiah who would be a "fountain...for sin and uncleanness" for his people. The Hebrew word (*maqor'*) refers to a spring bubbling up from the ground. The prophet uses this to illustrate the double point that the Messiah will both *justify* and *sanctify* his covenant people.

That is, in the Messiah's saving his people from their sins, God first declares them righteous with a righteousness not their own. How? By having laid their sins on the Messiah and accounted the Messiah's righteousness to them, he *justifies* them before himself.

Then, he sets them apart to live and grow in holiness under the ministry of the indwelling Holy Spirit and the Word of truth (Eph. 1:13). He *sanctifies* them in the course of their lives as they walk with the Lord (Col. 1:10). This is salvation effected for and applied to his people in this world.

In the immediate context, Zechariah has already been outlining the great victory of God's people in the Messiah. The first part of this is about true gospel repentance, while the second focuses upon true sanctification (12:10–14; 13:1–6). The fountain theme illumines the transforming work of God's grace in and through his Son, our Savior.

Christ Pours Out Saving Grace

"In that day" the fountain is to be opened. The day referred to is the same day and time in which God pours out the "Spirit of grace and supplication" upon his people, and they will "look on [Christ] whom they [have] pierced" (Zech. 12:10). This is not simply a description of the people who were witnessing the crucifixion of Jesus at Calvary, but it is a figurative reference to the messianic era—the "day" of the New Testament gospel in Christ. To "look" on him is best understood as looking to Christ as the author and finisher of personal and saving faith (Heb. 12:2). The "Spirit of grace..." points to Pentecost and the definitive coming and continuing presence and work of the Holy Spirit with the Church (John 14:26; 15:26; 16:13; Acts 2:33).

Formerly hidden but now revealed.

The "fountain...opened" also carries the idea of a *hidden* spring that is dug out and opened up to allow free access. Someone is providing the fountain so that its flow will be a gift and a blessing to those who receive it. And is not this exactly what happens with Jesus's death on the cross? When Jesus says, "It is finished!" (John 19:30), the spring or fountain is enabled to gush forth with new life for the whole world. In contrast to this, the Old Testament ceremonies signified forgiveness but did not and could not actually secure forgiveness (compare with Heb. 9:7–15). These only granted remission of sin in terms of the retroactive power of the Great High Priest "of the good things to come" (Heb. 9:11; compare with Lev. 1:4, 9, 13; 2:2, 9; 16:16, 22–34; 2 Sam. 12:13; Ps. 32:5; and Isa. 1:18).

People were saved in the Old Testament period, but it was by Christ's sacrifice and not that of the animals in the temple. These pointed to the need of a Savior who would effect the salvation of sinners by his death and substitution for sin. Jesus Christ is the fountain. He is the *source* of forgiveness, as that was promised in the Old Testament. This continues to be proclaimed to us in the Word and sacraments.[1]

Water for thirsty souls.

When we think of a fountain, we naturally think of the power it takes to propel vast quantities of water up into the air. It may be geothermic, as with "Old Faithful," or a mighty pump, as in the fountain at "the Point" in Pittsburgh, Pennsylvania. Natural springs are mostly nowhere as spectacular. The wonder of more ordinary springs is that they can be so reliable. The Spring of Gihon in Jerusalem, for example, has poured out fresh water for thousands of years without a break. It is no wonder, then, that such springs, especially when they exist in dry lands, are so highly valued.

Not surprisingly, springs have provided us with some of the most powerful images in Scripture. In Psalm 42:1, the psalmist uses this picture to illustrate his spiritual thirst: "As the deer pants for the water brooks, so pants my soul for You, O God." In John 7:37–38, Jesus portrays himself as the source of "living water"—that is, new life—in the believer's soul: "If anyone thirsts, let him come to Me and drink. He who believes in Me, as the Scripture has said, out of his heart will flow rivers of living water." This language begins to paint a picture of how Jesus Christ makes sinners righteous in their hearts and lives. It also poses the question as to what he accomplishes in us as our fountain and spring.

Opened for the Church.

The fountain is opened for "the House of David and for the inhabitants of Jerusalem" (Zech. 13:1). As in Zechariah 12:10, reference is being made to the New Testament Church. Jesus sends out his forgiveness and peace everyday in the life of the Church and the experience of believers. He is with us by the indwelling Holy Spirit.

For sin and uncleanness.

Christ is the fountain opened for sin and for uncleanness. The coverage is comprehensive, for this includes all sin—everything from "secret faults" committed even unknowingly (Ps. 19:12, compare with 90:8), to "the works of the flesh," which are overt and gross sins (Gal. 5:19ff.; Eph. 5:3ff.). Contrast this with Jeremiah 2:13: "For my people have committed two evils: They have forsaken Me, the fountain of living waters, and hewn themselves cisterns—broken cisterns that can hold no water."

Here is the challenge of the gospel of Christ to your soul: will you be a well of living water or just another dry cistern? You see, Jesus is the fountain who makes his converts fountains also. Remember what he said to the woman of Samaria: "whoever drinks the water that I shall give him will never thirst. But the water that I shall give him will become in him a fountain of water springing up into everlasting life" (John 4:14).

Christ is the fountain of our *regeneration*. The new life of the Christian begins with the "washing of regeneration" (Titus 3:5). It is also called the new birth (John 3:3, 7). This is where the fountain of the shed blood of Jesus is applied in the washing of the sinner so as to renew his dead human nature, purge his conscience from dead works, and so enable him to turn to Christ in the conscious act of saving faith. William Cowper's powerful words expound this marvelous work of God's grace:

There is a fountain filled with blood
drawn from Immanuel's veins,
And sinners plunged beneath that flood
lose all their guilty stains.

The shedding of the blood of Christ, in its application here under the figure of a fountain, cleanses from all sin (1 John 1:7; see also Rev. 1:5; Heb. 9:14). It is a sovereign work of God. We cannot bear ourselves again, as Nicodemus correctly noted in his response to Jesus's telling him he needed to be born again (John 3:4).[2] Our believing and calling upon the name of the Lord Jesus as our Savior is, not the act, but the fruit of being born again. Peter also notes that work of God's sovereign grace when he says believers have "been born again, not of corruptible seed but incorruptible, through the word of God which lives and abides forever" (1 Peter 1:23).

Christ is also the fountain of our *justification* before God "wherein He pardons all our sins, and accepts us as righteous in His sight, only for the righteousness of Christ, imputed to us, and received by faith alone" (*Shorter Catechism*, Answer 33).

Christ is the fountain of our *sanctification*. Jesus says, "He who believes in me, as the Scripture has said, out of his heart will flow rivers of living water" (John 7:38). Jesus is speaking of the Holy Spirit working in us. In other words, it is not just sins committed that are washed away, but sin itself in the heart—its guilt and defilement. And in its place we are given new life in the Holy Spirit, who is himself a fountain of the gospel grace of Christ.

Christ Continues to Purify His Church

We have already seen that the fountain is open for the people of God. "The House of David and the inhabitants of Jerusalem" refer to the then future New Testament Church. Jesus sends out his forgiveness and peace every day in the life of the Church and the experience of his saints. Forgiveness of sin is not simply in the believer's past when he trusted in Christ for his salvation. It is a recurring application of God's grace in the ongoing experience of the believer, as is the repentance, which must follow our sins and precede our appropriation of Christ's forgiveness as won on Calvary's cross.

The Lord removes sin progressively.

Israel's two great failings of old receive dishonorable mention: idolatry and listening to false prophets. "In that day," when the Messiah comes, the "names of the idols" will be obliterated (Zech. 13:2). The false prophets also will be discredited. Even though they deny being prophets, their self-mutilation will give them away (vv. 3–6). Zechariah's point is that in the time of the coming Messiah, the era of the New Testament, the Lord will purge the covenant community (the Church) of gross idolatry and false prophets. This is ongoing while the world lasts. This means that God will maintain the opened fountain so that Christ continues to be preached by a sound gospel ministry. All this flows from the cross and the finished work of Christ.

Jesus Christ, therefore, is still the fountain who fulfills Zechariah's prophecy: he was appointed from all eternity, revealed in the fullness of the time, and is opened to us here and now for our salvation. We must be washed in this fountain or we are lost. A. M. Toplady confesses his living faith in the fountain, Christ:

Nothing in my hand I bring
Simply to Thy cross I cling.
Naked, come to Thee for dress.
Helpless look to Thee for grace.
Foul, I to the Fountain fly.
Wash me, Saviour, or I die!

In her lovely poetic rendition of the words of Samuel Rutherford, Anne Ross Cousin testifies to the blessing of walking in Christ the fountain:

O Christ, He is the Fountain
the deep sweet well of love.
The streams on earth I've tasted
more deep I'll drink above.
There, to an ocean fullness
His mercy doth expand.
And Glory, Glory dwelleth
in Immanuel's Land.

Philip Henry has a sweet exhortation for us in his sermon on our text. "The best way to keep yourself clean and your way clean," he says,

> is by taking heed thereto according to the divine word…If any pollution happens…make hast to your fountain and wash speedily: I mean to the Lord Jesus, confessing bewailing, believing. As in the case of other dirt, the sooner the better. Go wash seven times.[3] You that have never been with him for mercy, for grace, have most need of all… there is a fountain just by thee.[4]

The Lord Jesus Christ is that fountain, and he calls to all who will hear him:

Ho! Everyone who thirsts,
Come to the waters;
And you who have no money,
Come, buy and eat.
Yes, come, buy wine and milk
Without money and without price.
(Isa. 55:1)

Jesus Is Our

Great High Priest

We have a great High Priest
who has passed through the heavens, Jesus the Son of God.
—Hebrews 4:14

READ HEBREWS 4:14–5:4

No New Testament book explains how the types of the Old Testament are fulfilled by Christ more clearly or systematically than the Epistle to the Hebrews, and no portrait of Christ receives more attention from its writer than that of the priesthood. Whereas Israel's prophets represented God to man, her priests represented man to God; that is, they performed the function of *mediators*, offering sacrifices to God to atone for the sins of his people. Among their ranks, the high priest played an especially exalted role as the one chosen to symbolically bring the Israelites into the Holy Place once a year on the Day of Atonement (Lev. 16:1ff.; Heb. 9:6–7). Hebrews 4:14–5:4 constitutes just the beginning of the writer's great discourse explaining how these priests were but shadows and types of the perfect priesthood of Christ.

The majestic themes that will later burst forth in greater detail are here found in the bud. But they contain the essence of all that follows, painting a compelling portrait of Christ our Great High Priest in three dimensions: his *qualifications*, his *work*, and the *benefits* that accrue to you because of them.

The Qualifications of Our Great High Priest

A brief sketch of the Old Testament priestly office is drawn in Hebrews 5:1–4, which reveals three qualifications for all who aspired to it—qualifications that Christ has now fully and perfectly met:

Christ is suited to your need.

Warring factions in the world today often make use of international mediators to arbitrate a cessation of hostilities and achieve reconciliation. And that is precisely what a priest is commissioned to be: an arbitrator between you and the God from whom you have estranged yourself by sin. As Hebrews 5:1 says, "Every high priest taken from among men is appointed for men in things pertaining to God, that he may offer both gifts and sacrifices for sins." Job expresses your need this way: "[God] is not a man, as I am, that I may answer Him, and that we should go to court together. Nor is there any mediator between us, who may lay his hand on us both" (Job 9:32–33).

You need One who can put his hand on God's shoulder and yours and restore the broken relationship, who can arbitrate an end of hostilities between you and your Creator. And only Jesus is suited to this need, for he alone is both God and Man, a truth illustrated in the name he is given in Hebrews 4:14: "Jesus the Son of God."

Christ is sympathetic to your weakness.

When people face a severe illness, their initial shock and uncertainty is often eased when they meet others who have faced the same thing and emerged safely on the other side. Hospitals often form support groups for people facing cancer or other diseases and addictions. Why? Not as a venue for their adherents to hear the doctor issue orders. Rather, it is so patients can share and talk with fellow sufferers who have been there and can identify with their specific trial in a way perhaps even the doctor cannot. They can give case-specific advice from personal experience.

Likewise, Christ possesses a compassion and understanding that can only come from shared experience. This is the second qualification of our Great High Priest, and it is stated clearly in Hebrews 4:15 and 5:2:

> For we do not have a High Priest who cannot sympathize with our weaknesses, but was in all points tempted as we are, yet without sin.... He can have compassion on those who are ignorant and going astray, since he himself is also subject to weakness.

Most vocations require certain *strengths* in order to be qualified. Students seek to qualify in their fields by obtaining a college degree and then their job interviews will assess their strengths to ascertain whether or not they are qualified to take a position. In contrast, Jesus is qualified as your High Priest because of his *weakness*. Indeed, his weakness is his glory. It is in his weakness that he ministers to the weak, and in his weakness that he finds favor with his Father (see John 10:17). It is because Christ "humbled Himself to the point of death on the cross" that God has exalted him to the highest place at his right hand (Phil. 2:8–9). On this basis, he is qualified to petition the Father on behalf of his needy people with great persuasion.

Christ is set apart by God.

Finally, according to Hebrews 5:4, Jesus is called to this priestly office: "No man takes this honor to himself"; it was in obedience to his Father's will (see also 5:5–6). And so, according to the terms of the covenant of grace, the Son of God would agree to become the seed of the woman and crush Satan's head, thereby granting access once again to the Tree of Life for all who would trust in him (Gen. 3:15).

The Work of Our Great High Priest

We have considered the qualifications of our Great High Priest: Jesus is suited, sympathetic, and set apart. But *to what*, exactly? We must next enquire about the actual *work* of Christ as priest, which the text outlines for us in three stages: past, present, and future.

The work of our Great High Priest in the past.

There are several aspects of Christ's high priestly work in the past (i.e., when he was here among us—what is sometimes called his "Estate of Humiliation"). Let us look at them in the order in which he accomplished them:

Jesus's earthly life: We are told that "He was in all points tempted as we are, yet without sin" (Heb. 4:15). Jesus endured suffering during the entire course of his life as the Man of Sorrows; he was tempted by the flesh, the world, and the devil, "yet without sin." Here is a declaration of Christ's "active obedience": that is, as your sinless High Priest, he lived a life of perfect conformity to God's law. That is why, unlike the Old Testament priests, he had no need to offer a sacrifice for his own sins (Heb. 5:3)—he did not have any.

Jesus's earthly death: We are told that he "[offered] both gifts and sacrifices for sin" (Heb. 5:1). The terms "gifts and sacrifices" refer to the many offerings God's law demanded to atone for sins.[1] Jesus's sinless life ended with his sufferings on the cross, which is his "passive obedience." As High Priest, he both *offered* the sacrifice and *was* himself the sacrifice for the sins of his people. Thus Jesus makes atonement for you—an "*at-one-ment*"—to make you at one again with an estranged God.

Jesus after his death: We are told something about what happened after Jesus's death. He "passed through the heavens" (Heb. 4:14). This refers to what is sometimes called our Lord's "Estate of Exaltation": his resurrection and ascension into glory, assuming the place of authority at the right hand of God until his glorious return to judge. Later in Hebrews

10:11–13, the writer explains this position: "Every priest stands ministering daily and offering repeatedly the same sacrifices, which can never take away sins. But this Man, after he had offered one sacrifice for sins forever, sat down at the right hand of God, from that time waiting till His enemies are made His footstool." All of these elements of Christ's priestly work have been fully accomplished in the past.

The work of our Great High Priest in the present.

Christ's priestly ministry is not confined to the past, however, for the writer says, "we *have* a great High Priest" (Heb. 4:14, italics added). Jesus's high priestly work continues in his present estate of exaltation, and we are later told by the writer just what this consists of: "He, because He continues forever, has an unchangeable priesthood. Therefore He is also able to save to the uttermost those who come to God through him, since He always lives to make intercession for them" (Heb. 7:24–25; compare with Rom. 8:34). Christ presently intercedes for all those he died for. He has passed through the heavens, and now his work as mediator between God and man continues.

The Apostle John explains, "We have an advocate with the Father, Jesus Christ the righteous. And he Himself is the propitiation for our sins" (1 John 2:1–2). Notice the interplay between Christ's *earthly* and *heavenly* high priestly works; his completed earthly work as High Priest centers on his "propitiation" (his shed blood that "propitiates" God towards you). His ongoing heavenly work as High Priest centers on his pleading the propitiation on your behalf. So Jesus's earthly high priestly work is finished; his heavenly high priestly work is ongoing. And the latter is based upon the former.

The work of our Great High Priest in the future.

Much of the Book of Hebrews deals with the matter of Christian perseverance: your continuing in faith to the end of the race. In the context of Hebrews 3:7–4:13, the writer has been comparing the Hebrews to their ancestors in the wilderness, warning them to endure lest they fall short of the rest promised in the heavenly Canaan. Your assurance of persevering into the future and finally entering this rest also depends on Christ's priestly work: "Seeing then that we have a great High Priest… let us hold fast our confession" (Heb. 4:14).

Maybe you struggle with assurance and wonder, "how do I know I'll not abandon the faith altogether? How will I persevere to the end?" The answer lies in Christ's ongoing work of intercession for you until he finally brings you home. Jesus your High Priest prays for your perseverance. We find a beautiful example of this in Luke 22:31–32: "Simon, Simon! Indeed, Satan has asked for you, that he may sift you as wheat. But I have prayed for you, that your faith should not fail." Just as Christ's priestly work of atonement in the past brought you into a right relationship with God, so his priestly work of intercession in the present and future enables you to persevere in that right relationship with God to the end of your pilgrimage.

Discussing this inseparable link between the atonement and intercession of Christ, the nineteenth-century Scottish theologian William Symington makes the following helpful comparison:

> they stand to each other in much the same character as do the ideas of creation and providence. The providence of God consists in upholding all things, or maintaining in being the creatures he has made…So the intercession of Christ is the continued efficacy of His expiatory merit…If the Providence of God were suspended, all created being must be annihilated; and if Jesus were not to make intercession, the merit of his atonement would prove utterly unavailing.[2]

So just as God upholds what he has created by his works of providence, so Christ upholds whom he has redeemed by his work of intercession. If you have been definitively bought by his precious blood in the certain past, you will assuredly be sustained by his ongoing intercession into the uncertain future.

The Benefits of Our Great High Priest

So far we have been admiring Jesus in his priestly office, as it were, from a distance. And in a very real sense, all you *can* do is be a spectator, for what your High Priest has done only he can do for you: "While we were still sinners, Christ died for us" (Rom. 5:8). But while you behold him accomplishing what you cannot, this text mentions many glorious benefits of Christ's priestly work that accrue to you, which bring this teaching down to earth in the practicalities of living the Christian life. We shall mention just three of them by way of application.

Jesus is a High Priest for you.

It may seem obvious, but Hebrews 4:14 declares, "We have a great High Priest"! Perhaps all the doctrine we have considered in this chapter seems distant and academic, but in reality it is not. Nothing could be more practical and immediate. "*We* have a great High Priest"—you and I. If we are passive spectators of what he has already done, we are certainly *not* spectators when it comes to participating in the benefits he bought for us.

Jesus your High Priest gives boldness to your prayers.

"Let us therefore come boldly to the throne of grace" (Heb. 4:16). If you have been reconciled to God through Jesus, then you come to his throne as a throne of grace, not a throne of judgment, for God's judgment has already fallen upon your High Priest instead.

What holds you back from prayer? Point your doubts and timidity to the blood of your High Priest that mingles with the incense of your prayers before the mercy seat and demands the attention of the Father (see Lev. 16:3, Rev. 5:8; 8:3–4). The words, "in Jesus's name, Amen," must never degenerate into a vain liturgical repetition. One writer puts it like this: "'Asking in Jesus' name' isn't just another thing I have to get right so my prayers are perfect. It is one more gift from God because my prayers are imperfect. Jesus not only guarantees that my package gets through, but it also transforms the package."[3]

Since your great High Priest has gone to such great lengths to make the way open for your prayers to be heard (compare with Heb. 9:24), will you not also go to great lengths to pray through him?

Jesus your High Priest promises you timely help.

We are assured here "that we may obtain mercy and find grace to help in time of need" (Heb. 4:16). If you are injured or suddenly taken ill in the middle of the night, it is a relief to know there is a doctor on call or an emergency room nearby where you can go and receive immediate help. Thanks to your High Priest, the throne of grace is open 24/7. Hebrews 4:16 literally reads, "that we may receive timely help." And isn't that what you need? Instant resort to the throne of grace at any time of day or night, any time zone, any hemisphere! And knowing that, when you get there, there is someone qualified with authority, skill, and sympathy to give you the help you need.

Perhaps you worry about the future: what future temptations and trials will you face? You do not need to know; all you need to know is that there will be "timely help" from One "who was in all points tempted as you are" (Heb. 4:15), and can therefore relieve you. There is no temptation you can face about which you can say, "Jesus wouldn't understand this." Even those temptations that are offered in twenty-first-century wrapping paper by your culture are the same root temptations to sin that Jesus faced. Temptations that seem unique to your age, stage, and era of history are really as old as the Fall and have been confronted and conquered by your High Priest.

We all face different "times of need," but one time we will all face is when we come to die. And when the hour of death comes to you, Jesus is the priest you must call for—not some human priest to mumble last rites, which accomplish nothing. You will need a priest who has paid for your sins in full, has passed through the heavens ahead of you, "to prepare a place for you...that where I am, there you may be also" (John 14:2–3). In that moment, he will bid you follow him "through the heavens," so that in that "time of need," you will certainly "obtain mercy and find grace."

> Therefore, brethren, having boldness to enter the Holiest by the blood of Jesus, by a new and living way which He consecrated for us, through the veil, that is, His flesh, and having a High Priest over the house of God, let us draw near with a true heart in full assurance of faith, ...Let us hold fast the confession of our hope without wavering, for He who promised is faithful. (Heb. 10:19–23)

Jesus Is Our

Hope

The Lord Jesus Christ, our hope.
—1 Timothy 1:1

READ 1 TIMOTHY 1:1–2

If you visit the National Portrait Gallery at the Smithsonian Institute in Washington D.C., you can see the picture by which graphic designer Shepard Fairey earned his fame in 2008. You may not have heard his name, but you have probably seen the picture: a stylized stencil portrait of Barack Obama with one word prominently printed at the bottom, HOPE. It became iconic during Obama's first presidential election campaign, and its message was simple: ascribing hope to a single person—one man who would lift a people from the valley of despair and set them on the mountaintop of hope.

Whether or not the subject of Mr. Fairey's artwork succeeded will, I suppose, be left to the verdict of the history books. But in a fallen, messed-up world, it should not surprise us that its inhabitants are desperately in search of hope. They look for that hero who will break their pessimism and offer them a new life. We see it, for example, in the enormous growth of blockbuster superhero movie franchises. Such an instinct is not necessarily a bad thing; the sad part is they are looking in all the wrong places, because ultimately, in such a world, hope can only express a wish, not a certainty. And despite the short-lived hype over any given hero, the search goes on year after year, because no son of Adam can bring lasting hope, only a *second* Adam. And just such a hero is found in the Bible. In 1 Timothy 1:1 we find his portrait: "The Lord Jesus Christ, our hope."

Jesus brings hope to unbelievers.

It is not the same hope most people are looking for (more wealth, more worldly happiness, more license to express their sinful egos). "Hope" will be defined by your understanding of the condition from which you want to be rescued. So if your pessimism primarily has to do with high taxes, unemployment, loved ones overseas in foreign wars, then understandably you might search for hope in a politician. But suppose your real problem is much deeper; suppose it is not a sick country, but your own sick soul, a soul afflicted with the virus of sin, which rejects its Creator and his law. In that case, you have defined the problem quite differently, and the solution must be found elsewhere. Redemption from this underlying sin problem is where the Bible's hope for unbelievers is drawn from—what 1 Thessalonians 5:8 calls, "the hope of salvation."

Jesus brings hope to believers.

However, in 1 Timothy, Paul is not writing to an unbeliever who knows nothing experientially of this salvation. Timothy is a Christian, one who has already found hope in Jesus. Yet as a Christian, he still needs to be reminded that Jesus Christ is his hope. Ralph Robinson explains why: "Hope is a saving grace of God's Spirit, worked in a regenerate person, whereby he firmly and patiently expects the certain accomplishment of all future good which God has promised and faith believes."[1] So Christian hope confidently anticipates future aspects of our presently possessed salvation that have yet to be tasted

(Rom. 8:24–25). For example, we hope for further sanctification in this life: increasing victory over sin and Satan, and increasing Christ-likeness by the work of the Holy Spirit. We hope for our souls' entrance into the presence of God when we die. We hope for the resurrection of our bodies when Christ returns. We hope for our vindication before the judgment throne of God, and we hope for the joys of God's presence in heaven forever.

If you are a Christian, you have not yet experienced these things, but you hope for them eagerly—and not in the same way as a child "hopes to receive something for Christmas" or "wishes upon a star." The Greek word implies something that is certain and assured; the writer to the Hebrews calls it "the full assurance of hope" and further declares, "this hope we have as an anchor of the soul, both sure and steadfast" (6:11, 19). In the opening verses of 1 Timothy, Paul demonstrates its source, object, and fruit.

The Source of Hope: "God our Savior"

Notice in verse 1 how Paul distinguishes between "God our Savior" and "the Lord Jesus Christ," that is, between God the Father and God the Son. It is not as common in the New Testament that God the Father is distinguished as "our Savior" (compare with 1 Tim. 2:3 and 4:10), but of course that is what he is. Salvation is the work of the triune God. Specifically, how is God the Father the *source* of our hope?

God the Father is the source of hope because he is the God of election.

Peter connects your eternal hope with the Father's election in the introductory greeting of his first epistle: "elect according to the foreknowledge of God the Father...Blessed be the God and Father of our Lord Jesus Christ, who...has begotten us again to a living hope" (1 Peter 1:2–3). God alone is the author of salvation: He might have chosen to withhold salvation from such undeserving rebels; instead, "whom He foreknew, He also predestined to be conformed to the image of His Son" (Rom. 8:29).

God the Father is the source of hope because he is the sender of Christ our hope.

In the eternal covenant of redemption, the Father determined to send his only begotten Son into the world to save those he had graciously elected. Jesus says, "As the living Father sent Me, and I live because of the Father, so he who feeds on Me will live because of Me" (John 6:57). The source of our hope of life is the Father's sending Christ that you might feed upon him by faith and so be saved.

God the Father is the source of hope because he lays our punishment on Christ our hope.

"God our Savior" struck "Christ our hope," that you might have the hope of sins forgiven: "Surely He has borne our griefs and carried our sorrows; yet we esteemed Him stricken, smitten by God, and afflicted. But he was wounded for our transgressions…" (Isa. 53:4–5; compare with Titus 3:4–5).

For these reasons, God the Father is said to be our Savior and the source of our hope. Take time to thank your heavenly Father, without whom you would have no hope.

The Object of Hope: "The Lord Jesus Christ Our Hope"

Many human hopes are not what they seem. Shepard Fairey, who produced the Obama poster, was subsequently the focus of a federal lawsuit, in which it was proved his "HOPE" portrait was plagiarized from a photo taken by an Associated Press photographer and that he destroyed the original to cover his steps.[2] In contrast, the portrait of

Christ our hope proclaimed by Scripture is not fabricated, neither is it false advertising. Three observations may be drawn from this portrait of our Lord.

The Lord Jesus Christ is our hope because he has accomplished the salvation for his people.

> But let us who are of the day be sober, putting on the breastplate of faith and love, and as a helmet the hope of salvation. For God did not appoint us to wrath, but to obtain salvation through our Lord Jesus Christ, who died for us, that whether we wake or sleep, we should live together with Him. (1 Thess. 5:8–10)

Paul here shows us that our hope is grounded upon Jesus's finished work, which is why he calls it elsewhere "the hope of the gospel" (Col. 1:23).

We have already listed the future aspects of salvation you still eagerly await and hope for: increasing victory over sin and Satan, your soul's entrance into the presence of God when you die, the resurrection of your body, your vindication before the throne of God, and the joy of God's presence in heaven forever. Jesus is your hope because he has *preceded you* in each of them as your pioneer: he has overcome every temptation and sin for you, crushed Satan's head on the cross for you, died and gone to heaven to represent you, has been raised bodily the third day for you, has been vindicated by God for you, and presently sits at the right hand of the Father to intercede for you.

And Christ is your hope because you are united to him by faith, so that "where [He has gone], there you may be also" (John 14:3). The blessed assured hope that you too will one day be victorious over sin and triumph over death is not because you are up to the task, but because you are spiritually one with the person who has completed this task in your stead. Where Christ our head has gone, the Church his body must follow. It would be a gross miscarriage of divine justice if you who are united to Jesus were robbed of your hope and failed to be with him in glory. He is the firstfruits; if he is there, you too will be soon.

If the Lord Jesus Christ is our hope,
then he is hope personified.

If I say to my wife, "you're beautiful," she appreciates the compliment. But if I say, "you are beauty itself," I have really scored points by saying she is the very *embodiment* of beauty. Likewise, Paul's portrait of Christ does not convey merely that Jesus inspires hope or is a role model for hope; he is *hope itself*!

The hope of salvation is not achieved by acquiring good grades in a catechism quiz, impressive church attendance, or finding some secret mystery in the Bible that only the initiated can obtain. It is achieved by trusting a person, the Lord Jesus Christ our hope. Suppose Paul had said, "the Lord Jesus Christ who teaches a philosophy of hope," or "the Lord Jesus Christ who can give you hopeful feelings." How long do you suppose your hope would last? This would reduce hope to an abstract concept that you have to constantly remind yourself of in order to possess it.

Rather, Paul says that hope is a *person*—someone you can talk to, pour your fears out to, depend upon. Hope is a friend who can relate to you, who understands your feelings of hopelessness, and who loves you. Hope is a trustworthy surety who has purchased your salvation by his atoning blood, and holds your title deed to heaven in his hand. Hope is the eternal Son of God, whose promise of eternal life is dependable and unchangeable. In short, your hope is as solid as he is. Your hope is as unshakable as God, because it relies not on how you feel, but on what another has done for you.

Christianity is not a religion that simply creates hopeful feelings among the hopeless. Every day, lots of world religions stimulate positive feelings in the hearts of their devotees. But Christianity does not offer just another religious crutch. It offers a permanent relationship with the divine Son of God, who actively works in you every day to bring you to be with him. Once you reduce the Bible's hope to a subjective feeling that resides only within your own fickle heart, then what does Jesus offer that the world does not? But if you discover a hope that is an objective, rock-solid reality *outside of yourself*, safe in the hands of the Son of God who cannot lie, and does not change, regardless of how you feel, then you have a treasure beyond compare.

Of course, this is not to deny that hope is something that we subjectively experience as Christians. Naturally, hopeful feelings should flow from this. Joy should characterize your life: "Now may the God of hope fill you with all joy and peace in believing, that you may abound in hope by the power of the Holy Spirit" (Rom. 15:13). But the joyful reality of Christ our hope is that whatever hope-robbing afflictions may come your way in this life—sickness, unemployment, disappointed expectations, an untimely death—your eternal hope is secure in Jesus, who is hope personified.

If the Lord Jesus Christ is our hope,
then all other hopes are hopeless.

The American restaurant chain Steak 'n Shake recently had a billboard campaign featuring a giant 10-foot milkshake and the slogan, "Earth's Last Hope for Survival." Of course, this was meant to be funny and so ludicrous as to be unforgettable. All the same, it serves to illustrate the sad reality that our world has an extensive catalog of misplaced hopes: external religion, possessions, military strength (Job 27:8; 31:24–25, 28; Ps. 33:16–19). Your unbelieving friends and family shop in this catalog regularly, buying hope cheaply, with the result that they feel a temporary sense of comfort and security, but in the end they will get what they paid for. "If in this life only we have faith in Christ, we are of all men most pitiable" (1 Cor. 15:19).

If Christ is your hope, then he is your *only* hope. Since God our Savior is the author of salvation, he alone has the right to appoint the hope of that salvation, and he has appointed his Son and no other. If you are trusting instead on this world's substitutes for hope, you must run from them all and not rest until you can confidently testify that he is "Christ in you, the hope of glory" (Col. 1:27).

The Fruit of Hope: "Grace, Mercy, and Peace"

Paul's greeting in 1 Timothy 1:2 contains more than just the epistle's addressee and a blessing. It also contains four distinct fruits enjoyed by those who have this hope of glory: "To Timothy, a true son in the faith: grace, mercy, and peace from God our Father and Jesus Christ our Lord."

The fruit of adoption.

Paul describes Timothy as a "true son in the faith." While he had been the young pastor's mentor, the relationship was not merely academic; the bonds of family love between them were cemented deeply because they shared a common Savior. That is because in conversion, Christ becomes our hope—Paul's and Timothy's, yours and mine. We are no longer spiritual orphans but are adopted into the family of God, the Church, where together we share "one hope…one faith" (Eph. 4:4–5). When a couple are expecting a baby, there is a joyous hope and expectation for the happy parents-to-be. But that joyful hope does not stop there; it is shared by the family: brothers, sisters, parents, grandparents. Likewise, in the family of God, a hope shared is a joy shared. We are true sons, daughters, brothers, and sisters in the faith, who enjoy the shared hope of life together here and life together with him in glory.

The fruits of grace and mercy.

Paul begins each of the pastoral epistles with the same greeting and benediction: "grace, mercy, and peace" (1 Tim. 1:2). Significantly, there is not a single epistle from his pen that lacks a prayer that *grace* may be with the recipients. But this is not a prayer for *saving grace* to come to Timothy; he had already received such grace and mercy in his justification. Rather, it is a prayer for fresh supplies of grace and mercy throughout his Christian walk, precisely because Jesus Christ was now his hope. He is applying the exhortation of Hebrews 4:16: "Let us therefore come boldly to the throne of grace, that we may obtain mercy and find grace to help in time of need." If Christ is your hope, you have both the hope of heaven and the hope of daily supplies for your pilgrimage there.

The fruit of peace.

The same may be said of the final fruit of hope Paul prays for: "Grace, mercy, *and peace*." In one sense, we have peace already: "Therefore, having been justified by faith, we have peace with God through our Lord Jesus Christ" (Rom. 5:1). But in another sense, we still need ongoing supplies of peace: not the *positional* peace of being right with God, but the *personal* peace within when facing life's trials. And this, too, Christ our hope guarantees for us, because the "peace of God" (Phil. 4:7) is only enjoyed by those who have tasted God's grace and mercy in Christ.

Is Christ your hope? Are these fruits of grace, mercy, and peace discernible in your life? If so, then rejoice in the hope of the promises of God: "For I know the thoughts that I think toward you, says the LORD, thoughts of peace and not of evil, to give you a future and a hope" (Jer. 29:11). As Ralph Robinson reminds us, we have a great treasure in Christ our hope: "The steadfastness of hope is from the certainty of faith. Faith believes the truth of the thing, and hope waits for the accomplishment of it...Faith is the mother of hope and hope is the daughter of faith; faith discovers the treasure and hope gathers and lays it up."[3]

However, if Christ is not your hope, then in God's estimation you are in a hopeless state: "without Christ...having no hope and without

God in the world" (Eph. 2:12). You needn't remain this way. Do not look to a superhero or a presidential candidate for hope; look instead to the Savior. No Christ, no hope. Know Christ, know hope.

Jesus Is Our

Horn

Blessed is the Lord God of Israel, for He has visited and redeemed His people, and has raised up a horn of salvation for us in the house of His servant David.—Luke 1:68

READ LUKE 1:67–79

Of all the metaphors applied to Jesus Christ, the horn of an animal may seem the most strange and distant. Two illustrations may bring it a little closer to us. In Dunvegan Castle in Scotland's Isle of Skye there is a drinking horn named "Sir Rory Mor's Horn" after a seventeenth-century chief of Clan McLeod. The legend is that this horn was cut from a wild ox that had confronted a fourteenth-century McLeod one dark night. In spite of being armed only with a dagger, he managed to kill the beast. Ever since, the chiefs and their heirs are required to demonstrate their "manhood" by draining the horn of claret, all in one go.[1] The horn is a symbol of power and coming of age. Another example is in the logo of the great American insurance company, The Hartford. It is the picture of a large red deer stag, lifted from Edwin Landseer's famous painting "The Monarch of the Glen." The majestic animal with its impressive rack of antlers positively breathes an image of nobility, stability, and security. It declares that you can trust The Hartford.

This image of power is exactly what is represented in Scripture by the horns and antlers of large and impressive animals. This horn metaphor is applied to Jesus when he is described, as in our text, as "a horn of salvation for us" (Luke 1:69). This naturally poses the question, "In what way(s) is Jesus a horn for us?"

The Promise of Salvation

How then is Jesus a horn for us? The primary answer is clearly that he is the one and only Savior in whom there is the *promise* of salvation. Notice how this promise is unfolded in the text.

What is God doing?

Zacharias speaks after nine months of silence (Luke 1:67–68). "This was a remarkable witness of the goodness of God," observes John Calvin, "that not only did Zacharias recover the power of speech, which he had not enjoyed for nine months, but his tongue became the organ of the Holy Spirit."[2] As he speaks, he himself is a sign and a wonder from God. Why? Because he had been struck dumb for doubting the promise of the son who would be John the Baptist (vv. 18–22). Now he is "filled with the Holy Spirit" and prophesies.

We should note that this remains the pattern for all "prophecy"—from the new revelation of Bible times to faithful proclamation and witness in all ages since—first, the indwelling Spirit and then the outgoing "word of the truth of the gospel" (Col. 1:5). We are not given new direct revelation or predictive prophecy. Scripture is the complete and sufficient revelation of God's will, but we do "prophesy" in preaching Christ from all the Scriptures and witnessing personally to the gospel of saving grace in Christ.

Zacharias' prophecy is that God "has visited and redeemed His people" (Luke 1:68). The tense of the verb indicates an accomplished fact, or, perhaps we should say, an ongoing reality. God has visited and redeemed his people throughout history. What Zacharias is specifically referring to is the advent of the promised Messiah in the person of Mary's son. This is obvious from what follows. It is, however, always true that, before and after Jesus coming and dying his death on the cross as an atoning sacrifice for sin, God saves sinners. What Zacharias realizes is that this Jesus is the long-promised Messiah who saves his people past, present, and future. Jesus is the Savior that the godly had been waiting for. He is the Savior we must believe upon if we are to be saved. He is the center and meaning of world history and of every human being's personal destiny, whether they accept him or reject him.

How does God redeem his people?

The answer is that he "has raised up a horn of salvation for us in the house of His servant David" (Luke 1:69). The Davidic kingdom was, of course, long gone. The house of David was reduced to a carpenter and his wife. It is out of this weakness—or, rather, *into* this weakness—that God sends his only begotten Son to raise up one who is "mighty to save" (Isa. 63:1). This fulfills the prophecy of the psalmist: "There I will make the horn of David grow; I will prepare a lamp for My Anointed. His enemies I will clothe with shame, but upon Himself His crown shall flourish" (Ps. 132:17–18). All this implies a desperate need of a Savior, not only for David's fallen house, but for every fallen human being (Amos 9:11; Acts 15:16). In short, we all need a Savior.

Can we be sure?

The world has seen many visionaries predicting amazing things—and seen them come to nothing. Perhaps many old men have been bold enough to predict great things for an infant relative. This is why understanding the biblical theology of God's unfolding plan is so important. The fact is that this baby is all over the Scriptures from Genesis 3:15 to Malachi 4:2. God has spoken multiple times "by the mouth of His holy prophets, who have been since the world began" (Luke 1:70). We saw this already in Psalm 132:17–18, but there are other prophecies of Christ as our horn, most notably in Psalm 89 and Ezekiel 29:

> But My faithfulness and My mercy shall be with him, and in My name his horn shall be exalted. (Ps. 89:24)

> In that day I will cause the horn of the house of Israel to spring forth, and I will open your mouth to speak in their midst. Then they shall know that I am the LORD. (Ezek. 29:21)

Besides these, there are innumerable references to the Messiah throughout the Word of God, many, as you are discovering in this book, in a wide range of metaphors and similes. The very same Jesus revealed to us by these and other means is also the horn of salvation raised up for our redemption.

The Accomplishment of Salvation

Zacharias goes on to explain, in Luke 1:71ff., as Calvin puts it, "more clearly the power and office of Christ."[3] This speaks to the question, "How does Jesus as a horn accomplish the salvation of lost sinners of mankind?"

Jesus defeats his enemies.

The horns of a bull and the antlers of a deer are not just for show. Each is a fearsome defensive weapon.[4] When I was a boy, the most famous bullfighter in the world was a matador named Manoleté, whose forté was to allow the bull to pass him four or five times, while he never moved from the one spot. One day, a bull caught him and gored him in his right thigh, from which injury he died, aged just 30.

This image of a bull goring an attacker and tossing him in the air evokes an image of Jesus's power to save. The "horn of salvation" equals "mighty salvation." "Their Redeemer is strong," says the prophet, "The LORD of hosts is His name" (Jer. 50:34). "Israel shall be saved by the Lord with an everlasting salvation; you shall not be ashamed or disgraced forever and ever" (Isa. 45:17). Through Zacharias, the New Testament prophet, the Lord assures us we who believe will be "saved from our enemies and from the hand of all who hate us" (Luke 1:71).

The image is turned around in Zechariah 1:21, where the wicked are the ones with the horns: "These are the horns that scattered Judah so that no one could lift up his head, but the craftsmen are coming to terrify them, to cast out the horns of the nations that lifted up their horn against the land of Judah." Sooner or later, the divine *force majeur* of the horn who is Christ the King will overthrow all the horns of wickedness. And, of course, it is this same power that overcomes "the law of sin and death" in the hearts and lives of those he comes to save (Rom. 8:2). The salvation of the repentant runs parallel with the condemnation of the reprobate who refuses to bow the knee to Jesus.

Jesus gives mercy to his own.

As the horn of salvation, Jesus came "to perform the mercy promised to our fathers and to remember His holy covenant" (Luke 1:72). Notice the link between promised mercy and the holy covenant of grace. Mercy is promised in God's gracious covenant, and that covenant pre-dates the coming of Christ. Having come as the incarnate Son and promised Messiah, Jesus actually performs the stipulations of the covenant of grace. He fulfills the promise in space and time as he does the will of the Father who sent him (John 5:30). John Calvin has a wonderful comment on this:

> Forgiveness of sin is promised in the covenant, but it is in the blood of Christ. Righteousness is promised, but is offered through the atonement of Christ. Life is promised, but it must be sought only in the death and resurrection of Christ.[5]

Jesus's power to save comes down to his death and resurrection (Rom. 4:25). Our Redeemer needs to be strong, because he has to deal not only with his own enemies and the spiritual blindness and deadness of sinful people, but with the just anger of God against sinners in their sin. Philip Henry perceptively points out that God's "justice is our enemy"[6] and that Jesus must bear that enmity to atone for our sin. To be saved from our sins means being saved from the justice of a holy God who cannot look upon sin. God's "holy covenant" sets the way by which our Savior secures the promised mercy of the God who "so loved the world that he gave His only-begotten Son, that whoever believes in him should not perish but have everlasting life" (John 3:16).

Jesus gives new life with which to serve him.

Jesus keeps the covenant to keep his promise for all eternity, according to "the oath which He swore to our father Abraham" (Luke 1:73). Zacharias refers back to the covenant with Abraham, in this way reminding us that Christ is the "seed" of Abraham (Gen. 12:3, 7; 13:15; 22:18; 24:7). Paul points out that Jesus is the true seed of Abraham to whom the promise is made: "Now to Abraham and his seed were the promises made. He does not say, 'And to seeds,' as of many; but as of one, 'And to your seed,' who is Christ" (Gal. 3:16). Redemption is vested in the person and work of the Son of God.

Jesus does not keep the covenant only for himself. He does so in order that believers do really and effectually believe and follow him: "To grant us that we, being delivered from the hand of our enemies, might serve Him without fear, in holiness and righteousness before Him all the days of our life" (Luke 1:74–75). The fruit of deliverance from all the enemies of our soul is service to the Lord as his disciples. And that service is happily given. "His purpose," says Calvin, "was, that, being redeemed, they might dedicate and consecrate themselves entirely to the Author of their salvation...This deserves careful attention, that we may remember our calling, and so learn to apply the grace of God to its proper use."[7] We are saved to serve, and we serve to bring glory to his name. This service will be characterized by four distinct blessings that will shape our Christian experience, service, and witness.

First, we are saved that we may serve the Lord "without fear" (Luke 1:74c). The connection with deliverance from "the hand of our enemies" seems obvious enough. Jesus does indeed charge us not to "fear those who kill the body but cannot kill the soul" (Matt. 10:28). He adds, however, "But rather fear Him who is able to destroy both soul and body in hell." This is a word of warning leveled at backsliders, hypocrites, and unbelievers. But it is also directed at we who love God to the end that we never take God for granted but offer due reverence to him in our hearts. Jesus died not only to deliver us from wicked enemies, but to deliver us from the holy God who does not tolerate sin. Yes, there is a sense in which we are delivered *from* God—even though we are saved *by* and *for* him—for his perfect holiness, righteousness, and justice is the greatest enemy of sin. Jesus suffered and died to save us from the just and righteous divine wrath—to reconcile us to God. Serving God "without fear" also means worshiping him with what Calvin calls "composure of mind" and "peace of conscience," because when we are reconciled to God through Christ we are "delivered by his grace from fear."[8]

Second, we are saved that we may serve the Lord "in holiness" (Luke 1:75a). This is generally taken to refer to the first "table" of the law—the first four of the Ten Commandments—which concerns our relationship to God. We are to have no other gods before him. We are to make no images of him to aid our worship of him. We are never to take his name in vain. And we are to keep his Sabbath day holy to rest from our work and devote ourselves to his worship and service. In Christ we are free to love the God who first loved us. And because we now love him, we delight to keep his commandments (1 John 4:19; John 14:15, 23).[9]

Third, we are saved that we may serve the Lord "in…righteousness" (Luke 1:75). Righteousness, as Calvin comments, "extends to all the duties of charity; for God requires nothing more from us in the second table of the law, than to render everyone what belongs to him." Parents, life, marital fidelity, truthfulness, property rights, and contentment—and all the godly application of commandments six through ten—form the road map for the practical love of our neighbors and even our enemies. We are free in Christ to abound in the work of the Lord and not to grow weary in doing good by others (2 Thess. 3:13; 1 Cor. 15:58).

Fourth, we are saved that we may serve the Lord "all the days of our life" (Luke 1:75). The Lord who assures us, "I will never leave you nor forsake you," also assures believers that their calling is life-long and for all eternity (Heb. 13:5). We are called to unending faithfulness in covenant with our Savior. Persevering in the faith is the evidence of a true conversion to Christ. Knowing the Lord Jesus Christ personally is a joyous inheritance that is all of grace and has changed us forever, for "if anyone is in Christ, he is a new creation; old things have passed away; behold, all things have become new" (2 Cor. 5:17).

Is Jesus Your Horn of Salvation?

The reason we need Jesus as the horn or mighty power of salvation is because we do not have the power to save ourselves or even live faithfully as Jesus's disciple. We need Jesus as our horn, or mighty strength, every hour and every day. The psalmist recognizes he is not self-sufficient just because he happens to be a believer: "The LORD is my rock and my fortress and my deliverer; my God, my strength, in whom I will trust; my shield and the horn of my salvation, my stronghold" (Ps. 18:2). How then shall we live day by day? The psalmist points the way: "I will call upon the LORD, who is worthy to be praised; so shall I be saved from my enemies" (v. 3).

Jesus is a horn of salvation for us. Let us then rejoice in his salvation and trust ourselves to him. In Christ, *your* horn will be exalted and *you* will gain the victory by his grace. God's Word says of the faithful believer, "He has dispersed abroad, he has given to the poor; his righteousness endures forever; his horn will be exalted with honor" (Ps. 112:9). In calling us to faithfulness, God commands and promises,

Arise and thresh, O daughter of Zion;
For I will make your horn iron,
And I will make your hooves bronze;
You shall beat in pieces many peoples;
I will consecrate their gain to the LORD,
And their substance to the Lord of the whole earth.
(Mic. 4:13)

Peace, perfect peace, in this dark world of sin?
  The blood of Jesus whispers peace within.
Peace, perfect peace, with loved ones far away?
  In Jesus' keeping we are safe, and they.
Peace perfect peace, our future all unknown?
  Jesus we know, and He is on the throne.
(Edward H. Bickerstaff, 1825–1906)

Jesus Is Our

King

Yet I have set My King on My holy hill of Zion.
—Psalm 2:6

READ PSALM 2

As an undergraduate student of British history in the U.K., I soon discovered that its pages are filled with rebellions. I encountered, for example, the Jacobite rebellions of 1715 and 1745, the Irish Rebellion of 1798, and the Indian Rebellion of 1857 and learned how each was eventually suppressed by the reigning British monarch, whose authority was again restored. Some years later, as a high school history teacher in the U.S.A., I discovered that there seems to be something quite romantic in the American psyche about the idea of "rebelling against the king." After all, this nation owes its existence and consequent liberties to just such a rebellion. This is particularly evident when Hollywood is the storyteller: when the king wins, the crushed rebels are often depicted as martyrs, the downtrodden victims of tyranny. Whatever the relative merits of such an interpretation in each case, rarely is the triumph of the king over rebels portrayed in a positive light.

But in biblical terms, there is nothing cool about being a rebel. Adam is a rebel; mankind is a rebel; I am a rebel by nature. And the Sovereign against whom I rebel is not some oppressive dictator or tyrannical pretender to the throne of my heart. He is a loving, beneficent, even indulgent Ruler, whose rule is rightful and just and whose mercy and grace towards his subjects knows no limits. God is your rightful Sovereign; he has created you, and you are his. And he has appointed a King through whom he exercises this dominion over his creation—his only begotten Son, Jesus Christ. This is the message of Psalm 2, which describes the enemies, coronation, victory, and subjects of Christ our King.

The King's Enemies

The first section introduces us to the rebels and the rightful King.

The rebels.

The psalm begins with the hatching of a rebellion, and the conspirators are clearly identified for us. They are listed as nations and people (v. 1). It is a global rebellion of ordinary men and women, boys and girls, but it is also composed of kings and rulers (v. 2)—the governments of the world. So the conspiracy takes in the whole sweep of humanity; in the words of Revelation 19:18, it is a collusion of "kings…captains…mighty men…all people, free and slave, both small and great."

This is the greatest rebellion of all time, making the great revolutions of history seem like petty playground squabbles; it is the great rebellion of man against his Maker. They "set themselves" and "take counsel together" against him. The psalmist calls their rebellion "rage" or "tumult" (v. 1); it is an ill-conceived conspiracy, foolish and self-destructive. It began in Eden, when Satan persuaded us to question our Maker's goodness, justice, and generosity. Ever since, God has been in the business of redeeming us from our deep-rooted suspicion of his motives. So in his blindness, man sees the gracious rule of his Creator as bondage: "Let us break their bonds in pieces and cast away their cords"

(v. 3). How foolish to exchange the easy yoke of Christ for the brutal yoke of Satan and consider it freedom (Matt. 11:29–30; Rom. 6:20–23).

Little wonder, then, that in God's view, this rebellion is "a vain thing" (Ps. 2:1): a phrase that not only suggests man's pride, but the hopelessness of his coup. Paul echoes this verdict when he writes, "although they knew God, they did not glorify Him as God, nor were thankful, but became futile in their thoughts, and their foolish hearts were darkened. Professing to be wise, they became fools" (Rom. 1:21–22). Such are the rebels. But who are they rebelling against?

The rightful King.

They rebel "against the LORD and against His Anointed" (Ps. 2:2). The mob of the world's villagers grab their torches and pitchforks and march against their omnipotent Creator. Mankind sets himself against the One that gave him being and takes counsel against the One he depends upon for his very next breath. God has given man a mouth; man uses it to blaspheme him. God has given man a brain; he uses it to concoct a plan to outwit and overthrow the omniscient One that invented the human brain.

But there is another authority identified as the object of man's rebellion. You will recall that God gave Adam a mandate to rule over the creation (Ps. 8:5–6). Since he chose instead to rebel, God provided a second Adam to have dominion instead (Rom. 5:12–21), who is described in Psalm 2 as the Lord's Anointed, his King, his begotten Son, and the Son. This King that the human insurrection raises its standards against is none other than Jesus Christ.

The battle lines are drawn. Are you with the LORD and his Messiah or with the rebellion against him?

The King's Coronation

In the next stanza of the psalm, we are taken away from this earthly scene of wicked scheming and attempts to dethrone God, and are transported by the psalmist far above to a heavenly scene where we behold God himself enthroned. And what is he doing? "He who sits in the heavens shall...*weep*?"—perhaps in wounded self-esteem because his creatures do not like him very much? "He who sits in the heavens shall...*evacuate*?"—fearful that his heavenly abode is about to be overrun by hordes of human revolutionaries? "He who sits in the heavens shall...*abdicate*?"—surrendering his sovereignty to the whims of his rebellious creatures? Absolutely not. "He who sits in the heavens *shall laugh.*" That is because man's pretensions to sovereignty are frankly laughable.

What man fails to understand is that the LORD "sits in the heavens"; He is enthroned in power. It is the same vision Isaiah saw in Isaiah 6:1: "I saw the Lord sitting on a throne, high and lifted up, and the train of His robe filled the temple." He is serene, calm, unmoved, immovable. He is not in the slightest threatened by the puny display of defiance he is witnessing: "The LORD reigns; let the peoples tremble! He dwells between the cherubim; let the earth be moved!" (Ps. 99:1). And so he laughs at them and "holds them in derision" (Ps. 2:4). The laughter of God is not the laughter of a funny joke, but his just and holy mockery of man's arrogant mutiny.

But this divine mockery soon turns to anger: he "speaks to them in His wrath" (v. 5). God is not laughing anymore; as Thomas Adams muses, "Oh, what are His frowns, if His smiles be so terrible!"[1] Man's rebellion is no laughing matter in a comedic sense; it is not the bold and brave attempt of a band of freedom fighters to throw off the yoke of slavery, but the wickedness of beloved children disgracing their compassionate Father, rejecting his glorious inheritance in favor of dirt, and then attempting to murder him, dethrone him, and set themselves up as masters of their own destiny. Thus, the LORD will "distress them in His deep displeasure" (v. 5).

That brings us to the turning point in the psalm, which is contained in the words, "Yet I." God sits, God mocks, and now, God speaks: "Yet I have set My King on My holy hill of Zion" (v. 6). This verse describes the coronation of Christ by his Father. Now, you may be thinking, "Isn't He King already? After all, he is the Son of God, the second person in the Trinity; doesn't that make Him sovereign?" Of course, that is perfectly true. As God, he always has and ever will be sovereign over all; this is what theologians sometimes call Christ's *essential kingship*. But the psalmist is prophesying that he will also become flesh and earn as a man what already belonged to him as God by his death on the cross (Phil. 2:5–11). Jesus is King as Redeemer as well as Creator. Upon his ascension, he will be crowned to rule by conquest what he already ruled by right: "All authority has been given to Me in heaven and on earth" (Matt. 28:18). This is sometimes called his *mediatorial kingship*.[2]

This is what so distresses the nations: that Jesus Christ will triumph over Satan and thus receive his crown (John 3:35). When a monarch is crowned, he has a "seat of power"—a place where his throne is established—from which he exercises his authority. For Queen Elizabeth II, it is Buckingham Palace; for King Carl XVI Gustav of Sweden, it is the Royal Palace of Stockholm. And for King Jesus, it is "My holy hill of Zion" (Ps. 2:6). Mount Zion is the place where God dwelt on earth among his people, which, in the New Testament, is applied to the Church (1 Peter 2:4–6; Rev. 14:1). It is from *the Church* that Christ's dominion will extend to the ends of the earth and vanquish his enemies. The Church, God's Zion, is the visible outpost of King Jesus's rule in this rebellious world, so it is little surprise that the "rage" of governments and peoples should fall on the visible Church throughout history. But it will all prove "a vain thing," because following his coronation, God's King gets busy in quelling man's rebellion.

The King's Victory

We have heard the King's enemies speak, and we have heard God speak. Now, we hear a third voice: that of the King himself! "I will declare the decree: the Lord has said to Me, 'You are My Son, today I have begotten You'" (Ps. 2:7). He recites his Father's promise of the great victory he will win over the rebels. The historical background to this promise is God's covenant with David, which includes the following words:

> When your days are fulfilled and you rest with your fathers, I will set up your seed after you, who will come from your body, and I will establish his kingdom. He shall build a house for My name, and I will establish the throne of his kingdom forever. I will be his Father, and he shall be My son. (2 Sam. 7:12–14)

God has promised to establish Christ's throne; this is the decree that Jesus is speaking about in Psalm 2:7: *He* is "the Beloved Son in whom [God is] well pleased" (Matt. 3:17). God appointed his King for a purpose: "Ask of Me, and I will give You the nations for Your inheritance, and the ends of the earth for Your possession" (Ps. 2:8). Christ has been promised the nations as his inheritance—the very same "nations" from Psalm 2:1, which are in a state of rebellion. And how will he inherit them? "You shall break them with a rod of iron; you shall dash them to pieces like a potter's vessel" (v. 9).

As God's anointed King, it is certain that Jesus will accomplish victory over the rebels—a victory resulting in one of two outcomes: either he will subdue the rebellion in their hearts, and win them back to allegiance, or else he will subdue unrepentant rebels by destroying them. Jesus will be victorious over you with either a victory of redemption or a victory of judgment. These are the only two options for natural-born rebels like ourselves. You must either surrender and embrace him as your rightful King, or else be dashed to pieces and go to the grave in your rebellion. The first time Jesus came, it was to secure the victory of redemption, but the next time will be to secure the victory of judgment (Luke 9:56; John 3:17).

How do the kings of history quell rebellions? All the examples of rebellions we began with were subdued by brute force. It is striking that the decree of God for Jesus is a mandate *not* to go and exterminate rebellious mankind and start afresh, *not* to go and brutally suppress the rebels and force them to live in a spiritual police state under Jesus's dictatorial rule. It is something far more glorious: to enter this rebellious world and change hearts of rebellion into hearts of loyalty and devotion, to remove fear and suspicion and win hearts back again, so that the once-rebellious nations might be his inheritance. In other words, Jesus takes rebels against his kingdom and turns them into model citizens of his kingdom: "For God so loved [the nations of] the world, that He sent His only begotten Son that [they]...might not perish but have eternal life."

The greatest crime on the statute books in many nations is that of treason; typically it is considered a capital offense. In God's kingdom, it is no different. Sin is cosmic treason, and it brings the curse, which was symbolized by hanging on a tree (Gal. 3:13). Christ our King obtained the treacherous nations as his inheritance by taking upon himself the penalty of treason against the Most High God that we rebels deserved—dying on the cursed tree. The cross declares that Jesus became the criminal that committed no crime, the sinner that committed no sin, the traitor that committed no treachery. And he did this so that you might become the upright citizen that plotted rebellion, the obedient one that committed disobedience, the faithful one that committed spiritual adultery. What lengths Christ our King went to, to receive "the nations for [his] inheritance, and the ends of the earth for [his] possession" (Ps. 2:8–11)!

The King's Subjects

In Psalm 2's final section, the psalmist returns as narrator with words of practical application: "Be wise...be instructed." How shall you respond to this King? We have seen that there are only two options: He will either have a victory of redemption or a victory of judgment.

The King's subjects are those who have been subdued by his work as Savior and are being ruled by his work as Lord.

- They are *a wise and instructed people* who have heeded the psalmist's advice: "Now therefore, be wise, O kings; be instructed, you judges of the earth" (v. 10).

* They are *a serving people* not out of raw obligation as slaves, but as free citizens: "Serve the LORD" (v. 11).
* They are *a rejoicing people* and redeemed citizens of Christ's kingdom have something to be joyful about: "Rejoice with trembling" (v. 11b)
* They are *a reverent people*; they know the dread Sovereign they serve is worthy of their awe and wonder: "Serve the LORD with fear, and rejoice with trembling" (v. 11).
* They are *a covenanted people*; that is, they have entered into a covenant of grace with him and love him: "Kiss the Son" (v. 12).
* They are *a blessed people* and happy because they have found salvation: "Blessed are all those who place their trust in Him" (v. 12).
* They are *a trusting people* justified by faith alone: "Blessed are all those who place their trust in Him" (v. 12).
* In short, the King's subjects are *a Christ-centered people*. They are what they are because of what Christ is for them, and that is a matter for celebration.

In contrast to the King's subjects, the King's enemies are objects of his warning: "Kiss the Son, lest He be angry, and you perish in the way, when His wrath is kindled but a little…" (v. 12). Psalm 2 predicts that unrepentant rebels will be captured and face justice; it is an eschatological psalm, which speaks of the end, warning rebels of the approaching judgment day. It therefore comes as no surprise that it is frequently cited in the last book of the Bible:

> Now I saw heaven opened, and behold, a white horse. And He who sat on him was called Faithful and True, and in righteousness He judges and makes war. His eyes were like a flame of fire, and on His head were many crowns…He was clothed with a robe dipped in blood, and His name is called The Word of God. And the armies in heaven, clothed in fine linen, white and clean, followed Him on white horses. Now out of His mouth goes a sharp sword, that with it He should strike

> the nations. And He Himself will rule them with a rod of iron. He Himself treads the winepress of the fierceness and wrath of Almighty God. And He has on His robe and on His thigh a name written: KING OF KINGS AND LORD OF LORDS. (Rev. 19:11–16)

Let all rebels heed the King's warning of that coming day. And since that day has not yet come, let them also heed his *invitation* to return their allegiance to him and become his loyal subject: "Kiss the Son, lest He be angry, and you perish in the way....Blessed are all those who put their trust in Him."

Jesus Is Our

Lamb

Christ, our Passover, was sacrificed for us.
—1 Corinthians 5:7c

READ 1 CORINTHIANS 5:1–8

Try calling someone a lamb and you are sure to get a strange look. Lambs are cuddly, wee things and all that, but no one would take the epithet as a compliment. Yet just as Jesus bursts on the scene of his public ministry, he is famously hailed by John the Baptist as "the Lamb of God who takes away the sin of the world" (John 1:29). And it was not only a compliment, but a proclamation heralding a man who would change the world forever. Fast forward to the last book of the Bible and you will find no fewer than twenty-seven references to Jesus as "the Lamb."[1]

Calling Jesus the Lamb is as deliberate as it is profoundly significant. This is so on two counts, which every Jew would instantly have recognized. One is, of course, *innocence*. Peter describes Jesus as "a lamb without blemish and without spot" (1 Peter 1:19). Closely related is the element of *sacrifice*. Jesus is "the Lamb slain from the foundation of the world" (Rev. 13:8). These images tie into the universal symbol of the lamb as the symbol of new life, of the spring of the year and the promise of future growth and blessing. These come together in Paul's affirmation that Christ is "our Passover" that is "sacrificed for us" (1 Cor. 5:7). The "Passover" refers to the sacrificial lamb central to that feast. That lamb points ahead to Jesus, as God's appointed way of salvation. Jesus Christ the Passover Lamb is the bringer of new life. He is the eternal spring of saved souls.

How Is Jesus Our Passover Lamb?

Paul's words, "For indeed Christ, our Passover, was sacrificed for us," take us to the Bible's account of Israel's exodus from Egypt after four centuries in that land, the last of these spent in slavery, and to the first Passover feast that occasioned that deliverance (Ex. 12).

The Passover in Egypt.

God "passed over" Israel one night in 1446 BC when his judgment fell upon the first-born children of Egypt. Connected with this was a ceremonial meal, called the *Pesach* in Hebrew (hence the Greek *pascho* and our English "paschal"). This was a *sacrificial* meal, which is what "paschal" signifies. It involved several finely focused elements:

* It centered on a *paschal lamb* (Ex. 12:6–10)—a male lamb, unblemished, killed and eaten the same night (all of it), and the blood sprinkled on the lintels of the doors.
* It was a *heavy* meal to prepare for a hard journey (Ex. 12:31–33).
* It was a *symbolic* meal in which the bread represented Israel's separation from corruption and their speedy exodus from Egypt (Ex. 12:34). This was unleavened bread, Hebrew *matzah*, made in a hurry without yeast.

These elements all have powerful meanings. In them you can see wonderful examples of how theology and practice are bound up together: the lamb, the meal, and the bread all teach us about what we are to believe about God, Jesus, and the plan of salvation. The lamb is a *sacrifice*, and its being completely consumed teaches us that Jesus is a complete offering for sin. The lamb is also a *substitute* sacrifice in which it dies to "redeem" sinners, teaching us that Jesus, the Lamb of God, is the true Redeemer, whose death actually saves sinners from their sins. Blood—that is, life—is shed so as to take away sin, for "without shedding of blood there is no remission" (Heb. 9:22). The sprinkling of the lamb's blood on the lintels of the doors takes the exercise of *faith* in the Lord who declares the way of "salvation" (from Egypt) for the first born of his people and points to the Savior who was still to come, of whom John writes, "the blood of Jesus Christ...cleanses us from all sin" (1 John 1:7).

The Passover meal in Egypt anticipates and points to Christ fifteen-hundred years before his birth in Bethlehem. This also teaches us that God does not save us by our "good" works, nor by lambs or their blood as such, but by his grace through the mediation of the beloved Son in whom he is well-pleased, whose sacrifice of himself as the sin bearer is the uniquely sufficient and effectual sacrifice acceptable to God. All the lambs of Israel's Passovers were shadows pointing to the substance who is Jesus Christ.

An annual Passover.

Why did the Passover continue year after year as a central focus of the life of the church in the Old Testament period? The answer is that God established it as an annual event with the purpose that his people remember their deliverance from Egypt: "So this day shall be to you a memorial; and you shall keep it as a feast to the LORD throughout your generations" (Ex. 12:14ab). It was repeated through a millennium and a half to remind them of their constant and continuing need of a divine Savior. This taught them that lambs could never really atone for sin and that they needed what the lambs signified: a Savior whose death could actually wash away their sins. Jesus is that once and final Lamb.

A perpetual Passover.

You will notice that the Passover was not only to be an annual celebration for Israel, but also an "everlasting" one: "You shall keep it as a feast by an everlasting ordinance" (Ex. 12:14). But in what sense can this be everlasting—whether on earth or in heaven? Paul addresses that question when he says that "Christ, our Passover, was sacrificed for us" (1 Cor. 5:7). The little lambs came and went and saved nobody, whereas the Lamb of God comes in the fullness of the time and saves sinners from every nation and generation, right now and forevermore. Christ was "slain from the foundation of the world," and his mercy "is from everlasting to everlasting on those who fear Him, and His righteousness to children's children" (Rev. 13:8; Ps. 103:17). He is the true Passover Lamb, and his is the blood that cleanses all who trust in him from all sin.

The final Lamb.

Jesus identifies himself as the final Lamb when he declares at his institution of the Lord's Supper that his blood is the "blood of the new covenant which is shed for many" (Mark 14:24). As the Passover was the sacramental seal by which God signified and sealed his adoption of Israel as his covenant people, so the Lord's Supper is that sacramental seal of the new age in which God seals believers in Christ as his own people.

In Christ, the Old Testament Passover graduates into the Lord's Supper because of the death of the final Lamb on the cross. This is the force of Paul's later words to the church in Corinth: "Is not the cup of blessing which we bless a sharing in the blood of Christ? Is not the bread which we break a sharing in the body of Christ? Since there is one bread, we who are many are one body; for we all partake of one bread" (1 Cor. 10:16ff. NASB).

Jesus is our Passover Lamb. The lamb of the Passover points forward to Christ, while the bread of the Supper points back to him as "crucified for you" (compare with 1 Cor. 1:13). All earlier Passover lambs foreshadowed the Savior. Jesus's very institution of the Lord's Supper is an identification of himself as the Lamb of God. He who is without blemish and without a broken bone (compare Ex. 12:5, 46 with 1 Peter 1:18–19 and John 19:36) dies for his people that they might be saved and made "free from the law of sin and death" (Rom. 8:2). "For indeed, Christ, our Passover, was sacrificed for us."

The next question is, "What practical implications does this truth have for those for whom Christ died?" Paul's answer in a nutshell is that we are to "keep the feast" (1 Cor. 5:8). But what exactly does that mean?

What Is It for Us to "Keep the Feast"?

Before we can keep the feast, we must, says Paul, "purge out the old leaven." The reference to the Passover feast with its unleavened bread is unmistakable. In the immediate context, however, the apostle is using the normal operation of yeast in leavened bread to illustrate the effects of sin in the life of the church in Corinth. To understand its application to ourselves we will need to unpack this ancient imagery.

Purge out the old leaven.

The old leaven to which Paul refers to in 1 Corinthians 5 is, in general, sin in the human condition and, in particular, a peculiarly perverted case of sexual immorality in the church (vv. 1–5). The sheer hypocrisy in the church galled Paul all the more because they patted themselves on the back for being such a faithful group while refusing to deal with the sinner and his sin. "Your glorying is not good," expostulates the apostle with obvious exasperation, "Do you not know that a little leaven leavens the whole lump?" (v. 6). Just as a little yeast spreads through the dough and raises it to a large loaf, so a little sin multiplies to engulf a whole life. Changing the metaphor, it takes only one rotten apple to spoil the whole barrel.

When it comes to sin in the Christian's life, we are to be like the unleavened bread of the Passover. We are therefore to "purge out the old leaven, that [we] may be a new lump, since [we] truly are unleavened" (v. 7). Paul is saying in effect, "Be new men and women in your behavior and your choices, because this is what you already are in Christ. You are washed in the blood of the Lamb in virtue of your saving faith in Christ" (see Rev. 1:5; 7:14). So be what you are in Christ and purge out the old life of sin. Jesus "Himself bore our sins in His own body on the tree, that we, having died to sins, might live for righteousness—by whose stripes you were healed" (1 Peter 2:24). Die to sin and live to godliness. Christians, we are already the citizens of heaven.

Keep the feast.

To keep the feast is to live in a way that flows from love for Jesus (1 Cor. 5:8). It is not about formal observance of the Passover in the Old Testament or the Lord's Supper in the New. The continuous present tense of the verb points to a constant, continuing, and open-ended obedience to the Lord.

When you love the Lord Jesus Christ, you will not follow him "with old leaven"—as in the case of the sexual immorality of the backslidden brother in Corinth (vv. 1–7)—"nor with the leaven of malice and wickedness" (v. 8). Malice translates from the Greek *kakos*, which means "bad" as conceived in the heart and practiced with the hand. Wickedness is the Greek *poneros*, which refers to "evil" engaged in with deliberation, determination, and delight. This is why Satan is called "the evil one"—in Greek, *ho poneros* (Luke 11:4; compare with Luke 6:45).

Our lives ought rather to be lived with "the unleavened bread of sincerity and truth" (1 Cor. 5:8). Sincerity and truth must be inseparable twins. Sincerity without truth is a delusion. Truth without sincerity is hypocrisy. Truth is more than truthfulness, and sincerity more than commitment. Both, as Charles Hodge points out, represent an inward state and moral condition "which is conformed to the law and character of God."[2] Keeping the feast is simply practical godliness practiced by Christians as individuals and together as a body. This is what being united to Christ as our Passover Lamb means for both soul and body, in time and for eternity. Philip Henry asks his readers,

> Is Christ your Passover, is his blood sprinkled on your souls? If not, sprinkle it quickly; you know not how near the destroyer may be. If it be done in God's name, take the comfort of it.[3]

And as Paul writes;

> There is therefore now no condemnation to those who are in Christ Jesus, who do not walk according to the flesh, but according to the Spirit. For the law of the Spirit of life in Christ Jesus has made me free from the law of sin and death. For what the law could not do in that it was weak through the flesh, God did by sending His own Son in the likeness of sinful flesh, on account of sin: He condemned sin in the flesh, that the righteous requirement of the law might be fulfilled in us who do not walk according to the flesh but according to the Spirit. (Rom. 8:1–4)

The Lamb Is All the Glory

Before leaving for the Mount of Olives and his betrayal and arrest, Jesus and the disciples sang a portion of the Hallel (Ps. 116–118). This was a prophetic rehearsal of what was to come: from the fulfillment of his vows, even to death, to his victory as the stone the builders rejected that would nevertheless become the capstone of God's church (Ps. 116; 118:22). All this speaks of God's love for his people as he calls them out of all the nations to be his holy nation (Ps. 117).

In Christ their Lamb, believers share in this new order of things established by God in terms of his covenant, his kingdom, and his everlasting glory. Jesus underscores this at his last Passover in this world, when in prospect of his death on the cross he says to his followers, "Assuredly I say to you, I will no longer drink of the fruit of the vine until that day when I drink it new in the kingdom of God" (Mark 14:25). In that glorious feast at the consummation of all things, Christ our Lamb will be—in Anne Ross Cousin's adaptation of Samuel Rutherford's words—"all the glory of Immanuel's land":

The bride eyes not her garment,
  But her dear Bridegroom's face;
I will not gaze at glory
  But on my King of grace.
Not at the crown He giveth
  But on His pierced hand;
The Lamb is all the glory
  Of Immanuel's land.

Jesus Is Our Life

When Christ who is our life appears,
then you also will appear with Him in glory.
—Colossians 3:4

READ COLOSSIANS 3:1–17

You will sometimes hear someone say, "Sports are my life"; or, speaking of another, "He lived for speed"; or, perhaps, "His family was his life." Such statements suggest to us what is really important in people's lives. This is what makes them "tick." This also comes out in extreme circumstances, as Satan cynically informs God when the former aims to subvert Job, "Skin for skin! Yes, all that a man has he will give for his life" (Job 2:4). Satan was wrong with respect to Job and the many others who have been ready to die before giving up what they regard as central to their life. On the other side of the equation, there are many who choose to die rather than give up their darling sins, because some sin is their life and they are in bondage to it.

The apostle Paul says that Jesus Christ is the Christian's life. There is no more profound statement of the identity of the believer. It is not only a definition of the saint in his relationship to his Savior, but a challenge to be applied to the conscience of every living soul, "Is Christ *your* life? Is Jesus *your* passion? Is the Son of God the Lord of your very being?" In Colossians 3:1–4, the apostle addresses the specific question, "How is Christ the believer's life?" In his use of this metaphor, he gives us a portrait of Jesus that highlights four essential truths about "Christ who is our life": you were dead in sin, you are now dead to sin, you are truly alive to God, and you will appear with Christ in glory.

You Were Once Dead in Sin

If you are a Christian, Paul is saying you know this because you "were raised with Christ" (v. 1). He earlier laid the groundwork for this when he wrote:

> In Him you were also circumcised with the circumcision made without hands, by putting off the body of the sins of the flesh, by the circumcision of Christ, buried with Him in baptism, in which you also were raised with Him through faith in the working of God, who raised Him from the dead. And you, being dead in your trespasses and the uncircumcision of your flesh, He has made alive together with Him, having forgiven you all trespasses, having wiped out the handwriting of requirements that was against us, which was contrary to us. And He has taken it out of the way, having nailed it to the cross. (Col. 2:11–14)

This says that without Christ you had no life. You were hopelessly condemned before the unassailable righteousness of God—"dead in your trespasses" (v. 13). But Christ died and rose again and you "were raised with Him through faith," the penalty of the law having been "nailed...to the cross." This in turn is a motive to follow the Savior who "has called you out of darkness into His marvelous light" (1 Peter 2:9).

We Christians inevitably understand that our calling is to "seek those things which are above, where Christ is, sitting at the right hand of God" (Col. 3:1). It is written on our renewed hearts and reformed consciences. This is what God wants us to do every day in life. This is what the Christian experience is about, simply because we know in heart, mind, and soul that we were once dead and now have new life in our risen Savior. The old "natural" was spiritual deadness and going our own way, without reference to God or in deliberate rejection of his known will. The new "natural" is a desire to follow the Lord and a delight in doing so. There is no neutral gear between the two.

You Are Now Dead to Sin

Paul repeats his exhortation of the first verse to seek the "things which are above," but adds a second motive: "for you died" (vv. 2–3). This is the other side of being "raised with Christ." Formerly dead *in* sin, the believer is now dead *to* sin. As the apostle has already explained in chapter 2, "you died with Christ from the basic principles of the world" (v. 20). So what does this mean?

One thing it does not mean is that Christians are dead to the *influence* of sin. We are still tempted and we still fall into sin. Our best words, thoughts, and deeds are still tainted by sin (Isa. 64:6). Paul speaks frankly of this in his own Christian life, bemoaning the reality that though he delights in God's law, he finds himself slipping into sinful behavior (Rom. 7:19ff.). Practical sinless perfection awaits in the world to come. Being "dead to sin" is not the same thing as sinless perfection.

Believing in Jesus Christ as your Savior means that you have entered into newness of life. That means that sin cannot kill you. Saving faith in Christ saves you from sin in a number of ways. In Christ, you are no longer a slave to sin (Rom. 6:6, 14). In Christ, there is no longer any condemnation for sin (Rom. 8:1). Therefore, Paul tells us, "reckon yourselves to be dead indeed to sin, but alive to God in Christ Jesus our Lord" (Rom. 6:11). Faith in Christ unites the believer to Christ in his death, so that "the world has been crucified to me, and I to the world" (Gal. 6:14). Christ is our life because by his death on the cross he has borne away our sin and removed the death penalty it entailed upon us; he has given us a life that is real and eternal and cannot be taken away (compare with 1 Peter 1:4). Everyone who is truly "in Christ" is a "new creation" and therefore "dead to sin" (2 Cor. 5:17; Rom. 6:2).

You Are Truly Alive to God

Being united to Christ in his death—that is, by believing in him as your Savior—means you died to sin and now have a new life: "your life is hidden with Christ in God" (Col. 3:3). You may, however, still question if anything like the fullness implied in these glorious words has touched your own life experience. You look at your life and wonder what this is supposed to mean for you. For example, you find yourself still struggling with sin and also with the assurance of your faith.

The short answer is that experientially you have some way to go until you will enjoy the fullness and perfection of God's glory. That is still hidden with Christ and awaits his coming and your resurrection on the last day. But even if this is hidden from you in some measure, your life is nevertheless with Christ constantly. Yes, you are short of perfection in the eyes of the world and yourself (Rom. 7:22–23). But every day, through thick and thin, you are held for sure in Jesus's hand (John 10:28–29). And like the Apostle Paul, you "have learned in whatever state [you are], to be content" and can testify with him, "I know how to be abased, and I know how to abound. Everywhere and in all things I have learned both to be full and to be hungry, both to abound and to suffer need. I can do all things through Christ who strengthens me" (Phil. 4:11–13).

You are consciously committed to seeking the "things above"—that is, following the Lord's will in your life. To that end, you continue to pray with the psalmist from the depth of your being, "Create in me a clean heart, O God, and renew a steadfast spirit within me" (Col. 3:1–2; Ps. 51:10). Christ is our life, because—through his life, death, and resurrection—he has secured both grace and glory for all who will believe upon him as their Savior and follow after him as their Lord. Whatever the buffetings and apparent uncertainties in life, the Christian is so related to God in Christ that his life is actually, and eternally, "hidden with Christ in God."

You Will Appear with Christ in Glory

Jesus is not only our life now, in our life in this world, but also in the world to come: "When Christ who is our life appears, then you also will appear with Him in glory" (Col. 3:4). Jesus is seated in his body "at the right hand of the throne of God" and is the "firstborn among many brethren" (Heb. 12:2; Rom. 8:29). Because he died, rose again, and lives in heaven in his body, so a this-life-only faith in Jesus is as empty as it is unbiblical: "If in this life only we have hope in Christ, we are of all men the most pitiable" (1 Cor. 15:19).

The "Jesus" who is a great man who lived, died, and inspired us to do good things, but who was not truly God and man, never actually paid for sin and never rose from the dead except in our minds, is no better than any other inspiring myth or psychological crutch to help us cope with life. The real Jesus Christ is the one and only living Savior.

He gives life to us.

Jesus is the "Christ who is our life." Thomas Brooks notes that "life here is by a metonymy, put for the author of life."[1] Metonymy is a figure of speech in which something is called by the name of something intimately associated with it. In this case the "something" is a person, Jesus, and the association being made is with the life that he gives to those he saves.[2] Scripture abounds with instances of this theme:

> Love the LORD your God, that you may obey His voice, and that you may cling to Him, for He is your life and the length of your days. (Deut. 30:20)

> In this the love of God was manifested toward us, that God has sent His only begotten Son into the world, that we might live through Him. (1 John 4:9)

> And this is the testimony: that God has given us eternal life, and this life is in His Son. (1 John 5:11)

> Believers are to be "giving thanks to the Father who has qualified us to be partakers of the inheritance of the saints in the light." (Col. 1:12)

Jesus Christ is the one who secures life for his people that is physical, spiritual, and eternal. He *is* our life.

He will come for us.

"When Christ...appears" refers to his coming again at the end of this present world. He is hidden for now, and our life is, as we have already seen, "hidden with Christ in God" (Col. 3:3). It is hidden to us simply because we have not seen it yet as it will be seen when Jesus comes: "For now we see in a mirror, dimly, but then face to face. Now I know in part, but then I shall know just as I also am known" (1 Cor. 13:12). In the meantime, we wait with all the saints in the whole of history for this great consummation of all things:

> For I know that my Redeemer lives, and He shall stand at last on the earth. (Job 19:25)

> In a moment, in the twinkling of an eye, at the last trumpet. For the trumpet will sound, and the dead will be raised incorruptible, and we shall be changed. (1 Cor. 15:52)

> Finally, there is laid up for me the crown of righteousness, which the Lord, the righteous Judge, will give to me on that Day, and not to me only but also to all who have loved His appearing. (2 Tim. 4:8)

That day, when Jesus our life appears, is surely coming. Believers wait expectantly for him because they are alive with new life wrought by him in their hearts. Those who do not know him are still dead in trespasses and sins and urgently need to come to him that they might have life, "For He is coming to judge the earth. With righteousness He shall judge the world, and the peoples with equity" (Ps. 98:9).

He will share his glory with us.

In Jesus Christ, says John Davenant, we "have a certain expectation of future glory."[3] When Jesus comes at the end of human history, writes Paul, "then you also will appear with Him in glory." Our bodies will be "raised incorruptible" and reunited to our spirits: "For this corruptible must put on incorruption, and this mortal must put on immortality" (1 Cor. 15:53). "Then," we read in Matthew 13:43, "the righteous will shine forth as the sun in the kingdom of their Father."

How shall we apply this to our hearts and lives?

Philip Henry urges us, "Rest not in having life, but press after liveliness."[4] Pray daily with the psalmist, "revive me according to Your lovingkindness, so that I may keep the testimony of Your mouth" (Ps. 119:88). Make Christ your own Savior and so your own life, because, as Henry challengingly but rightly says, "Christless souls are lifeless souls."[5]

> He who has the Son has life; he who does not have the Son of God does not have life. These things I have written to you who believe in the name of the Son of God, that you may know that you have eternal life, and that you may continue to believe in the name of the Son of God. (1 John 5:12–13)

Jesus tells us plainly, "I am the way, the truth, and the life. No one comes to the Father except through Me" (John 14:6). Jesus came to die on the cross as a substitute for sinners. "I have come," he says, "that they may have life, and that they may have it more abundantly" (John 10:10). Without a saving relationship with Christ, we are condemned already and dead in sin. Knowing him in a personal saving faith means he is our life now and forever. Augustus Montague Toplady captures this wonderful truth so memorably:

Lord! it is not life to live
 if thy presence Thou deny:
Lord! if Thou thy presence give,
 'tis no longer death to die.
Source and giver of repose!
 Singly from thy smile it flows.
Thee to see and Thee to love
 perfects bliss below, above.

Jesus Is Our

Light

I am the light of the world.
—John 8:12

READ JOHN 8:12–29

Lamech was the world's first great boaster. "If Cain shall be avenged sevenfold," he bragged, "then Lamech seventy-seven fold" (Gen. 4:23–24). This archetype of braggadocio has had a prolific progeny. His spirit echoes down the centuries everywhere from bar-rooms to boardrooms. Since we are not strangers to these things ourselves, we are quite sensitive to those who have a penchant for blowing their own trumpets. It should not surprise us that when Jesus boldly claims to be "the light of the world" eyebrows were raised and questions asked. It is a stupendous assertion, not least because here is a man claiming of himself what is only attributable to God. John acknowledges this fact elsewhere when he says that "God is light and in Him is no darkness at all" (1 John 1:5). To be this particular Light, Jesus must be God.

The practical implications of Jesus's self-identification are very far reaching. John follows through on some of these when he writes:

> If we say that we have fellowship with Him, and walk in darkness, we lie and do not practice the truth. But if we walk in the light as He is in

> the light, we have fellowship with one another, and the blood of Jesus Christ His Son cleanses us from all sin. If we say that we have no sin, we deceive ourselves, and the truth is not in us. If we confess our sins, He is faithful and just to forgive us our sins and to cleanse us from all unrighteousness. If we say that we have not sinned, we make Him a liar, and His word is not in us. (1 John 1:6–10)

The Light in question is not mere human enlightenment or some particular wise insight, but is a figurative reference to God himself, his eternal truth, and his infinite wisdom. *Not* to have this Light of God—namely, to reject the truth of his Word—is to be in denial of God himself and therefore to be a guilty rebel against his revealed truth. It is therefore vital for every one of us, for both time and eternity, to grasp what Jesus is saying about himself when he says he is "the light of the world." Then we will be able to apply it rightly to ourselves for our everlasting benefit.

Jesus's words in John 8:12–29 speak to the *substance* of his claim, his *authority* for making it, and its *practical relevance* for every human being past, present, and future. The answers to these issues are not academic. They are at the heart of the gospel and bear upon our very relationship to God.

What Is the Substance of Jesus's Claim?

You can well imagine the electric reaction of the disciples to Jesus's words: "I am the light of the world. He who follows Me shall not walk in darkness, but have the light of life" (v. 12). Two basic doctrines are set out in this astounding and complex claim.

Who is this Jesus?

When Jesus says, "I am the light of the world," he is telling us something about who he really is. He has come as "the light" into "the world."

This was in fact not the first time this claim had been made: Simeon identified the newborn Jesus as "the Lord's Christ" and declared him to be "a light for revelation to the Gentiles, and for glory to your people Israel" (Luke 2:26, 32 ESV).

Jesus is the Light in himself, because he is the Son of God incarnate. God in the flesh cannot be anything but the Light. God has spoken to us by his Son (Heb. 1:2). He reveals God to us. Entering the darkened room of this fallen world, he inevitably sheds his light abroad. Like every word from God, Jesus the living Word is "light that shines in a dark place" (2 Peter 1:19).

What has Jesus come to do?

Darkness always cries out a certain need for light. "Darkness" in Scripture is also a figure of speech, always evoking the spiritual darkness of lost souls and a world of sin and misery. The only light in hell is that of a "lake of fire," itself a figurative representation of the relentless darkness of eternal punishment (Rev. 19:20; 20:10, 14–15).

Sin *is* darkness. Consequently, the heart of the sinner is "darkened" because, as Paul says of the Gentiles he was sent to reach with the gospel, "although they knew God, they did not glorify Him as God, nor were thankful, but became futile in their thoughts, and their foolish hearts were darkened" (Rom. 1:21). It was to the dark world, our world, that Jesus came. He is "the true Light which gives light to every man coming into the world" (John 1:9).

This gospel era was prophesied long before Jesus was born to Mary: "The people who walked in darkness have seen a great light; those who dwelt in the land of the shadow of death, upon them a light has shined" (Isa. 9:2). This tells us what Jesus has come to do in our lives. Everyone who "follows" him—that is to say, believes in him as Savior and Lord—"shall not walk in darkness, but have the light of life" (John 8:12). John is here referring us back to what he wrote at the beginning of his gospel when he noted that John the Baptist was a "witness of the Light…

the true Light which gives light to every man coming into the world" (John 1:7–9). This Light is the Christ, the Word or Logos of God, who came so that "as many as received Him, to them He gave the right to become children of God, to those who believe in His name" (v. 12).

Because Jesus is the Light, he is the good news this darkened world desperately needs. He says it himself: "I have come as a light into the world, that whoever believes in Me should not abide in darkness" (John 12:46). He fulfills that prophecy in which God says, "to you who fear My name, the Sun of Righteousness shall arise with healing in His wings." This is good news, for, as the Lord continues, "you shall go out and grow fat like stall-fed calves" (Mal. 4:2). This is what the apostles preached concerning Christ:

> For we did not follow cunningly devised fables when we made known to you the power and coming of our Lord Jesus Christ, but were eyewitnesses of His majesty. For He received from God the Father honor and glory when such a voice came to Him from the Excellent Glory: "This is My beloved Son, in whom I am well pleased." And we heard this voice which came from heaven when we were with Him on the holy mountain. And so we have the prophetic word confirmed, which you do well to heed as a light that shines in a dark place, until the day dawns and the morning star rises in your hearts. (2 Peter 1:16–19)

Jesus is "the Root and the Offspring of David, the Bright and Morning Star" (Rev. 22:16). Jesus came to sinners "to open their eyes, in order to turn them from darkness to light, and from the power of Satan to God, that they may receive forgiveness of sins and an inheritance among those who are sanctified by faith in [Him]" (Acts 26:18).

What Is the Authority for Jesus's Claim?

Anyone who makes a claim for himself, or just wants a hearing for what he has to say, had better be prepared to deal with objections. It must be said with reverence, but this is as true of the incarnate Son of God as it is for anyone else in the human race. Who says Jesus is the Light of the World and by what authority? Jesus anticipates a chorus of questions and proceeds to address two of the most obvious ones head-on: namely, "You are a liar," and, "Your evidence falls to the ground" (John 8:13–20).

Objection #1 — "Your witness is not true." (John 8:13–18)

This objection probably arises from the thought that Jesus's testimony is not valid because it falls short of the Mosaic requirement of at least *two* witnesses (Deut. 17:6; 19:15). "You bear witness of Yourself," they note (John 8:13). We quite rightly raise the question in response to "the word" of an individual. We know it is dangerous to accept uncorroborated testimony as to someone's suitability for a job or even their profession of faith in Christ. This is also true for the way witnesses are heard in a court of law. The Mosaic law guards against deceit in the speaker and gullibility in the hearer. It establishes a minimal level of evidence and credibility.

Jesus first asserts that his witness is *uniquely valid* (vv. 14–16). He acknowledges that he is a single witness to himself but insists he speaks the truth: "Even if I bear witness of Myself, My witness is true" (v. 14). He then makes three points relative to this statement that serve to make the objectors think more deeply. Remember that his critics were Pharisees who were well versed in the Scriptures and the prophecies of the coming Messiah. None of them came to the subject completely cold. Centuries of biblical and rabbinic study had given them a rare background to assessing any messianic claim. Jesus says:

* First, "I know where I came from and where I am going..." (John 8:14). Here is an example of Jesus teaching "as one having authority, and not as the scribes" (Matt. 7:29). In anyone else this would have sounded pretentious and even delusional, but Jesus could never be dismissed as a village idiot or a mad visionary. His words had weight and were not to be summarily dismissed.

* Second, "...but you do not know where I come from and where I am going" (John 8:14). He prods their consciences; they had no clue! They were certainly "astonished," but before the "light of the world" they were completely in the dark. The (veiled) implication is that God does not need anyone else to vouch for him. But that was beyond them at this point.
* Third, "I am not alone..." (vv. 15–16). He does not judge by human standards—that is, by subjective human conviction—but rather in terms of God's wisdom: "I am with the Father who sent Me." Jesus is saying that he has the objective testimony of divine revelation, namely the Word of God.[1]

Jesus further asserts that he does fulfill the Mosaic requirement of two witnesses (vv. 17–18). He admits that the law requires "the testimony of two men" and affirms that the first witness is himself and the second is God the Father for, he says, "the Father who sent Me bears witness of Me." This naturally begs the question as to how the Father bears objective witness to Jesus. For the answer, we turn to John 5:31–39, where he addresses this question in some detail. He admits that if he is the only witness to what he claims, then it all falls to the ground (v. 31). He has another witness, but it cannot be a man, not even a great man like John the Baptist (vv. 32–35). He has "a greater witness" and he is God the Father: "The very works that I do—bear witness of Me" (v. 36). This principally refers to His miracles of healing. Jesus later emphasizes this same point: "If I do not do the works of My Father, do not believe Me; but if I do, though you do not believe Me, believe the works, that you may know and believe that the Father is in Me, and I in Him" (John 10:37–38).

"The Father Himself" has testified of Jesus in words, but they "neither heard his voice at any time, nor [saw] his form" (John 5:37). This refers to his identification at his baptism by John the Baptist as the "beloved Son" in whom the Father was "well pleased" (Matt. 3:17). Jesus also notes that "the Scriptures...these are they which testify of Me" (John 5:39).

The gist of it is that both God's works and his Word bear an incontrovertible witness to the validity of Jesus's claim to being the Light of the World.

Objection #2—"Where is Your Father?" (John 8:19–20)

This objection follows from Jesus's appeal to his Father-God. It is a valid question; just try claiming your father as the justification for your great ideas. These Pharisees were not looking for Jesus to produce his earthly father, Joseph, as a witness. He was dead and gone. Besides, Jesus had already been dismissed by his own people in Nazareth because they knew his ancestry: "'Is this not the carpenter, the Son of Mary, and brother of James, Joses, Judas, and Simon? And are not His sisters here with us?' So they were offended at Him" (Mark 6:3). The school playground taunts about "my dad's better than your dad" echo in the prejudices of adult life. In any case, they knew that Jesus was referring to God as his Father, and they would not countenance that for a moment. They could not accept that *their* God, the Yahweh of their Torah, had anything to do with Jesus of lowly Nazareth and his grand claims.[2]

Jesus's answer is searching and uncompromising. He lays down two practical implications, each presenting a challenge to his critics, ancient and modern. He replies, "You know neither Me nor My Father. If you had known Me, you would have known My Father also" (John 8:19). The fundamental fact is that if we do not recognize Jesus for who he is, we do not know the real God either. The obverse of this coin is that if we are ever to know God truly, we will first need to know Jesus as our Mediator. The failure to recognize Jesus's authority is the fruit of spiritual blindness to the true character of God. People can use the word "God" all they like, but this does not prove they know him personally, inwardly, and savingly. They are lost in the midst of all their religious verbiage and empty ritual. But they also protest too much, for all unbelievers that ever live actively "suppress the truth in unrighteousness" (Rom. 1:18). There is no innocence in the ignorance of unbelief. It is willful, and therefore culpable, ignorance that denies the authority of God as it is revealed in the person and work of Jesus Christ.

We are told that "these words Jesus spoke in the treasury, as He taught in the temple; and no one laid hands on Him, for His hour had not yet come" (compare John 8:20 with 8:59). We can read this simply as a piece of historical detail recorded to inform us as to where Jesus's encounter took place. It is that, to be sure. It also serves as his answer's final curtain call to those who question his authority to declare himself as the Light of the World. Jesus has just *said* that his authority was his own witness and that of the Father. Now, as he passes unmolested from his enemies, the Father *acts* with divine authority to restrain them. The reason given is that "His hour had not yet come." This is a parable of God's power validating the truth of Jesus's self-identification as the Light.

What Is the Practical Relevance of Jesus's Claim?

What is it to us that Jesus is the Light? The short answer is that it all adds up to the simple, searching truth about your spiritual state and your need of salvation now and forevermore (John 8:21–29). Jesus, the Light of the World, is the only Savior of sinners: "Nor is there salvation in any other, for there is no other name under heaven given among men by which we must be saved" (Acts 4:12). Jesus's answer unfolds this truth in three steps, rather obviously preparing the hearers for his coming crucifixion.

"You will die in your sins." (John 8:21–24)

If you do not believe that Jesus is "He"—the promised, divine Messiah—then you will die in your sins (v. 24). At that moment, Jesus was with them. As such, he was Savior-in-waiting. As yet, he had made no atonement for anyone's sin. The gospel was a promise all the way from Genesis 3:15 to his coming, but he still had a death to die and a grave to conquer.

But the crisis is at hand. Jesus will not always be with them (John 8:21; 13:33; 16:28). What then? Their response proves that they had never even thought about his dying. But was he not the Lamb of God? Could they not put two and two together? Centuries of sacrificial lambs—the Passover itself—surely meant that *the* Lamb has to die as a sacrifice for sin? No, they had no grasp of the vital fact that he must die. All they could do was mumble about him maybe taking his own life. Incredible! But that is what spiritual blindness does: "seeing they do not see, and hearing they do not hear, nor do they understand" (Matt. 13:13). And the only answer to this kind of darkness is the Light of the World. Faith in Christ is absolutely crucial. Time is short and Jesus tells us most clearly that it is a matter of repenting or perishing (Luke 13:3, 5).

"Who are you?" (John 8:25–26)

Jesus's claims just get more breathtaking: "Who are you?" they gasp. The answer? Jesus says simply that he is who he claims to be and who his Father proclaims him to be. Is it so unclear? Is God's Word obscure? What do you read in your Bible about Jesus? His very name is Yeshua ("God saves"), and he is given that name because "He will save His people from their sins" (Matt. 1:21).

"Then you will know that I am He." (John 8:27–29)

Still they were flummoxed for they did not grasp that he was speaking of God the Father (v. 27). Will they ever get it? Jesus gives a hint: "When you lift up the Son of Man, then you will know that I am He" (v. 28). The cross will tell the story. The Light will dawn in a new way for the world.

What of you and me in the meantime? Come to the Light. And "if we walk in the light as He is in the light, we have fellowship with one another, and the blood of Jesus Christ His Son cleanses us from all sin"

(1 John 1:7). In the words of John Brown of Edinburgh, "If we follow Christ on earth, we shall follow Him to heaven."[3] The Apostle Peter still exhorts us across the centuries:

> For we did not follow cunningly devised fables when we made known to you the power and coming of our Lord Jesus Christ, but were eyewitnesses of His majesty. For He received from God the Father honor and glory when such a voice came to Him from the Excellent Glory: "This is My beloved Son, in whom I am well pleased." And we heard this voice which came from heaven when we were with Him on the holy mountain. And so we have the prophetic word confirmed, which you do well to heed as a light that shines in a dark place, until the day dawns and the morning star rises in your hearts. (2 Peter 1:16–19)

Is Christ *your* Light?

Jesus Is Our

Lion

Do not weep. Behold, the Lion of the tribe of Judah, the Root of David, has prevailed to open the scroll and to loose its seven seals.—Revelation 5:5

READ REVELATION 5

Symbols are rarely insignificant, and often are very potent and weighty. For example, in the 1960 British movie *Sink the Bismark!*, the first image you see is the Nazi Swastika in a newsreel of Adolf Hitler launching the great German battleship on February 14, 1939, some months before World War II broke out. The very last image—after the Royal Navy sank the ship on May 27, 1941—is of one of the massive bronze lions that grace the plinth of Nelson's column in Trafalgar Square, London. The British lion, evoking the spirit of Britain's greatest naval hero, presides over the defeat of yet another of the nation's enemies.

Anyone who has seen lions on the hunt and on a kill understands why the lion is known as "the king of beasts" and has throughout history been a symbol of power and sovereignty. In Scripture, lions represent various qualities, some good and some bad.

* One theme is the *voice of God*: "A lion has roared! Who will not fear? The Lord God has spoken! Who can but prophesy?" (Amos 3:8; see also Hos. 11:10; Rev. 10:3).

* Another is *strength and courage*: "Saul and Jonathan...were stronger than lions" (2 Sam. 1:23).
* Still another is *oppression*: "my soul is among lions" (Ps. 57:4; see also 7:2; 10:9; 17:12; 22:13, 21; 35:17; 58:6; 91:13).
* And then there is the *devil* himself: "your adversary the devil walks about like a roaring lion, seeking whom he may devour" (1 Peter 5:8).
* God on occasion used lions as *instruments of his judgment* on particularly egregious sinners (1 Kings 13:24–26; 20:35–36; 2 Kings 17:24–26; compare with Hos. 13:8).

With all of this in mind, let us ask who the Lion of the tribe of Judah is, how he came to be such, and what it is that he came to accomplish.

Christ Is the Lion of Judah

There is no mystery as to the identity of the Lion of Judah, who is also the Root of David. When the elder says to John, "Behold, the Lion of the tribe of Judah, the Root of David," his use of these titles clearly points to the Messiah promised in the Old Testament.

The title "Lion of the tribe of Judah" harkens back to Genesis 49:9–12, which records Jacob's blessing of his sons at the end of his life. The patriarch likens Judah to a young lion. Judah will be the strongest of the tribes and will exercise rule for "the scepter will not depart from Judah, nor a lawgiver from between his feet" (vv. 9–10). Notice, however, that this will not last forever; the scepter shall not depart from Judah "until Shiloh comes," after which "to Him shall be the obedience of the people" (v. 10bc). The word "Shiloh" appears thirty-three times in Scripture and all but this one refer to the place where the Tabernacle had been located before moving to Jerusalem. Here, however, Shiloh is a person and not a place. He is the future scepter holder and lawgiver who replaces Judah in the age to come—which now is—the New Testament era.

And who is he? Jacob's next words are a prophecy of that future messianic age. That time will be so full of blessing that "Shiloh" will be "binding his donkey to the vine, and his donkey's colt to the choice vine, he washed his garments in wine, and his clothes in the blood of grapes. His eyes are darker than wine, and his teeth whiter than milk" (vv. 11–12). The only conceivable candidate for this personage is the final Davidic king, Jesus Christ the incarnate Son of God. The kingdom it describes is one of plenty and glory, such that vines can be hitching posts and wine can be used for washing. The language is poetic, of course, but it points to a dispensation of grace the world had not seen and would not see until the coming of the Messiah-Shiloh. Jacob's last words are best seen as a prophecy of Christ's reign as the Mediatorial King with whom is abundance and glory. The Lion of Judah is Christ the King.

The title "Root of David" takes us to Isaiah 11:1–10: "There shall come forth a Rod from the stem of Jesse, and a Branch shall grow out of his roots....in that day there shall be a Root of Jesse, who shall stand as a banner to the people."[1] The linking of the Lion of Judah with the line of the Davidic monarchy points to the Messiah who is David's greater Son, Jesus Christ the Son of God and Son of Man. "He is the royal King," observes Richard Brooks, "to whom is given all power and authority in heaven and earth."[2] Jesus Christ, and him alone, is uniquely and forever the Lion of Judah.[3]

Christ Is Worthy to Open the Scroll

The Lion "has prevailed to open the scroll and to loose its seven seals." This tells us what Jesus has done in virtue of being the Lion of Judah and also why he needs to be the Lion in order to do so.

The bad news about the scroll.

Before addressing these questions, we need to understand what the scroll with the seven seals is.

The scroll first appears in God's hand. We are told that it is written "inside and on the back" and is kept closed by seven seals (Rev. 5:1). The seals remind us that "known to God from eternity are all His works" (Acts 15:18). This, comments Matthew Henry, is the "transcript of so much as was necessary to be known in the book of the scriptures in general, in the prophetical part of the scripture especially, and in this prophecy in particular." The scroll is God's blueprint for the church, the kingdom, and the salvation of sinners.

John weeps because he cannot see how it can be opened and its contents revealed. The apostle clearly understands that whatever is in that scroll is essential for the salvation of lost humanity. We need to be saved. We need to know God's salvation. We need to know the truth about his purposes of grace and the mysteries of his kingdom. We need to know how to come to him that we might be saved.

Remember that this is a vision and not a video of a particular event in history. The vision and its vivid images present a picture of the great themes of the human predicament and the divine provision of redemption. To be deprived of this knowledge would be devastating—indeed, hopeless. It would mean being left in the dark forever, condemned to being irremediably lost. The sealed scroll that no man is good enough to open is saying that lost, unregenerate human nature cannot understand its own plight, its own world, or the way of salvation and reconciliation to God. We are, by nature, "wretched, miserable, poor, blind, and naked" (Rev. 3:17). This is God's sober truth, and it is why John "wept much." There is no one found worthy to know God, to know his salvation, and to be one with him as a redeemed son of a Father in heaven (Rom. 3:10–11). This is the bad news: no opening of the scroll means no possibility of salvation for anyone.

The good news about the scroll.

There is, however, good news and it is that the "Lion…the Root of David has prevailed to open the scroll…" How has he prevailed? The answer is that Jesus, as our Lion, has won the victory over all that has alienated us from God and rendered us helpless to save ourselves. In Christ our Lion, God has provided a way of salvation that satisfies both his perfect justice and righteousness and his perfect love and compassion for sinners. "God," says Paul, "gives us the victory through our Lord Jesus Christ" (1 Cor. 15:57). On that horrible cross at Calvary, he paid the penalty of sin; not his sin, but that of others. No one else could pay the price of his sin, never mind the sin of the world.

Jesus is *worthy* to take the scroll because his merits as the sin bearer and perfect lawkeeper justify his breaking the seals and revealing God's plan of redemption.

God, having accepted Jesus's atonement for sinners, is pleased to give him authority to open the scroll and *execute* its contents. Jesus marks this moment when he says, "All authority has been given to Me in heaven and on earth" (Matt. 28:18). Jesus is the Lion for the salvation of sinners, which is why, as he opens the seals, we see him going out "conquering and to conquer" (Rev. 6:2).

Life-giving Lion.

This is reinforced by the picture of Christ as the "Root." The root is the life of the plant. No root generally means no life, as, for example, with the seed that fell on stony ground in Jesus's parable of the seeds and the sower. The seeds germinated but their growth was soon terminated: "because they had no root, they withered away" (Matt. 13:6). The believer is "like a tree planted by the waters (Jer. 17:8; Ps. 1:3). The church is like "a vine out of Egypt" that is caused by God "to take deep root [so that] it filled the land" (Ps. 80:8–9). Christ is "a root out of dry ground" who suffers so as to "[bear] the sins of many" that he might "see of the labor of His soul, and be satisfied" (Isa. 53:2, 11–12).

Christ is therefore the life-giving Lion,[4] who through the death of the cross is able to prevail as the Mediator between God and lost humanity.

Christ Wipes Away the Tears of Believers

In Revelation 1:5, the discouraged John is told by the visiting elder: "Do not weep." The reason is that Christ's prevailing is what opens the redemptive purposes of God to his people. This is how there is a gospel (literally "good news"). The key is in the transition from verse 5 to verses 6 and beyond. John, having heard that the Lion is worthy to open the scroll, turns toward the throne of God to witness the Lion take the scroll and unlock the purposes and mysteries of God's kingdom. But what does he see? Not a lion, but a "Lamb as though it had been slain" (v. 6). Where he, and we, expect to see a lion, we see a Lamb. What could this mean? I would suggest at least two things.

The Lion conquers by the sufferings of the Lamb.

Jesus says: "My kingdom is not of this world," adding that if it were, his "servants would fight so that [He] should not be delivered to the Jews" (John 18:36). God's kingdom is not built by naked power or even mere divine omnipotence. Instead, it is built by *effectual sacrifice*: "For the weapons of our warfare," says Paul, "are not carnal but mighty in God for pulling down strongholds, casting down arguments and every high thing that exalts itself against the knowledge of God, bringing every thought into captivity to the obedience of Christ" (2 Cor. 10:4–5).

The salvation of sinners is not won by the force of a divine decree—like some heavenly clerical amendment to a final report—but by the atonement for sin in which Christ expiates the penalty of sin and propitiates the just wrath of God. It is "the Lamb of God who takes away the sin of the world" (John 1:29).

Salvation is given by God's free and sovereign grace in Christ and it issues in the most profound personal transformation of those who believe upon Christ and are saved (Acts 16:31). Throughout the Book of Revelation, we are given glimpses of "the exalted and judging Christ.

But John will never let us lose sight of the true source of this mighty rule in the Lamb's suffering."[5]

The Lamb rules "with all the power of the Lion."[6]

The kingly rule of the Risen Christ, the Lamb that was slain, is strikingly evident at certain crisis points in his earthly ministry. When Jesus taught in the synagogue in his hometown of Nazareth and declared himself to be the fulfillment of the prophecy of Isaiah 61:1–2, the mob grabbed him and took him up a hill intending to throw him off a cliff to his death. All we are told is that "passing through the midst of them, He went on His way" (Luke 4:30). Once, when Jesus taught in the temple in Jerusalem, the authorities sent officers to arrest him. But they were so astonished by Jesus's words that they could not bring themselves to apprehend him (John 7:45–47).

Only on two occasions does Jesus resort to violence against his enemies, and these are startling intimations of what the reprobate lost will face when they come unrepentant, unbelieving, and unsaved to the last judgment. Twice, Jesus clears the "money changers and...those who sold doves" from the Temple precincts (Matt. 21:12–13; John 2:13–16). When Jesus comes again, he comes as a King who "judges and makes war." Indeed, he is "King of kings and Lord of lords" (Rev. 19:11, 16).

It would be a mistake, however, to categorize Jesus's actions as sometimes lion-like and most times lamb-like. He is both Lion and Lamb at all times, although, as in the above instances, he exercises main force to secure his vital interests. The power of God is constantly in play, however gentle Jesus may be. When he urges his disciples, "Take My yoke upon you and learn from Me, for I am gentle and lowly in heart, and you will find rest for your souls" (Matt. 11:29), it is surely obvious that the promise of this verse will only be effective when it is undergirded by real supernatural power from the Lord acting upon people and circumstances.

Christ is our Lion—"Do not weep."

Jesus may be both Lion and Lamb at all times, but human experience of Jesus's dealings will differ widely from time to time. The Lion's roar calls us to account; the Lamb's gentle bleat calls us to rest in him. What is essential for every one of us is that we know the Lion as the Lamb slain for sin. No one knows Jesus as Savior without knowing him personally from the heart as "the Lamb of God who takes away the sin of the world" (John 1:29). When Paul testifies, "I am not ashamed of the gospel of Christ, for it is the power of God to salvation for everyone who believes," he is acknowledging that Christ who went "as a lamb to the slaughter" is able save him as the Lion acting in the omnipotence of God himself (Rom. 1:16; Isa. 53:7). Believers who know the Lord cannot but know him as both Lion and Lamb.

On the other hand, all who will not receive Jesus as the Lamb who died on the cross to save lost sinners, will meet him as the Lion who comes to them in judgment. Jesus's gloves will come off for determined reprobates who refuse his rule over them. Not one will escape Jesus the Lion of Judah in the Judgment.

So here is the issue for your eternity and present blessedness: Will it be Lion *and* Lamb? Or just Lion alone? Jesus is the believers' Lion-Lamb, but the unbelievers' Lion-Judge. Which will it be? "Believe on the Lord Jesus Christ and you will be saved" (Acts 16:31).

Jesus Is the

Master of the House

Then the master of the house…said to his servant, "Go out…
and bring in here the poor and the maimed and the lame and the blind."
—Luke 14:21

READ LUKE 14:15–24

One of the richest but most overlooked portraits of Christ in the New Testament is tucked away in a few of the parables, where our Lord depicts himself as the Master of the house.[1] It is found in the parable of the wheat and tares, the workers in the vineyard, the wicked tenants, and in this parable of the great banquet (Matt. 13:27; 20:1; 21:33; Luke 14:21); but its oversight is perhaps explained by the tendency of many modern translations to render a rich Greek word by the somewhat bland terms "owner," "landowner," or "householder." The term is just one word in the original language (*oikodespotēs*), but it is composed of two words that carry a lot of theological freight, and so it merits inclusion in our gallery of portraits.

The first word in this title of Christ is "house." This Greek term (*oikos*) can mean a literal house, but more specifically it refers to the residents of that house—the family who lives there; the household. Throughout the epistles, this word is used to define the Church: "You also, as living stones, are being built up a spiritual house" (*oikos*,

1 Peter 2:5); and Paul elsewhere describes the Church as "the household of faith" (*oikeous*, Gal. 6:10, compare with Eph. 2:19). The second word is "master." This term (*despotēs*) refers to a ruler or governor who has absolute sovereignty (from which we derive the less-than-happy English word *despot*). In Roman times, the master of the house was the one who possessed, managed, and governed the family, servants, and slaves of the household.[2]

Put these two words together, and you get a powerful portrait of Jesus as Master of the household of God and of the Church as the Household of the Master. Christians are the family and household of God, and Jesus is our Lord. We discover four aspects of Christ's identity as Master of the house in the parable of the great banquet.

The Banquet of the Master

We learn something about the Master of the house by the banquet that he hosts. Jesus tells a parable about "a great supper" (Luke 14:16). The immediate context of this parable is Sabbath dinner at the home of a particularly high-ranking Pharisee, where Jesus has been invited as a guest (v. 1). The other guests are self-righteous religious leaders—people of religious and biological pedigree, who presume to hold a special place in God's favor. We also read that "they watched Him closely" (v. 1). The atmosphere is not one of warm, jovial friendship, and the invitation is not motivated by fellowship and goodwill. Jesus does not disappoint them; he heals a man with dropsy that Sabbath day, and then lectures them on their selfishness in seeking the place of honor at the feast while disregarding "the poor, the maimed, the lame, and the blind" (vv. 2–6, 7–14).

But there is also a much broader context to this parable. Seven hundred years previously, the prophet Isaiah had prophesied that in the last days, the days of the Messiah, God would host a great banquet:

> On this mountain the LORD Almighty will prepare
> a feast of rich food for all peoples,

a banquet of aged wine—
  the best of meats and the finest of wines...

The Sovereign LORD will wipe away the tears
  from all faces;
He will remove the disgrace of His people
  from all the earth. (Isa. 25:6, 8 NIV)

This was the great "messianic banquet" that every Jew looked forward to. It was literally the "party to end all parties." God would gather all the nations to his banqueting house at the end of time, and they would feast with the Messiah himself. Jesus spoke of it with his disciples at the Last Supper: "Assuredly, I say to you, I will no longer drink of the fruit of the vine until that day when I drink it new in the kingdom of God" (Mark 14:25; Luke 22:29–30). John caught a glimpse of it in his vision: "Let us be glad and rejoice and give Him glory, for the marriage of the Lamb has come, and His wife has made herself ready...Blessed are those who are called to the marriage supper of the Lamb!" (Rev. 19:7–9). It is precisely this blessedness that Jesus's host assumes he will someday personally enjoy when he declares in Luke 14:15, "Blessed is he who shall eat bread in the kingdom of God!" But Jesus's parable in response suggests quite a different outcome for the Pharisee and his friends.

With this background, we can proceed to interpret and apply Jesus's parable to ourselves: The great supper is the great messianic banquet for God's household in heaven (v. 16); the host is the Master of the house, Jesus the Messiah (v. 21); and the guests are all whom this Master of the house invites that respond to his gospel invitation. The Pharisees assume it will be an exclusive, black-tie event, with a limited guest list for only the most holy—no "riff-raff" allowed. But Jesus is going to remind them that his guest list is far more extensive than they would ever have dreamed: "a certain man gave a great supper and invited many" (v. 16).

This is the first lesson this portrait of Christ teaches you: that as Master of the house, Jesus alone has the right to admit or refuse entrance to his great supper. If you would be at his table in the kingdom of heaven, if you would be found in the Household of Faith, you must have personal dealings with the Master of the house, Jesus Christ. Sadly, as we proceed into the heart of the parable, we find that not everyone he invites is willing to do that.

The Rejection of the Master

We learn something more about the Master of the house by the rejection he faces. He generously invites a chosen people to feast with him: He "invited many and sent his servant at supper time to say to those who were invited, 'Come, for all things are now ready' " (v. 17). It was a great personal expense for any master of the house to host such a feast, and therefore a great honor to be invited.

If you have had the pleasure of receiving a wedding invitation, you will know that the first thing to do is send an RSVP. These are necessary so the host has a head count to know how much food to prepare. This was also the custom in the first century: the master of the house would send out an initial invitation to know what preparations to make. The assumption in Jesus's parable is that these guests had already responded positively to that initial invitation, because he has prepared the food and now sends out a servant to announce that everything is ready for them. But what a shock awaits the Master of the house.

"They all with one accord began to make excuses" (v. 18). To reject the invitation of the master of the house was not just ill-mannered, but also a deep personal insult, and the greater the person insulted, the greater the insult. They had initially said they would come, so what profound reasons do they have for suddenly rejecting this summons to sit at the table where the food is even now getting cold? Three reasons are offered:

* "I have bought a piece of ground, and I must go and see it. I ask you to have me excused" (v. 18). Even today, no one in

their right mind would buy a plot of land without having first inspected it.

* "I have bought five yoke of oxen, and I am going to test them. I ask you to have me excused" (v. 19). No one would even bid on such expensive farming equipment without first testing them out to make sure they work well together.[3]
* "I have married a wife, and therefore I cannot come" (v. 20). This reason is worst of all. Not to put too fine a point on it, he is basically saying, "Tell your Master, I'm busy on my honeymoon."

Of course, these are three excuses, not three reasons. What is more, they are utterly unconvincing excuses. No one is pulling the wool over anyone's eyes; these people have no desire to be in the company of the Master of the house. It is him they are rejecting, not his sumptuous food. Jesus is teaching that, as Master of the house, he faces rejection. In the Old Testament, Israel had RSVP'd positively to God's gracious covenant invitation, saying they would attend his messianic banquet. But now that they see just who this Messiah is—Jesus, the carpenter from Nazareth, no less—they want to shut down his banquet altogether.

But the rejection of the Master of the house is not limited to first-century Pharisees. By nature, all men alike make excuses, and like these three examples, they are unanimous in their rejection of the Master of the house: They will not enter his house, and they will not accept his mastery. "They all with one accord began to make excuses." Are you making excuses too? To do so is to reject Jesus as Master of the house and to show contempt for the great expense he has paid to furnish the banquet. It is to say there is other company you would rather keep than his, other houses you would rather occupy, and other masters you would rather serve.

Often these rival masters are not bad things in themselves. After all, there is nothing wrong about owning property, buying tools for your trade, or enjoying the wife of your youth (Prov. 5:18–19). But what happens when property, work, and relationships become "the masters of your house"? These three men were busy doing good, lawful things. It was not so much the wicked things they were doing, but the great quantity of good things that squeezed out the most important thing of all.

If you want to sit with Jesus at the messianic banquet in glory, you must realize that while the invitation is free, there is a very real cost, a cost these men were not willing to pay. The Lamb's Bride must "[make] herself ready" (Rev. 19:7). She must turn from all other admirers and worldly entanglements and be joined to the Master of the house. Does your affection for Christ trump all the other lawful pleasures of this fleeting life?

The Generosity of the Master

We learn something about the Master of the house by the generosity he shows. He may be the "Despot of the house," but he is a benevolent despot.

Have you ever invited a family to dinner and they stood you up? While there is obviously disappointment for all the work that has seemingly gone to waste, perhaps someone in the family finds a silver lining and, trying to cheer everyone up, says, "Oh well, all the more for us." But this Master of the house, displaying understandable anger at this snub, also displays astonishing generosity of spirit. He does not say, "all the more for Me," but "all the more for others." And *which* others does he have in mind? "The poor and the maimed and the lame and the blind" (Luke 14:21).

So the Pharisees, who presume they have dinner reservations, are shown the door, and those *they* had shown the door are ushered in.[4] Who are these people that fill the Master's house? There are actually three specific groups of invitees in the parable. First are the Jewish religious leaders who want nothing to do with the Master of the house.

The second group are those in "the streets and lanes of the city," that is, the outcast Jews of Jesus's day: "the poor, the maimed, the lame, and the blind" (v. 21). These were the people Jesus came for: the spiritually poor, those diseased and blinded by sin who knew their condition and trusted Christ to save them. Then there is a third group of invitees: those *outside* the city in "the highways and hedges" (v. 23), the Gentiles, who will come "from the east and the west, from the north and the south, and sit down in the kingdom of God" (Luke 13:29), just as Isaiah had prophesied seven hundred years before. The Master's food will not go to waste; he will lavish it on a people who know they do not deserve it, even though they may be written off by their social and religious superiors.

In Eastern cultures, dining with a host is a sign of friendship, fellowship, and goodwill.[5] How generous that this Master of the house should want to dine with you! We do not consider it an unexpected generosity if one millionaire says to another millionaire, "come over to my mansion for a great supper," for he eats with an equal. But it certainly is unexpected generosity when the millionaire extends that invitation to the middle-school kid who mows the lawn on one of his many villas, lavishing his riches upon a nobody. For someone used to hob-nobbing with kings, sultans, and Hollywood stars, to cherish the company of little Jimmy the sixth grader! Surely it would be beneath him?

Not for this Master. Listen to what Jesus says: "Behold, I stand at the door and knock. If anyone hears My voice and opens the door, I will come in to him and dine with him, and he with Me" (Rev. 3:20). And again, "If anyone loves Me, he will keep My word; and My Father will love him, and We will come to him and make Our home with him" (John 14:23).

Jesus is an uncommonly generous Master who invites nobodies like you and I to be a member of his household and then desires to eat and drink with us. He does so each time we celebrate the Lord's Supper as a prelude to the messianic banquet in glory. Yes, it is simple fare: bread and wine. But these elements on his table were bought at a great price, and the realities they point to are more costly than anything you could ever taste at the table of any earthly king. Shall we not joyfully accept his invitation to "take, eat, and drink"?

The Compulsion of the Master

Finally, we learn something about the Master of the house by the loving persuasion with which he urges people into his household. There is one character in Jesus's story that we have not mentioned yet. Who is the servant, scurrying about the city, speaking on behalf of his Master? He represents those of us who *have* accepted the invitation of the Master, who are now members of his household, and delight to do his bidding. And what is his bidding? It is to compel others to come to his banquet. Jesus says to you and me: "Go out into the highways and hedges, and compel them to come in, that my house may be filled" (v. 23).

The Master of the house reveals an *evangelistic urgency*. His faithful servants are commanded to go out and proclaim, "still there is room." (v. 22). We do not know who will sit in those seats, but we do know who is on the Master's invitation list: "whosoever believes in Him" (John 3:16). The means by which Jesus brings into his banqueting house those who will feast with him forever is the free offer of the gospel. One free, generous invitation; two responses: either lame excuses or glad acceptance. Are you faithfully compelling people to come to the Master of the house, so that they may be members of his house and he may be their Master? "Still there is room!"

The Master of the house reveals *an evangelistic deadline* (Luke 14:24). In another of the "Master of the house" passages, Jesus says,

> Strive to enter through the narrow gate, for many, I say to you, will seek to enter and will not be able. When once the Master of the house has risen up and shut the door, and you begin to stand outside and knock at the door, saying, "Lord, Lord, open for us," and He will

> answer and say to you, "I do not know you, where you are from." (Luke 13:24–25)

The Master of the house "rises up and shuts the door" daily as millions are taken away in death. And he will rise up and shut the door definitively when he returns to welcome his elect into his banqueting house on the last day.

When you respond to a wedding invitation, there is always an RSVP deadline. I suppose if you missed that deadline slightly you might still get in, but there is one deadline you certainly cannot afford to miss: the hour of the wedding itself. Once the door is shut, it is too late. In the same way, the marriage supper of the Lamb has a fixed day and time.

Will the door be closed on you? The last verse contains a most solemn declaration from the Master: "For I say to you that none of those men who were invited shall taste my supper" (Luke 14:24). They were invited, but they will never enter. You see, a personal invitation from the Master of the house himself is not enough to taste his supper. It is not enough to be well-acquainted with the terms of the gospel offer to be admitted to the Master's house; you must respond personally by faith to his gracious invitation. Jesus, the Master of the house, gives a great supper, and he has now sent his servant at supper time to say to you, "Come, for all things are now ready."

Jesus Is Our

Peace

For He Himself is our peace...
—Ephesians 2:14

READ EPHESIANS 2:14–18

"Where they make a desert, they call it peace," is the famous comment of the Roman annalist Tacitus on the *Pax Romana*—the so-called Roman Peace—a "peace" that was established and maintained by the force of relentless military conquest.[1] Something similar may be said for a lot of the peace in human hearts. People will say they are OK while inside they are tortured by confusion or anger. This is a false peace built on delusion or denial. Scripture warns us with stark realism: " 'There is no peace,' says the LORD, 'for the wicked' "—whether in time or eternity. Consequently, "the wicked are like the troubled sea, when it cannot rest, whose waters cast up mire and dirt" (Isa. 48:22; 57:20).

This does not mean that many do not persuade themselves they have peace of mind and conscience, even before God. Jeremiah decries the self-deceived peace of people in his own day who thought themselves right with God: "For they have healed the hurt of the daughter of My people slightly, saying, 'Peace, peace!' when there is no peace"

(Jer. 8:11). False peace is in one way or another the currency of all false teaching:

> They continually say to those who despise Me, "The Lord has said, 'You shall have peace' "; and to everyone who walks according to the dictates of his own heart, they say, "No evil shall come upon you." (Jer. 23:17)

They will discover, sooner or later, that God's just judgment will blow away their illusions of peace. God is not mocked and tells the false teachers in the Old Testament Church,

> Because, indeed, because they have seduced My people, saying, "Peace!" when there is no peace—and one builds a wall, and they plaster it with untempered mortar—say to those who plaster it with untempered mortar, that it will fall. There will be flooding rain, and you, O great hailstones, shall fall; and a stormy wind shall tear it down....Thus will I accomplish My wrath on the wall and on those who have plastered it with untempered mortar; and I will say to you, "The wall is no more, nor those who plastered it, that is, the prophets of Israel who prophesy concerning Jerusalem, and who see visions of peace for her when there is no peace," says the Lord God. (Ezek. 13:10–11, 15–16)

The fundamental problem, as Paul says in Romans 8:7, is that "the carnal mind is enmity against God; for it is not subject to the law of God, nor indeed can be." This is the root of human nature's *dis*peace with God, with others, and with itself. The natural man is at war with God and will not and cannot get out of it by himself (1 Cor. 2:14). From this stems all the dispeace in this sadly fractured world of ours. If any of us is to have real peace with God, it will only be on his terms as revealed in his Word and not on the basis of what we decide is sufficient to the task. We therefore need, says Paul, a divine makeover of our very nature with "the peace of God, which surpasses all understanding," which "will guard [our] hearts and minds through Christ Jesus" (Phil. 4:7).

Christ Is Our Peace

The source of the peace we all need is the Lord Jesus Christ, savingly believed and lovingly followed. He is God's answer to all the unrest in our souls, in our personal relationships, and in our relationship to the holy God who is "of purer eyes than to behold evil, and cannot look on wickedness" (Hab. 1:13). Paul gloriously asserts that Christ *is* exclusively that peace. He is peace in himself and in his work as the Mediator (1 Tim. 2:5). He is peace personified. He is the one-and-only peace for this world of ours, as the angels sang at his birth in Bethlehem: "Glory to God in the highest, and on earth peace, goodwill toward men!" (Luke 2:14). But if he is the answer and we are to be blessed with his peace, we must first grasp the nature of our problem of dispeace with God and man.

Hopeless aliens.

Paul's initial focus is not upon man's estrangement from God, but on the historical difference between Jew and Gentile and their relationship to one another (Eph. 2:11). In other words, he starts with the concrete estrangement between the two groups of people—a common problem, you will agree, in the modern world—and then sets it in its theological context to bring us all to the larger question of the estrangement between God and man and the state of our own present personal relationship to God. "Therefore remember," he says to the Ephesian Christians, "that you [were] once Gentiles in the flesh." They were accordingly called "the Uncircumcision" by those called "the Circumcision," that is, the Jews (v. 11). But what exactly does this mean?

Paul cuts to the chase: "at that time you were without Christ" (v. 12). This was just a fact. The Gentile peoples had no Messiah. Why? For two reasons: they were separated from "the commonwealth" (Greek, *politeia*) of God's people and were strangers to "the covenants of promise." That promise is Christ the Son, the Risen Savior and the Seed of Abraham (Acts 13:32ff.; Gal. 3:16). Because of this, they were "without

God"—literally "atheists" (Greek, *atheoi*). The Gentile problem "at that time"—that is, before Jesus came into the world—is not merely that they were separated from the Jews, but that they were alienated from God. Because they were outside the promise of God's covenant, and so did not receive the sign of the covenant and hence were called the uncircumcision, they therefore were a people "having no hope." They were well and truly in the dark and really needed Jesus.

Brought near.

The remedy is "the blood of Christ" (Eph. 2:13). This is the way by which those who "once were afar off" are "brought near" (compare with Isa. 59:1; 57:19; and Acts 2:39). This takes us back to the earlier assertion that "in Him we have redemption through His blood, the forgiveness of sins" (Eph. 1:7). This is simply the gospel of "Jesus Christ and Him crucified" (1 Cor. 2:2). Hence he is our peace.

Christ Makes Our Peace

If Christ *is* our peace, how does he *make* that peace to be ours in our hearts and in our lives? How is his peace accomplished so that it may become transferrable to us? Let us remind ourselves that Jesus came to secure a real peace that actually ends a real war that afflicts human beings spiritually and physically in time and for eternity.

Both made one.

Notice how concrete Paul is as he addresses this question. Jesus, he says, "has made us both one and has broken down in his flesh the dividing wall of hostility" (v. 14 ESV). In other words, Jews and Gentiles are brought together *by* Christ in his person and work and made one *in* Christ on account of shared faith in him. Because of this, real barriers that formerly came between them are taken away. The "dividing wall" may be a reference to the physical barrier in the Jerusalem Temple that separated the court of Israel from the court of the Gentiles, but it reaches far beyond that to the barrier between God and sinful humanity. Jesus came to secure a reconciliation that is both "vertical"—between alienated God and alienating humanity—and "horizontal"—between people united in "like precious faith" (2 Peter 1:1).

Enmity put to death.

The *ability* of Jesus to be our peace arises from three amazing things he has done to abolish the enmity that blights human nature and relationships with God and man. The basic human problem is a natural condition of spiritual death, which has its origin in our minds being set on "the flesh"; it is "because the carnal mind is enmity against God; for it is not subject to the law of God, nor indeed can be" (Rom. 8:7; compare with 1 Cor. 2:14; Eph. 2:1; and Col. 2:13).

First of all, Jesus abolishes this enmity "in His flesh" and so satisfies, fulfills, and abolishes "the law of commandments contained in ordinances" (Eph. 2:15). The Old Testament ceremonial law and its sacrificial system was the sole preserve of the Jews. Jesus perfectly fulfills it through his death on the cross, bearing the penalty of the law for all he will save. If he dies for us, we will live forever in him. He suffers as the substitute for all those he saves. Princeton's Charles Hodge comments that "Christ has freed us from the law as a covenant of works by being himself made subject to it, Gal. 4:5; by bearing its penalty, Gal. 3:13; by his body, Rom. 7:4; by the body of his flesh, Col. 1:22; by his cross, Col. 2:4."[2] Jesus bears the just enmity of God against sinners in order to kill the unjust but endemic enmity of man toward God. Jesus "Himself bore our sins in His own body on the tree, that we, having died to sins, might live for righteousness—by whose stripes you were healed" (1 Peter 2:24).

Second, Jesus was thereby able to "create in Himself one new man from the two, thus making peace" (Eph. 2:15). He is able to regenerate the old nature so that "if anyone is in Christ, he is a new creation, old things have passed away, behold all things have become new" (2 Cor. 5:17). People nowadays often talk about re-inventing themselves, or having a makeover. What we need most is a divine re-creation, a new birth that is not of our making but comes from the gracious and powerful hand of the Lord. This is what Jesus is able to do for all who will follow him.

Third, Jesus reconciles us "to God in one body" by the death he died on Calvary's cross (Eph. 2:16). He dies to kill sin dead so as to remove the enmity that flows from it—between Jew and Gentile and between God and people. He saves sinners one by one to build them as one body, his church: "Christ is the head of the church: and He is the Savior of the body" (Eph. 5:23).

When we draw all these threads together, we can see what Jesus is to us as our peace. He saves you "by grace...through faith," and it is "not of yourselves; it is the gift of God" so that you may be united in peace to God and believers (Eph. 2:8). He regenerates dead souls and calls and converts them to himself to be new creations in him as Savior and Lord. And we are remade as the body of Christ, for Jesus's purpose is "that the Gentiles should be fellow heirs, of the same body, and partakers of His promise in Christ through the gospel" (Eph. 3:6). Only Jesus could make this peace for restless sinners. Only Jesus makes us one body and does so only by his shed blood and sinless life.

Christ Gives Us His Peace

Having told us how Jesus is peace in himself for us, and how Jesus secures peace through the cross for us, the apostle turns to how Jesus conveys his peace to us and sustains us in it. He does this by two great means.

He comes and preaches peace to the whole of humanity.

The angels declared Jesus's birth as the harbinger of a new era of peace: "Glory to God in the highest, and on earth peace, goodwill toward men!" (Luke 2:14). Jesus is the "Prince of Peace" (Isa. 9:6) whose ministry to all who followed him was one of peace. Just prior to his crucifixion, he tells his immediate disciples, "Peace I leave with you, My peace I give to you; not as the world gives do I give to you. Let not your heart be troubled, neither let it be afraid" (John 14:27; compare with Ps. 72:3, 7; Luke 1:79; 7:50; 8:48; John 16:33; 20:19–21; Rom. 5:1; 10:15; 14:17; Col. 1:20; and Heb. 6:20–7:2).[3]

He does this still by the ministry of the gospel, which is a ministry of reconciliation. "God," says Paul, "has reconciled us to Himself through Jesus Christ, and has given us the ministry of reconciliation, that is, that God was in Christ reconciling the world to Himself, not imputing their trespasses to them, and has committed to us the word of reconciliation" (2 Cor. 5:18–19). This is the great message of true gospel preaching. "We are ambassadors for Christ," says Paul, "as though God were pleading through us: we implore you on Christ's behalf, be reconciled to God" (v. 20). We must keep this in the front of our minds: the reconciliation of the lost to the Lord is the great goal. We are perhaps too prone to preach and argue *against* things...to take on great issues without pressing through to that goal of peace with God. Jesus Christ is still proclaiming peace on earth.

He secures access to the Father by the one Holy Spirit.

When Jesus is our peace, we are reconciled to God and to everyone he saves. The goal and fruit of this is access to God as our Father (Eph. 2:18). Having adopted us as his children, he brings us into that personal relationship in which we may cry to him, by the Holy "Spirit of adoption," as our "Abba, Father" (Rom. 8:15).

You will notice that this is the work of all three persons of the triune God: "through Him [Jesus Christ] we both have access by one [Holy] Spirit to the Father." In the economy of salvation, God the Father represents absolute Godhead—he plans and purposes, chooses whom he will save, and sends his Son to save them. Then the Father and the Son send the Holy Spirit to apply salvation to sinners in time and space. He "predestined us to adoption as sons by Jesus Christ to Himself, according to the good pleasure of His will" (Eph. 1:5).

Access to the Father is, then, the fruit of a peace in Jesus. It begins when you come to Christ in saving faith. It is fed and grows in the body life of believers in connection with the "means of grace," both public and private—the preaching of the Word, the sacraments, and prayer—for " 'the word is near you, in your mouth and in your heart' (that is, the word of faith which we preach): that if you confess with your mouth the Lord Jesus and believe in your heart that God has raised Him from the dead, you will be saved" (Rom. 10:8–9). Martyn Lloyd-Jones, commenting on Ephesians 2:18, observes,

> If only every Church member, every Christian in the Church, realised the truth of this statement, the Church would be so different that we would scarcely recognize her. But oh, how different is the Church from what we find here! How many think of Christianity and of the Christian Church simply as a place where they attend now and again, and that perhaps in a perfunctory manner...or as a place in which they may exercise certain gifts that they have, and be busy—a kind of club, an institution, a human society. What a contrast to what we have here! This is Christianity, this is what makes one a Christian. The Christian Church really consists of a people who realize that this is the whole object and purpose of—access by one Spirit unto the Father.[4]

Jesus Christ is the peace that brings believers to a living access to his Father—the same "God and Father of our Lord Jesus Christ, who according to His abundant mercy has begotten us again to a living hope through the resurrection of Jesus Christ from the dead" (1 Peter 1:3). Ezekiel Hopkins (1634–90) vividly illustrates the nature of the peace Christ has secured for believers. He first likens the wall of sin between God and man to a wood fence that keeps out the light but cannot survive the heat of God's wrath. Jesus breaks down that wooden wall we have put up between us and God and becomes himself the shield of his people. He stands between believers and God's wrath against sin, like a wall of crystal that keeps us from the heat of wrath but lets the light of truth and grace through to our hearts.[5] Let us therefore embrace Christ together, rejoicing in him who is our peace, and "the peace of God, which surpasses all understanding, will guard your hearts and minds through Jesus Christ" (Phil. 4:7).

Jesus Is Our
Physician

Those who are well have no need of a physician, but those who are sick.—Matthew 9:12

READ MATTHEW 9:9–13

Each year, autumn hails the arrival of flu season. Families shuffle off to pharmacies and doctor's offices to be vaccinated in the hopes of dodging the bullet for another year. Sickness is of course an inescapable reality of life, whether we face comparatively minor infirmities or serious disabilities and diseases. Our bodies feel the curse. This means that physicians with their skills and medicines are a gift of God's common grace to a fallen world. The Fall necessitates physicians; we shall certainly have no need of them in heaven. But the Scriptures teach that bodily illness is really only a symptom. The real pandemic that affects the human race is sin; and its wages, Paul reminds us, is death (Rom. 6:23).

It is no surprise, then, that the Savior of this fallen world should call himself a physician. And as with any good physician, Jesus does not simply address the symptoms; he supplies the cure for the underlying disease. This is the lesson of Matthew chapter 9, which relates several of Jesus's miraculous healings, specifically, those of the paralytic, the bleeding woman, the ruler's daughter, the two blind men, and the demon-possessed mute, all of whom are restored by the Lord. But Matthew's purpose is to demonstrate that Jesus is the healer of the *spiritual* ailment of sin. For example, in Matthew 9:5–6, we find Jesus asking the skeptical scribes, "For which is easier, to say, 'Your sins are forgiven you,' or to say, 'Arise and walk'? But that you may know that the Son of Man has power on earth to forgive sins—then He said to the paralytic, 'Arise, take up your bed, and go to your house.'" Jesus thus gives us his own hermeneutic for properly understanding his miracles of healing the *body*; they attest to his mission as physician of the *soul*.

The Sick Sinner

The "sick" sinner in the story is Matthew himself. We are told he was a tax collector, which means he worked either for Caesar or Herod. As such, he belonged to a class despised by Jewish patriots and the general public alike.[1] They were regarded as cut-throat social climbers and were pariahs for their greed and robbery. The Jewish Talmud even disqualified them from being judges or witnesses in a court of law, declaring "repentance was particularly difficult" for this class of "sinners."[2] So Matthew is a social outcast, an incurable traitor to Israel. And while it is true that there is nothing pretty about the Jewish hatred of these outcasts (as we shall see), it is equally true that there is nothing pretty about Matthew's heart. Matthew is *sick*.

Sin is a sickness. In terms of the conditions Jesus healed in Matthew chapter 9, we see that it is paralyzing, polluting, painful, blinding, controlling, and terminal. Sin is endemic to man; it is more widespread, devastating, and infectious than any disease. Sin makes the AIDS epidemic in Africa appear like a common cold. The casualty rate is 100 percent, and the death rate is 100 percent. It is so virulent that its victims are said to be dead while still alive; Matthew is "dead in trespasses and sins" (Eph. 2:1). He must therefore be raised; a Lazarus-like command must be issued by the giver of life. And this very command falls from Jesus's lips in the words "follow me" (Matt. 9:9). Here is the Lord's divine summons to this sick sinner, and Matthew's response is immediate: "So he arose and followed Him." In theological terms, this was not the programmed response of a robot but the willing response of a new heart transformed by the effectual calling of Christ.[3] This is Matthew's conversion story, and it is not so much Matthew's decision for Christ, as it is Christ's decision for Matthew.

But the *inward calling* of a sick sinner in Matthew 9:9 is quickly followed by the *outward testimony* of a healed sinner in verse 10. The scene has suddenly changed from a dusty street to a lavish dining room. Luke's account tells us, "Then [Matthew] gave him a great feast in his own house. And there were a great number of tax collectors and others who sat down with them" (Luke 5:29). As with many an eager new convert, he wants to introduce his friends to Christ. The invitees include Jesus as the guest of honor, his disciples, and a crowd from Matthew's old spheres of friendship: "many tax collectors and sinners" (Matt. 9:10). In other words, the guest list is filled with other "sick" people. Matthew has been healed, and so he schedules an appointment for his sick friends with the physician.

Historians tell us that in the fourteenth century, the Bubonic Plague (or Black Death) killed about one-third of the population of Europe.[4] In the twenty-first century, if caught in time, the same condition is treatable with a simple course of antibiotics. Imagine what a difference it would make if you lived back then and had a great supply of medicine. Would you not offer it to as many people as possible? The healed sinner does not keep the antidote to himself. He shares it with others who are as he once was. If you are a Christian, you too have the testimony of a healed sinner; you know the physician who can cure your sinful-sick friends and family. So do you tell them, or are you guilty of keeping your knowledge of the Great Physician to yourself?

The "Healthy" Self-Righteous

The "healthy" self-righteous in our story are the Pharisees. In Matthew 9:11, the religious police crash the party. The public conduct of the young rabbi from Nazareth is out of line with their rabbinical code of conduct. In fact, it is nothing short of scandalous. The whole village would learn of such a feast, and so in no time the Pharisees challenge Jesus (through the Twelve): "Why does your Teacher eat with tax collectors and sinners?" Instead of rejoicing that notorious sinners like Matthew are repenting, they are mortified. The essence of their objection is found in a two-fold comparison of themselves with others.

It is the others who are sick.

They first compare themselves to the sick sinner. The tacit assumption is, "Others are sick. We're not sick at all. We are *righteous*!" Whereas the sinner might compare himself to the Pharisee and deem himself unworthy of salvation, here the Pharisee compares himself to the sinner and deems himself unneedful of salvation.

It is Jesus who has a problem.

Far more seriously, they compare themselves to Jesus. They consider themselves more righteous even than Christ. After all, what sort of a teacher would risk contamination by associations with tax collectors and sinners! But in doing so, they are the standard of their own righteousness; they erect their own petty fences to the level of God's law, and then, holding the very Son of God to the standard of their own legal code, promptly fail him. In other words, they presume to be physicians themselves and make terminal diagnoses of others while ironically condemning themselves in the process. Their misdiagnosis is a self-diagnosis. And if self-medication is dangerous in the physical realm, then it is far more dangerous in the spiritual.

Such is the attitude of the healthy self-righteous, but the "righteousness of the healthy" is of course an oxymoron. The Pharisees consider themselves righteous, but it is a righteousness of their own, which Paul in Philippians 3:8 declares to be "dung." So when Jesus says, "I did not call the righteous" in Matthew 9:13, he means the self-righteous, or those who are righteous in their own esteem.

Those who do not feel the need for a doctor are often those who need one most. When I was in high school, I woke up one summer morning with a sharp chest pain. My family told me not to worry about it—that it was probably indigestion. I continued for a couple of days without medical attention, until it was eventually diagnosed as an eighty-percent lung collapse, requiring surgical intervention. If you put off that dentist visit, that blood pressure check, or ignore that lump you thought you felt last year, it may cost you dearly in the end. Procrastination in the spiritual realm is just as deadly as in the physical. You say, "I feel fine," but unless you have had personal dealings with the Great Physician, you are most certainly *not* fine.

The Compassionate Physician

What do we learn about Christ from his response to these two sets of characters in the story?

Jesus is a physician for the sick sinner.

First, and most obviously, we need to learn that Jesus is a physician for the sick sinner. He says, "Those who are well have no need of a physician, but those who are sick" (v. 12). Notice how he turns the incredulous question of the Pharisees on its head; they are rather like a group of nurses entering a hospital ward and gasping, "Doctor! What are *you* doing here among all the *patients*?" But exactly what kind of physician is Jesus for the sick sinner?

Jesus is a *qualified* physician for the sick sinner. He understands the anatomy of your soul; he has been "tempted as [you] are, yet without sin" (Heb. 4:15). But he also knows you individually—he knows your medical history in all its hideous detail, and he matches his medicine to suit your condition perfectly. He knows which soothing balm to prescribe for your particular wounds, which treatment to apply to your spiritual cancers, which diet for your inordinate lusts, and which disciplines for your addictions.

Jesus is a *skillful* physician for the sick sinner. He heals by the medicine of Scripture applied effectually by his Spirit. First, he takes on your individual case and schedules surgery (election). He then gives you a new heart—not "fixing" the old one, but giving you a heart transplant: "I will take the heart of stone out of your flesh and give you a heart of flesh" (regeneration; Ezek. 36:26). He thus gives you new life, just as he did to Matthew, and clothes you with his health—by his shed blood and perfect righteousness—declaring a once-for-all "clean bill of health" (justification). This clean bill of health will never be contradicted (though many rival physicians will try to convince you that you need their supplemental remedy too). And when your regular spiritual ailments threaten your confidence in his "clean bill of health," he will remain your physician still until he perfects you. It is in the confidence that he *has* made you whole that you can live as a whole person (sanctification and glorification).

Jesus is a *compassionate* physician for the sick sinner. He administers good medicine and a good bedside manner, as is evidenced in Matthew 9:36: "But when He saw the multitudes, He was moved with compassion for them, because they were weary and scattered, like sheep having no shepherd." You are never a mere statistic in Christ's hospital; you are a well-beloved family member who receives tailored care and individual attention.

Jesus is a *sufficient* physician for the sick sinner, and that is because he is the *only* physician for the sick sinner. His treatment does not need to be supplemented with any human medicines; home remedies are insufficient (i.e., your good works and personal performance—see Isa. 64:6). Other physicians' remedies will not suffice; there are many spiritual equivalents of alternative medicines out there—alternative religions, the mystical experiences of "spiritual formation" practices, etc. The Christian must beware of false teachers peddling their spiritual snake oils; they are costly, and may even seem to bring a measure of relief to symptoms for a time, but they cannot solve the root problem. Placebos will not work either:[5] religious works such as penance or any spiritual disciplines that you perform to try to eradicate your sin problem. Indeed, any remedy other than the gospel of Christ is certain to fail. Even after we become Christians, we may fall prey to some of these false physicians. Beware of any book or teacher that says he has the foolproof answer to a sin problem—some method or mantra or mystery—rather than coming to Christ who alone is the physician for sick sinners. Do you know this physician? Can you personally testify with Matthew to Jesus's healing power, skill, and grace?

Jesus Is Not a Physician for the "Healthy" Self-Righteous

Second, we need to learn that Jesus is not a physician for the "healthy" self-righteous, for he says, "Those who are well have no need of a physician" (Matt. 9:12). As we have seen, these healthy self-righteous are anything but healthy. Rather, they have compared themselves to others and *diagnosed themselves* as righteous. Jesus does two things for such people.

For one thing, *he accepts their sinful misdiagnosis*. This is a chilling thought. It is not blindness on Jesus's part, as if he accepted the lie himself, but rather his acceptance of the sentence they have passed on themselves. They are "self-condemned men" (Titus 3:11); the self-righteous will have nothing of Jesus, and so Jesus will have nothing of them.

Maybe you have examined yourself, and, while you know you are not perfect, you really do not think you are *that* sick. "Isn't the writer exaggerating just a little bit? It's just another health scare like those 'bird and swine flu' warnings some years ago that came to nothing." But this is no health scare; Jesus is not given to exaggeration. We read in John 9:41: "Jesus said to [the Pharisees], 'If you were blind, you would have no sin; but since you say, "We see," therefore your sin remains.'" Jesus is the Savior of *sinners*. If you are not a sinner, Jesus cannot be your Savior. So be warned: your opinion of yourself before God will have eternal consequences. "Those who are well have no need of a physician."

But notice that our Lord also sends these Pharisees to their Bibles. He says, "Go and learn what this means," and cites Hosea 6:6: "I desire mercy and not sacrifice." In Hosea's day, Israel had displayed sham righteousness by a rigorous outward conformity to the ceremonial law, but a horrible inward disposition to their neighbor (expressed in adultery, robbery, and murder). The Pharisees were essentially doing the same thing: pitting the stipulation of the law against the moral essence of the law. What is striking, though, is that Jesus does not expound the text; he simply asks these "Bible teachers" to go and do their own Bible study. If they do their homework, they will find themselves condemned of a pedantic preoccupation with ritual over a genuine, heartfelt concern for those in need.

How many of us does Jesus need to send back to our Bibles? "Go and learn," he says to these Pharisees. And he really wants them to learn! He does not send them off in the wrong direction; he points them to his surgery, the place where they will find him. Jesus may not be a physician for the "healthy" self-righteous, but he sends them to the place where they may learn of their terminal condition. There, even the misdiagnosed Pharisee may receive the right diagnosis and so be healed.

Is Jesus your physician? Are you relying on his diagnosis or your own self-diagnosis? There is no healing for your terminal condition without this physician; therefore, whatever keeps you from him will kill you. Christ our physician still calls sinners to repentance (Matt. 9:13), and he accepts new patients all the time. So will you be like the Pharisee and stand at a distance and protest your health? Or will you be like Matthew and acknowledge your sickness, receive his cure, and follow him?

Jesus Is Our Prophet

The Lord your God will raise up for you a Prophet like me from your midst, from your brethren. Him you shall hear.
—Deuteronomy 18:15

READ DEUTERONOMY 18:9–22

For forty years, God's people had been tested in the wilderness, led by Moses, who was a prophet, a priest, and (in a sense) a king to them; he had taught them God's law, instituted the priestly rituals of the Tabernacle, and ruled them with justice.

But now Moses was about to die. As the people assembled on the border of Canaan, the book of Deuteronomy would record Moses's last words to them, review their wilderness testing, and instruct them in their expected conduct in the Promised Land. In this part of the book, (chapter 18, verses 9–22), Moses addresses the subject of communication from God.

First, in verses 9–14 he warns how the Canaanites sought revelation by the occult practices of witches, mediums, astrologers, etc. But then, in verses 15–22 he shows how Israel was to seek revelation: God promised to raise up his own spokespersons, the prophets, and one Great Prophet in particular. He is described in verse 15, and, as we shall see, he is none other than our Lord Jesus Christ.

Jesus Is Our Prophet

Moses tells Israel, "The LORD your God will raise up for you a Prophet." But what does a prophet actually do? The answer is found in verse 18: "I will put My words in His mouth, and He shall speak to them all that I command Him." First, God puts his own words in the prophet's mouth, something that presupposes a close relationship. The prophet then *speaks* those words (and those words only) to God's people. In other words, the prophet has a *mediatorial* role. He is a man under orders: "He shall speak to them all that I command Him." He is not at liberty to change or embellish the Lord's message; his office is not to tell the people what he thinks but what God commands. Thus, the prophet is also fundamentally a preacher. As such, he is not at liberty to change the message or the medium. It matters not what the hearers would like their itching ears to hear, or how they would like their ears to be tickled; the prophet must speak God's Word, God's way. All these things are found true of Jesus; he is our *prophet*.

But Jesus is also *our* prophet: "The LORD your God will raise up *for you* a Prophet." Why do you and I need a prophet? Let Jesus himself answer: "The words that I speak to you are spirit, and they are life" (John 6:63). You need a prophet because your life depends upon it. The *Westminster Shorter Catechism*, Answer 24, instructs us, "Christ executes the office of a prophet, in revealing to us, by his word and Spirit, the will of God for our salvation." Peter understood how critical this matter is when he said, "Lord, to whom shall we go? You have the words of eternal life" (John 6:68). A farmer in a desert land needs to irrigate his fields or his plants will die. He may have a great reservoir of water, but without a conduit or pipeline to convey the life-giving drink, all will perish. God has a plan of salvation for our dying world, but if he did not "raise up for you a Prophet" to reveal it to you, you would likewise perish under the burning heat of his wrath. Jesus is *our* prophet.

A brief survey of subsequent Scripture also makes clear that *Jesus* is our prophet. While this passage may doubtless be applied to all the true prophets that came after Moses, it supremely refers to a single great prophet yet to come. By the end of this book, he has still not been revealed: "But since then there has not arisen in Israel a prophet like Moses, whom the LORD knew face to face, in all the signs and wonders which the LORD sent him to do" (Deut. 34:10–11). And so the Israelites began correctly to associate Deuteronomy 18:15 with the person of the coming Messiah. For example, the Pharisees asked John the Baptist: " 'Are you the Prophet?' And he answered, 'No' " (John 1:21).

When Jesus began his public ministry, however, there was no doubt in many of his hearers' minds that it was he that fulfilled Moses's prophecy: "And they glorified God, saying, 'A great prophet has risen up among us' " (Luke 7:16); "We have found Him of whom Moses in the law, and also the prophets, wrote—Jesus of Nazareth, the son of Joseph" (John 1:45); "Then those men, when they had seen the sign that Jesus did, said, 'This is truly the Prophet who is to come into the world' " (John 6:14).

Finally, the apostles would formally declare Jesus to be God's great, final prophet: Of "Jesus Christ, who was preached to you before... Moses truly said to the fathers, 'The LORD your God will raise up for you a Prophet like me from your brethren. Him you shall hear in all things, whatever He says to you' " (Acts 3:20, 22). The Scriptures thus show beyond doubt that what we have in Deuteronomy 18:15 is a beautiful picture of our Lord Jesus Christ in his prophetic office. But this identification raises several important questions.

Who Sent Jesus Our Prophet?

The answer to who sent our propeht is also found in Deuteronomy 18:15: "The LORD your God will raise up for you a Prophet." This tells us that Jesus is the Father's gift to you. *You* do not have to raise up or hire prophets to speak to you as the Canaanites did (vv. 9–14). God has made adequate provision for you. Christ speaks with all the authority of the One who sent him. And this was his own testimony:

> My doctrine is not Mine, but His who sent Me. If anyone wants to do His will, he shall know concerning the doctrine, whether it is from God or whether I speak on My own authority. He who speaks from himself seeks his own glory; but he who seeks the glory of the One who sent Him is true, and no unrighteousness is in Him. (John 7:16–18)

His prophetic message is an *authoritative* message because of whose it is.

But what is the message Christ speaks to you? To quote the *Shorter Catechism*, Answer 24, again, it is "the will of God for our salvation"; it is the *gospel*. It teaches you that God is holy, that your sin must be punished, and that God has provided reconciliation to himself through Christ's body broken and his blood shed for you on the cross. In short, Christ our prophet has as the subject of his message…himself! Christ commends himself to you as the only Mediator between God and men: "These [things] are written that you may believe that Jesus is the Christ, the Son of God, and that believing you may have life in His name" (John 20:31).

Do *you* consider Jesus's message authoritative? Or do you have a "take-it-or-leave-it" attitude? What do you say about him? Is he just another good teacher? Is there merely *some* truth in him (along with Mohammed, Confucius, Buddha, etc.)? No! He is *the* prophet whom *God* himself has raised up.

What, then, do you say about his message? Jesus our prophet infallibly presents us with a theology—a doctrine of God and all things, a definitive revelation of the gospel from God. How tragic, therefore, that even many professing Christians adopt Jesus into the postmodern pantheon as one among many roads to truth. This is often subtle. For example, one "emergent church" leader has written, "[Theology] is the story of God in play with the story of our lives…our stories change and [so] our understanding of God's story changes. When this happens our theology should change too."[1] In contrast, when you understand who it is that sent Jesus our prophet, you realize that the unchangeableness of the message flows from the unchangeableness of its author. This is precisely why Moses issues the subsequent warning in Deuteronomy 18:20–22 about "the prophet who presumes to speak a word in My name, which I have not commanded him to speak, or who speaks in the name of other gods."

There are false prophets who send themselves out on a presumptuous errand. You need to listen instead to the voice of Jesus, God's prophet, because there are lots of competing voices, and a lot of them sound a lot like Jesus. Take, for example, Islam's Shahada: "There is no god but Allah, and Mohammed is his prophet." Well, Moses begs to differ. He says clearly that all such prophets are "presumptuous," because they claim to speak in God's Name (v. 22). John Calvin concurs: "This is impious and intolerable audacity, to set forth the offspring of man's earthly brain as if it were a divine revelation."[2] And yet, is it not an "unpardonable sin" in our society (and one fast becoming punishable by law in the West) to declare that if Jesus is the prophet raised up by God, then the others are, in the terms of our text, imposters, self-imposed, and not to be feared? Let us "beware of false prophets" (Matt. 7:15).

Israel was about to inhabit a polytheistic culture whose cultural icons and celebrity spokespersons were idolaters. The list in Deuteronomy 18:9–14 bears a striking resemblance to our own contemporary society. You must resist the allure and dazzle of false religions, cults, politicians, and celebrities that lead you away from God with different gospels. It is astonishing that professing Christians today should even consult horoscopes and flirt with the occult in its pop-culture forms. (Surely if this were not a real possibility, then God would not have warned us against it here.) False prophets can be physically and intellectually intimidating. According to a poll published recently, devotees of the prophet Mohammed now make up a quarter of the world's population.[3] It is important that Moses follows his warnings about the false prophet with a reassurance in verse 22, "you shall not be afraid of him." We must place our full confidence in our prophet and the God who sent him.

What Kind of Prophet Is Jesus?

Moses declares that God's prophet will be "a Prophet like me" (vv. 15, 18). So if we want to know what our prophet is like, we should look at Moses. Like Moses, Jesus is a Mediator between God and his people; he speaks to God face to face; he performs signs and wonders to attest to his authority; he is ruler over God's people; he gives us God's law. Jesus is thus, in a sense, the "New Moses." But he is far more besides: the writer to the Hebrews declares, "Consider the Apostle and High Priest of our confession, Christ Jesus, who was faithful to Him who appointed Him, as Moses also was faithful in all His house. For this One has been counted worthy of more glory than Moses" (Heb. 3:1–3).

What kind of prophet is Jesus? He is also a prophet "from your midst, from your brethren" (Deut. 18:15). In the immediate context (vv. 9–14), God is warning Israel not to look to the nations around them and their soothsayers for revelation, because the prophet would come from among themselves. But as this relates to Jesus, it reminds us that God's prophet is one of us. Jesus is a prophet suited to our needs. This is critically important: why did the Israelites need a prophet?

> The LORD your God will raise up for you a Prophet...according to all you desired of the LORD your God in Horeb in the day of the assembly, saying, "Let me not hear again the voice of the LORD my God, nor let me see this great fire anymore, lest I die." (vv. 15–16)

Israel needed this prophet because they had faced a major problem at Mount Horeb (Sinai). Let us go back to the foot of the mountain and see what this problem was in more detail:

> So it was, when you heard the voice from the midst of the darkness, while the mountain was burning with fire, that you came near to me, all the heads of your tribes and your elders. And you said: "Surely

> the LORD our God has shown us His glory and His greatness, and we have heard His voice from the midst of the fire. We have seen this day that God speaks with man; yet he still lives. Now therefore, why should we die? For this great fire will consume us; if we hear the voice of the LORD our God anymore, then we shall die. For who is there of all flesh who has heard the voice of the living God speaking from the midst of the fire, as we have, and lived? You go near and hear all that the LORD our God may say, and tell us all that the LORD our God says to you, and we will hear and do it." (Deut. 5:23–27)

Israel's problem is our problem: "If we hear the voice of the LORD our God, then we shall die." Neither God's holiness, nor man's sin, has changed since Sinai. You cannot approach a holy God in your sin. Face to face with the divine holiness, the prophet Isaiah cried out, "Woe is me, for I am undone! Because I am a man of unclean lips" (Isa. 6:5); the Apostle Peter cried, "Depart from me, for I am a sinful man, O Lord!" (Luke 5:8); and the Apostle John tells us: "When I saw Him, I fell at His feet as dead" (Rev. 1:17). And that is why you need a Mediator: one "from your brethren" who can relay God's words to you, yet at the same time be close to God, to enter his presence and receive the message. This is your fundamental problem, but God has a fabulous solution: "No one has seen God at any time. The only begotten Son, who is in the bosom of the Father, He has declared Him" (John 1:18).[4] Jesus is "in the bosom of the Father," sharing his nature, yet he is also intimate with us, sharing our flesh. He is "one of our brethren," and thereby uniquely qualified to "declare the Father to us," which is just another way of saying he is uniquely qualified to be our prophet.

Like any gifted teacher, Jesus is able to take difficult truths and complex teachings and explain them with accuracy, precision, and clarity to little children who can only grasp the simplest of concepts. And are we not all children? Babbling infants before the majesty and wisdom of God in his plan of redemption, with all of its breathtaking scope? And what better teacher than Jesus Christ, who as God's Son and partaker of human flesh, takes from God's infinite mind and simply and patiently conveys it to us in language we can understand? He is wise with his spiritual first graders; he is patient with the slowest students, and all who are taught by him are sure to graduate. But first let us be sure that we are indeed students in his class.

What Is Your Response to Jesus the Prophet?

According to our text, there are only two possible responses to this final question of responding to Jesus our prophet.

You will hear Jesus.

The first is, "Him you shall hear" (Deut. 18:15). Moses's command was echoed by the Father at the transfiguration, "This is My Son…Hear Him!" (Matt. 17:5). His gospel message must be heard. Are you grateful that you have a prophet at all? Even as you read this, millions of people have not heard the voice of God's prophet, and "where there is no prophetic vision the people cast off restraint" (Prov. 29:18 ESV). God might have chosen to remain silent and sent you no prophet at all. Then you would have to face the voice from Sinai that struck the people with terror. You would have to say with Israel, "let Moses speak to us, but do not let the LORD speak to us lest we die!" (see Deut. 18:16). But there would be no Moses, no intercessor, no Christ to speak to you in words that you could stand. You would be undone—turned over to your sins without the restraint God's Word brings.

You should be grateful that you have a prophet. Since you do have a prophet, you should strive to be found under his tutelage. Do not be content to remain in spiritual kindergarten, but make every effort to progress, to grow in grace, and mature. And strive to introduce others to God's prophet for without him, they wander around like sheep without a shepherd; they "are destroyed for lack of knowledge" (Hos. 4:6). All they have is the prospect of the terrifying voice of judgment.

But where may I hear God's prophet speaking today? We no longer hear the voice of Christ *audibly* on earth; rather, he has gone to his Father and sent his *Holy Spirit* to be his prophetic voice. Practically speaking, that means we hear Jesus our prophet speaking in his Word, the Bible, and we hear Jesus our prophet speaking in his sacraments—what John Calvin called God's "visible Words."[5] At the Lord's Table, Christ our prophet once again preaches most eloquently to us of his finished work as Mediator, so that we might not tremble at his voice, but instead be welcomed into his banqueting house, like the elders who ate and drank on Mount Horeb with God (Ex. 24:9–11).

You will answer to Jesus, having not listened to him.

There is a second possible response: "It shall be that whoever will not hear My words, which he speaks in My name, I will require it of him" (Deut. 18:19). In our city of Indianapolis, the tornado sirens are tested every Friday at 11 a.m. The city residents may not think it important to hear the sirens at that hour, week in, week out, but only when a tornado is actually headed their way. Familiarity can breed contempt; they can hear it every week, become oblivious, and harden their hearts to it. *One can hear the siren but not truly listen to its message.* The problem is not with the siren, but with the hearer. The same is true of hearing the words of God's prophet. You may go week by week to church, but do you really hear his words? Every unheeded Scripture or sermon will demand a reckoning, because it is a rejection, not of a personal opinion, philosophy, or a religious option, but the rejection of a *person*. "Everyone to whom much is given, from him much will be required" (Luke 12:48).

God's prophet will not speak forever. There is perhaps nothing more terrifying than the thought of the silence of God, that God should withdraw his Word from you, that he should silence his prophet and his under-prophets, and that the tornado siren be made to cease and you be swept away. Here is a challenge to us all:

> Therefore we must give the more earnest heed to the things we have heard, lest we drift away. For if the word spoken through angels [i.e., the law given at Horeb] proved steadfast, and every transgression and disobedience received a just reward, how shall we escape if we neglect so great a salvation, which at the first began to be spoken by the Lord…? (Heb. 2:1–3)

What is your response to Jesus the prophet? "The LORD your God will raise up for you a Prophet like me from your midst, from your brethren. Him you shall hear."

Jesus Is Our

Propitiation

He loved us and sent His Son to be the propitiation for our sins.
—1 John 4:10

READ 1 JOHN 4:7–11

"Propitiation" is a very big word. It is also a very rare word. It appears only three times in our Bibles. It is nevertheless a word we need to grasp and hide in our hearts, because it is where we meet Christ savingly. A Christ without propitiation is a savior who cannot save. A sinner without this propitiation is a sinner who cannot be saved, for he is without the only real Savior, "having no hope and without God in the world" (Eph. 2:12). Propitiation is a matter of life or death—in time and for eternity. These assertions obviously beg some questions: What is propitiation? How does Jesus become our "propitiation"? And how does propitiation apply to us? In examining these, we will find that this big word has big implications for every human life in both time and eternity.

As we look at this, you will soon notice that Christ as our propitiation is bound up with the love of God and how we can know and return that love. The Apostle John tells us that "he who does not love does not know God for God is love" (1 John 4:8). How do we know God *is* love? The short answer is that he showed that love in the real world by sending his Son to be the propitiation for sins. We so easily sentimentalize love and imagine it as an ethereal, spiritual feeling in abstraction from real-world, real-time actions. But it is what is *seen* and *real* that tells us what love is. God so loved "that he gave his only begotten Son, that whoever believes in Him should not perish but have everlasting life" (John 3:16). Propitiation by the Son was an essential part of God's eternal purpose of love.

What Is "Propitiation"?

As already noted, there are only three places in the Bible where this word "propitiation" is found. Our English word comes from Latin *propitiare*, "to render favorable." From that we have the more familiar English word "propitious," which simply means "favorable." When circumstances are propitious, they are favorable to whatever project is in view. Christ's propitiation on behalf of believers means that his Father-God becomes propitious toward them and adopts them as his own sons and daughters.

Propitiation: Three Vital Verses.

The three Scripture passages on propitiation are as follows:

* 1 John 4:10, "He loved us and sent His Son to be the propitiation [Greek, *hilasmon*] for our sins."
* 1 John 2:2, "He Himself is the propitiation [Greek, *hilasmos*] for our sins, and not for ours only but also for the whole world."
* Romans 3:25, "Whom [Christ Jesus, v. 24] God set forth as a propitiation [Greek, *hilasterion*] by His blood, through faith, to demonstrate His righteousness."

The doctrine taught in these verses is unfolded in three phases:

* First of all, it is the *love of God*, wholly undeserved by us, that

causes him to provide his Son, the crucified and risen Christ, to be the propitiation necessary to our salvation (1 John 4:10).

* In the second phase, Christ's propitiation for sin is *sufficient* to cover not only Jewish believers ("ours only"), but also "the whole world" of Gentile believers from "every nation, tribe, tongue, and people."[1]
* Finally, God is favorable to sinners who through faith receive Christ as the propitiation for their sins (Rom. 3:25). God accepts believers because he accepts Jesus's death in their place. He is reconciled to them through Jesus's propitiation as the Mediator between God and man (1 Tim. 2:5).

The Mercy Seat: A Vital Link

The same word used in Romans 3:25 for propitiation (Greek, *hilasterion*) is used in reference to the "mercy seat" in Hebrews 9:5. This was the gold cover and lid of the Ark of the Covenant with the cherubim at either end (Ex. 25:17ff.): "and above it were the cherubim of glory overshadowing the mercy seat." The point is that the same word that means propitiation in Romans clearly means mercy seat in Hebrews. The theological significance of this is that the Christ who is our propitiation is also our mercy seat. The mercy seat is both a picture of propitiation and a picture of Christ. Jesus is our mercy seat because he is the propitiation for our sins.

The Hebrew word for mercy seat is *kapporeth*, which simply means "covering." This clues us into the reason why the mercy seat and propitiation are united by the one Greek word *hilasterion*. Notice four things about this mercy seat:

* The covering on the ark was made of pure gold—pure, perfect, and spotless. Jesus is the sacrifice that is "without blemish and without spot" (1 Peter 1:19).
* The covering completely hid the contents of the ark, which included symbols of both divine law and divine

deliverance—respectively, the proof of our being lost in sin and the provision of God's grace to save us (Heb. 9:4).

* The covering had two angels between which God manifested himself as the *Shekinah* (glory).
* The covering was sprinkled with the blood of sacrifice each year on the Day of Atonement.

This mercy seat, sprinkled with blood, comes between us in our sins and the God who, in his righteousness, cannot look upon sin. Above the mercy seat is the holy God. Below it are the symbols of man's failure and his consequent condemnation before God (that is, the tablets of the law of Moses, Aaron's rod that blossomed, and manna from the wilderness). Sprinkled blood covers the sin, pointing to Jesus's once-for-all atoning sacrifice. He is the mercy seat for us; he is the propitiation for sin. He is the acceptable sacrifice. Sin is covered and God is propitiated. Christ is the gospel of salvation by grace, received through faith, and the acceptance and favor of God is secured for all who receive Christ as their Savior and Lord.

How Is Jesus Our Propitiation?

The root of the matter is that God loves the lost enough to send Jesus, the enfleshed divine Son, to be our Savior: "For God so loved the world that He gave His only begotten Son, that whoever believes in Him should not perish but have everlasting life" (John 3:16). The basis for this is laid out in 1 John 4:7–8, where John roots the imperative for us to love one another in the very character of God: "Beloved, let us love one another, for love is of God; and everyone who loves is born of God and knows God. He who does not love does not know God, for God is love." Because God is love, those who are "born of God and know God" will and do love others. This is a window on God's essential being and as such it provides us with the underpinning for Jesus's work of propitiation.

A Savior sent by God.

Jesus is the propitiation for saved sinners because the God who is love sent him to bring many from death to life: "In this the love of God was manifested toward us, that God has sent His only begotten Son into the world, that we might live through Him. In this is love, not that we loved God, but that He loved us and sent His Son to be the propitiation for our sins" (1 John 4:9–10).

Evidence of God's love.

The evidence of God's love is his sending "His only begotten Son into the world, that we might live through Him" (v. 9). This is the objective basis of the divine love. God reveals this objectively in his Word and in his Son. We too easily make this a matter of our subjective feelings and imagine that the proof of God's love toward us is that we "feel loved" or "feel forgiven," or it may be that we just "believe" he loves us. The proof of his love, however, is not tied to our subjective convictions or feelings. The proof is Jesus sent, crucified, and risen. That God gave his Son is an objective fact.

Confirmation of God's love.

The confirmation of God's love to us in Christ is that he loved us first and loved us freely (v. 10). It is "not that we loved God, but that He loved us." Your felt love for God, full and sincere as it may be, is not the benchmark. His love is sovereign, all of grace, and from eternity. It is also in Christ, and it is an article of faith to be accepted as such and acted upon in the obedience of your faith. That said, the truth of God's words about his love for us require confirmation in the reality of the salvation promised. Hence, John adds that God "sent his Son to be the propitiation for our sins" (v. 10). He provides in Jesus a rational and effectual basis for a real salvation. Jesus actually saves. His death covers sin. Therefore, when you believe, you will be saved. You are not saved because you feel saved, but are saved because in *believing, receiving, and trusting Jesus,* you really are saved.

A Savior accepted by God.

We know that Jesus's propitiation was and is accepted by God. Everything about the cross proclaims this truth. Jesus is the Lamb without spot and blemish (1 Peter 1:19; Heb. 9:14). Jesus's blood "cleanses us from all unrighteousness" and reconciles believers to God: "Christ also has loved us and given Himself for us, an offering and a sacrifice to God for a sweet-smelling aroma" (1 John 1:9; Eph. 5:2). Jesus is the effectual atonement who *expiates* sin (that is, cancels its penalties) and so *propitiates* God (that is, secures acceptance with him). Both Jesus's active and passive obedience come together here: passively, he bears our sin and its penalty; actively, his perfect righteousness is accounted to us and reckoned to be ours. By these acts of free grace, he secures redemption for those who, coming to saving faith in him, are reconciled to God.

How Does This Apply to Us?

When we have believed and trusted in Jesus as our Savior, then, as God has "so loved us, we also ought to love one another" (1 John 4:11). Properly unpacked, what does this mean?

Live in the light of God's favor.

Why would you not "present your bodies a living sacrifice, holy, acceptable to God"? As the children of God in reconciled union with a heavenly Father, this is only "your reasonable service" (Rom. 12:1–2), because "now in Christ Jesus you who once were far off have been brought near by the blood of Christ" (Eph. 2:13). Be what you are in Christ.

Work at dying to sin.

You will surely pray with the psalmist, as he did after his sin with Bathsheba, "Purge me with hyssop, and I shall be clean" (Ps. 51:7). Jesus, says Peter, "bore our sins in His own body on the tree, that we, having died to sins, might live for righteousness" (1 Peter 2:24). In other words, since Christ is your propitiation, there remains no sin barrier between you and God. In Christ, you are already "dead to sin." This being the case, "do not let sin reign in your mortal body" (Rom. 6:11–12). Fight it off. Pray it off. Be the winner you are in Christ.

Only one way to go.

If you have not received Christ, you are incapable of both dying to sin and living for righteousness. In God's sight, all your best "righteousnesses are like filthy rags" (Isa. 64:6). There is only one way for you to be saved. Jesus must be your propitiation. Otherwise, you will be your own sacrifice for sin, and that can only end in eternal disaster. New sin cannot atone for old sin, but only confirm that you deserve judgment. Every living sinner is on probation. What happens to the criminal who commits a further crime while out on probation? Consider also that "our God is a consuming fire" (Heb. 12:29). By nature, "all who do wickedly will be stubble" (Mal. 4:1). What happens when fire meets stubble?

So today, as in the Old Testament, bring your sacrifice and lay your hand upon it (Lev. 1:4)—that is, in New Testament fulfillment, lay your hand upon Jesus Christ crucified as your sacrifice for sin. Go to Christ as the one and only propitiation for sin. Confess your sin to Jesus and repent toward God, trusting him for salvation, for "He loved us and sent His Son to be the propitiation for our sins" (1 John 4:10).

Jesus Is Our
Rain

He shall come down like rain upon the grass.
—Psalm 72:6

READ PSALM 72

Across the continental United States, July 2012 was the hottest month since records began, even breaking the previous record of 1936, the year of the infamous Dust Bowl. Almost 1,500 counties nationwide were declared natural disaster areas, meaning 64 percent of the country endured a moderate to exceptional drought.[1] Americans everywhere were praying for rain, and God graciously answered their prayers, eventually sending "rain on the just and on the unjust" (Matt. 5:45).

But there is another kind of rain that this country needs even more urgently, and the drought and famine that comes in its wake is taking a far greater human toll. The inspired psalmist speaks of the coming Savior, Jesus Christ, as being like rain: "He shall come down like rain upon the grass before mowing, like showers that water the earth. In His days the righteous shall flourish, and abundance of peace, until the moon is no more" (Ps. 72:6–7). It is a most welcome portrait to a thirsty nation enduring drought, and especially to one enduring *spiritual* drought.

The King Shall Reign

In order to fully appreciate this portrait, we need to first understand the context in which it is displayed. There is dispute over who wrote this psalm; the title in the original simply reads, "Of Solomon," but the final verse says it is a "prayer of David" (v. 20). Most likely, it was written *by* David but *about* Solomon.[2] There is no doubt when we read it that he is echoing the covenant God has made with him and praying that these promises will be fulfilled through his seed, Solomon:

> When your days are fulfilled...I will set up your seed after you, who will come from your body, and I will establish his kingdom. He shall build a house for My name, and I will establish the throne of his kingdom forever. I will be his Father, and he shall be My son....And your house and your kingdom shall be established forever before you. Your throne shall be established forever. (2 Sam. 7:12–16)

If this is the case, we might ask, is the psalm a prophecy or a prayer? If you read it in the New King James Version (NKJV) it sounds like a prophecy: "He will judge...he shall come down like rain...He shall have dominion..." If you read it in other versions, like the English Standard Version, it sounds more like a prayer: "May He judge... may He be like rain that falls...may He have dominion..." So is this a prophecy of future prosperity or a prayer for future prosperity? The answer is Yes! While it may be argued that the NKJV is a preferable rendering of the Hebrew, either way, we are being pointed to certain future events with prayerful confidence, and these future events have to do with a king.

The identity of the King (v. 1).

"Give the king Your judgments, O God, and Your righteousness to the king's Son." Here is a prayer that God would send forth his appointed king and equip him to judge and rule his people. But while this certainly applies in the first place to Solomon, the king's son,[3] the language of the psalm points beyond the earthly reign of David's son Solomon, to the heavenly reign of David's greater Son, Jesus Christ. Christ perfectly fulfills the terms of God's covenant with David, for all judgment has been entrusted to him by his Father: "For the Father judges no one, but has committed all judgment to the Son, that all should honor the Son just as they honor the Father" (John 5:22–23).[4] So this prayer is also a prophecy; Solomon's glorious reign of peace is a foreshadowing of Christ's even more glorious reign of peace.

The reign of the King (vv. 2–20).

A brief survey of the rest of the psalm reveals more about the glory of Jesus's reign. In verses 2–7 we are told that Jesus reigns over the Church: "He will judge your people with righteousness." Jesus is king and head of the Church, which is the "Israel of God" (Gal. 6:16), bringing them salvation and making them prosper. But the rule of this coming King will be much more expansive; verses 8–19 teach that his reign extends to all nations: "He shall have dominion also from sea to sea, and from the River to the ends of the earth." Jesus will bring salvation to the Gentile world, making them prosper too. The Church will be the means of bringing the gospel to all nations, which will then be incorporated into its numbers.

Psalm 72 thus speaks to what theologians call the "Mediatorial Kingship of Christ"—that dominion he has received as a gift from his Father because of his sufferings as mediator (Phil. 2:8–10).[5] It speaks of the post-Pentecost blessing of Jesus's building his Church throughout the world: "This gospel of the kingdom will be preached in all the world as a witness to all the nations, and then the end will come" (Matt. 24:14). In short, it speaks of the experience of today's Church. It speaks of what we should look for in global missions, in our own congregations, and in our own Christian lives, as Jesus judges His "people with righteousness" (Ps. 72:2).

The King Shall Be Like Rain

It is exciting to think that we now live in the age of this psalm's fulfillment; Jesus is reigning as mediatorial king in our era of world history, the "years of our Lord" (*Anno Domini*, AD). So it is in our day that we should be able to see clearly the psalmist's portrait of Christ: "He shall come down like rain upon the grass before mowing, like showers that water the earth" (v. 6). The weather forecast predicted by the psalmist for the New Testament is rain—and lots of it. In what sense should we look for Christ to be "like rain" to us?

Jesus is like rain in his "coming down" from heaven.

"He shall *come down* like rain." This verb is often used in Old Testament prophecy to speak of God descending to the earth in judgment and salvation. For an example, see Isaiah 64:1: "Oh, that You would rend the heavens! That You would come down!" Of course, the message of the New Testament is, "He has come down—in the person of Jesus Christ." Some suggest the "coming down" the psalmist refers to is the incarnation; Jesus came down to earth from heaven to live for us, and to die for us. This is what theologians call his "estate of humiliation," or his mediatorial work. However, we have already seen that Psalm 72 is not primarily describing Christ's estate of humiliation, but rather, the estate of *exaltation* that follows it: the rich blessings the Church enjoys in this age by virtue of his mediatorial work. He is no longer in the grave; he has been raised and has ascended and is seated in royal majesty at the Father's right hand, where he is building his Church and "[putting] all enemies under His feet" (Matt. 16:18; 1 Cor. 15:25). And it is in this present exalted state that we are told "He shall come down like rain."

The rain metaphor in Psalm 72:6 thus describes a *present* activity of the now-exalted King Jesus experienced by all his loyal subjects; he presently comes down from heaven on his Church like rain by the ongoing ministry of his Holy Spirit, following the once-for-all giving of the Spirit at Pentecost. George Horne writes of this metaphor, "What image can convey a better idea of those most beneficial and blessed effects which followed the descent of the Son of God upon the earth, and that of the Spirit, at the Day of Pentecost?"[6] The Old Testament commonly uses this image to describe the Messiah communicating blessing to his people in the present age following Pentecost (e.g., Isaiah 44:3–4: "For I will pour water on him who is thirsty, and floods on the dry ground; I will pour My Spirit on your descendants, and My blessing on your offspring; they will spring up among the grass like willows by the watercourses").

So, just like the rain, Christ still comes down to us from heaven. He rules, administers, and advances his Church from his heavenly throne above, but not like some distant monarch who rules from afar. Rather, he communicates daily grace to his subjects and communes with them by his Holy Spirit. But what does that look like *practically* in your daily Christian experience? How do you receive this rain from heaven and irrigate your life with Christ in this wilderness? The *Shorter Catechism* summarizes beautifully the Bible's answer: "The outward and ordinary means whereby Christ communicates to us the benefits of redemption, are his ordinances, especially the word, sacraments, and prayer; all which are made effectual to the elect for salvation."[7] This is how Christ comes down like rain on his Church: The Word, sacraments, and prayer are the ordinary means whereby Jesus showers his blessings upon you. These are the channels by which Christ, the life-sustaining rain, is fed to your thirsty souls.

Jesus is like rain in his life-giving power.

At the time of writing, NASA's space rover "Curiosity" continues its epic trek across the surface of Mars. Its mission? To see if there was ever liquid water on the Red Planet to sustain life. In his wisdom, God has decreed that water is essential for life in his creation. In times of drought your lawn, your flowers, your vegetable gardens, and your crops will die for lack of precipitation. Exactly the same may be said in the spiritual realm; Jesus is like rain in his *life-giving power*. Apart from him, there is no spiritual life or vitality. But in what ways does Christ our rain give life?

By regenerating his people when they were dead. The NKJV inexplicably translates this verse to say Christ "shall come down like rain upon the grass before mowing," whereas the Hebrew (and virtually all other English translations) talk about grass after it has been mowed. The NIV perhaps gives the best sense: "He will be like rain falling on a mown field." The grass is already cut down; it is dead, not merely dormant. Its stubble is withered, scorched by the hot sun. This image of mankind being as fragile and fleeting as grass that is cut down and burned is found everywhere in Scripture. It describes what you are physically. But more than that, it describes your spiritual condition by nature; you are dead in trespasses and sins, and yet, when Christ comes down to you like life-giving rain, he regenerates you, bestowing life from the dead. This he accomplishes through the ordinance of his Word: "having been born again, not of corruptible seed but incorruptible, through the word of God which lives and abides forever" (1 Peter 1:23). But your need for Christ as rain does not stop at conversion.

By reviving his people when they experience spiritual drought. Have you ever looked out your window at your parched garden on a hot summer day and thought to yourself, "that illustrates me"? The drooping leaves, the thirsty ground, the fruitless vines? On the outside, you may not look unhealthy, but on the inside, you know you are living in a spiritual disaster area. All of us from time to time experience a kind of spiritual drought; it may be moderate, or it may be severe. The fruits of the Spirit seem to wither on your vine. Your time with the Lord is not refreshing as it used to be. The heavens seem closed, and you feel unmotivated and lethargic as on a hot, sultry midsummer day. David experienced this, and sang about it in Psalm 63:

I'll seek you early, God my God;
My soul's athirst for You.

In dry, unwatered, weary lands,
My flesh longs after You.[8]

Perhaps you have been tolerating some secret sin; perhaps like the psalmist, you have been dwelling in "dry, unwatered, weary lands," far from the company of the Lord and his people. You have not been walking according to the statutes of the King and have grieved his Holy Spirit so that he has withheld the rain (Eph. 4:30).

At such times you need to call a state of emergency and do what everybody does in a drought: pray for rain. Resolve to return to the Lord with the psalmist's thirst and longing for Jesus, who alone is your rain. Pursue him in his ordinances like a storm chaser pursuing a heavy cloud across the plains of the American Midwest, expecting it to burst forth at any moment with life-giving power. Follow the example of God's backslidden people when they said, "let us press on to know the LORD; His going out is sure as the dawn; He will come to us as the showers, as the spring rains that water the earth" (Hos. 6:3 ESV). Press on, and chase that raincloud so that you might be revived; you will find that "the king's wrath is like the roaring of a lion, but His favor is like dew on the grass" (Prov. 19:12). What is true of individual believers is also true of the Church as a whole. Has not the Church in America and the West become a "dry, unwatered, weary land"? How we need revival! How we need Christ to "come down like rain…like showers that water the earth." Let us pray for rain.

Jesus is like rain in his fruit-yielding power.

The psalmist also predicts the consequences of Christ's rain-like properties: "The righteous shall flourish, and abundance of peace until the moon is no more" (Ps. 72:7). Christ our rain does more than give you spiritual life; he also *sustains* your spiritual life and makes it abound with fruit. In the words of Adam Clarke, "The influence of the doctrine and Spirit of Christ on the soul of man shall be as grateful, as refreshing, and as fructifying as the...[spring] showers on the cultivated lands. Without His influence, all tilling is vain; without him there can neither be seed nor fruit."[9] You depend on Christ as your spiritual rain not just when you are dead in sin and not just in those seasons of spiritual drought as a believer. You also need him when things are going well and when you are in your growing seasons. Sustained rain is essential, not just to stave off death, but to produce growth and a harvest of rich fruit.

Jesus bears fruit in you by the rain of his Word and doctrine. This verse references the last words of the two greatest Old Testament types of Christ: Moses and David. Moses's last words are found in Deuteronomy 32:2: "Let my teaching drop as the rain, my speech distill as the dew, as raindrops on the tender herb, and as showers on the grass." David's last words are these: "The Spirit of the LORD spoke by me, and His word was on my tongue...[Christ will be]...like rain that makes grass to sprout from the earth" (2 Sam. 23:2, 4 ESV). Both verses use exactly the same words—"rain" and "showers"—as Psalm 72:6, and both specify that their word and doctrine are like the rain that makes things grow. What they are saying is fulfilled by the word and doctrine of their great antitype, Jesus Christ. By Christ's word read and preached and by the visible word of the sacraments, Christ our rain comes down upon you with power and enables you to bear eternal fruit, just as the psalmist predicted: "Like showers that water the earth, in His days the righteous shall flourish" (Ps. 72:6–7).

Jesus bears fruit in you by rain of different degrees. It is said that the Eskimos have many different words for snow (because they have a lot of it).[10] Similarly, people from the British Isles have many different words for rain (because we have a lot of it). A heavy rain may be pouring, lashing, chucking, tipping, etc. A light rain may be spitting, sprinkling, dripping, etc. In a similar way, there are two different Hebrew words used to describe two different kinds of rain. The word translated "rain" in verse 6 refers to a sudden heavy downpour, whereas the word translated "showers" refers to regular, steady rainfall. It is not enough to just have a few downpours; rather, it is the sustained, steady, regular rainfall that will bring real fruit and recovery after a time of drought. The same is true in our spiritual lives. Christ occasionally comes in great downpours; we can experience times of revival nationally or personally. Perhaps you receive a great measure of blessing at a conference; you come back deeply refreshed with a renewed vision and zeal. This is something to thank God for, but it is no substitute for the steady, regular use of the ordinary means of grace, day by day, Sabbath by Sabbath, for you to yield lasting fruit in your Christian life.

Application

We have seen that Jesus is like rain in his "coming down" from heaven, in his life-giving power, and in his fruit-yielding power.

These truths present you with two personal challenges:

First, do not take this rain for granted. It is only when you have been deprived of the rain that you really value it. If you are ever guilty of taking the meteorological rain for granted, then how much more this spiritual rain? Have you despised the means of grace? Have you neglected them when you have possessed them? Have you failed to thank God for them? If we grieve the Holy Spirit, he may chasten us to teach us the true value of Christ the hard way, as he did back in Amos 8:11–13: " 'Behold, the days are coming,' says the Lord GOD, 'That I will send a famine on the land; not a famine of bread, nor a thirst for water, but of hearing the words of the LORD.' " Neglected means often become scarce means.

Second, avail yourself of this rain. You know where to find it; in fact, you can predict where it is going to fall. Your job as a Christian is to catch as much of this spiritual rain as possible in your reservoirs. The more vessels you can place under the raincloud of the ordinances the better. When you do, God has attached a promise to it:

> For as the rain comes down, and the snow from heaven, and do not return there, but water the earth, and make it bring forth and bud, that it may give seed to the sower and bread to the eater, so shall My Word be that goes forth from My mouth; it shall not return to Me void, but

> it shall accomplish what I please, and it shall prosper in the thing for which I sent it. (Isa. 55:10–11)

Living a fruitless Christian life is easy: neglect the worship services, avoid the prayer meetings, be too busy for your devotions, make excuses for ignoring family worship, and clutter the Sabbath with worldly pursuits. But know that this comes at a great cost. The Bible warns us,

> For the earth which drinks in the rain that often comes upon it, and bears herbs useful for those by whom it is cultivated, receives blessing from God; but if it bears thorns and briars, it is rejected and near to being cursed, whose end is to be burned. (Heb. 6:7–8)

If you are a member or adherent of a faithful local congregation, then "the rain often comes upon you": you have the Word preached weekly, you have corporate prayer weekly, you have the sacrament to nourish you, and you have Bibles and good Christian books, blogs, and sermons as often as you want them. Christ is falling upon you as rain. But do you drink in the rain that often falls upon you? Where is the fruit it is designed to yield? As we live in this age of Christ's kingly rule, may he continue to rain upon us with regular showers and increasingly regular downpours. And may we all avail ourselves of Christ our rain and so bear fruit to his glory.

Jesus Is Our

Refiner

He will sit as a refiner and a purifier of silver.
—Malachi 3:3

READ MALACHI 2:17–3:7

For millennia, raw ore has been refined into metal ingots, but only with searing heat, great blasts of air, and often powerful chemical agents. Getting rid of impurities is dirty and dangerous work for both the refiner and the refined. The process of refining people is not necessarily very "refined," nor is it less messy than refining iron or oil.

Malachi employs a simile to explain how the "Messenger of the covenant" will come to be a "refiner's fire" that will purify God's backslidden people in these days, and how this applies to us today. "This process," writes Henry Law, "is a mirror to show Christ" and is "a page of Gospel-lessons."[1]

Who Needs Refining and Why?

Malachi 2 is a searing indictment of the corruption of the priests of Judah and the marital unfaithfulness among God's people. It closes with the solemn challenge, "You have wearied the LORD with your words…" These were actually "weasel-words" aimed at justifying their sins. "They thought to evade the convictions of the word," observes Matthew Henry, "and to justify themselves by cavilling with God's proceedings; but their defence was their offence, and their vindication of themselves was the aggravation of their crime…"[2] Their open contempt for God's law doesn't stop them being "churchy" people. They are still able to "cover the altar of the Lord with tears, with weeping and crying" (v. 13).

The Lord who "searches all hearts and understands all the intent of the thoughts" will have none of it (1 Chron. 28:9; Heb. 4:12). "He does not regard the offering anymore," the writer of Malachi says, "nor receive it with goodwill from your hands" (2:13). God will not be denied: "the fierce anger of the Lord will not return until He has done it, and until He has performed the intents of His heart" (Jer. 30:24). Notice that he adds, "In the latter days you will consider it." In other words, if your heart's thoughts and intents run counter to his, don't imagine you will escape the reckoning.

Two practical points should be noted here. The first is that *God does not have to guess as to what we are really thinking*. Robert Murray McCheyne once told his congregation, "If every natural man here were to throw off his disguise, and appear as he really is, this church would look more like the gate of hell than the gate of heaven."[3] God already observes it all, every day, all over the world. Jesus pulls no punches: "I say to you that for every idle word men may speak, they will give account of it in the day of judgment" (Matt. 12:36). We have been warned.

Second, *this has the widest application to both believers and unbelievers*. Malachi is speaking to the problems of the Church of his day, and centuries later Jesus speaks to their descendants: "These people draw near to Me with their mouth, and honor Me with their lips, but their heart is far from Me" (Matt. 15:8). But this is not just for the Jews. The apostles take this message to the whole world, "testifying to Jews, and also to Greeks, repentance toward God and faith toward our Lord Jesus

Christ" (Acts 20:21). There is no comfort here for non-Christians who may enjoy the sad spectacles of hypocrisy in Christians and churches. You can be right about others' sins, but you are still lost if you lack the "one thing...needed" (Luke 10:42)—a saving knowledge of Jesus Christ. Who will protest that he has no need of the refining and purifying of his very being (compare with 1 Thess. 5:23)?

Why Is This Refining Necessary?

The Lord did not leave Israel in the dark. He sent Ezekiel to tell them: "The house of Israel has become dross to Me...they have become dross from silver...As men gather silver, bronze, iron, lead, and tin into the midst of a furnace, to blow fire on it, to melt it; so I will gather you in My anger and in My fury, and I will leave you there and melt you" (Ezek. 22:18–20). Isaiah had told them, "How the faithful city has become a harlot!...Your silver has become dross" (Isa. 1:21–22). Malachi sets out two principal maladies that afflict God's backslidden people (then and now): spiritual blindness and self-deceived self-righteousness.

Spiritual blindness (Mal. 2:17).

Malachi's hearers ask: "In what way have we wearied Him?" They have a blind spot—and it is not an innocent ignorance, but a dispositional incapacity to see themselves as God sees them. They are angry with God, dismissive of his Word as the rule for faith and life, and have persuaded themselves that they are right and God and his prophets are wrong. Paul later explains that "the natural man does not receive the things of the Spirit of God, for they are foolishness to him; nor can he know them, because they are spiritually discerned" (1 Cor. 2:14; compare with Gen. 6:5). Paul is referring to the *original sin*, endemic in fallen human nature, from which all actual sins flow. The effect of this is a practical atheism, whether in the Church or in the world.

Self-deceived self-righteousness (Mal. 2:17).

The sad fruit of self-deceived self-righteousness is hypocrisy recast as virtue: "Fervent lips with a wicked heart are like earthenware covered with silver dross" (Prov. 26:23). Here is the willful inversion of good and bad, right and wrong, and truth and error, all clothed in an apparently sincere conviction of being in the right. Notice how this works out in Malachi's two examples of the words that weary the Lord.

Excuse #1 is that God's promises have failed: "Everyone who does evil is good in the sight of the LORD, and He delights in them" (Mal. 2:17). T. V. Moore observes that this is "an ungodly challenging of divine Providence."[4] When bad things happen to people who believe they are "good," while outright wickedness seems to prosper, the blame is shifted to God—and this by church folks complaining about the God they ostensibly worship.

Excuse #2 is that God's justice has failed: "Where is the God of justice?" they ask (v. 17). Calvin comments that "they malignantly impeached God."[5] Their argument is that this evil is not prevented or judged; a just God would or should judge or prevent evil; therefore, a non-judging God is unjust and therefore effectively favors evil and evildoers. This was the temptation with which the psalmist wrestled when he saw "the prosperity of the wicked" (Ps. 73:3–14).

The fallacy in the argument is that a just God would and must judge or prevent all evil. But God has explained in his Word, the Bible, why sin exists in our fallen world and why he is taking his time about the judgment of sinners: "The LORD is longsuffering and abundant in mercy, forgiving iniquity and transgression; but He by no means clears the guilty" (Num. 14:18). God is not the author of human sin, but he is the author of salvation from sin (John 3:16). In fact, God defers many judgments so as to save more lost people in future generations (2 Peter 3:9; Ps. 78:1–8). This explains the necessity for God's messenger-refiner: "Today, if you will hear His voice, do not harden your hearts" (Heb. 3:15). Here is where personal refining must begin and why.

Who Is the Refiner?

Malachi describes five aspects of the coming refiner, by which we may identify him for sure.

His coming will be heralded (Mal. 3:1).

"Behold, I send My messenger, and he will prepare the way before Me." This refiner is clearly the second "Elijah" (Mal. 4:5) and also "the voice…crying in the wilderness: 'Prepare the way of the Lord' " (Isa. 40:3). These two prophecies are confirmed in Matthew 3:1 and Luke 1:17 (see also Matt. 11:10–15 and Luke 7:27). Calvin's summary is appropriately emphatic: "This passage ought doubtless to be understood of John the Baptist."[6] Anthony Selvaggio observes that "two messengers, Malachi and John the Baptist, both proclaim the same message: 'Repent!' "[7]

His coming will be looked for (Mal. 3:1).

This refiner is "the Lord whom you seek." People were looking for the Messiah, but not all of them were like Cleopas and his friend, who "were hoping that it was He [Jesus] who was going to redeem Israel" (Luke 24:21). The material point is that a heightened expectation of the Messiah's coming would exist at the time he actually came, even if God's people were confused as to his identity.

His coming will be unexpected (Mal. 3:1).

He "will suddenly come to His temple…" But, "He came to His own, and His own did not receive Him" (John 1:11). Jesus Christ is more than a merely human prophet and is more than the church leaders bargained for, then and now. "His temple" is best understood as referring to the physical temple in Jerusalem.[8] Charles Simeon rightly identifies him as God's promised "salvation"; Jesus is "a light to bring revelation to the Gentiles, and the glory of Your people Israel" (Luke 2:27–32; see also vv. 36–38). Charles Simeon notes that "it was in the temple that he delivered many of his instructive discourses, and wrought many stupendous miracles, and he repeatedly purged it from the profanations which the venal priests had allowed."[9] Indeed, *Christ is the meaning of his temple* and is the substance of everything it foreshadowed through its building, furniture, sacrifices, priests, and all. It is no accident that he here identifies himself as the Christ and is condemned to death by crucifixion (Matt. 26:61–66). Jesus comes suddenly, because he really is the promised Messiah.

His coming is in covenant fulfilment. He is, says Malachi 3:1, " 'the Messenger of the covenant, in whom you delight. Behold, He is coming,' says the LORD of hosts." Thomas Manton, commenting on Isaiah 53:10, notes that "the business of man's salvation was transacted by way of covenant between God and Christ," in which "Christ would make his soul an offering for sin." Because of this, says Manton,

> you shall see he is called a covenant: Isa. xlii.6, "And give thee for a covenant of the people, for a light of the Gentiles;" Isa. xlix. 8, "And give thee for a covenant of the people, to establish the earth"...His being given for a covenant is to be a means to redeem and reconcile them.[10]

The Messiah the Jews should have been looking for is the "man of sorrows" of Isaiah 53, whose soul is made an offering for the sin of sinners. But, as Charles Simeon observes, "the manner of his appearance was so contrary to the carnal notions which were entertained respecting him that he was overlooked; and, instead of being welcomed as the Messiah, was rejected as an imposter."[11]

His coming is powerful (Mal. 3:2).

"But who can endure the day of His coming? And who can stand when He appears? For He is like a refiner's fire and like launderer's soap." The "day of His coming"—which would be a day of God's wonderful grace for Elizabeth and Zacharias, Mary and Joseph, Simeon, Anna, John the Baptist, eleven of the twelve disciples, and millions from future generations—held no attraction for Malachi's complainers. It was no blessing in their eyes.

That day would nevertheless impact them and they would perish or be purged under the ministry of God's Christ. T. V. Moore notes that the "day" of his coming refers to no single 24-hour day in world history, but encompasses

> The mission of Christ...regarded as a whole, from the manger of Bethlehem to the throne of judgment, and declared to be for the fall as well as for the rising of many in Israel, a work that should separate the pure from the impure, just as the refiner's fire and the fuller's washing lye...This process began during the life of our Lord on earth; it has been going on ever since; and will continue until the final separation, of which we have so solemn a description from the lips of Christ himself in Matthew 25:31–46.[12]

This, in turn, leads us to ask what this refining will accomplish.

What Does This Refining Accomplish?

The prophet now speaks of the goals of Jesus the refiner: "He will sit as a refiner and a purifier of silver" (Mal. 3:3). It is a patient ministry. He will "sit." He begins where we are in whatever our state of soul is at the time. Henry Law, with his characteristic sweetness of spirit, says,

> The eye of Jesus marks those struggling motions of reviving evil. Is He indifferent? No; as He "forgiveth all their sins," so He "healeth all their diseases." The process of correcting may be painful, but still a gracious hand will firmly apply it. The furnace must be used, and the precious metal placed within. The needful heat must not be withheld.[13]

Grace in the furnace (Mal. 3:3).

But what is this furnace? God had told his people long before: "Behold, I have refined you, but not as silver; I have tested you in the furnace of affliction" (Isa. 48:10). This surely encompassed all the afflictions of their life and times—the things that get us down, like war, famine, disease, bereavement, poverty, and oppression, together with all the mental wrestling and anguish that goes with such trials. But why does God say he refined them, "but not as silver"? Matthew Henry explains:

> It was to refine them, but not as silver, or with silver, not so thoroughly as men refine their silver, which they continue in the furnace till all the dross is separated from it; if God should take that course with them, they would be always in the furnace, for they are all dross, and, as such, might justly be put away (Ps. 119:119) as reprobate silver, Jer. 6:30.[14]

The point is that if affliction is the way to perfect holiness acceptable to God, we would never be holy. We are, as far as our native acceptability to God, "all dross." There is no silver *in us* waiting to be discovered by our suffering in the furnace of affliction: "There is none righteous, no, not one" (Rom. 3:10). The rich man in Jesus's parable had no relief from the pains of hell. He was, sad to say, unrepentantly "all dross" on both sides of eternity (Luke 16:22ff.). Listen again to Matthew Henry:

> He therefore takes them as they are, refined in part only, and not thoroughly. "*I have chosen thee in the furnace of affliction*, that is, I have made thee a choice one by the good which the affliction has done thee, and then designed thee for great things." Many have been brought home to God as chosen vessels and a good work of grace has been begun in them in the furnace of affliction. Affliction is no bar to God's choice, but subservient to his purpose.[15]

Salvation is by grace through faith in the suffering Savior, not by our afflictions bringing out the best in us. The Lord uses affliction—as, for example, the prodigal son—to awaken us and teach us to come to an end of ourselves and rest for our salvation entirely and exclusively upon Christ, "who was delivered up because of our offenses, and was raised because of our justification" (Rom. 4:25). In the refining furnace of affliction, the Lord has surely brought many to saving faith in Christ, although not all believers come to faith in desperate and painful experiences. What Christ always does with the afflictions of his believing people is to grow them in grace.

He sanctifies his people (Mal. 3:3).

The ordinary fruit of refining fire and launderer's lye in the Lord's ministry is sanctification. The immediate focus in the text is upon the priestly "sons of Levi," who were historically the most faithful of the tribes of Israel and who, as Calvin says, "ought to have been guides to others" and "were to be in the Church, as it were, the pattern of holiness."[16] They too had backslidden. The Lord's promise is that "He will purify the sons of Levi, and purge them as gold and silver." His goal in this is that "they may offer to the LORD an offering in righteousness" (v. 3), that is, that priests and people "will come in a spirit of humble repentance and sincere gratitude" so that their offerings are pleasing to the Lord.[17] God wants no "dead works" from us: "How much more shall the blood of Christ, who through the eternal Spirit offered Himself without spot to God, cleanse your conscience from dead works to serve the living God?" (Heb. 9:14). The psalmist's testimony is surely on the heart of all who love Jesus Christ: "Before I was afflicted I went astray, but now I keep Your word" (Ps. 119:67).

He revives his Church (Mal. 3:4).

This refining from dross and dirt applies to the whole Church as an organism made up of "living stones" (1 Peter 2:5): "Then the offering of Judah and Jerusalem will be pleasant to the LORD, as in the days of old, as in former years." In New Testament terms, "foreseen here by Malachi," says Theodore Laetsch,

> there is no special priesthood; every believer is a royal priest (1 Peter 2:5, 9). Being washed, sanctified, justified (1 Cor. 6:11), they offer sacrifices acceptable to God (Phil. 4:18; compare with Rom. 12:1ff. and Heb. 13:15ff.). The spotless perfection of Christ's offering himself cleanses away, as does fuller's soap, every spot and blemish from their persons and offerings.[18]

This must also be true of the "body of Christ" as a whole—what Paul calls the "Israel of God" (Gal. 6:16).

He judges his enemies (Mal. 3:5).

In the cases of unbelievers, God says, "I will come near you for judgment; I will be a swift witness against sorcerers, against adulterers, against perjurers, against those who exploit wage earners and widows and orphans, and against those who turn away an alien—because they do not fear Me," (v. 5). In the New Testament terms, the apostle Paul urges us to transparent devotion:

> I beseech you therefore, brethren, by the mercies of God, that you present your bodies a living sacrifice, holy, acceptable to God, which is your reasonable service. And do not be conformed to this world, but be transformed by the renewing of your mind, that you may prove what is that good and acceptable and perfect will of God. (Rom. 12:1–2; see also 6:4)

How Should We Respond?

Does Malachi perhaps seem to you to be more brimstone than balm, more failure than faith, and more giving hell than opening heaven? If so, you are missing the fact that even *God's sternest warnings are calls to a new life* (Jer. 18:1–11). The Lord is certainly serious about judging sin and unbelief, but this never gets in the way of his primary goal of saving people from their sins and effecting reconciliation between God and man for all eternity (Matt. 1:21; 2 Cor. 5:19; Heb. 2:17). Malachi accordingly closes out this prophecy of the coming of Christ with an urgent call to all of us to be reconciled to God.

Waste no time! (Mal. 3:6)

The God of all grace is *calling us personally*: "For I am the LORD, I do not change; therefore you are not consumed, O sons of Jacob" (v. 6). There is still time. He has not changed. That is why he is slow to anger and why the last judgment is…last. Judgment can wait. The Lord has saving work to do—and our receiving Christ for salvation is on a tighter schedule. Urgency is on Jesus's mind on those many occasions when he says to us, "He who has ears to hear, let him hear!" (Matt. 11:15; 13:9).

Perhaps the most affecting of these calls is the one given in connection with Jesus's explanation of the Parable of the Tares;

> The Son of Man will send out His angels, and they will gather out of His kingdom all things that offend, and those who practice lawlessness, and will cast them into the furnace of fire. There will be wailing and gnashing of teeth. Then the righteous will shine forth as the sun in the kingdom of their Father. He who has ears to hear, let him hear! (Matt. 13:41–43).

Is this not a clear invitation for those who presently "offend" God and "practice lawlessness" to flee to Christ in repentance and faith without delay while there is still time?

Return to Me! (Mal. 3:7)

The God of all grace will *return to you*: "Yet from the days of your fathers you have gone away from My ordinances and have not kept them. Return to Me, and I will return to you," says the LORD of hosts."

The prophet sees they are putting off a right response to God: "But you said, 'In what way shall we return?' " (v. 7). You realize that, as the refiner, the Lord's ministry cuts both ways. He separates the wheat from the chaff: "For the word of God is living and powerful, and sharper than any two-edged sword, piercing even to the division of soul and spirit, and of joints and marrow, and is a discerner of the thoughts and intents of the heart" (Heb. 4:12); "And even now the axe is laid to the root of the trees. Therefore every tree which does not bear good fruit is cut down and thrown into the fire" (Luke 3:9). The ultimate answer is to return to the Lord and live.

Whether you know it or not Jesus's gospel message is refining you. He is calling us to a new life, a saved life, a holy life. His message is not some static circular email. It is a refining fire, in which God calls us: "Be holy, for I am holy" (1 Peter 1:16). His ongoing ministry of refining is about our personal and practical growth in grace and that progressive sanctification is a fruit of "looking unto Jesus, the author *and finisher* of our faith" (Heb. 12:2, author's emphasis). It all points to Jesus. And it is pointing *us all* to Jesus. Is Jesus Christ your refiner and purifier?

Jesus Is Our

Resurrection

I am the resurrection and the life.
—John 11:25

READ JOHN 11:25–27

Jesus's miracles were not just intended to improve the earthly lot of those on the receiving end; they validated who Jesus claimed to be and illustrated why he came. The well-known story of the raising of Lazarus provides a striking example: an unmistakable demonstration of Christ's power over death, as well as his intention to resurrect his beloved people from their graves. In a tender conversation with a bereaved Martha recorded in John 11:25–27, our Lord explains the miracle he is about to perform in raising her brother and applies its lessons to all of us, revealing himself as *Christ our resurrection.*

The Need for Resurrection

Our need for resurrection is found in four little words in verse 25: "Though he may die." You need the reality of a bodily resurrection because someday you are going to die. The context of Jesus's words is the funeral of a loved one. You may recall that Jesus had been east of the

Jordan when Mary and Martha sent word to him that "he whom You love is sick" (v. 3). Like so many of the Lord's people, these sisters are suddenly facing a terminal illness in the family, and they do the right thing with this upsetting news: they bring it to the Lord. Strangely, though, Jesus delays his journey, allowing the disease to run its fatal course, and Lazarus dies. It is puzzling to the disciples, the grieving sisters, and the mourners, but Jesus's timing is always perfect (vv. 6–16, 21, 37). His delay was in order that a powerful sign may be performed, so "that [they] may believe" (v. 15).

And so it is that we find Jesus in Bethany surrounded by mourners. The Lord of life is in the presence of death, and he is deeply moved:

> Therefore, when Jesus saw her weeping, and the Jews who came with her weeping, He groaned in the spirit and was troubled. And He said, "Where have you laid him?" They said to Him, "Lord, come and see." Jesus wept. Then the Jews said, "See how He loved him!" (vv. 33–36)

Not one of us enjoys funerals, yet every one of us will attend our own. As Ben Franklin reputedly quipped, death and taxes are the two great certainties in life. The death rate is one hundred percent. It is an unpleasant reality that confronts us all, yet not one that we naturally feel comfortable talking about. Death is a topic of conversation commonly avoided in polite company, but it is not one Jesus ever shied away from. He is realistic about it, and he confronts it because he has come to conquer it. What does the Bible teach about death?

Death is not natural, but a penalty.

Death is an intruder into God's created world. It is not "just a normal part of living." Paul explains that "through one man sin entered the world, and death through sin, and thus death spread to all men, because all sinned" (Rom. 5:12). Just as we all share in Adam's original sin, even so we all share in its penalty, for "the wages of sin is death" (Rom. 6:23).

Death is physical, but it is also spiritual.

Paul declares that we are by nature "dead in trespasses and sins" (Eph. 2:1). Adam and Eve did not physically keel over the moment they ate the forbidden fruit, but they did die *spiritually* by estranging themselves from God, and this spiritual death both preceded and guaranteed Adam and Eve's later *physical* death. Thus they rendered themselves and their offspring incapable of spiritual life—unless, of course, God found a way of bringing them spiritually back to life again.

Death has an eternal dimension.

The Bible teaches that if you remain spiritually dead in trespasses and sins, and die physically in this condition, then after the Judgment Day you will also die *eternally*, which Revelation 21:8 calls "the lake which burns with fire and brimstone, which is the second death."

Spiritual death, physical death, eternal death—a "threefold death"[1]—is the lot of every one of us by nature. Jesus's words, "though he may die," do not merely state a human possibility; they define our basic human condition and final destiny. And that is why you have a need for resurrection.

The Goal of Resurrection

Jesus then goes on to say, "Though he may die, he shall live. And whoever lives and believes in Me shall never die" (John 11:25–26). The goal of resurrection is *life*: being raised to new life and then being sustained in that life. We have seen that there is a spiritual death from which you need to be resurrected, and not just the physical death of your body. Jesus's words in verses 25–26 flesh this out: "Though He may die, he shall live." Jesus here clearly refers to *physical* death. He is speaking about someone coming to the end of their earthly life, being laid in the grave, and then being brought back to life again. This is what we most commonly think of when we speak of resurrection. The goal of resurrection is to raise your dead body on the Day of Judgment.

But then he says, "Whoever lives and believes in Me shall never die." Now he is speaking about someone who is *never going to die*—someone who possesses eternal life. He can't mean "never die" in a physical sense, because eventually everyone will. Rather, Jesus means someone who has been resurrected spiritually—who has been born again, receiving new spiritual life (Ezek. 37:1–14)—and who will thus never die *eternally*, even though he must one day die physically.

So there is a sense in which you need to experience resurrection in this life before your funeral. As George Hutcheson explains, "In a spiritual sense, [Jesus] is the 'resurrection' in His first giving spiritual life unto dead sinners...and [then] He is 'the life' in continuing and preserving that spiritual life which He conferreth."[2] Only the person who has been spiritually resurrected during the course of this brief earthly life by conversion can expect to one day be physically resurrected to an eternal heavenly life.

Suppose you had to emigrate to a distant country. You have your one-way ticket reserved for a certain seat, on a certain flight, on a certain day for your epic journey to a new and unknown land, leaving behind all that is familiar. However, having your flight confirmed is not enough; in a sense, your journey begins many months prior to that day. You will first have to receive an invitation from that far-off country in the form of a visa. You will want to begin learning the language of that land to be ready to settle there. You will try to wean yourself from this familiar place to better acclimatize to the new life that awaits you there. Yet without that visa and those subsequent preparations, you will make that flight to your destination, but you will never be granted entry. Instead, you will be turned away.

In a similar way, your day of departure from this world is fixed; your one-way ticket is booked, so your preparation for that day is vital. Unless you have accepted the invitation of Christ and been resurrected from spiritual death to life in this world, you cannot expect to be physically resurrected to life and eternal glory in the next. A Christian is someone who is already raised from spiritual death and who lives accordingly—not for the things of this world, but the things of the next world (Heb. 12:14). If this is true of you, then you are more likely to find a seamless continuity between your present life and the one you will experience after death, for eternal life began when you first believed in Jesus: "And this is the testimony: that God has given us eternal life, and this life is in His Son" (1 John 5:11).

The Source of Resurrection

Jesus Christ is so intimately connected with the work of resurrection that he assumes this great task as his own personal title: "I am the resurrection and the life." He is the very embodiment of resurrection power; he has in himself power over death; he is the source and procurer of your resurrection for "in Him was life, and the life was the light of men" (John 1:4). It is to Christ that you must come for resurrection, and it is to him that you must come for life. This raises a number of questions.

How is Christ both the resurrection and the life?

It may be helpful here to draw an analogy with God's works of creation and providence. First, God *creates*, but then he *sustains* what he has created by his providence.[3] He is both creator and sustainer. In a similar way, Jesus is both the resurrection and the life. First, he raises you from spiritual death to spiritual life as a new creation: Jesus is the resurrection. But then, he also sustains you in that new life by his Holy Spirit: Jesus is the life.

The same applies to your bodily resurrection. He will raise you from physical death to physical life on the last day: again, Jesus is the resurrection. But then he will also sustain you in that heavenly life: "For this perishable body must put on the imperishable, and this mortal body must put on immortality" (1 Cor. 15:53 ESV). Jesus is the resurrection. But he is also the life.

How is Christ qualified to be the resurrection and the life?

The Christian hope of resurrection is based on something sure and steadfast; it is not just "pie in sky when you die, by and by."

On the one hand, *Christ is qualified because he is God.* Notice how in John 11:21–22, Martha says to Jesus, "Lord, if You had been here, my brother would not have died. But even now I know that whatever You ask of God, God will give You." She has confidence in Jesus's persuasive power with God to ask him to raise her dead brother. But Jesus's reply calls Martha to trust not only on God the Father, but in himself as God the Son: he essentially says to her, No, Martha; "I am the resurrection and the life; He who believes in Me, though he may die, he shall live" (v. 25). Jesus is the divine Son of God and is thus himself qualified to raise the dead. He declares, "I lay down My life that I may take it again…I have power to lay it down, and I have power to take it again" (John 10:17–18).

On the other hand, *Christ is qualified because he is man.* We have seen that the need for resurrection arises from the penalty of Adam's sin that we all bear. That is why, in order to be the resurrection and the life, God must become flesh as the second Adam. There was simply no other way, as Paul makes clear in 1 Corinthians 15:21–22, "For since by man came death, by Man also came the resurrection of the dead. For as in Adam all die, even so in Christ all shall be made alive." Thus the conqueror of death submits to death, in order to defeat death (2 Tim. 1:10). Or, in John Owen's words, we behold "the death of death in the death of Christ."[4]

For whom is Christ the resurrection and the life?

The answer is, for all who are united to him as the second Adam. As Paul explains, "For as in Adam all die, even so in Christ all shall be made alive" (1 Cor. 15:25); and again,

> If we have been united together in the likeness of His death, certainly we also shall be in the likeness of His resurrection...Now if we died with Christ, we believe that we shall also live with Him, knowing that Christ, having been raised from the dead, dies no more. Death no longer has dominion over Him. (Rom. 6:5, 8–9)

Death is the penalty for your sin; it is the debt you owe and the wages you have earned. We might say that it is the dreaded collection agency that comes suddenly to repossess your entire life's earnings. First, it kills your body, and then after the judgment it kills your soul with an eternal death in hell. In the words of Jesus's parable, "Assuredly, I say to you, you will by no means get out of there till you have paid the last penny" (Matt. 5:26).

But the good news for the Christian is this: since Christ has paid your debt for you, the collection agency cannot harm you. Your body may die, but "death no longer has dominion over you" if you are united to Christ in his death, his burial, and his resurrection. The grave won't be able to keep you, for Christ's resurrection guarantees yours. The confident hope that you will one day experience a literal, historically verifiable, bodily resurrection is not wishful thinking; it is rooted in the literal, historically verifiable, bodily resurrection of another.

Is it any wonder then that, next to the cross, the confession of Christ's bodily resurrection on the third day has always been the central unique dogma of the historic Christian faith?

The Cost of Resurrection

We have seen what your resurrection cost Jesus: his atoning death on the cross. But what will it cost you to obtain it? What does Jesus say? "I am the resurrection and the life. He who believes in Me, though he may die, he shall live. And whoever lives and believes in Me shall never die. Do you believe this?" (John 11:25–26).

Jesus could not be clearer. What he asks of Martha, he asks of us all: faith in him. What a small price to pay for such an extraordinary blessing.

What would you be willing to pay on your death bed to keep on living? What have people given to try to attain immortality? The Pharaohs built pyramids on the backs of their people; millionaires have paid fortunes to freeze their remains in cryogenics programs; the famous have erected mausoleums and monuments to perpetuate their memory; Eastern mystics promise reincarnation if you will follow their karma-boosting strictures. But all of it is in vain; you cannot cheat death. Not even Jesus could cheat death; but only Jesus could conquer it. And it is precisely that victory which Christ won over the last enemy that all men and women in history want to share. Sadly, they are usually unwilling to pay the price.

Since Jesus alone conquered death, it is to Jesus alone that you must come if you would conquer death. Jesus offers for you to share the spoils of his victory by believing in him, entrusting your body and soul to him, submitting your life to his Lordship, and in return he promises you, "that everyone who sees the Son and believes in Him may have everlasting life; and I will raise him up at the last day" (John 6:40).

As we have seen, he who makes this promise is the only one qualified to make good his offer. Why would you entrust your soul to anyone else? Nobody else has ever died and been resurrected like Jesus. Suppose you needed a complicated, life-threatening surgery, and you knew that you might not come through it. If you had the choice of any surgeon in the world to perform this last operation, who would you choose? Would you not find the world's leading expert? The one with the greatest track record of success? The one who pioneered the procedure? The one who wrote the definitive volume on the subject? Why would you look elsewhere?

All of us are going to undergo this final operation. When your life comes to its final hurdle to whom will you turn? Your family and friends may be there by your side to comfort you, but they cannot help you. The worldly possessions that you have stored up over the decades of your life may be within your view, but they cannot bail you out, and you cannot take them with you. They are worthless to you now. Your memories of a life well lived that flash before your eyes—what you have contributed to mankind, what you have accomplished with the time and gifts God gave you—they cannot secure you. In that hour, there is only one that can help you: Christ our resurrection. The rock to which you must consciously cling in that hour is the same as Paul's: "I know whom I have believed, and am persuaded that He is able to keep what I have committed to Him until that Day" (2 Tim. 1:12).

If you understand your need of resurrection, the goal and only source of resurrection, will you not also count the cost of resurrection? Jesus says to you, "I am the resurrection and the life. He who believes in Me, though he may die, he shall live. And whoever lives and believes in Me shall never die...Do you believe this?" May your answer be that of Martha: "Yes, Lord, I believe that You are the Christ, the Son of God, who is to come into the world" (John 11:25–27).

Jesus Is Our

Righteousness

Now this is His name by which He will be called:
THE LORD OUR RIGHTEOUSNESS.
—Jeremiah 23:6

READ JEREMIAH 22:1–23:8

The prophet Jeremiah was called to preach at a very dark time in the history of Israel. The once great and godly nation that the world had looked to with respect in Solomon's day had become a decadent, immoral society infatuated with eastern religions. Instead of enjoying the peace that characterized the reigns of Solomon and some of her more godly kings, she had been engaged in a long series of wars with brutal and sadistic enemies from the east. The once-respected Davidic dynasty was now corrupt and wicked, making alliances with enemies, neglecting justice and righteousness, and legalizing unmentionable things that God's Word abominated. The once family-affirming nation had exchanged God's laws of the covenant home for promiscuity and infanticide. Each successive generation that arose was increasingly ignorant of God's Word. The once-central place of God's worship, the temple, was now run by greedy charlatan preachers whom God had not sent, preaching a message of self-indulgent idolatry and tolerance of wickedness.

This picture should sound familiar to many readers. Like Israel, we in the West live in increasingly "post-Christian" nations. We have rejected God and his Word, and so the basic structures of society continue to unravel: marriage is redefined, the weakest and most vulnerable are quietly disposed of, the knowledge of God and his Word vanishes from the public square, our rulers legalize wickedness, and we are at war with brutal and determined enemies.

So Jeremiah preached at a dark time to a nation in eclipse. But for all this, it was not a time devoid of the promises of God—and that meant *hope*. God is a covenant-keeping God. Even though an unrighteous people had broken faith with him, God still remembered the covenant he had made with David to raise up a righteous King. And that is who this passage is really all about; "the Lord our righteousness" is promised to an *unrighteous* people.

Israel's Problem

In Jeremiah 22, God summarizes Israel's problem as a problem of leadership, but as we shall see, the implications go far beyond that. Israel's problem (and the West's problem by extension) is not merely a political problem, but a spiritual problem—an unresolved problem of the heart.

God exposes the failure of David's dynasty (Jer. 22).

First of all, Israel has been spiritually hamstrung by a series of sinful and ineffectual heads of state, as a brief survey of this chapter demonstrates. Jeremiah 22:1–10 is a denunciation of David's dynasty in general:

> Hear the word of the LORD, O king of Judah, you who sit on the throne of David, you and your servants and your people who enter these gates! Thus says the LORD: "Execute judgment and righteousness, and deliver the plundered out of the hand of the oppressor. Do no wrong and do no violence to the stranger, the fatherless, or the widow, nor shed innocent blood in this place." (vv. 2–3)

This thundering indictment shows what God has always expected of heads of state: "For he is God's minister to you for good…an avenger to execute wrath on him who practices evil" (Rom. 13:4). But this calling was not being pursued by the house of David, as the itemized list of kings that follows makes clear. In Jeremiah 22:11–17, God indicts King Shallum (also known as Jehoahaz), who ripped off his subjects and would die in captivity. In verses 18 to 23, God indicts Shallum's brother, King Jehoiakim, who would be buried like a dead donkey with no one to lament him. In verses 24 to 30, God indicts Jehoiakim's son, King Coniah (also known as Jehoiachin), who would also be sent into captivity. So the problem for Jeremiah's generation was that Israel's kings had failed. Israel needed a *righteous* King as its head of state who would take after David: "a man after His [God's] own heart" (1 Sam. 13:14). But it is not just Israel's royal family that has a problem.

God exposes the failure of all Israel's shepherds (Jer. 23:1–2).

"Woe to the shepherds who destroy and scatter the sheep of My pasture!" These are the bankrupt political and spiritual leaders of the day: prophets, priests, and kings who have "scattered the flock, driven them away, and not attended to them." And so God ominously says he will attend to Israel's shepherds presently.

God exposes the failure of the sheep.

Now, it is very easy for us to just blame our leaders for our national sins. One thinks of the SS regiments posted at the Nazi death camps, whose defense at the Nuremberg war crimes trials was, "we were just following orders." But Jeremiah makes clear that this moral depravity was not simply at the top with the shepherds; it was *the sheep too* who were unrighteous: "My people have forgotten Me, they have burned incense to worthless idols. And they have caused themselves to stumble in their ways, from the ancient paths, to walk in pathways and not on a highway, to make their land desolate and a perpetual hissing" (Jer. 18:15–16). Where there are sinful heads of state, there is usually a sinful nation; where there are sinful shepherds in the Church, there is usually a sinful flock.

Do we not see a similar state of affairs in our own hearts? What may be said of Old Testament Israel may be said of us all in our natural state. Like Israel, we are stubborn and rebellious against God—made for his glory, yet "burning incense to worthless idols" and "straying from the ancient paths" to walk in dark byways. We may indeed be led into sin by unrighteous rulers like Coniah, who do not "execute judgment and righteousness," but if we are honest, we do not really need their help. We are by nature vulnerable, like sheep without a shepherd, and fleeced by the spiritual charlatans of this life. Like Israel, our sins threaten banishment and exile from the presence of the LORD.

God's Solution

God will do three things to address Israel's problem.

Solution #1: God will shepherd the people himself (Jer. 23:3–4).

If you visit Ireland, you do not have to look far before you see sheep scattered across the hills. And they are not always easily persuaded to come down off those hills. By nature stubborn, sheep will often not come without being led, driven, induced, forced, or even carried on the shoulders. God knew what he was doing when he created sheep to be a prime illustration of his people;[1] for here, God's sheep are every bit as stubborn, scattered, and difficult to reason with. So God himself must sovereignly and graciously intervene to resolve the problem and do for them what they cannot do for themselves.

He will "gather the remnant of [His] flock" from their scattered state of exile and bring them home again (v. 3). This refers first to the decree of Cyrus, where the exiles returned from Babylon in 538 BC. He will make them "fruitful and increase" (v. 3). The literal and spiritual barrenness they had brought upon themselves would be forgotten. This speaks to the success of the returning exiles in establishing themselves once more in the land. Furthermore, he will appoint good under-shepherds who will feed them. This refers to the new godly leadership the returned exiles would enjoy under Zerubbabel and Joshua, Ezra and Nehemiah, Haggai and Zechariah.

Solution #2: God will establish his own King (Jer. 23:5–6).

Jeremiah now comes to his central point. He contrasts Israel's unrighteous kings and shepherds who have failed with God's righteous King and shepherd who is to come. There are three things he wants us to consider in this regard: a person, a personal quality, and a personal possession.

A Person. How is God's King described to us in verses 4–6? He is called David's branch of righteousness: " 'Behold, the days are coming,' says the LORD, 'that I will raise to David a Branch of righteousness' " (v. 5). This is a common phrase the prophets use to describe the Messiah:

* "In that day the Branch of the LORD shall be beautiful and glorious" (Isa. 4:2);
* "Listen, O high priest Joshua, you and your associates seated before you, who are men symbolic of things to come: I am going to bring my servant, the Branch" (Zech. 3:8 NIV);
* "In those days and at that time I will cause to grow up to David a Branch of righteousness; He shall execute judgment and righteousness in the earth. In those days Judah will be saved" (Jer. 33:15–16).

This is the language of horticulture. When the prophets speak of shoots, seeds, growth, and branches, they are speaking symbolically of family trees, seed, offspring, and genealogies. And from whose stock will

God's King come? From *David's*. He will have royal blood in his veins. According to God's covenant with David (2 Sam. 7:13ff.), his dynasty will endure forever through one descendant who is also God's own first-born Son; God's love will never be removed from him (as it was from others); and his kingdom will never pass away. This entire description of the coming King is being contrasted with the worthless King Coniah. He will succeed where Coniah has failed. The people of Israel have broken the covenant; they do not deserve salvation. But God remembers the covenant he has made, and on this basis alone does he engage to save.

This coming King is also called "a King [who] shall reign and prosper," in contrast with Coniah, who is "a man who shall not prosper in his days" (Jer. 23:5; 22:30). He is called a Judge—One who will "execute judgment and righteousness in the earth" (Jer. 23:5)—unlike Israel's kings, who had fleeced the sheep. He is the bringer of salvation and security to God's people, for "in those days, Judah will be saved, and Israel will dwell safely" (v. 6). Finally, he is the bearer of God's own Name: "The LORD our Righteousness." In other words, he is a *divine* King. This description matches only one person in history: our Lord Jesus Christ. Jesus alone is David's branch of righteousness, the King who will reign and prosper, the Judge executing judgment and righteousness on earth, the Savior of his people, and the divine Son of God. But Jeremiah reveals to us more than his identity; he also tells us about his character.

A Personal Quality. Jesus Christ is glorious in all his attributes. But there is one particular attribute that must especially draw our attention, and that is his righteousness. What exactly does this word mean?

The term righteousness always refers to a *law*.[2] It is a measurement of conformity to a moral standard that we are bound to obey. Insofar as we measure up to that law, to that degree we are either deemed "righteous" or "unrighteous" by the lawgiver and judge. Now, the Bible describes all human beings born on God's earth as those under God's law (Gal. 4:5). We are born into God's creation, and so his moral law (summarized in the Ten Commandments) is the law of the land. So the personal quality of "righteousness" means perfect, active obedience to that law, every nanosecond of your life and existence. It is to be "right with God" in perfect, unbroken conformity to his will, whether awake or asleep, in your thought life, in every word you have ever spoken, and in every action you have ever performed. In short, it is to be like God, to possess a perfection on a par with God.

And this, of course, is the righteousness that Christ alone possesses. When Jeremiah calls him the LORD our righteousness, he is saying that Jesus is the *epitome* of righteousness, not merely Christ our righteous one, but Christ our righteousness—the very definition of righteousness. We intensify the attribute by making the object the epitome and definition of that attribute. So it is when Jeremiah calls Christ the LORD our righteousness.

Because Jesus is the incarnate Son of God, he is the incarnation of righteousness; he is righteousness in the flesh, the "Holy One of Israel" (Isa. 55:5). Nor is it simply that, as the eternal Son of God, he is already in perfect conformity to his own will and precepts. Rather, it is that as the *Mediator*—as God-made-flesh—he was "born of a woman, born under the Law" (Gal. 4:4), just as you and I are, and in our human nature has lived a life of perfect, active obedience to his own law, every nanosecond of his earthly life. As Peter says in 1 Peter 2:22: "[He] committed no sin, nor was deceit found in His mouth."

All this is why Jeremiah draws so much attention to this one personal quality of this coming King. He is God's solution to Israel's problem. He is the solution to unrighteous Shallum, unrighteous Jehoiakim, and the unrighteous Coniah. And he is the solution to every unrighteous citizen of Israel, Ireland, or Indianapolis, because he possess this personal quality: he is the LORD our righteousness. But critically, he does not simply possess it for himself.

A Personal Possession. Jesus is the LORD our righteousness. This righteousness is for you. You have a particular vested interest in it (and if you do not yet, you should). Why do you need Christ's righteousness as your personal possession?

* *Because you lack it.* You lack it in your father, Adam. Adam's sin was imputed to you. You have a sinful nature: an inclination to live unrighteous lives, and, consequently, all your best works are deeply flawed (Isa. 64:6; Rom. 3:10).
* *Because you need it.* Without it you will perish. God's standard has always been perfect obedience to his law, and he will never lower it. Either you must attain to a perfect righteousness on your own—which is the futile message of every other religion in the world—or else Christ must procure it for you. Only clothed in the righteousness of the LORD our righteousness can you dare appear before the Lord. And when you do, he will recognize the righteousness with which you are arrayed as his own and accept you in the Beloved.
* *Because you can have it.* Jeremiah thus brings the light of the gospel of Christ into the darkness of his own nation, in his own time, and freely offers an "alien righteousness" to an unrighteous people. To obtain it, they must look by faith to Christ, and so must we: "For I am not ashamed of the gospel of Christ…For in it, the righteousness of God is revealed from faith to faith; as it is written, 'The just shall live by faith' " (Rom. 1:16–17).

If all your worldly possessions were bet on a single round of golf, you would be happy to know Rory McIlroy was playing on your behalf and that his score would be credited to your scorecard. But this is no game, and the stakes are much higher. Your eternal soul is staked on your faultless obedience to God's law. It is your salvation that Jesus has kept perfectly in your stead and offers his "score" for your scorecard. And Paul tells us how we can obtain it: "that I may gain Christ and be found in Him, not having my own righteousness, which is from the law, but that which is through faith in Christ, the righteousness which is from God by faith" (Phil. 3:8b–9). It is *faith* that stretches out and receives the LORD as our righteousness. Have you renounced your own shabby good deeds, and rested upon his, that they may be made out to you?

Solution #3: God will Provide Redemption (Jer. 23:7–8).

God's third solution to Israel's problem is the promise of a new exodus in the likeness of the first exodus. Israel's redemption from slavery in Egypt, and now from Babylon, are metaphors for our exodus from slavery to sin. Do you want to join this exodus? If so, you must look to this heavenly King, and no earthly ruler, for redemption. Do not look for a political solution to a spiritual problem, as the Jews who looked to King Coniah as a "broken idol" (Jer. 22:28).

During President Obama's election campaign in 2008, journalist Caroline Glick wrote an article entitled, "Obama the Savior," and quoted the first-lady-elect as saying, "Barack Obama is the only candidate for president who understands that before America can solve its problems, Americans have to fix their 'broken souls.' Obama can do what his opponent...cannot do. He can heal his countrymen's broken souls. He will redeem them."[3] But neither a King Coniah or a President Obama can redeem souls. Only one King can break the bonds of slavery in our spiritual Egypt: the Lord our righteousness. Who are you depending on for redemption? Christ or someone else? Only in Christ will you find a righteousness sufficient to save.

As Archbishop James Ussher explains,

> Here we have assurance of the sufficiency of our redemption. That soul must be thoroughly acquitted that is [clothed] in such a righteousness, that debt must be fully discharged, that hath such a price laid down for it; our sins, though never so great, cannot weigh down his righteousness and merit (Rom. 8:33) and God having accepted his Son's righteousness for us, will not hold us anymore [to be] trespassers, but he disables his own justice from making any further demand.[4]

Is God's justice "disabled" from making any further demands from you? Only if Jesus is the Lord your righteousness.

Jesus Is God's

Servant

Who among you fears the Lord*? Who obeys the voice of His Servant?*
—Isaiah 50:10

READ ISAIAH 50:1–11

The message of the book of Isaiah is one of sin and redemption. Perhaps nowhere is it stated more beautifully than in the memorable words of the opening chapter, " 'Come now, and let us reason together,' says the Lord, 'Though your sins are like scarlet, they shall be as white as snow; though they are red like crimson, they shall be as wool' " (vv. 18–21). These words are really a summary of the message of the whole Bible: a world lost in sin against God and God coming into it to wash those sins away. This is God's master plan, and in order to accomplish it, he chose a special people who would be his agents of blessing to the world. And so it was that he entered into a covenant of grace with the nation of Israel: a special nation with a special calling to be a showcase people to the world, mediating God's blessings to the world, just as God covenanted with their forefather Abraham, "In you all families of the earth shall be blessed" (Gen. 12:3).

It is little wonder then that, throughout Isaiah, Israel is called God's *servant*: "But you, Israel, are My servant, Jacob whom I have chosen, the descendants of Abraham My friend. You whom I have taken from the ends of the earth, and called from its farthest regions, and said to you, 'You are My servant, I have chosen you and have not cast you away' " (Isa. 41:8–9; compare with 44:1–2, 21). As God's servant, Israel has a glorious mission to bless all nations, and the Old Testament provides their track record in carrying it out. Unfortunately, by the time we get to Isaiah 50, it is clear that Israel has failed terribly, and her tenure as God's servant is fast running out. But God's master plan is far from thwarted. He announces through the prophet that he will raise up another servant: One who will obey God's Word, proclaim God's Word, and be the blessing to all families of the Earth just as God promised—Jesus Christ our Lord.

Israel, God's Disobedient Servant

If you have ever had your job performance reviewed, you probably had the experience of sitting down with your employer to discuss the findings of the evaluation. Depending on your faithfulness to your contract, that may be very good or else very bad. After centuries in the employment of God as his servant, it is now Israel's turn to have her "job performance" evaluated. Had Israel been faithful to the covenant God had made with her through the patriarchs? In verses 1–3 we eavesdrop on the interview between God and his servant Israel and find that *both* have a predicament and a complaint.

Israel's predicament.

Israel's predicament is that she has been "put away," or sold into exile: "Thus says the LORD: 'Where is the certificate of your mother's divorce, whom I have put away? Or which of My creditors is it to whom I have sold you?' " (v. 1). The "mother" mentioned here is Zion, and those directly addressed are Zion's sons and daughters, but together they make up the people of Israel.[1] Clearly, they have failed as God's servant. Their job performance has, to say the least, been disappointing. To mix the two metaphors of this verse, they had been both a disobedient servant and a faithless bride to God. They had disobeyed their Master's instructions and committed adultery against their Husband, whoring after pagan gods. And so (in the words of prophecy) they find themselves exiled to Babylon; we might say they have been put on administrative leave. This predicament is the grounds for Israel's complaint.

Israel's complaint.

Israel has the gall to blame God for her predicament. They say to him: "You divorced me! You sold us!"[2] God has placed his disobedient servant on administrative leave, but they protest that they have been arbitrarily fired. Of course, God will not take this.

God's complaint.

On the contrary, God retorts that they have only themselves to blame: "For your iniquities you have sold yourselves, and for your transgressions your mother has been put away!" (v. 1). What we are reading here is not simply a lesson for ancient Israel. Here God is powerfully exposing our shared *human* predicament. It is our own sins that have estranged us from our Creator. "For all have sinned and fall short of the glory of God" (Rom. 3:23) and "your iniquities have separated you from your God; and your sins have hidden His face from you, so that He will not hear" (Isa. 59:2). We are like the bitter children of a divorce, blaming Dad for the grief and brokenness we are experiencing, when all the time we have the wrong analogy: we are not the child victims of a divorce, but rather an unfaithful bride who has abandoned her husband for other lovers. By nature, we feel the pain of our exile from our Maker, but we would rather blame him than accept our own responsibility.

But remarkably, even though we have failed God, he is still willing to save: "Is My hand shortened at all that it cannot redeem? Or have I no power to deliver?" (Isa. 50:2). He even offers historical proof, reminding Israel in verses 2–3 of their redemption from slavery in Egypt, hinting that what he did in the past to save his people, he is about to do again.

God's "predicament."

Of course, God never, strictly speaking, faces a "predicament"—the Almighty is never in a jam. But it is that kind of language he uses when he asks the question, "Why, when I came, was there no man? Why, when I called, was there none to answer?" (v. 2). God had been patient with Israel, sending her prophets to call her back to her mission, but they would not listen to God's voice or open their ears to his Word. When God sought a faithful man in Israel, he found none. Who then will be his obedient servant now that Israel has failed?

Jesus, God's Obedient Servant

After the opening dialogue between God and Israel in verses 1–3, a new voice speaks in verse 4: "The Lord GOD has given Me the tongue of the learned, that I should know how to speak a word in season to him who is weary. He awakens Me morning by morning, he awakens My ear to hear as the learned." This is not the voice of God's disobedient servant Israel, but we are told it is "the voice of His Servant," with a capital "S" (v. 10). It is the voice of one "who did not come to be served but to serve, and to give His life as a ransom for many" (Mark 10:45). It is the voice of Jesus Christ.

The New Testament applies these "Suffering Servant songs" of Isaiah chapters 42, 49–50, and 53 to the Carpenter of Nazareth. For example, "Great multitudes followed Him, and He healed them all…that it might be fulfilled which was spoken by Isaiah the prophet [Isa. 42:1–4], saying: 'Behold! My Servant whom I have chosen, My Beloved in whom My soul is well pleased!'" (Matt. 12:15–18).

So Jesus himself is the speaker in the remainder of the chapter, as he describes three distinct aspects of his own earthly ministry as God's servant: his *qualifications*, his *humiliation*, and his *exaltation*. It is a very intimate glimpse of the inner life of our Lord as he shares in his own words his "job description" as God's servant, succeeding where Israel, and we, have failed.

The qualifications of God's servant (Isa. 50:4).

God's servant Jesus has a learned tongue. Christ says, "The Lord GOD has given Me the tongue of the learned, that I should know how to speak a word in season to him who is weary." The Hebrew term is literally, "a disciple's tongue," or "the tongue of a scholar."[3] With such a tongue instructed by God, he brings a message of good news: "A word in season" for exiles, the spiritually "weary." Like any servant, Jesus spoke not his own words, but those of his Lord and Father (John 7:16, 14:10). God's servant Israel had ultimately failed to speak God's Word to the world, but instead had given cause for the Gentiles to blaspheme. But not Jesus. As exiles in this world, we need someone to bring us gospel tidings of redemption, someone who will say, "Come to Me, all you who are weary and heavy laden, and I will give you rest" (Matt. 11:28).

God's servant Jesus has a listening ear. "He awakens Me morning by morning, He awakens My ear to hear as the learned. The Lord GOD has opened my ear" (Isa. 50:4–5). Jesus's ears are always open to his Father's will, and that is because God's servant is also God's prophet. He first listens to God's Word and then declares it to his people. Jesus is uniquely qualified to be God's servant because of the intimacy between him and God. C. H. Spurgeon explains:

> Oh beloved, there was never One who had His ear so near the mouth of God as Jesus had. His Father had no need to speak to him in dreams or visions of the night, for when all his faculties were wide awake there was nothing in them to hinder His understanding of the mind of God.[4]

You have maybe watched movies depicting the household of some great Eastern sultan surrounded by a retinue of servants; he merely claps his hand, and, instantly, a servant hustles forward and seems to knows precisely what to do. So with Jesus: he is attentive to his Master's will. His ear is opened, and his will is subject to his Father. No wonder, then, that it was Jesus's practice to spend long hours communing with his Father in prayer (Matt. 14:23; Mark 1:35; Luke 6:12).

Jesus is eminently qualified to be God's servant. He has a learned tongue and a listening ear—and he still does today. If his listening ear is open to your feeble tongue as you pray to him, then be sure to afford him the courtesy of listening to his *learned* tongue as he speaks to you in his Word.

The humiliation of God's servant (Isa. 50:5–6).

It pleased God that in order for his servant to be able to speak good news to the weary sinner he must first suffer. Jesus is supremely the *Suffering* Servant. Indeed, the humiliation of the servant is the very heart of the good news he will preach. The *Westminster Shorter Catechism* summarizes it well: "Christ's humiliation consisted in his being born, and that in a low condition, made under the law, undergoing the miseries of this life, the wrath of God, and the cursed death of the cross; in being buried, and continuing under the power of death for a time."[5] It is by definition a servant's most basic task to be obedient to the tasks assigned by his Lord, or else (like servant Israel) he can expect to be sent packing. Systematic theology summarizes Christ's two tasks as servant into two categories: active obedience and passive obedience.

Active Obedience. What did God have to say about his servant Israel in verse 2? "Why, when I called, was there none to answer?" Now, what do we read about his servant Jesus in verses 4–5? "The Lord God has opened My ear; and I was not rebellious, nor did I turn away." God had given Israel his law at Sinai—moral, civil, and ceremonial—and they had failed to keep it. So Jesus took upon himself the same law on the same terms: "born of a woman, born under the Law, to redeem those…under the law" and obeyed its demands perfectly where Israel had disobeyed (Gal. 4:4–5). Christ's "active obedience" was thus vicarious (on behalf of others, not merely for himself). And neither was it only for Israel: you and I too have fallen short, and have no righteousness of our own (Isa. 64:6). But the good news is that his perfect righteousness can be yours if you will believe in him (Rom. 1:17). His active obedience provides infinite credit in your spiritual bank account, entitling you to come out of exile, and into his glorious presence. What God's law demands, God's gospel supplies through Christ's active obedience imputed by faith.

Passive Obedience. But if Christ's active obedience is accomplished for you, what about the debt you owe for sins you have committed and continue to commit? Didn't God begin by saying, "For your iniquities you have sold yourselves, and for your transgressions [you have] been put away" (Isa. 50:1)? For these there must be a reckoning, for "because of these things the wrath of God comes upon the sons of disobedience" (Eph. 5:6). Our text tells us that God's servant Jesus has taken care of this for you too. For your sake, the wrath of God came upon the Son of *obedience*: "I gave My back to those who struck Me, and My cheeks to those who plucked out the beard; I did not hide My face from shame and spitting" (v. 6). Here is a vivid autobiographical account of the *passion* of the Christ, that is, his sufferings, from which we derive the term "passive obedience"—his obedience to suffer for the sins of his people.[6] And it was *voluntary* suffering: "I gave my back to those who struck me." These and other prophesied elements of our Lord's humiliation are found in the Gospel narratives of Matthew 26:63–67 and 27:26–31. All that God's obedient servant suffered was because of all that God's disobedient servant had committed, which is another way of saying, the blessed servant, God's Son, suffered for your sins and in your place.

Remember God's complaint against Israel: "For your iniquities you have sold yourselves, and for your transgressions your mother has been put away" (v. 2). This was your predicament by nature, yet the gospel says, "For your iniquities Jesus has sold Himself, and for your transgressions Jesus has been put away." He was treated without mercy because *you* deserve no mercy. In the words of Psalm 129:3, they "plowed deep furrows in His back" with a Roman whip. Human spittle landed on his face. Tufts of hair were cruelly torn from his blessed face. He was hanged by nails driven through his hands and feet. And all the while his agony was mocked. But worse than all this, he endured exile from God, crying out, "My God, my God, why have you forsaken me?" (Matt. 27:46).

In Isaiah's day, God had asked his people in verse 2: "Why, when I came, was there no man? Why, when I called, was there none to answer?" But today, God can say, "When I come, there is a Man! When I call, there is One who answers!" Today, when God asks you, "Is My hand shortened that it cannot redeem? Or have I no power to deliver?" you can answer: "Yonder hangs God's obedient Servant in agony on a cross! His flesh is torn. His blood pours out upon the ground. 'The heavens are clothed with blackness, and the sackcloth is their covering' (v. 3). He cries out in his solitariness, exiled from God in my place. Surely God's hand is not shortened that it cannot redeem. He has power to deliver!"

The exaltation of God's servant (Isa. 50:7–9).

In the Gospels we read, "Jesus took the Twelve aside and told them, 'We are going up to Jerusalem, and everything that is written by the prophets about the Son of Man will be fulfilled. He will be handed over to the Gentiles. They will mock him, insult him, spit on him, flog him and kill him'" (Luke 18:31–32 NIV). How did Jesus endure such humiliation? Jesus continues in verse 33, "and the third day He will rise again." He endured by looking to the vindication he would receive from God, or as Hebrews 12:2 explains, "for the joy that was set before Him [He] endured the cross, despising the shame, and has sat down at the right hand of the throne of God." Jesus's humiliation is followed by his *exaltation*.[7] And this too Isaiah predicts in our text:

> For the Lord GOD will help Me; therefore I will not be disgraced; therefore I have set My face like a flint, and I know that I will not be ashamed. He is near who justifies Me; who will contend with Me? Let us stand together. Who is My adversary? Let him come near Me. Surely the Lord GOD will help Me; who is he who will condemn Me? Indeed they will all grow old like a garment; the moth will eat them up. (vv. 7–9)

Both cross and tomb are empty. God's obedient servant has been justified by the Lord God and vindicated as a "good and faithful Servant." Despite his disgraceful treatment at the hands of men, Jesus is not disgraced anymore. He presently reigns as King. Who dares contend with him?

Which Servant Will You Identify with?

Isaiah 50 has presented us with two contrasting portraits. The first is of God's disobedient servant Israel, which is a picture of us all in our sinful condition. The second is that of God's obedient servant Jesus, who is God's solution to our predicament. The closing verses leave us with a decision: which servant will you identify with?

By nature, you "walk in darkness and have no light," and so Isaiah gives four clear instructions to you in verse 10: "Fear the Lord. Obey the voice of the Servant. Trust in the name of LORD. Rely upon God." Fear, obey, trust, rely: these must be the vital characteristics of your life if you identify with God's servant Jesus, not relying on your *own* obedience but on his.

But there is also a word to you who stubbornly continue to identify with God's unfaithful servant by relying on your own efforts: "Look, all you who kindle a fire, who encircle yourselves with sparks: walk in the light of your fire and in the sparks you have kindled—this you shall have from My hand: You shall lie down in torment" (v. 11). Are you trying to create your own light, to kindle a feeble fire of sparks?

What foolishness to behold the Suffering Servant of the Lord dying on the cross for sinners and yet imagine that you do not need his help. Why, when he comes to *you*, is there "no man?" Why, when he calls, is there "none to answer?" (v. 2). If you refuse to "trust in the name of the Lord," you shall yourself bear the penalty of your sins—the flogging and the spitting, the solitary exile from God—and you will "lie down in torment." Far better to obey the voice of his servant and live.

Jesus Is Our
Shelter

Behold, a king will reign in righteousness...a shelter from the storm.
—Isaiah 32:2 ESV

READ ISAIAH 31:1–32:2

"National calamity!" What images do these words bring to your mind? For the prophet Isaiah, it meant an incompetent national government and economic meltdown. It meant war, invasion, and occupation by a brutal enemy. It meant massive civilian casualties, orphaned children, and endless lines of shuffling refugees with nowhere to run: an entire population gripped with panic.

Now, to such an afflicted people, what does the word "shelter" convey? Surely, it conveys relief and a hiding place from the pursuer, a place of safety you can run to where you and your family can finally be at rest and fear the enemy no more. Isaiah lived through some of the most turbulent years of the kingdom of Judah; he witnessed the terror of the Assyrian invasion, the burning of the cities and villages of Judah, and subsequent siege of Jerusalem. But against this terrifying backdrop, God gave him a message of hope: the provision of shelter from the violent storm not only of a national and political kind, but of a spiritual kind.

While you may not live to see such national calamity in your day, it is almost certain that you will see (or have seen) personal calamity. All of us live under the calamity of sin—a human calamity so profound that all the storms of life have their origins in this great fount of all human misery. And it is this great calamity and its fallout that God has done something about. He has provided a shelter, and that shelter is a person:

> Behold, a king will reign in righteousness, and princes will rule with justice. A man will be as a hiding place from the wind, and a [shelter, ESV] from the tempest, as rivers of water in a dry place, as the shadow of a great rock in a weary land. (Isa. 32:1–2)

Here is another glorious portrait of our Lord Jesus Christ: He is our "shelter from the tempest."

A Shelter Foretold

In order to fully appreciate the beauty of this portrait of Christ as our shelter, we first need to get to grips with the storm from which his people need to be sheltered. This is found in Isaiah 31. Israel is facing a major national crisis; the storm clouds of war are gathering on her northern borders. The restless Assyrian Empire under King Sennacherib—a nation still recognized today as one of the most brutal military regimes of history and specialists in torture and butchery—is amassing its armies.

By chapter 31, the northern kingdom of Israel has already fallen, and Judah is the next target. God's people in Judah, ruled by King Hezekiah, give in to their fears and do something foolish, which is recorded in verse 1:

> Woe to those who go down to Egypt for help, and rely on horses, who trust in chariots because they are many, and in horsemen because they are very strong, but who do not look to the Holy One of Israel, nor seek the LORD!

Hezekiah makes a critical mistake: he seeks shelter from Egypt, forming an alliance with her and trusting in horses, chariots, and horsemen instead of the Lord (compare with Deut. 17:16). No wonder God scoffs in Isaiah 31:3: "The Egyptians are men, and not God; and their horses are flesh, and not spirit."

But in Isaiah 31:4–9, God lays out his far better plan: "The LORD of hosts will come down to fight for Mount Zion and for its hill. Like birds flying about, so will the LORD of hosts defend Jerusalem. Defending, He will also deliver it; passing over, He will preserve it." God foretells a coming day of power when he himself, and not the puny Egyptian army, will defend Israel. And when he does so, he will "pass over" them, just as he "passed over" them in Egypt.[1] In other words, deliverance for God's people will be in the form of atonement for their sins, which will coincide with the destruction (described in graphic detail in the rest of chapter) of their arch-enemy, Assyria.

And that brings us to this portrait of Christ in Isaiah 32:1–2. Following this great victory, God will establish King Hezekiah's rule in Jerusalem, and he and his princes will govern with justice. A new era of safety will be ushered in; Assyria will never again trouble Judah. Instead of the *storm*, there will be *shelter*.

This brief overview of Isaiah 31 reminds us that in times of calamity in our lives, be they national or personal, God expects us to patiently believe his promises and not to take matters into our own hands. "The Lord is not slack concerning His promise, as some count slackness, but is longsuffering toward us" (2 Peter 3:9). That is the way it was for Israel. God foretold that shelter was going to come.

A Shelter Fulfilled

Isaiah has foretold a day when God will shelter his people and destroy their enemy: "In that day every man shall throw away his idols" (Isa. 31:7). But this begs the question, "In what day?" When would the shelter foretold be a shelter *fulfilled*? As with all Old Testament prophecy, we see different layers of fulfillment: a more immediate fulfillment and a more distant messianic fulfillment.

The immediate fulfillment.

In 701 BC, the inevitable finally happened: the dreaded Assyrian army under King Sennacherib invaded Judah, and, just as Isaiah had predicted, Egypt was powerless to help (compare with Isa. 36:18–20). Having crushed the Egyptian army, Sennacherib captured no fewer than forty-six walled cities in Judah[2] and finally came and besieged Jerusalem itself. It seemed as if it was all over for God's people. Where was this "shelter from the tempest" he had foretold? A few chapters later in Isaiah 36–37 we find the answer. Hezekiah finally calls on the Lord, and the Lord miraculously overthrows the enemy:

> Then the Angel of the LORD went out, and killed in the camp of the Assyrians one hundred and eighty-five thousand; and when people arose early in the morning, there were the corpses—all dead. So Sennacherib king of Assyria departed and went away, returned home, and remained at Nineveh. (37:36)

Thus God fulfilled his Word: He showed up Egypt as a worthless help, he jealously guarded his own people, and he did it without any help from human armies (Isa. 31:3–4, 8–9). And after this truly astonishing act of deliverance, Hezekiah went on to have one of the most glorious reigns of all the Old Testament kings who sat on David's throne, "reign[ing] in righteousness, and princes will rule with justice" (Isa. 32:1).[3] So a shelter foretold became a shelter fulfilled for that generation. But there is also a more glorious fulfillment we must consider.

The messianic fulfillment.

The rescue of Jerusalem is not the only "day" of power that God wants us to see here. The mighty deliverance of Israel from Assyria is an

Old Testament picture of your deliverance from sin and Satan by Jesus Christ. This is seen through a closer look at Isaiah 32:1–2. The Hebrew literally reads in verse 1, "Behold, according to righteousness there will reign a King";[4] and in verse 2, "The man (or *this* man) will be as a hiding place from the wind, a shelter from the tempest."[5] The ESV and NIV translations of verse 2 unfortunately obscure the fact that a particular man is in view. The prophet is saying that David's heir Hezekiah foreshadows the perfect King Jesus, who will "reign in righteousness" (compare with Isa. 9:6–7 and 11:1–4) and be for his redeemed people "a hiding place from the wind, and a shelter from the tempest."

When we read the words of Isaiah through the lens of the New Testament, we find the gospel written large. It is a short prophetic step from the Angel of the Lord's supernatural act of redemption from Assyria in the Old Testament, to Christ's mightier act of spiritual redemption in the New Testament, in which our sins are "passed over" (Isa. 31:5). You, God's people, are oppressed by an evil enemy that is far too powerful for you, who would enslave you. But God, because of his covenant love, unilaterally descends to bring salvation to you: in the words of verse 4, "The Lord of hosts will come down to fight for Mount Zion and for its hill." God's Son—who appeared as the Angel of the Lord to crush the Assyrians outside the gates of Jerusalem (Isa. 37:36)—has now come down in human flesh to rescue his Church and crush our great enemy Satan on the cross, so that God might "pass over" your sins and that he might reign as King in righteousness.[6]

Are you trusting in Christ our shelter? Have you been sheltered from the wrath of God? Has he passed over your sins? If not, will you cry out to him as Israel did and find salvation, or are you perhaps still betting on the help of your "Egyptians"—that is, your own earthly alliances and securities: your possessions, friends, or good works—instead of the Lord? But if you have been passed over, what then? Then Christ is still your shelter from the storms of life until you join him in glory. That is the thrust of Isaiah 32:2, which contains much by way of practical application.

A Shelter for You

Explaining how the Old Testament should be read by Christians, the apostle Peter writes, "Of this salvation the prophets have inquired and searched carefully…To them it was revealed that, not to themselves, but to us they were ministering the things which now have been reported to you through those who have preached the gospel to you" (1 Peter 1:10, 12). Our text in Isaiah was written not only for the original hearers, who lived under the rule of Hezekiah, but for you and me, who presently live under the rule of Jesus Christ. Specifically, it shows why you still need shelter and how Christ is a shelter for you.

Why you still need shelter.

Christ does not turn the tide of the war and then leave his soldiers to fend for themselves on the battlefield. You may have been definitively saved from sin and Satan at the cross, but until you come to heaven, you must expect these enemies to harass your every step there. Yes, Satan is defeated and awaits his final sentence, but in meantime, "he is filled with great wrath, because he knows his time is short" (Rev. 12:12). Yes, you died to sin with Christ, but until you put off this mortal body, your sinful nature, the "law of sin," "wars" within your members (Rom. 6:10–11; 7:23). Yes, Christ has "overcome the world," but this world in which you live is at enmity with your King. So we are told, "Do not marvel, my brethren, if the world hates you" (1 John 3:13).

Isaiah describes this fact vividly when he writes, "A man will be as a hiding place from the wind, and a [shelter] from the tempest, as rivers of water in a dry place, as the shadow of a great rock in a weary land" (32:2). These common biblical metaphors (usually found in the Psalms) vividly describe the afflictions you regularly face as a subject of the King and why you still need Christ as your shelter. As Thomas Boston explains,

> The world is spiritually to Christ's subjects, the people of God, a "weary land", that is, a "thirsty land", a scorching country, a stormy

> place, with many inconveniences, which make travelers weary and faint. It is a wilderness, wherein there is no water, which makes people weary, and long for shelter and refreshment.[7]

So as you trek like the Israelites in the wilderness, thirsty travelers in a thirsty land, you walk through "dry places," singing with David, "O God, You are my God; early will I seek You; my soul thirsts for You; My flesh longs for You in a dry and thirsty land where there is no water" (Ps. 63:1). And yet, to make matters worse, you must also endure "winds" and "tempests"—yet more common biblical metaphors for trials we face as Christians. The weather forecast for the committed Christian is stormy: "chance of precipitation, 100 percent." These storms may take the form of outward trials—physical afflictions, bereavement, economic troubles, strife in personal relationships, even the effects of war, like Israel experienced. Or they often take the form of inward trials, such as struggles with sinful habits, temptation, a wounded conscience, or a sense of distance from God. "Winds, tempests, dry places, a weary land"—this is your lot as a subject of the King, and this is why you still need him as your shelter.

How Christ is your shelter.

Christ's once-for-all deliverance from "the Great Assyrian Storm" does not immunize you from further storms in life, but it does guarantee you will have a shelter in them. For each trial Isaiah mentions, he shows how Christ is a shelter from the storm for you. So what storms are you facing? You may not have 185,000 Assyrian warriors at your doorstep, but you do have days where you feel surrounded by enemies. Are you struggling with temptations that threaten to engulf you? Are you filled with a sense of guilt over your many failings? The nineteenth-century revival preacher Edward Griffin reminds you, "When the lightning of conviction flashes upon the soul, and guilt with its thundering voice spreads its dark folds over the mind, nowhere but in Jesus can be found a covert from the bursting storm."[8] And that is because he has withstood every temptation and borne the tempest of God's wrath in your place on the cross: "reckon yourself therefore as dead to sin, but alive to God in Christ" (Rom. 6:11).

What afflictions are you suffering in your body, your family, your material well-being? Christ is a shelter from these storms too: "You have been a strength to the poor, a strength to the needy in his distress, a refuge from the storm" (Isa. 25:4).

But what about the times when you find yourself spiritually in "a dry place and a weary land?" Here too, Jesus will be for you "a river of water" and "the shadow of a great rock," respectively (Isa. 32:2). The metaphor changes, but this is another vital element of Christ's work as shelter. A shelter is a place of refreshment in a long and arduous journey, which, as we have seen, is through a wilderness. If you visit the Grand Canyon, there are many trails you can take down into that desert oven. And for each of them, the printed tour guides warn you how many bottles of water you will need to take with you in order to complete the journey safely. They also strongly recommend completing most of your trek in the early morning or evening, because that is when you are more likely to find shadows from the escarpment to shelter you from the blazing sun. Likewise, in your Christian journey, you can easily grow faint and "weary in well doing": tired from endless battles against sin or exhausted from long nights of watching in prayer (2 Thess. 3:13 KJV). At such times, Jesus supplies not just a feeling of rest but he *is* our rest; he supplies you with himself.

The Hebrew word translated "rivers of water" refers not so much to a welcome oasis or a spring in the desert, but to an irrigation system built to supply copious water directly to its needed recipients. Each plant in the vineyard is thus guaranteed its own supply of water by channels that direct the life-giving water to its roots. Instead of shriveling up under the blazing sun, the plant grows and produces fruit in an otherwise forbidding environment. Likewise, for his vineyard the Church, your Master has provided "channels of water" that direct his life-sustaining grace to you: the means of grace. It is not the channels themselves that refresh and water the thirsty plants, but rather the water that is conveyed through them.[9] In the same way, you must make use of the Word, sacraments, and prayer. You must do so not because you automatically receive grace in partcipating in the Lord's Supper or the discipline of daily Bible reading. Rather, you must take hold of these ordinary means because *through* them you commune with Christ, are refreshed by Christ, and receive Christ as your shelter, so that the desert may bloom and flourish with the fruits of the Spirit.

In your day of calamity, will you run to the many inadequate shelters this world offers? Or will you instead flee to Christ? He alone is a competent shelter for You because he has faced all the "winds, tempests, dry places and weary land" on your behalf. For just as Isaiah foretold, he "came down to fight for Mt. Zion and for its hill," taking your flesh and blood, and exposing himself to the ferocious blast of God's wrath, so that you too might have shelter.

Jesus Is Our

Shepherd

I am the good shepherd.
—John 10:11

READ JOHN 10:11–30

My fifth-grade Latin teacher was Mrs. Weatherup. She seemed to us as old as Rome itself and had little control of her unruly class. I am sorry to say that students would sleep, slip out of class, and perform all sorts of pranks (and usually get away with it). Then there was Mrs. Cree, who taught fifth grade history. She was altogether different, for she knew well the nature of fifth grade boys. She was vigilant in class, fed us fascinating (and often grisly) stories from the past, chased truants, commanded our complete attention, and cared enough to tutor the straggling class clown. (It will not surprise you that I subsequently became a history teacher and not a Latin teacher.)

Sheep are like fifth-grade boys; they have stubborn, wandering hearts, are vulnerable to distraction and danger, and they can tell the difference between a good shepherd and a bad one. This is the familiar biblical imagery our Lord uses in John chapter 10: God's people may come under the influence of bad shepherds to their harm, but Jesus alone is the Good Shepherd of the sheep, and the sheep will hear and respond to his voice.

In the previous chapter of this Gospel, Jesus was exposing the sham shepherding of the Pharisees. Now he contrasts his own ministry with theirs by using two metaphors. First, in John chapter 10 he says, "I am the door of the sheep," that is, through him they may come in and out and find pasture. But we want to focus on the second metaphor found in verse 11, "I am the good shepherd," examining first the assertion itself, and then considering the proofs of the assertion, so that we may better admire this well-loved portrait of our Lord.

Jesus's Assertion: "I Am the Good Shepherd"

When Jesus uses this well-known metaphor, he is drawing deep from the wells of the Old Testament. Throughout the Hebrew Scriptures, God revealed himself as the shepherd of Israel, a truth his people sang frequently in the worship songs he put on their lips:

> The LORD is my shepherd, I shall not want....You led Your people like a flock by the hand of Moses and Aaron....Give ear, O Shepherd of Israel, You who lead Joseph like a flock; You who dwell between the cherubim, shine forth!...Know that the LORD, He is God; it is He who has made us, and not we ourselves; we are His people and the sheep of His pasture. (Ps. 23:1; 77:20; 80:1; 100:3)

For Jesus to assert that *he* is the shepherd of God's flock is therefore to make an unmistakable claim to divinity. But it is more than a divine assertion; it is also a messianic assertion. The prophets repeatedly described the coming Savior using the same language:

> He will feed His flock like a shepherd; He will gather the lambs with His arm, and carry them in His bosom, and gently lead those who are with young...I will establish one Shepherd over them, and He shall feed them—My servant David. He shall feed them and be their shepherd. And I, the LORD, will be their God, and My servant David a prince among them. (Isa. 40:11; Ezek. 34:23–24)

Jesus's claim, "I am the good shepherd," is more than a heart-warming image to splash on a Hallmark card. It is an assertion that he is Israel's divine Shepherd-King, prophesied of old. And if anyone disputes the point, he drives it home with the bombshell of John 10:30: "I and My Father are one." The implications were not lost on his hearers: "The Jews took up stones again to stone Him." And they explain why: "for blasphemy, and because You, being a Man, make Yourself God" (vv. 31, 33). So what proofs does Jesus give us of the veracity of his stupendous claim?

Five Proofs of Jesus's Assertion

Proof #1: Jesus is not like false shepherds (John 10:12–13).

Long ago, Ezekiel had also denounced the false shepherds of his own generation in no uncertain terms:

> Therefore, you shepherds, hear the word of the LORD: "as I live," says the Lord GOD, "surely...My flock became a prey, and My flock became food for every beast of the field, because there was no shepherd, nor did My shepherds search for My flock, but the shepherds fed themselves and did not feed My flock." (Ezek. 34:7–8)

Things had not changed by Jesus's day, nor indeed is the Church free of them today. So it is that Jesus warns against hirelings, who contrast sharply with his own unique office as the "great Shepherd of the sheep" (John 10:12–13; Heb. 13:20). What does Jesus's condemnation of the bad shepherds teach us about himself as the Good Shepherd?

The hireling "is not the shepherd," in contrast to Jesus, who is. Hirelings may dress, speak, and act like shepherds, but are in fact imposters, as Jesus reminds us in Matthew 7:15: "Beware of false prophets, who come to you in sheep's clothing, but inwardly they are ravenous wolves." Today's hirelings are cult leaders, pagan priests, leaders of apostate churches, and unconverted clergy within the visible Church. Our Christian duty is to test such shepherds against the Good

Shepherd and cling to him: "Beware lest you also fall from your own steadfastness, being led away with the error of the wicked; but grow in the grace and knowledge of our Lord and Savior Jesus Christ" (2 Peter 3:17–18).

The hireling is "one who does not own the sheep," in contrast to Jesus, who does. If you are a Christian, Jesus *owns* you; he has bought you, and his investment is one that will never be lost, because the currency with which he paid can never lose its value. No global recession can diminish the returns of Jesus's blood. You were unpromising stock, but he placed such a value on you that he invested his very lifeblood for you (1 Peter 1:18–19).

The hireling "sees the wolf coming." Jesus sees the wolf coming too—this much they have in common. But Jesus is vigilant for his *sheep's* sake; the hireling is vigilant for his *own* sake. When wolves go out to hunt, they don't wave a sign and say "Danger! Wolf!" They are camouflaged, subtle, and thus very dangerous predators. The sheep are often not aware of the threat until it is too late. But Jesus is always on guard duty; you may indeed "lie down in green pastures," for "His rod and staff will comfort you." A rod for discipline when you stray, and a staff to fight off your wolf-like enemies (Ps. 23:2, 4).

The hireling "leaves the sheep and flees; and the wolf catches the sheep and scatters them." Again, the hireling's pastoral infidelity highlights our Good Shepherd's faithful pastoral protection. Jesus sticks by his flock and withstands all their enemies. Consequently, the wolf does not catch the sheep or scatter the flock. For two thousand years Christ has faithfully defended his own against the most ferocious onslaughts.

The hireling "flees because he is a hireling and does not care about the sheep." Jesus, on the other hand, cares intensely for them. John uses the same word as 1 Peter 5:7: "casting all your care upon Him, for He cares for you." Jesus is a tender shepherd; he "leads [you] beside the still waters. He restores [your] soul" (Ps. 23:2–3). Whereas the hireling's self-serving goal is to save his own life, the Good Shepherd's selfless goal is to lay his down for the sheep he cares for.

In summary, we know Jesus is the Good Shepherd because his character is utterly unlike that of false shepherds. Here is comfort for the flock of God, but here also we find a warning to all hirelings: do not provoke the wrath of the shepherd! He will guard his lambs jealously, even to the death. Either the wolf will die or the shepherd will die slaying him.

Proof #2: Jesus knows and is known by his sheep (John 10:3–5, 14).

Jesus's sheep are not like a faceless herd identified only by ear tags and impersonal serial numbers. Rather, "the sheep hear His voice; and He calls His own sheep by name and leads them out." It does not matter if you are a nobody in the world's eyes; it matters that you are known personally by your shepherd. We feel honored when we are noticed by someone important. My father was a minister of the Free Church of Scotland when the Queen personally visited the General Assembly in Edinburgh in May 1977. As the Assembly rose, and Her Majesty entered the hall, he happened to catch her eye, and she smiled and nodded. It was just a momentary glance, but he felt honored all the same. King Jesus gives each of his subjects a good deal more than just a passing nod. If you have no more acquaintance with Christ than that, perhaps you need to reassess whether you belong to him.

Not only does Jesus know each member of his flock personally, but he adds, "and I am known by my own." There is thus a reciprocal relationship between shepherd and sheep, which calls us to examine how well we actually know our shepherd. It is quite possible to simply know facts about Jesus and not know him by personal relationship, to know him as a doctrine and not as a friend.

As a normal part of the application procedure for the "Green Card" to live as a permanent resident in the US, my American wife and I had to interview with an immigration officer after two years of marriage. We needed to prove that our relationship was *bona fide* and not just a marriage of convenience to sneak into the country. During that interview, I could have given my wife's vital statistics: birthday, place of birth, social security number, etc. But this would not have proven a relationship, just a good memory for regurgitating facts. Instead, I brought our marriage license, photos of our wedding, and ultrasound pictures of the baby we were expecting—plenty proof of a fruitful relationship. If you claim to know the Good Shepherd, a stockpile of memorized verses and catechism answers will not in itself prove the reality of a saving relationship. Where is the fruit of a transformed life?

Proof #3: Jesus seeks his sheep (John 10:16).

Jesus further proves that he is the Good Shepherd when he declares, "other sheep I have which are not of this fold; them also I must bring, and they will hear My voice." Jesus graciously *calls* sheep into his fold; he is "moved with compassion for them, because they [are] weary and scattered, like sheep having no shepherd" (Matt. 9:36; compare with Isa. 40:11). And when he calls them to himself it is an *effectual* call; he says "they will hear My voice" (John 10:16). The *Shorter Catechism*, Question and Answer 31, explains this transaction:

> Effectual Calling is the work of God's Spirit, whereby, convincing us of our sin and misery, enlightening our minds in the knowledge of Christ, and renewing our wills, he doth persuade and enable us to embrace Jesus Christ, freely offered to us in the gospel.

This shepherd's call is not a *suggestion*; it is a divine summons that will brook no refusal. When he determines to redeem a lost soul, he leaves the ninety-nine and seeks the one that is lost, a search that has never yet come up fruitless (Luke 15:4–7).

Furthermore, Jesus declares that his flock will be a very diverse one, comprising "other sheep not of this fold" (see Isa. 55:4–5). He will fill it with believing Jews and Gentiles, forming "one flock," not two. Any flock of sheep in a pasture will be very diverse—fat sheep, skinny sheep, white sheep, black sheep. The sheep are not uniform, but they are *united* in following the same shepherd. So it is in the Church; our identity is not defined by any particular ethnicity or social status, or ensuring everybody looks exactly the same (such cloning is more characteristic of cults), but rather our identity in following the same shepherd. "And there will be one flock and one shepherd" (John 10:16). Other "flocks" are not true flocks of sheep, but herds of goats (Matt. 25:32–33). What defines us as sheep is our shepherd; what defines the goats is that they follow a hireling. Has Jesus sought and found you yet? You can tell by who you are following.

Proof #4: Jesus redeems his sheep (John 10:17–18, 25–30).

The greatest proof of the assertion that Jesus is the Good Shepherd is that "the good shepherd lays down His life for the sheep." Christ has not left us as prey to the wolf but has redeemed his flock, and in this discourse he shows us how:

Jesus dies for his sheep: "I lay down My life that I may take it again." This would be a little shocking to the original hearers. Whoever heard of a shepherd sacrificing his life for the sake of his domestic animals? Although a flock of sheep was certainly very valuable—a man's livelihood, in fact—they were not worth more to him than his very life. How much value did the Lord place on you that he came to willingly die in your place? That such a one as he should willingly die for such a one as you? That his body should be broken for you and his blood spilled for you? That his soul should be anguished and his intimacy with the Father broken? And that he should rise again from the dead, triumphant over death so that you might not taste its sting? "Therefore My Father loves me, because I lay down my life" (10:17). Yet at the apex of his sufferings, he cries out, "My God, my God, why have you forsaken Me?" (Matt. 27:46). He suffers alone; no human, angelic, or divine help supports his agony. He bears the full weight of the sins of his sheep and drinks the full cup of his Father's wrath on their behalf. But that is not the end of the story.

Jesus is raised for his sheep: "I lay down My life that I may take it again. No one takes it from Me, but I lay it down of Myself. I have power to lay it down, and I have power to take it again." At seemingly his weakest point—the point of death on the cross—Jesus is in perfect control. In an age of increasing euthanasia in the West, we commonly hear people espouse "death with dignity" by asserting "control" over their death. Jesus was in perfect control at Calvary, yet he bore the most undignified death, hanging naked upon a cross with the jeers of the world ringing in his ears. Those who sinfully take their own lives can do no more, but on the third day, Jesus took up his life again and rose victorious over death.

Jesus gives his sheep eternal life. Christ has power to rise from the dead so *you too* might be victorious over death: "If we have been united with Him like this in His death, we will certainly also be united with Him in His resurrection" (Rom. 6:5 NIV; compare with 1 Cor. 15:20–23). But what about every day of a sheep's vulnerable life between now and glory? What assurance is there that you will not stumble before the finish line? Jesus gives a glorious promise to his flock: "They shall never perish; neither shall anyone snatch them out of My hand. My Father, who has given them to Me, is greater than all; and no one is able to snatch them out of My Father's hand" (John 10:28–29). The Good Shepherd will lose *none* of his own, and he will not rest until all have been brought into his fold. And when that day comes, as it most assuredly will, he will judge between sheep and goats as the divine shepherd: "When the Son of Man comes in His glory, and all the holy angels with Him, then He will sit on the throne of His glory. All the nations will be gathered before Him, and He will separate them one from another, as a shepherd divides his sheep from the goats" (Matt. 25:31–32). Where will you stand on that day?

Jesus is the Good Shepherd. He is not like the world's false shepherds. He knows and is known by his sheep; he seeks each one of them and fully redeems them. When he comes again to gather them to himself, may each of us be identified as his sheep indeed—not as hirelings, not as goats, but as true members of his flock.

Jesus Is Our
Strength

"So I will strengthen them in the LORD, and they shall walk up and down in His name" says the LORD.
—Zechariah 10:12

READ ZECHARIAH 10

Superheroes are tremendously popular in our day. We must have our happy endings, but we know these will only come with intervention of someone with god-like powers. Popeye eats spinach and anvils appear in his biceps. If David Banner gets angry enough, he turns green and miraculously bulks up to become the Incredible Hulk, and so on, down to the Guardians of the Galaxy of recent movie fame. The other side of this is that we are not in love with our physical limitations, but are only too aware of our weakness and consequent vulnerability. We need strength from outside of ourselves.

Politicians, pundits, and psychiatrists are fertile sources of a myriad of proposed remedies. Often, we are told to look into ourselves for the resources to cope with life's challenges. Self-reliance is certainly an aspiration of many, but it is too obviously a temporary expedient that proves itself to be a broken reed. Most people, whether they like it or not, soon discover to their chagrin that the prophet Jeremiah hits the mark when he says, "O LORD, I know the way of man is not in himself;

it is not in man who walks to direct his own steps" (Jer. 10:23). Man dreams on, but his dreams are not reality.

If all the laws and government programs, the armies and the pharmaceuticals, and the palliatives without number that are designed to deliver us from a myriad of threats are anything to go by, you could be forgiven for concluding that the human race believes it is the most endangered species on the planet. With every lurid headline, our twenty-first-century world looks less and less like the "brave new world" of the twentieth-century secular optimists and more and more like the same old real world it truly is. It is a world that the Bible explains with infallible accuracy as being blighted by the natural man's number one problem—he is by nature not alive, but spiritually "dead in trespasses and sins." Because of this endemic condition, we humans walk "according to the course of this world, according to the prince of the power of the air, the spirit who now works in the sons of disobedience" (Eph. 2:2), and are alienated from the God who created us.

We are fallen in Adam and by nature in a state of war with the Lord: "Because the carnal mind is enmity against God; for it is not subject to the law of God, nor indeed can be" (Rom. 8:7). We need a new nature that is regenerated, renewed, and redeemed by the only living God who is both able and determined to save people from themselves and their sins so as to be reconciled to him in glorious and everlasting fellowship (John 3:5–8, 14–21).

A Word of Hope from the Living God

The prophet Zechariah brought God's Word to the dark and scary world of his time. It was in essence no different from our own, both as to problems and solutions. What his world needed—and every generation after him also needs—he proclaims from the mouth of God. He heralds the coming of the kingdom of the promised Messiah, who is revealed six centuries later in the person of Jesus of Nazareth, the incarnate Son of God. In Zechariah 9–11, the prophet looks at this promise of the Messiah in terms of a "burden" against a place called "Hadrach." This Hadrach is thought to have been a small kingdom near Damascus, Syria. It seems it had become a byword for hostility against God's people. It represents those politico-religious powers that array themselves against God, his people, and his cause and kingdom in the world.[1] The "burden" describes God's dealings with the "big battalions" that oppress his people.

In Zechariah 9:10–17, the prophet speaks of the Messiah's kingdom of peace and shows that it is a *reality at present* in the hearts of believers and in the Lord's sovereign superintendence of his creation. This kingdom will become *a full and visible reality* in "a new heaven and a new earth" at the second coming of our Lord Jesus Christ (Rev. 21:1).

The kingdom of Christ is therefore both *now* and *not yet*. The risen Jesus rules now as mediatorial King in virtue of the fact that his Father-God "put all things under His feet, and gave Him to be head over all things to the church" (Eph. 1:22). Jesus's rule over everything subserves his saving purposes. In the fullness of time, at Jesus's second coming, "Then comes the end, when He delivers the kingdom to God the Father, when He puts an end to all rule and all authority and power" (1 Cor. 15:24).

Meanwhile, as we await Jesus's return and the complete unfolding of the kingdom of heaven spoken about in Zechariah 9:10, there is *work* to be done. The Church (i.e., the body of believers) is the visible expression and the vanguard of Christ's kingdom. As such the Church operates in a world filled with spiritual and moral darkness. That kingdom of darkness persists also in the hearts of people until and unless they are saved. Its baleful work continues until its destruction at Christ's second coming. The period between the first and second comings of Christ is the arena for the clash of "the prince of this world" and the Prince of Peace (John 12:31; 14:30; 16:11; Eph. 2:2). Zechariah 10 tells us how we can have strength enough to live and serve the Lord in the work of his kingdom in this difficult world.

Strength is needed.

The assumption behind the instruction, "Ask the Lord for rain," is that we cannot snap our fingers and produce the goods. In ourselves we are not equal to the task of the work of God's kingdom.

We are weak in many ways.

Philip Henry, father of the more famous Matthew, has a quaint, but touching, sermon on Philippians 4:13, "I can do all things through Christ who strengthens me." He speaks of our universal weakness and says, "We are all over weak. I mean in the inner man; spiritually weak." Then he goes on to show that we are weak in various aspects of our character and our carriage. We are weak in the *head*; our understanding is dull and our thoughts of low quality. We are weak in the *heart*, in that we love our ignorance, and worse, we cling to our dearest sins. We are weak in our *hands*:

> The hand is the part that we hold with, when we have received. Suppose a man taking hold of Christ, good hold, justifying hold, saving hold, can he keep that hold by any strength of his own? No, he cannot... [only] as Christ is his strength. He is weak.[2]

We are also weak, he says, in the *back and shoulders*; we cannot bear either the cross or our afflictions. We are weak in the *feet*; we neither stand fast in the faith (Phil. 4:1), nor do we walk in the Spirit, but we "stumble at straws." We are slow, and we tire easily.

All this is not exactly flattering. There is not much here for the self-esteem the world loves to conjure up for itself. Worldly wisdom tells us incessantly that we need to "believe in ourselves," as if all we need is hiding inside us waiting for discovery. But the lie in such claims is only too obvious in human experience in the real world. Jesus tells the truth when he says, "without Me you can do nothing" (John 15:5). Jesus's followers know this is true. We certainly have our weaknesses and must unashamedly confess our need of strength from outside ourselves.

What can we do about our weaknesses?

Two things must be done, says Zechariah: ask the Lord to help you and avoid false teaching and teachers like the plague.

Ask the Lord for help without reserve. The illustration is beautiful: "Ask the LORD for rain in the time of the latter rain" (Zech. 10:1). The idea is that he will give more rain than we ask for, with the result that there will be "grass in the field for everyone." When receiving blessing, ask for even more. The Lord is not some celestial Scrooge. Paul will later write that the Lord "is able to do exceedingly abundantly above all that we ask or think, according to the power that works in us" (Eph. 3:20).

Our awareness of personal weakness should send us post haste to the throne of grace for "grace to help in time of need" (Heb. 4:16). So ask him. Seek him in prayer—personally and from the heart—in the spirit of Jacob at Peniel, who declared, as he literally wrestled with God, "I will not let You go unless You bless me!" (Gen. 32:26).

Avoid the false shepherds most intentionally. Zechariah is asking the post-exilic returned remnant of Judah: "What did idols, diviners, and dreams get you?" The answer is that they wandered like sheep "in trouble because there is no shepherd" (Zech. 10:2). They reaped as they had sown. If you do not listen to God, you are already listening to the wrong people. Confusion is the currency of itching ears (2 Tim. 4:3–4). Believing anything false is bound to hurt you sooner or later.

The language of lost and straying sheep is, of course, integral to the language of the gospel of Christ.

- Isaiah 53:6—"All we like sheep have gone astray; we have turned, every one, to his own way; and the LORD has laid on Him [Christ] the iniquity of us all."
- Matthew 9:36—"But when He [Christ] saw the multitudes, He

was moved with compassion for them, because they were weary and scattered, like sheep having no shepherd."

* 1 Peter 2:25—"For you were like sheep going astray, but have now returned to the Shepherd and Overseer of your souls [Christ]."

The Savior we need to save us is the same Savior we need to strengthen us and sanctify us in our lives as his disciples. That Savior is the Christ prophesied by Zechariah and revealed in the gospel.

Strength Is Promised

It takes no genius to grasp that false teaching has been lamentably destructive of many an individual, family, community, church, and state in the course of human history. The love affair of the governing elites of the pseudo-Christian West, in both church and state, with the progressive redefinition of an ever-larger list of manifest immoralities as good is remarkable as it is startling. There is a growing doctrine of toleration that seeks to place these immoralities beyond any criticism. This can and already is leading to personal and societal tragedies as innumerable as they are sadly predictable.

To reverse such woes will take a mighty work of God among us. To be armed against the dangers that threaten us personally will take spiritual discernment to distinguish truth from error and love from and for the Lord Jesus Christ that enables us to cleave to him in the full assurance of a living, saving faith.

Jesus assured Paul, "My grace is sufficient for you, for My strength is made perfect in weakness," and Paul responds, "Therefore most gladly I will rather boast in my infirmities, that the power of Christ may rest upon me" (2 Cor. 12:9). When we trust Christ, we are neither left to ourselves, nor condemned to be the dupes of false teachers and teaching. The Lord promises to be our strength and overcomer of our weaknesses.

God is angry with the shepherds.

"My anger is kindled against the shepherds, and I will punish the goatherds," says the Lord in Zechariah 10:3. There is no clearer or more searching application of this text than the challenge of Brownlow North (1810–75)—the great lay-evangelist of the 1859 revival in Scotland and Ireland—to the "careless, godless ministers" whom he addresses as "hireling shepherds":

> In the name of the Lord Jesus Christ, then once more I say, *Beware!* And may the Lord Jesus Christ forgive you, have mercy on you and turn you. Woe to you if He does not; for I do not believe there exists a more miserable being, even amongst the lost themselves, than a lost minister shut up in hell with his congregation.[3]

To those who are not lost ministers, but are church-going folk to some degree, Bishop J. C. Ryle (1816–1900) has equally trenchant words:

> The saddest road to hell is that which runs under the pulpit, past the Bible, and through the midst of warnings and invitations. Oh, beware, lest like Israel at Kadesh, you mourn over your mistake when it is too late; or, like Judas Iscariot, find out your sin when there is no space for repentance. Arise and call upon the Lord.[4]

False teaching is the cancer of the church, and false teachers are the carcinogens that bid to corrupt and snuff out the lives of God's people. Jesus warns us that "false christs and false prophets will rise and show great signs and wonders to deceive, if possible, even the elect" (Matt. 24:24). False teachers are frequently better scholars—and usually faster more persuasive talkers—than most of the Lord's people. We therefore have a vital need to learn to discern truth from error and so to follow Christ as faithful disciples who take seriously the doctrine of the Holy Scriptures. If God is "angry" with the false shepherds, our first line of defense is to give them and their teaching a wide berth. How this is achieved is now further explained: God will visit his "flock" and he will be with his "mighty men" (vv. 3–5).

God will visit his flock.

Zechariah predicts that "the LORD of hosts will visit His flock, the house of Judah, and will make them as His royal horse in the battle" (v. 3). This recalls the prophet's earlier declaration of God's promise to raise up Zion's sons—against the sons of "Greece" (Zech. 9:13).

The *immediate* reference is to the Maccabean revolt of 167 BC against the Seleucid emperor Antiochus Epiphanes, which was to restore the Jewish state/church until AD 70. The "house of Judah" is Zion—the covenant people, the Jews. As the Lord's "royal horse" ("majestic steed" ESV), they will go forth to the "battle," which includes spiritual as well as physical warfare. The emphasis is on the corporate nature of the covenant people of God. God has not deserted his people. He is bound to them in his covenant of grace. He is determined to have and to save "a people" in this world. Zechariah anticipates what Peter says of the New Testament church:

> You are a chosen generation, a royal priesthood, a holy nation, His own special people, that you may proclaim the praises of Him who called you out of darkness into His marvelous light; who once were not a people but are now the people of God, who had not obtained mercy but now have obtained mercy. (1 Peter 2:9–10)

The *ultimate* reference is accordingly to the coming of the era of the Messiah: "From him comes the cornerstone, from him the tent peg, from him the battle bow, from him every ruler together" (Zech. 10:4). The cornerstone, tent peg, battle bow, and ruler are raised up from the people of God to counter the powers of darkness. Zechariah's language reaches beyond the future earthly rulers of the Jews to none other than the promised Messiah, the Christ, and blends seamlessly into the teaching of Scripture as a whole.

Jesus is the ultimate *cornerstone* of whom the psalmist declares, "The stone which the builders rejected has become the chief cornerstone" (Ps. 118:22; also Isa. 28:16; Matt. 21:42; Acts 4:11; Eph. 2:20; 1 Peter 2:6–7).

Jesus is the ultimate *peg* of our salvation, as Ezra, in his wonderful prayer for the returned exiles from Babylon, employs the bronze pegs that held up the curtains of the Tabernacle in the wilderness as emblematic of salvation by God's free unmerited grace: "And now for a little while grace has been shown from the LORD our God, to leave us a remnant to escape, and to give us a peg in His holy place, that our God may enlighten our eyes and give us a measure of revival in our bondage" (Ezra 9:8; see also Ex. 27:19).

Jesus is the once and final victorious messianic *ruler* prophesied by Micah when he says, "But you, Bethlehem Ephrathah, though you are little among the thousands of Judah, yet out of you shall come forth to Me The One to be Ruler in Israel, whose goings forth are from of old, from everlasting" (Mic. 5:2). The baby of Bethlehem is Jesus the Christ, the Lamb who wins the battle over sin and the grave with the kings and the beast (Rev. 17:12–14). Zechariah's prophecy ultimately points to the crucified and risen Jesus as the mediatorial King over all of human history and its outcomes for both time and eternity. The apostle John realizes with dismay that humanity is incapable of saving itself, but records that: "One of the elders said to me, 'Do not weep. Behold, the Lion of the tribe of Judah, the Root of David, has prevailed to open the scroll and to loose its seven seals'" (Rev. 5:5). Jesus is the ruler to end all rulers.

God will be with his mighty men.

The rulers that God will raise up from a reviving Israel "shall be like mighty men" and "shall fight because the LORD is with them," with the result that "the riders on horses shall be put to shame" (Zech. 10:5). Once again, the immediate reference is to the defeat of the Seleucids by the Maccabees some four centuries after Zechariah's time. T. V. Moore reminds us, however, that

> these temporal blessings of the Theocracy...symbolize the higher blessings of the Church, whose triumph is bloodless and tearless, and whose strength is that of the spirit, mighty to the pulling down of strongholds, and the subduing of principalities and powers. (compare with 2 Cor. 10:4 and Eph. 6:12)[5]

This word is ultimately the promise to the church militant that she will prevail in the era of the Messiah. That is, in the time between the first and second comings of Christ, the time in which we presently live. This promise of strength from the Lord stands for every generation of his people from the first Pentecost until the last trumpet. Human history unfolds under the sovereign superintendence of the risen Christ in the interest of his Church, for God "put all things under His feet, and gave Him to be head over all things to the church, which is His body, the fullness of Him who fills all in all" (Eph. 1:22–23).

Strength Is Provided

God's promises are always backed by his powerful provision. Zechariah points to three ways in which the Lord will extend and impart his enabling strength to his faithful people. He does this by revitalizing churches, restoring backsliders, and evangelizing lost people.

God strengthens the church as a body.

The work of God's grace in the church will be observed, experienced, and enjoyed congregation by congregation and believer by believer. God says: "I will strengthen the house of Judah, and I will save the house of Joseph....Those of Ephraim shall be like a mighty man." Judah and even the long-lost northern kingdom of Israel will experience a genuine revival and restoration.[6] The faithful remnant will see good things happening and will see the mercy of God in answered prayers, and "their heart shall rejoice as if with wine. Yes, their children shall see it and be glad; their heart shall rejoice in the LORD" (Zech. 10:6–7). God's gracious presence can only rejoice those who love him and see his mercies for what they really are. When his appointed means of grace are soundly carried forth in the church, his people will rejoice that God is truly in his holy temple (Hab. 2:20).

God gathers his people to himself.

The church will grow and the backsliders will return. God says, "I will whistle for them and gather them, for I will redeem them; and they shall increase as they once increased" (Zech. 10:8). The "whistle" may refer to the Middle East equivalent of our hello or our familiar whistle that calls someone's attention to ourselves.[7] It has even been suggested that this alludes to the practice of beekeepers in ancient times who made certain sounds to induce swarming bees to land in a particular hive. In any event, the idea is simple. As Isaiah states it, "He will lift up a banner to the nations from afar, and will whistle to them from the end of the earth; surely they shall come with speed, swiftly" (Isa. 5:26).

God sends his people out to the nations and gathers them again.

The message will go out to the world with those the Lord "will sow…among the peoples, and they shall remember Me in far countries; They shall live, together with their children, And they shall return" (Zech. 10:9). The Maccabean fulfillment cannot exhaust the scope of this prophecy, even though "the pride of Assyria" and "the scepter of Egypt shall depart" (vv. 10–11). This surely prefigures the gospel of the coming Messiah, the evangelization of the world, and the final consummation of God's plan of salvation in the New Testament era.

All of this underlines our perennial need of a strength that is not our own, even if we are, by the world's reckoning, strong characters. There is no doubt that the apostle Paul was a man of strong and single-minded character. This was true when he hated Christ and persecuted his followers. But then he neither recognized his true weakness, nor understood the paradox in the true strength of the Christians he so despised. The Lord however taught him through his trials, both external and internal, that his weaknesses were real, and that self-reliance was an illusory source of real staying power. This brought him to a place of confessing freely: "Therefore I take pleasure in infirmities, in reproaches, in needs, in persecutions, in distresses, for Christ's sake. For when I am weak, then I am strong." The Lord makes his strength complete in our weakness (2 Cor. 12:9–10).

Christ Must Be Your Strength

However great the promises of God and the glory of the stated provision of his power to sustain us, there remains the question of our conscious appropriation of his enabling grace. Charles Simeon notes that "In ourselves, we remain as weak as ever." Becoming a Christian does not magically invest us with superpowers so that, like mild-mannered Clark Kent, we only need to duck behind a tree for a quick wardrobe change before zooming off as Superman to fight for "Truth, Justice, and the American Way!"

The strength of a Christ-centered life.

The most important words in Zechariah 10:12 are the words "in His name." This is the essential component of true faith and true obedience to God. Notice that God is here talking to himself in our hearing, solemnly committing himself to his purpose of grace for our lives: "So I [God] will strengthen them [you believers] in the LORD [God]." Remember, however, that the triune God is speaking here. The New Testament, as we have seen, makes it clear that it is God the Son incarnate, the Lord Jesus Christ, through whom the strength is given, and that the Holy Spirit seals this strength to the believer. That is just to say that God the Father dispenses strength to those who truly believe in God the Son (Christ) as their Savior, and that this is effected by the ministry of God the Holy Spirit in the believer's heart.[8] The words "in His name" emphasize the vital role of *personal commitment* in the matter of receiving strength from the Lord.

In the fullness of the New Testament, this is a trinitarian experience of God and his grace. And it centers in the cross of the Son whom God sent out of his great love to be the Savior of sinners. Christ secures our salvation by his death and resurrection and the supply of God's strength for our ongoing weakness. Christ can be and must be the strength of each and every one of God's people. Here is the only possible source of the true strength we need both to be saved and to live our salvation. Our "walk" is not a merely moral exercise—deciding what is right from what is wrong—but an intimate engagement with Christ in both "the power of His resurrection and the fellowship of His suffering" by already "being conformed to His death" (Phil. 3:10). This is union and communion with Christ experienced and applied in fighting "the good fight of faith" (1 Tim. 6:12). Jesus's "yoke is easy and [His] burden is light," but that does not mean we can ever go at it alone in our Christian discipleship (see Matt. 11:28–30). Sin's yoke is difficult and its burdens heavy. Jesus lightens the load.

The fruit of a Christ-centered life.

Those whom the Lord strengthens will "walk up and down in His name" (Zech. 10:12). Too many think they are Christians, and therefore right with God, because they say so or said so on some occasion in the past. *Walk* is vastly more than *talk*. In fact, our walk is the only evidence that our talk has any credibility. The believer in Christ not only has a heart desire for personal godliness, but actually experiences the Lord's enabling grace and power in the transformation of heart, mind, and actions.

Jesus tells us how to discern his true followers from the false: "You will know them by their fruits. Do men gather grapes from thornbushes or figs from thistles?" (Matt. 7:16). This test must be equally applied to ourselves. There is nothing shallow about a true commitment to Christ; "all things have become new" and that is because "if anyone is in Christ, he is a new creation" (2 Cor. 5:17). Since this is so, the fruit and evidence of a saving knowledge of Jesus cannot but be as visible and observable, as are the thorns and thistles of the unconverted and the hypocrite. What is the fruit in your life? Do you who profess Christ sincerely, heartily, clearly, and observably "walk up and down in His name" in the daily course of your life? The evidence of a saving interest in Christ in Paul's life ought to be the most powerful encouragement to every Christian, young or old, struggling or assured. After all the twists and turns and challenges in his life, he tells us with humble confidence, "I can do all things through Him who strengthens me" (Phil. 4:13).

The enjoyment of a Christ-centered life.

In what vein will we advance in the strength of the Lord? The psalmist's answer is full of joy: "I will go in the strength of the Lord GOD; I will make mention of Your righteousness, of Yours only...My lips shall greatly rejoice when I sing to You, and my soul, which You have redeemed." It is also significant that he closes his song with the commitment that his "tongue also shall talk of Your righteousness all the day long" (Ps. 71:16, 23–24).

The joy of the Christian is to walk with Christ in actual obedience to his will for living as his disciple. Some will ask, "How can this be?" Paul answers so simply yet profoundly that "it is God who works in you both to will and to do for His good pleasure" (Phil. 2:13). His pleasure must surely be joy and satisfaction for the Christian. Matthew Henry has a beautiful comment on the eighth verse of Psalm 40:

> *I delight to do thy will, O my God!* It was to Christ his meat and drink to go on with the work appointed to him (Jn. 4:34); and the reason here

> given is, *Thy law is within my heart*; it is written there, it rules there. It is meant of the law concerning the work and office of the Mediator, what he was to do and suffer; this law was dear to him and had an influence upon him in his whole undertaking. Note, When the law of God is written in our hearts our duty will be our delight.[9]

Let us go forth in the strength of the Lord, praying and praising as we work: "O LORD, be gracious to us; we have waited for You. Be [our] arm every morning, our salvation also in the time of trouble" (Isa. 33:2). And let us not merely pray "about" something without doing anything. *Ora et labora:* pray as you work, as you step out in faith. The glory of the gospel is that it is "the power of God to salvation for everyone who believes, for the Jew first and also for the Greek" (Rom. 1:16). This is so because, as Peter proclaims, "Him [Jesus] God has exalted to His right hand to be Prince and Savior, to give repentance to Israel and forgiveness of sins" (Acts 5:31). This is so because Christ, who is "just and having salvation," is able to save we sinners and forever after be Christ our strength (Zech. 9:9).

Jesus Is Our

Sun

But to you who fear My name, the Sun of Righteousness
shall arise with healing in His wings.
—Malachi 4:2

READ MALACHI 4

One winter in this writer's Scottish teaching career, we had over a month of unbroken gray, sunless days. It was January, so it was dark when the students got to school, almost dark when they headed for home, and fairly dark in between. Everyone became observably listless as one dull week succeeded another. There were no discipline problems. Classes were lifeless. Then one day things changed. The banner headline in the *Edinburgh Evening News* that day declared in huge block capitals: "SUN SIGHTED!" Blood stirred in the veins and life began to return to some normality.

There can be very dark days in the spiritual experience of God's people. The light of a new day seems impossibly remote. Sorrows close in and bid to blot out all our hopes. You may have asked yourself, "Will there be light at the end of this tunnel? Will there ever be a fresh dawning of God's light and favor and joy?" The prophet Malachi spoke to God's people at a dark time in their history. The Old Testament Church had become corrupt and backslidden, very much like many modern churches. Those that truly "feared the Lord" were a remnant, hoping against hope for a better day, a day of real revival, a new day of blessing at the Lord's right hand (Mal. 3:16). They would readily have identified with the martyrs "under the altar" who cry out, "How long, O Lord, holy and true...?" (Rev. 6:9–10). Perhaps you have sometimes prayed such a prayer yourself.

The answer of God's Word is, in one name, Christ! Christ is our light at the end of the tunnel. Christ is our dawn. Christ is our sun of healing righteousness. Christ is our Savior. In his light we see light (Ps. 36:9). He is our light in the tunnel and he lights up our way even "unto the perfect day" (Prov. 4:18). As Malachi speaks of the "Sun of Righteousness" he uses the metaphor to tell us three things we need to grasp about him: Jesus is the *sun*, he is the Sun of *Righteousness*, and he has *healing* for those whom he saves.

Jesus Is the Sun

The prophet said that a time was coming when "the Sun of Righteousness shall arise." What does the sun in our solar system do for us every morning? It does at least two things:

The sun dispels the darkness of the preceding night. Notice the context in Malachi; he prophecies in the days of Nehemiah to a corrupt church with corrupt clergymen and corrupted members, and predicts the future destruction of Jerusalem and the end of the old order. The downside is dark indeed. But light is coming, because this Sun of Righteousness also rises.

The sun warms the land, gives life to the vegetation, and spurs activity in living organisms. Here is the upside. The Sun of Righteousness heralds the coming of a new age, of good news, and reveals a Savior who can be likened to the sun in the sky.

What is Malachi saying? Just this: that a Savior is to *arise* one day. Charles Simeon has a comment that is as lovely as it is sound. "Christ," he says, "is 'the Sun' of the spiritual world, and the one fountain of light and life to all that believe in him."[1] As you will have noted already in these present studies, Jesus identifies himself as "the true light" and "the light of the world" (John 1:9; 8:12). How then may he be said to be the "sun," as distinct from the "light"? The metaphor suggest several ways:

As the sun rises each day and *dispels the darkness* of the night, so Christ has risen from the dead to conquer death and the grave (Ps. 18:28). Light dies with the departing day, as life departs with death. The sun evokes the miracle of resurrection. This applies to the dead soul made alive in Christ and to the dead body raised to life in the last day when Christ comes.

As the sun rises and *warms the earth*, so Christ as the sun warms the coldness of hearts, making stony hearts into hearts of flesh (Ezek. 36:26; Ps. 119:11). Unaware at the time that Jesus was the one speaking with them, his companions on the road to Emmaus later testify, "Did not our heart burn within us while He talked with us on the road, and while He opened the Scriptures to us?" (Luke 24:32).

As the sun *reveals the scene* before us each morning, so Christ as the sun causes light to dawn in dull minds (Ps. 119:105). We constantly need light, even in the most mundane matters of each day: "The entrance of Your words gives light; it gives understanding to the simple" (Ps. 119:130).

As the sun is the *dependable, life-sustaining source* of heat and light for our world, so Christ as our sun is faithful, "the same yesterday, today, and forever" (Heb. 13:8).

For whom is Jesus the sun? Speaking from very dark days for God's people, the prophet Malachi records the response of those who loved the Lord and were looking for a new dawn,

> Then those who feared the LORD spoke to one another,
> And the LORD listened and heard them;
> So a book of remembrance was written before Him
> For those who fear the LORD
> And who meditate on His name.

"They shall be Mine," says the LORD of hosts,
"On the day that I make them My jewels.
And I will spare them
As a man spares his own son who serves him."
Then you shall again discern
Between the righteous and the wicked,
Between one who serves God
And one who does not serve Him.
(Mal. 3:16–18)

In Christ, that day has dawned. So it remains until the coming of the perfect day, that last day when he returns to judge the living and dead (Prov. 4:18).

Jesus Is the Sun of Righteousness

Nobody ever objects to the idea that Jesus has light for us. Even those who reject the gospel message with its incarnate divine Son, blood atonement, bodily resurrection, and last judgment, will say nice things about his abilities as a teacher. Some will routinely attribute to Jesus the light they think they have.

But Jesus is too often treated like Christmas lights that are bright, dazzling, pretty, and make us feel good. When expedient, he is frequently appreciated loudly by those who disregard what he actually has said and done. This is standard fare from politicians trying to win votes on the right. This underscores why the qualification "of righteousness" is so essential.

The Christ who is our sun is also our righteousness. He is inseparable from his person and work as revealed in the Scriptures. To believers, he is made "wisdom from God—and righteousness and sanctification and redemption" (1 Cor. 1:30). This has immense significance for our grasp of who Jesus is and our relationship to what he has done as the Sun of Righteousness.

Jesus is righteousness in himself.

He is the "Branch of righteousness," whom God promised to "grow up to David" and subsequently "execute judgment and righteousness in the earth" (Jer. 33:15). The branch is our "Advocate with the Father, Jesus Christ the righteous" (1 John 2:1).

Jesus is righteousness revealed to the world.

Zacharias, in his prophecy, declares with reference to Christ, "the Dayspring from on high has visited us" (Luke 1:78). Jesus is "the Word" who "was with God...was God...was in the beginning with God... became flesh and dwelt among us" and is revealed to be "the only begotten of the Father, full of grace and truth" (John 1:1–2, 14).

Jesus is righteousness for believers.

He is "the Lord our righteousness" (Jer. 23:6). As we read earlier, Paul assures the believers in Corinth, "But of Him you are in Christ Jesus, who became for us wisdom from God—and righteousness, sanctification and redemption" (1 Cor. 1:30). This was accomplished by his atoning death on the cross, "He [God the Father] made Him who knew no sin [God the Son incarnate] to be sin for us, that we might become the righteousness of God in Him" (2 Cor. 5:21).

Because he is the Sun of Righteousness who saves his people from their sins, then "the path of the righteous is like the light of dawn, which shines brighter and brighter until full day" (Prov. 4:18 ESV).

Jesus Heals His Believing People

God says plainly that the coming of the Sun of Righteousness will have tangible practical benefits for all "who fear My name" (Mal. 4:2). It will, of course, also have terrible consequences for all who do not devote themselves to him. He will render them "stubble" in the day when he will "come and strike the earth with a curse" (Mal. 4:1, 6). The Son who is the Sun of Righteousness will do three things for those who love and follow him.

Jesus gives healing (Mal. 4:2).

He "shall arise with healing in His wings." Here you have the coming of the sun as "the wings of the morning" (Ps. 139:9). The wings are the light and warmth of the sunlight as they embrace us in the dawn.

This is a picture of *conversion to Christ*: "You He made alive who were dead in trespasses and sins" (Eph. 2:1). I once spent a night sleeping in the open in Adana, Turkey. Even though it was not frigid weather, the warmth of the sun that morning is unforgettably imprinted in memory. The Lord finds sinners cold, numb, inactive, shivering, depressed, and dead, and he shines his healing light abroad in their hearts to revive and to renew and to redeem. Coming to Jesus in saving faith is a kind of resurrection in which a new warmth courses through a body hitherto in the grip of a cold deadness.

This is also a picture of *sustaining grace*:

> How precious is Your lovingkindness, O God! Therefore the children of men put their trust under the shadow of Your wings. They are abundantly satisfied with the fullness of Your house, and you give them drink from the river of Your pleasures. For with you is the fountain of life; in Your light we see light. (Ps. 36:7–9)

Jesus came to "baptize you with the Holy Spirit and fire," and that Spirit is the Comforter, "the Spirit of truth [who]...dwells with you and will be in you" (Matt. 3:11; John 14:16–17).

This is a picture of *transforming power*. We are more than merely cold and hungry. We are sick and in need of healing. This is true of the unconverted. Why did Jesus eat with tax collectors and sinners? His answer is that they needed a physician (Matt. 9:11–13). Peter testifies to his persecutors, "Nor is there salvation in any other, for there is no other name under heaven given among men by which we must be saved" (Acts 4:12). If you are unconverted, you need to be saved: and if you are a believer and are saved already you still need healing daily in your life as a disciple of Christ. The psalmist speaks to believers for their encouragement when he sings, "Who forgives all your iniquities, who heals all your diseases" (Ps. 103:1–3).

Jesus gives healthy growth (Mal. 4:2).

The fruit and evidence of healing—that is, of a saving knowledge of Christ—is that "you shall go out and grow fat like stall-fed calves."

To "go out" is to live as those who are healed and all to the glorious purpose of Christ for your life, for, as Peter says, "you are a chosen generation, a royal priesthood, a holy nation, His own special people, that you may proclaim the praises of Him who called you out of darkness into His marvelous light" (1 Peter 2:9).

To "grow fat" is to grow in grace and prosper, as opposed to wasting away through what ailed you hitherto. Sin is a wasting disease. Over against that, the evidence of really being saved is spiritual health that is observable, verifiable, and therefore credible. This is what Scripture calls the fruit of the Spirit, which is the Holy Spirit's work in the heart and life of the Christian:

> The fruit of the Spirit is love, joy, peace, patience, kindness, goodness, faithfulness, gentleness, self-control; against such things there is no law. And those who belong to Christ Jesus have crucified the flesh with its passions and desires. If we live by the Spirit, let us also keep in step with the Spirit. (Gal. 5:22–25 ESV)

There is more. When the prophet says that God's children will be "like stall-fed calves," he emphasizes that there will be quick progress in grace. "The trees of the LORD are watered abundantly, the cedars of Lebanon that he planted" (Ps. 104:16 ESV).

Jesus gives victory to believers (Mal. 4:3).

The good news of the gospel is bad news for those who steadfastly reject God and his Christ. Charles Wesley, in his famous carol, "Hark! The Herald Angels Sing," declares:

Glory to the newborn King!
  Peace on earth and mercy mild
God and sinners reconciled.

Here is the glorious call and promise of the gospel of Christ. But what if God and some sinners are not reconciled? God is not a universalist. He is full of grace, "keeping mercy for thousands, forgiving iniquity and transgression and sin," but "by no means clearing the guilty, visiting the iniquity of the fathers upon the children and the children's children to the third and the fourth generation" (Ex. 34:7). The victory of Christ heralds the defeat of his enemies, which includes those of his people (outwardly) who are really his enemies (inwardly). Failure to heed the gospel call has results every bit as predictable as those promised to all who come to Jesus and are reconciled to God.

Malachi completes the picture of the blessedness of salvation in the lives of the believing people of God by setting out how the victory of the Sun of Righteousness impacts both the elect and the reprobate. Speaking to the children of God, he says: " 'You shall trample the wicked, for they shall be ashes under the soles of your feet on the day that I do this,' says the LORD of hosts" (Mal. 4:3). Three things will happen as human history draws to its consummation:

* The wicked will not prevail over Christ's cause, kingdom, and people, but will be vanquished forever (v. 3a).
* The church will be vindicated as the wicked become "ashes under the soles of your feet" (v. 3b). Paul says, "the saints will judge the world" (1 Cor. 6:2).
* This will happen on a day of God's appointment and will be seen clearly to be God's doing (Mal. 4:3cd; Rev. 6:17).

> Then the King will say to those on His right hand, "Come, you blessed of My Father, inherit the kingdom prepared for you from the foundation of the world:"...Then He will also say to those on the left hand, "Depart from Me, you cursed, into the everlasting fire prepared for the devil and his angels." (Matt. 25:34, 41)

This last great Day is coming. In one sense it is "now," even though it is "not yet," for each person's day of reckoning is his day of judgment (small "d") and Christ is dealing with each one of us purposefully through all our days. Your world will end quite soon and your eternal destiny will be sealed by your relationship to God in Jesus Christ.

Is he your sun, your righteousness, and your healing? Then his promise for you is glory forever in heaven, where there will be "no need of the sun or of the moon to shine in it, for the glory of God illuminated it. The Lamb is its light" (Rev. 21:23). The Sun of Righteousness will shine forever, and in him "the righteous will shine forth as the sun in the kingdom of their Father. He who has ears to hear, let him hear!" (Matt. 13:43).

Jesus Is Our

Temple

But I saw no temple in it, for the Lord God almighty and the Lamb are its temple.
—Revelation 21:22

READ REVELATION 21

In his epic canvas, "The Plains of Heaven," John Martin[1] imagines the scene on that great day at the end of history when the saints will see "the holy city, New Jerusalem, coming down out of heaven from God, prepared as a bride adorned for her husband" (Rev. 21:2). The city itself is hardly discernable in the blaze of light that fills the sky in the picture. This echoes something of the careful way the Bible handles the ineffable character of the event. It reaches back to Ezekiel's prophecy, where the prophet is taken in "visions of God" to "a very high mountain," of which it is said that "on it toward the south was something like the structure of a city" (Ezek. 40:2). It also recalls Isaiah's vision of "The City of the Lord" (Isa. 60:14, 19–20), which has clear parallels with Revelation 21:22–27:

> But I saw no temple in it, for the Lord God Almighty and the Lamb are its temple. The city had no need of the sun or of the moon to shine in it, for the glory of God illuminated it. The Lamb is its light. And the nations of those who are saved shall walk in its light, and the kings of

> the earth bring their glory and honor into it. Its gates shall not be shut at all by day (there shall be no night there). And they shall bring the glory and the honor of the nations into it. But there shall by no means enter it anything that defiles, or causes an abomination or a lie, but only those who are written in the Lamb's Book of Life.

This city—and the new heavens and the new earth as a whole—is a picture of the final destiny of God's people. It represents the glory of the age to come and what it will be like when Christ returns. It is, however, not all future or only future, for it is also a picture of what the church already is and what it is progressively becoming. We, the people of God here and now, are "God's building" (1 Cor. 3:9). Christ came and lived amongst us. He died upon the cross and rose again, victorious over sin and the grave. He subsequently sent the Holy Spirit to live within all who are saved by grace through faith in Christ and transform them after the image of the One who has created them (Col. 3:10).

We who are alive today are living between the first and second advents of Christ. This is the era of the New Testament age, often called "the last days" (Acts 2:17; 2 Tim. 3:1; Heb. 1:2; Jas. 5:3; 2 Peter 3:3). "The city shown her," writes Michael Wilcock, "is what we shall be in the age to come, what in a sense we already are…and what in our earthly experience God is presently making of us."[2] Bearing this general perspective in mind, let us look at one remarkable reality about this city, this bride of Christ, namely, that it has no temple. The obvious question is, "Why no temple?"

Why No Temple?

First we must ask why there was a temple in the life of Old Testament Israel in the first place. The answer is that this was the physical place where God chose to presence himself with his people and where they were to gather to meet with him, to offer sacrifices for sin, to worship him as a people, and to seek his will. Here are some pertinent Scriptures:

* 1 Kings 6:11–13: God says, "I will dwell among the children of Israel."
* 2 Chronicles 5:14: God manifested himself visibly, "for the glory of the Lord, filled the house of God."
* 1 Samuel 4:4: God describes himself as "the Lord of hosts, who dwells between the cherubim."
* 2 Chronicles 7:12: God assures his people, "I have heard your prayer and have chosen this place for Myself as a house of sacrifice."

The temple is where God hears his people and answers their prayers. That is why Daniel turns toward Jerusalem when he prays (Dan. 6:10). This is, however, not a reason for us to look to Jerusalem today. In fact, we today must *never* look to Jerusalem in the way the Old Testament saints did for reasons Scripture makes plain.

God and the Lamb are the temple.

In Jesus Christ, the temple and its sacrifices are *superseded*. Any idea of "the Holy Land" and "the Holy Places" is therefore no better than a superstition. Why? Because all of this in the Old Testament era pointed ahead to the coming Messiah, Jesus Christ, and his perfect holiness. The holiness of the land and the temple was not in the things themselves, but in the God who revealed himself in and through them. This is why in the New Testament gospel era there are no more animal sacrifices and there is no place for external ritualism. The ceremonies of the temple are now "weak and beggarly elements" and therefore completely obsolete (Gal. 4:9).

In Jesus Christ our temple, the "new covenant" is *fully revealed* (compare Jeremiah 31:31ff. with Hebrews 8:8, 13 and 12:24). Here is what God says through Jeremiah:

> But this is the covenant that I will make with the house of Israel after those days, says the Lord, I will put my law in their minds, and right

> it on their hearts: and I will be their God, and they shall be My people. (Jer. 31:33)

Gone are the days of "smells and bells" and types and shadows. Gone should be all suggestions that the temple in Jerusalem be rebuilt and the sacrifices reinstituted. It is not for nothing that God has allowed the Muslims to erect the Dome of the Rock and the Al-Aqsa Mosque on the Temple Mount in AD 705. This is not the first time in history that God has used his enemies to teach his people some serious truth.[3]

Jesus is the risen and final temple.

The essential reason for this is that Jesus Christ is the *risen temple*. You may remember his words in John 2:19, "Destroy this temple and in three days I will raise it up." Jesus is both temple and sacrifice.

In his death and resurrection, he is the last once-for-all sacrifice and therefore the last once-and-forever temple. That is why God let the Romans destroy the Old Testament Temple in AD 70 and why any thoughts of rebuilding it and reviving the animal sacrifices ought to be banished from our minds as constituting nothing less than a denial of the cross. The cross is the last and only sufficient sacrifice, and Christ, as the one-and-only Savior, is the final and eternal temple.

How Is Jesus Our Temple?

The temple in the Old Testament was the one and only place of mediation between God and man. Only there, by God's appointed priest employing God's appointed means, did God accept sacrifices for sin and so mediate his grace and forgiveness of sin to his people. The provision of salvation was vested in the ceremonial system that was observed in the temple.

In the succeeding ages and in heaven itself there is no temple with its sacrifices because "the Lord God almighty and the Lamb are its temple."

God, who both requires and accepts sacrifices, is at the heart of the Jerusalem Temple. He is still the one who requires and accepts sacrifice in the heavenly temple. In this sense he *is* the temple, its meaning and its embodiment. How then does Jesus become our temple? The answer is that he is the Mediator whose sacrifice bridges the gap between the holy God and the unholy sinner. He offers the acceptable sacrifice.

Christ is the one and only Mediator.

"There is one God and one Mediator between God and men, the Man Christ Jesus, who gave Himself a ransom for all, to be testified in due time" (1 Tim. 2:5–6). In him we have "one Lord, one faith, one baptism" (Eph. 4:4–6). As the temple was unique in its day, so Jesus is the unique living temple in our time, in the primary sense that he came for the precise purpose of fulfilling all the promises of the Old Testament Temple. He did so by being the true, final, and effectual go-between for God and humanity: "For the law appoints as high priests men who have weakness, but the word of the oath,[4] which came after the law, appoints the Son who has been perfected forever" (Heb. 7:28).

Christ is the one and only Savior.

Christ is accordingly revealed by God "exalted to His right hand to be Prince and Savior, to give repentance to Israel and forgiveness of sins" (Acts 5:31). He is *the only Savior* who is able to save sinners and who actually does save his people from their sins (Matt. 1:21). This is accomplished by his sufferings and death upon a cross: " 'And I, if I am lifted up from the earth, will draw all peoples to Myself.' This He said, signifying by what death He would die" (John 12:32–33).

Christ is given the title "Lamb of God" because he is the *sacrifice* whose *blood* cleanses from all sin. We are saved "with the precious blood of Christ, as of a lamb without blemish and without spot" (1 Peter 1:19). He is "the Holy One," promised in the Old Testament, who in virtue of the purity and efficacy of his sacrifice does not "see corruption" (Acts 13:35; quoting Ps. 16:10). This is the great exchange of the gospel; God "made Him who knew no sin to be sin for us, that we might become the righteousness of God in Him" (2 Cor. 5:21).

Christ is therefore the giver of everlasting life. He says, "I am the way, the truth, and the life" (John 14:6). "And so it is written, 'The first man Adam became a living being.' The last Adam became a life-giving spirit" (1 Cor. 15:45). When we believe in Christ for who he is and what he has done in his death and resurrection, we receive his life in place of our death: "Coming to Him as to a living stone, rejected indeed by men, but chosen by God and precious, you also, as living stones, are being built up a spiritual house, a holy priesthood, to offer up spiritual sacrifices acceptable to God through Jesus Christ" (1 Peter 2:4–5).

This new life is now and ongoing, because Jesus is building his people up both individually and corporately. We, "hav[e] been built on the foundation of the apostles and prophets, Jesus Christ Himself being the chief cornerstone, in whom the whole building, being fitted together, grows into a holy temple in the Lord, in whom you also are being built together for a dwelling place of God in the Spirit" (Eph. 2:20–22). In Christ our temple, we who are his are made temples of the Holy Spirit ourselves—one by one as individual disciples and together as his body the church. Christian, "Do you not know that you are the temple of God and that the Spirit of God dwells in you?" and "that your body is the temple of the Holy Spirit who is in you, whom you have from God, and you are not your own?" (1 Cor. 3:16; 6:19). "Therefore, if anyone is in Christ," 2 Corinthians 5:17 says, "he is a new creation; old things have passed away; behold, all things have become new." In other words, be what you are in Christ. Live like the new creations Jesus has made you.

It Is All about the Gospel

Every word-picture of Jesus in Scripture, whether metaphor, simile, type, office, or allusion, is designed to reveal more of his character as the only Savior of sinners, proclaim the good news of salvation, and apply the truth as it is in Jesus to our spiritual needs and eternal destiny (Eph. 4:21). They invite us to ask ourselves leading questions about our relationship to him and, in and through him as the Mediator, with his God and Father.

These smaller vignettes combine into a larger canvas of Christ as the "beloved" who "is white and ruddy, chief among ten thousand," and of whom it can be said, "His mouth is most sweet, yes, he is altogether lovely. This is my beloved, and this is my friend, O daughters of Jerusalem!" (Song 5:10, 16). Everything about Jesus calls us with warmth and urgency to embrace him as "the Beloved" who is "a friend who sticks closer than a brother" (Eph. 1:6; Prov. 18:24). So here are some vital questions.

Trusting in Jesus?

Are you actively *trusting* in Jesus day by day? Do you know the Lord Jesus Christ as your Savior? Not, do you accept there was a Jesus who lived long ago and was a good teacher? Not, did you "accept" him in your youth at a rally or by praying a prayer, but he makes little or no difference in your life? Many treat Jesus and "faith" like a fire-insurance policy kept in a drawer or in a back pocket of the mind, where it can always be dug out if there is a crisis.

It has to be said that such lives are not transformed and such "converts" are not converted. You need to know Jesus personally and experientially, in your heart, and you should not rest until this is an assured reality in your soul. And you need to be following him in the obedience of faith.

So ask yourself, "Do I have faith in Christ and in his finished work?" Trust in Jesus as your atonement for sin. Commit your whole life to him in the obedience of faith. Live out of his perfect righteousness. If you are not personally and practically a disciple of Jesus, where is the evidence that you are Christian at all? The fruit of a saving knowledge of Jesus, or the lack of such fruit, is not so mysterious that we cannot discern if it is in our own lives (see Matt. 5:1–16; Gal. 5:19–26). But we must come to him in saving faith if we are to "have life, and...have it more abundantly" (John 10:10).

Rejoicing in the Lord?

Are you rejoicing in the Lord day by day? Not just generally happy, but happy "in the Lord" consciously and conscientiously. Our calling is to "rejoice in the Lord always" (Phil. 4:4). Psalm 146:5 says, "*Happy* is he who has the God of Jacob for his help, whose hope is in the LORD his God" (author's emphasis). The real Christian has a lot to be happy about, notwithstanding the troubles in this fallen world. Christians should be the happiest people in the world. They have everything to live for presently and an eternal glory for which to die in the future. And we can say with Paul, without the slightest taint of a morbid attitude, "For to me, to live is Christ, and to die is gain" (see Phil. 1:21–26).

Hoping for heaven?

Are you hoping for glory? Many professed Christians think little about heaven, and if they do they often have strangely sentimental views of it. They imagine reunion with a spouse so that their married life will be renewed and they will continue eternally as a nuclear family in a home that needs no maintenance and in bodies forever young and healthy. Never mind what Jesus actually says in Matthew 22:30: "For in the resurrection they neither marry nor are given in marriage, but are like angels of God in heaven."

So many people seem to want a heaven that preserves their middle-class lifestyle from this world into the next—minus, needless to say, the disabilities and disagreeable people of the present time. But is heaven just a sanitized version of this world? Here is something of what God tells us in his Word:

> The city had no need of the sun or of the moon to shine in it, for the glory of God illuminated it. The Lamb is its light. And the nations of those who are saved shall walk in its light, and the kings of the earth bring their glory and honor into it. Its gates shall not be shut at all by day (there shall be no night there). And they shall bring the glory and the honor of the nations into it. But there shall by no means enter it anything that defiles, or causes an abomination or a lie, but only those who are written in the Lamb's Book of Life. (Rev. 21:23–27)

The sheer majesty of the language indicates that "the glory that will be revealed" in heaven is of an order vastly above anything we have ever seen in our fallen world (1 Peter 5:1). The point is that, whatever heaven may look like, it is *glorious*, and that sets our hope on a higher plane than any we might entertain for the greatest of blessings on this side of eternity. Do you actively hope for that day when you will depart this scene to be present with the Lord? Can you be excited with Paul when he testifies, "We are confident, yes, well pleased rather to be absent from the body and to be present with the Lord" (2 Cor. 5:8). Heaven is not "Plan B" for those who love the Lord, as if heaven can only be a kind of demotion after the loss of this world. For you who love Jesus, he is, "Christ in you, the hope of glory" (Col. 1:27). The realization of that hope is simply glory itself.

Living life in Christ?

Are you living life in a risen Savior together with the people of God? When Paul asks us all, "Do *you* not know that *you* are the temple of God and that the Spirit of God dwells in *you*?" his every "you" is a plural (1 Cor. 3:16, author's emphasis). He is not addressing us as individuals, but as the fellowship of the church of which we are an organic part. This is as searching as it is significant. If you respond to this individualistically and you are one of the many people who think they are Christians but are not committed to any particular church, then you are missing Paul's point. If you are not involved in body-life activities in a congregation, like a prayer meeting or a Bible study group, and perhaps even do not attend church, you may well be deceiving yourself as to your walk with the Lord. The "you" that is the temple of the Holy Spirit in this verse is the body of Christ in the sense of the local congregation where you are a member together with other believers (2 Cor. 6:16). Of course it is true that Scripture tells us our physical bodies are individually temples of the Holy Spirit, which is why we are to turn them to godly behavior (1 Cor 6:19). But the touchstone of Paul's teaching is in the corporate dimension of our life in Christ.

If we are indeed Christ's and therefore individually temples of the Holy Spirit, then the first and obvious practical evidence will be our also being living stones in the larger temple of the Holy Spirit. This "temple" is the real church where you worship and serve as a committed member of the body. Why? Because "you have come to Mount Zion and to the city of the living God, the heavenly Jerusalem" (Heb. 12:22–24).

We have come full circle to Jesus our final temple who lives in us by the Holy Spirit and so makes us alive in him as his temples, both individually and together as his church in the world.

How blessed is the person
  Who is Your chosen one,
The one You have brought near You
  And made Your courts his home.
Within Your holy temple
  We will be satisfied,
And filled with all the goodness
  Your holy house provides.[5]

Jesus Is Our

Truth

I am the way, the truth, and the life.
—John 14:6

READ JOHN 8:31–59

The *locus classicus* in which Jesus is identified as "the truth" is John 14:6 where he declares of himself: "I am the way, the truth and the life. No one comes to the Father except through Me." The immediate context is Jesus's prediction of his departure in death on the following day. Thomas's response is to say "Lord, we do not know where you are going, and how can we know the way?" Jesus answers that he is "the way." It is all about following him. The triple theme of "the way, the truth, and the life" gives us Jesus's GPS directions for discipleship; he is the road (way), the guide (truth), and the destination (life). Jesus *is* salvation for lost people: the way, truth, and life.

Our focus in this study is the sense in which Jesus is the truth. He is "the only Son from the Father, full of grace and truth" (John 1:14 ESV). We are also told that while "the law was given by Moses; grace and truth came through Jesus Christ" (v. 17 ESV). Jesus's grace and truth defines salvation and the discipleship that flows from it. He is the truth that guides the new life of faith along the way to glory. For further light on the subject, we turn to John 8:32: "You shall know the truth, and the truth shall make you free."

What Has Jesus Come to Do?

First we must answer some basic questions. To say, "The truth shall make you free," begs the question as to what truth Jesus is talking about. All sorts of people, especially politicians and pundits, love this saying, but they clearly use it of *their* truth, *their* outlook, and *their* view of reality. It is invariably "truth" in the abstract—something "true" in generic terms, as opposed to something "false." No standard is given by which the truth is to be established beyond the notion that it is somehow self-evident and we must have a problem if we cannot see that.[1] Jesus's truth is not a thing in itself in abstraction from God, but the truth of God as revealed by God.

This point is illustrated in the immediate context, where we learn that as Jesus predicted his departure, "many believed in Him" (v. 30). It is clear that while they "believe" in some sense, they have at best a rather vague grasp of who Jesus really is. You can see that there is faith, truth, and freedom here, all tied together. Not any old faith, any old truth, or any old freedom, but God-wrought faith, God-revealed truth, and God-given freedom experienced in the heart and practiced in daily life. The key question then is, What *faith* is necessary to the freedom in the truth that Jesus is talking about? This is where he himself comes in, for Jesus is the truth who sets people free. This just means that Jesus makes free disciples. This is gospel freedom.

To make free by the truth.

Jesus defines the true disciple when he says, "If you abide in My word, you are My disciples indeed. And you shall know the truth, and the truth shall make you free" (vv. 31–32). Notice the parallels in these verses:

TEACHING		DISCIPLES
"abide in My word"	then you are	"My disciples indeed"
KNOW THE TRUTH		FREEDOM
"know the truth"	then this will	"make you free"

Notice that *doctrine grasped* results in *doctrine lived out.* A real believer is a real disciple. A disciple is not a super-believer; every believer is a disciple. Freedom in the truth believed is your Christian experience, as Paul puts it, "if indeed you have heard Him and have been taught by Him, as the truth is in Jesus" (Eph. 4:21).

It is worth noting, in passing, that many today will "accept Jesus" and then go on living as if nothing has happened, but they are subject to the same strictures that Jesus applies to superficial commitments in his own day (compare with John 2:23–24). The issue may be summed up in this way: "So you say you have accepted Jesus? But has Jesus accepted you?" There is more to saving faith than a flutter of emotional or intellectual approval and acceptance of Jesus. You must have a knowledge of his claims about himself, a heart acceptance of these claims for yourself, and a personal trust in him as your Savior and Lord.

To make sons out of slaves.

These "Jews who believed Him" objected: "We are Abraham's descendants, and have never been in bondage to anyone. How can you say, 'You will be made free'?" (John 8:31, 33). Their answer to Jesus is that they are free already as children of Abraham. In other words, "What are you talking about, Jesus? And who do you think you are?" Behind this is at least some awareness that Jesus is claiming that he alone can set sinners free from what ails them.

Jesus's answer does not give away any wiggle room; everyone who commits sin is a "slave of sin" (v. 34). This means that an external relationship to Abraham does not free you from sin. Paul will later point out this universal truth: "Do you not know that to whom you present yourselves slaves to obey, you are that one's slaves whom you obey, whether of sin leading to death, or of obedience leading to righteousness?" (Rom. 6:16). That is why God can say in his Word without the slightest possibility of refutation: "There is none righteous, no, not one" (Rom. 3:10).

The *remedy* is that you need to be a son and not a slave, for "a slave does not abide in the house forever, but a son abides forever" (John 8:35). It is the true children that remain in a "house," in the sense of household or family.[2] God's family is in view and what is crucial is to be a true child of God, united to him through living faith.

In a play on words—from "son" to "the Son"—Jesus drives home his point: "Therefore if the Son makes you free, you shall be free indeed" (v. 36). Jesus is the divine Son, whereas Abraham was not. Jesus is the Messiah come to save sinners. Jesus makes sons of God—by adoption—and it is in this saving work that he confers the true freedom. The apostle Paul describes the work of the Holy Spirit in this connection in terms of the distinction between "the spirit of bondage" and "the Spirit of adoption":

> Therefore, brethren, we are debtors—not to the flesh, to live according to the flesh. For if you live according to the flesh you will die; but if by the Spirit you put to death the deeds of the body, you will live. For as many as are led by the Spirit of God, these are sons of God. For you did not receive the spirit of bondage again to fear, but you received the Spirit of adoption by whom we cry out, "Abba, Father." The Spirit Himself bears witness with our spirit that we are children of God, and if children, then heirs—heirs of God and joint heirs with Christ, if indeed we suffer with Him, that we may also be glorified together. (Rom. 8:12–17)

The dreadful reality is that until and unless we receive the Lord Jesus Christ as our Savior and Lord, we are subject to the "spirit of bondage" and "again to fear." This is more than the unbeliever's own subjective spiritual state. It is a work of God's Spirit in the unbeliever's heart, applying the law of God in such a way as to stir up a nagging and foreboding fear in those who resist and reject the gospel. This is made plain by Jesus when he teaches the disciples about the work of the Holy Spirit: "And when He has come, He will convict the world of sin, and of righteousness, and of judgment: of sin, because they do not believe in Me; of righteousness, because I go to My Father and you see Me no more" (John 16:8–10). Paul describes the condition of the lost who are "in the flesh" as being bound to God's law, in that "the sinful passions that were aroused by the law were at work in our members to bear fruit to death" (Rom. 7:5). God's law dogs the very people who despise it, so that they live their lives in reaction against it. It is from this bondage that Jesus who is the truth sets believers free.

How Is Jesus Able to Set You Free?

You can well imagine the shock and outrage of Jesus's hearers: "How can he say any of Abraham's descendants are not free? Is Abraham of no account? And how can you, Jesus, make true freedom dependent upon you? Who are you to make such claims?" Jesus answers along three lines:

What is your present relationship to God?

Jesus first points to the Jews' true (that is, spiritual) parentage (John 8:37–38). Yes, he knows that they are "Abraham's descendants," but they "seek to kill" him, because, as Jesus confronts them, "My word has no place in you" (v. 37). Jesus's argument is to take them to what they are doing (plotting his death), and to what they are thinking (rejecting his word to them), and then ask what this says about their claim to being the spiritual children of Abraham. The underlying assumption is that our actions will generally reveal our true spiritual paternity. The specific charge is their rejection of the self-revealing and therefore self-evident

Word of God (John 1:1–5, 14–18). If any people should have recognized the Word of God and the promised Messiah, it should have been those sons of Abraham. But "He came to His own, and His own did not receive Him" (v. 11).

Jesus explains that he has spoken "what I have seen with My Father," and adds the clincher, "You do what you have seen with your father" (John 8:38). His implication is inescapable; whatever they may say about Abraham being their father, he and they have different fathers and the patriarch is quite evidently not their father.[3] When the Jews "answered and said to Him, 'Abraham is our father,'" Jesus further pressed his point: "If you were Abraham's children, you would do the works of Abraham" (v. 39). Do they actually *do* what Abraham did? On the contrary, says Jesus, "now you seek to kill Me, a Man who has told you the truth which I heard from God. Abraham did not do this. You do the deeds of your father" (vv. 40–41). Abraham had received both the Lord and his Word (Gen. 12:1, 7; 15:1, 6; 17:1ff.; 18:1ff.). They did neither. Whoever their "father" may be, he is neither Abraham nor Abraham's God.

What is the heart of the problem?

Jesus's hearers are typical. They push back: "We were not born of fornication; we have one Father—God" (John 8:41). They realize that Jesus is saying they are not acting like legitimate children of God and they are grossly offended. Yet this is precisely the issue not only for them, but for every human being. It gives the lie to the message on a church sign in Indianapolis that read: JESUS CHRIST—SALVATION—IT'S THAT EASY. However simply the connection between Jesus and salvation may be stated, neither the accomplishment of salvation by Jesus nor its application to sinners by gospel proclamation may be described as "easy."

As the apostle Peter points out, "If the righteous one is scarcely saved, where will the ungodly and the sinner appear?" (1 Peter 4:18).

Sin dies hard in sinners. Sin nailed Jesus to the cross. Salvation requires a divine Savior and a work of the divine Spirit. None of this is easy.

Jesus first answers their protestation by asserting that *loving him is the test* as to whether God is your father: "If God were your Father, you would love Me, for I proceeded forth and came from God; nor have I come of Myself, but He sent Me" (John 8:42). If the living God really is your God and Father, you will love Jesus. This test rests on two objective presuppositions: namely, that Christ and the Father are one (John 10:30); and that the fruits of loving Jesus will be evident in your thoughts, words, and deeds (Matt. 7:20; Gal. 5:19–24). Applying this test, who then is their true father? Jesus answers this in verses 43–45 of our text:

First of all, they do not understand Jesus because of their spiritual state. They "are not able" to listen to Jesus's word (v. 43). They need to be "born again" (that is, be regenerated by the Holy Spirit, John 3:3, 7), so that they might hear, repent, and be saved (that is, be converted to Christ, Acts 16:31; Rom. 10:9). The heart of the matter is the matter of your heart.

Second, they are in fact on the same spiritual wavelength as Satan (John 8:44–45). How do we know? Jesus pulls no punches: "You are of your father the devil, and the desires of your father you want to do. He was a murderer from the beginning, and does not stand in the truth, because there is no truth in him. When he speaks a lie, he speaks from his own resources, for he is a liar and the father of it" (v. 44).

Finally, Jesus drives home the fact that they cannot face or handle the truth. Jesus spells it out: "because I tell the truth, you do not believe Me" (v. 45). All protestations to the contrary, Jesus asserts that their true father is neither God nor Abraham, but is none other than Satan." Jesus is the truth, and sinners cannot by nature accept that truth.

Jesus then turns the *test of truth upon himself*: "Which of you convicts Me of sin? And if I tell the truth why do you not believe Me?"(v. 46). Jesus is appealing to the facts of his ministry among them. Do his words and deeds stand the test of God's truth? Or is he manifestly a heretic and a trickster? These people love the miracles of Jesus and the idea of a political Messiah. But the truth as it is in Jesus exposes their hearts and calls them to repentance, faith, and commitment to a new life of costly discipleship. Jesus's conclusion exposes the reality of their unbelief before the bar of God's truth: "He who is of God hears God's words; therefore you do not hear, because you are not of God" (v. 47). Confessing sin is an essential step in the conversion of lost sinners. Jesus's hearers on this occasion were not prepared to recognize, far less rectify, their problem. This is in the very nature of mankind's war with God, which is to "suppress the truth in unrighteousness" (Rom. 1:18).

How can you have everlasting life?

People cannot be expected to take kindly to being informed that they are "not of God." The Bible's message is like a diagnosis of terminal illness allied to a promise of successful radical surgery. If you deny you are really ill or refuse to believe the surgeon can save you, you will either plunge into hopeless resignation or act as if your truth is better than those who propose to save your life. Then you will die—and what a waste it will be!

Jesus does not stop with the delineation of the human predicament. *He reveals his saving truth*, which stands forever as an invitation to believe on him and be saved. His imperatives are three in number:

Imperative one: Believe that I can give you everlasting life. Jesus assures everyone, including his would-be executioners, that he has come to give new life to believers (John 8:48–51). In the face of being dismissed as a heretic and a demoniac, Jesus denies any thirst for glory and gently affirms that "if anyone keeps My word he shall never see death" (v. 51).

Imperative two: Believe that I am the promised Messiah. Jesus is able to make this promise of new life, against their vehement objections that he can be greater than Abraham, because he is the one sent by God his Father—the Savior Messiah, whose day Abraham rejoiced to see (vv. 52–56). All that Abraham—and the prophets and faithful believers down the Old Testament centuries—hoped for is being fulfilled in the person and work of Jesus of Nazareth. They must accept Jesus as the Messiah or reject the God of Abraham.

Imperative three: I am the only divine Savior. Jesus concludes with the revelation that he is God incarnate "before Abraham was, I AM" (v. 58). Not only did Jesus exist before Abraham, but he was and is the great eternally self-existent "I AM" (Ex. 3:14; Isa. 41:4; 43:10, 13). Jesus is God! He is God the Son. He is the enfleshed God: "Nor is there salvation in any other, for there is no other name under heaven given among men by which we must be saved" (Acts 4:12).

Jesus Is the Truth

On that day in the temple long ago, Jesus's claims go unheeded. Many take up stones to kill him, but Jesus "hid Himself and...going through the midst of them, and so passed by" (John 8:59). Jesus's remarkable escape may be seen as a miraculous acted-out parable authenticating, before the eyes of his enemies, the truth of his messianic purpose to proclaim "liberty to the captives" (Luke 4:18). Jesus is saying to us still, "I am the way, the truth, and the life. No one comes to the Father except through Me" (John 14:6). He is the truth that saves. Fob him off at your eternal peril. Hear him and live forever.

Jesus Is Our

Vine

I am the vine, you are the branches.
—John 15:5

READ JOHN 15:1–8

It is the night of Jesus's betrayal and the Last Supper is over. So also is the "supper discourse" that followed it. Jesus then says, "Arise, let us go from here." He and the disciples leave the upper room and head through the city on the way to the Garden of Gethsemane, where Jesus would be arrested (John 14:31).

Sometime before they cross the Kidron brook to Gethsemane, Jesus pauses and gathers them around him to offer more parting counsels (John 15–16). He then leads them in his great high-priestly prayer (John 17). In this extended discourse, Jesus teaches them about their relationship both to him and to one another, their relationship to the world, and their relationship to the work of the Holy Spirit (John 15:1–7; 15:18–16:4; 16:5–18). This was to prepare them for future trials and ministry. It all applies as vitally to us today as it did to these first disciples.

He begins with one of the most vivid pictures in all of Scripture: "I am the true vine, and My Father is the vinedresser" (John 15:1).[1] He goes on to say, "I am the vine, you are the branches" (v. 5). In this way,

Jesus establishes the relationship between himself and his believing people in terms of the simple image of a grape vine: a vine, its branches, and the fruit (the grapes). He is the Savior, the life, and the glory of the branches (v. 8). He is everything to everyone he saves.

Savior of the Branches

The characters in the drama are as follows: Jesus is the Vine; God is the Farmer; and Jesus's followers are the branches. What happens in the vineyard illustrates what it means to be saved by Jesus and to live a fruitful Christian life. It is an allegory, a metaphor, of what union with Christ is all about.[2]

Jesus is the true Vine.

The Old Testament uses the vine to symbolize the church of that period (Israel) and also the mothers of the church (Ps. 80:8, 14; 127:3; 128:3). Now Jesus says, "I am the true vine." In other words, he is the real thing, while the others are just symbols. He is the focus and fulfillment of the promise of these ancient symbols of fruitfulness. But what does this mean in specific terms? Jesus had just used the fruit of the vine in the Last Supper as the symbol of his blood of the new covenant (compare with Matt. 26:28 and 1 Cor. 11:25–26). Jesus, then, is the embodiment of everything promised in the symbolism of the vine with respect to union with him as Savior and Lord. This teaches us three essential truths:

New life comes for dead souls through union with Christ. The blood of Christ "cleanses us from all sin" (1 John 1:7); and "God so loved the world that he gave His only begotten Son that whoever believes in Him should not perish but have everlasting life" (John 3:16). Jesus saves. Only Jesus. Only Jesus crucified, risen, and believed upon as Savior and Lord. Proclaiming this message is going to be the great mission of Jesus's disciples. As they themselves are to be fruitful branches, so others will become new branches with their own fruit as the Lord brings them from death to life in Christ the Vine. This, says Paul, "has now been revealed by the appearing of our Savior Jesus Christ, who has abolished death and brought life and immortality to light through the gospel" (2 Tim. 1:10).

New life grows through ongoing union with Christ. Jesus says in John 14:19, "Because I live, you will live also." The sap in the Vine gives life to the branches. It is not so much a matter of "once saved," but rather the ongoing experience of being saved and continuously walking with the Lord all the way to heaven. Believers are united to Christ in both "the power of His resurrection and the fellowship of His sufferings" (Phil. 3:10).

New life bears fruit in Christ. This comes from feeding upon Christ and following after Christ actively, intentionally: "those who are Christ's have crucified the flesh with its passions and desires. If we live in the Spirit, let us also walk in the Spirit" (Gal. 5:24ff.). Obedience multiplies holiness in the Christian life. We must spiritually feed on Christ as "the bread of life" (John 6:35; 7:37–38).[3]

God the Father is the Vinedresser.

While Jesus is the Vine, his Father is *ho georgos*, "the Vinedresser." The Greek word *georgos* is the root of the common boy's name George. It means simply "farmer." The sobriquet "Farmer George" was famously applied to King George III on account of his passion for agriculture—an acknowledgement of that connection. In this Scripture, God is the Farmer cultivating his field, which is of course the world. How is God the Farmer? Jesus emphasizes three things:

God cuts off fruitless branches: "Every branch in Me that does not bear fruit He takes away" (John 15:2). See also Matthew 15:13, where Jesus says, "Every plant that my heavenly Father has not planted will be pulled up by the roots." The application is plain as a pikestaff.

God prunes fruitful branches for more fruit: "Every branch that does bear fruit he prunes, that it may bear more fruit" (John 15:2). Please note that this is "cutting back" not "cutting off." God loves his people, and "whom the Lord loves He chastens" (Heb. 12:6). Sanctification is principally effected by means of "doctrine...reproof...correction" and "instruction in righteousness" (2 Tim. 3:16).

God accomplishes this by the word of truth, for as Jesus tells his disciples, "You are already clean because of the word which I have spoken to you" (John 15:3). The Word of God is "sharper than any double-edged sword" (Heb. 4:12). He cultivates the soil of our souls by the Holy Spirit speaking in the Scriptures. Matthew Henry intriguingly suggests,

> Perhaps here is an allusion to the law concerning vineyards in Canaan; the fruit of them was as unclean, and uncircumcised, the first three years after it was planted, and *the fourth year* it was to *be holiness of praise unto the Lord*; and then it was clean, Lev. 19:23, 24. The disciples had now been three years under Christ's instruction; and *now you are clean*.[4]

Herman Ridderbos rightly notes that this "does not mean they have already attained a degree of spiritual or moral perfection, but that he [Jesus] has so deeply bound them to himself by his word that in virtue of that fellowship they are able and ready to do his word and to bear fruit."[5]

Can you say this is true of you?

Life of the Branches

Jesus immediately applies the doctrine that he is the Savior of the branches by setting before us the basic and essential truth that new life is to be found exclusively in him.

First principle: life is to be found in Christ.

Jesus the Vine says to his branches, "Abide in Me, and I in you" (John 15:4). Because some branches will remain and others be cut off, this must be addressed to the Church as the *external* covenant community. The Church is always a mixture of the saved and the unsaved, for as Paul says, "They are not all Israel who are of Israel" (Rom. 9:6). The gospel is not just to be sent out to the unchurched, but must be proclaimed to the church itself for the conversion of the lost within its community. This is an imperative applying to every man, woman, and child under heaven.

For all who hear these words of Jesus, this is a call to cultivate your personal relationship with Christ. To "abide in" him means loving him and doing his will. It implies of course that Christ is already in the heart of the believer. In Christian experience it is this that comes first, because we can only "love Him because He first loved us" (1 John 4:19). The logic is: "As you abide in Me, you can be assured that I am abiding in you." As we actively follow Jesus, he makes his strength perfect in our weakness (2 Cor. 12:9).

Jesus sharpens his point by setting out the alternatives: "As the branch cannot bear fruit of itself, unless it abides in the vine, neither can you, unless you abide in Me" (John 15:4). It all boils down to this: there is no fruit outside the Vine. Just as you cannot *enter* the kingdom of God without being *born again* by the Spirit, so you cannot *bear fruit* unless you *abide in* Christ. The metaphor of vine and branches holds as surely for the downside as for the upside. Branches can have no life outside the vine. They are plants without roots. That is, they are not real Christians, even if they look like they are. They are outside of Christ and there is no other Savior: "There is salvation in no one else, for there is no other name under heaven given among men by which we must be saved" (Acts 4:12). The great first principle is that new life, eternal life, is to be found in Christ alone.

Practical application: you must be abiding in Christ.

In pressing home his application of this principle, Jesus draws the contrast between those who abide in Christ and those who do not.

In Christ, you can and will bear fruit. How so? Jesus answers: "I am the vine, you are the branches. He who abides in Me, and I in him, bears much fruit" (John 15:5). He is saying that when we are united to him by faith, we will go on to bear "much fruit." Philip Henry notes that "the church is a great tree inverted, its root is in heaven, its branches here on earth, multitudes of them."[6] On the other hand, without Christ "you can do nothing" (v. 5). Cut off a vine branch and see what grapes grow. Or cut off water or oxygen from yourself and see how long you last. Can you generate these essentials for yourself?

Outside of Christ you are bound to be fruitless. Jesus spells out the five-step descent to self-destruction: "If anyone does not abide in Me, he is cast out as a branch and is withered; and they gather them and throw them into the fire, and they are burned" (v. 6). It begins in this life and ends in a lost eternity.

Step one is being "cast out" as a branch that is severed from the vine. Of course, that is where human nature always starts. No one is born sinless. Sin alienates us from a holy God. But being cast out is a judgment on an established pattern of life that has turned away from the Lord. Make no mistake, "It is a fearful thing to fall into the hands of the living God" (Heb. 10:31). If this truth does not lead you to be concerned about your soul and to flee to Jesus, then you are in deeper trouble than you know.

Step two finds a branch "withered" from being left to itself. If you leave the Lord out of your life, do not be surprised if nature takes its course and you wither away spiritually. God knows when he is not wanted. The cost is his judicial withdrawing from the backsliders and the rebels who deny him (Gen. 6:3). He gives them their heart's desire, which is to be left alone by God and the gospel.

Step three is the arrival of death, when God will "gather" the resolutely unbelieving, unrepentant, and lost branches for the final accounting. Jesus warns of this moment in his parable of the rich fool: "But God said to him, 'Fool! This night your soul will be required of you; then whose will those things be which you have provided?' "

(Luke 12:20). It is not for nothing that people do not like being reminded that "it is appointed for men to die once, but after this the judgment." But this is more than a mere warning, for it is God's grace calling us to Christ that we might have eternal life through saving faith in his Son (Heb. 9:27).

Step four is the moment at the last judgment, when unrepentant reprobates will be thrown "into the fire" of hell, under the just judgment of God. "The wicked shall be turned into hell, and all the nations that forget God" (Ps. 9:17). These will include many who, in spite of their actual beliefs and behavior, think they are branches of Jesus's Vine, but are not: "Many will say to Me in that day, 'Lord, Lord, have we not prophesied in Your name, cast out demons in Your name, and done many wonders in Your name?' And then I will declare to them, 'I never knew you; depart from Me, you who practice lawlessness!'" (Matt. 7:22–23).

Step five is the eternal condition of these cut off branches: "and they are burned." Speaking of his own role in the last judgment, Christ the true Vine reveals that he will "say to those on the left hand, 'Depart from Me, you cursed, into the everlasting fire prepared for the devil and his angels'" (Matt. 25:41). That day will confirm that "anyone not found written in the Book of Life was cast into the lake of fire," and that "the cowardly, unbelieving, abominable, murderers, sexually immoral, sorcerers, idolaters, and all liars shall have their part in the lake which burns with fire" (Rev. 20:15; 21:8).

Jesus sets out the issues of life this starkly not only because this is the truth, but also because you still have time to flee from the wrath to come. What track do you think you are on?

Christ is calling you to living faith and faithful living. "If you abide in Me, and My words abide in you, you will ask what you desire, and it shall be done for you" (John 15:7). With Christ's words in us—believed, understood, remembered, loved, and obeyed—we will pray effectually and the Lord will answer with his blessings. Jesus is most earnestly calling you to follow him all the way to heaven.

This answers the question as to how the Christian will bear fruit and abide in Christ Jesus. The answer is to embrace him in faith, giving yourself to the Word and to prayer, trusting him for every outcome, promise, and blessing—that is, for the fruits of his free grace in a life of faithful discipleship.

Glory of the Branches

The goal and glory of "the branches" is the glory of God: "By this my Father is glorified, that you bear much fruit" (v. 8). Not to live for the Lord is to rob God of his glory and pilfer it for ourselves. On the other hand, to live for the Lord is to give him glory and so become in a real sense *his* glory. Bearing spiritual fruit is a glorious testimony to Jesus's saving grace, as Paul tells the Romans: "But now having become slaves of God, you have your fruit to holiness, and the end, everlasting life" (Rom. 6:22).

This is simply Christian discipleship—"so you will be my disciples." William Hendrikson remarks that "It takes a disciple to become a disciple."[7] In Jesus Christ, every believer is a disciple and every disciple evidences this by bearing fruit. Is Christ your Vine? Then branch out in him day by day and on to glory itself. Like the grapes of Eshcol, which were so full that it took two men to carry one cluster (Num. 13:23ff.), Christians have the promise of abundant fruit both in this world and the one that is to come. "That famous cluster" observes Matthew Henry, "was to Israel both the earnest and the specimen of all the fruits of Canaan. Such are the present comforts which we have in communion with God, foretastes of the fullness of joy we expect in the heavenly Canaan. We may see by them what heaven is." The psalmist anticipates the future glory the church when he prays,

> Return, we beseech You, O God of hosts; Look down from heaven and see, and visit this vine and the vineyard which Your right hand has planted, and the branch that You made strong for Yourself. (Ps. 80:14–15)

Jesus Christ is that branch, or root, of the Vine, made strong to the salvation of its many branches and all to the glory of our Father in Heaven. "By this My Father is glorified, that you bear much fruit; so you will be My disciples" (John 15:8).

Jesus Is Our

Way

I am the way, the truth, and the life.
—John 14:6

READ JOHN 14:1–7

The annual family vacations of this writer's childhood were usually two weeks by the seaside in what we optimistically (or better, euphemistically) called "the Scottish summer." It was the 1950s and, since we had no car, we would sometimes go on a "Mystery Tour" operated by a local bus company. You pay your "5 bob" and off you go knowing neither the way nor the destination. It was all great fun, even for small boys, because we knew we would arrive at some ancient castle along the way and get to run around imagining ourselves to be "knights of old, when men were bold."

When Jesus announced that he was soon to go away, his disciples did not like the idea one bit. The news really rattled them, and it was no consolation when he told them that he was going to "prepare a place" for them where they would be reunited at some time in the future (John 14:2–3). He tried to allay their fears by assuring them, "where I go you know, and the way you know" (v. 4). It was as if Jesus's leaving was going to plunge them into an ominous mystery tour of the future.

Thomas says, "Lord, we do not know where You are going, and how can we know the way?" (v. 5). He and the others were mystified. Both the journey and the destination, whatever they were, seemed shrouded in forebodings of danger and they were gripped by nagging worries.

Jesus had told them he was going to his "Father's house" and although he had been preaching the gospel way of salvation to them for three years they were pretty clueless. He might have roundly rebuked their incomprehension and doubting fear. But he is full of grace. He knows what trials are ahead for them, so he simply yet profoundly explains the mystery as to both the way and the destination. In short, his Father is the destination and he, the Son, is the way, and the way of salvation is not, after all, a mystery tour.

Jesus Is the Way

The way to heaven and reconciled fellowship with God the Father is not a set of values, a standard of morality, a list of religious rules and regulations, a mental discipline, or a submission to pietistic religious forms and rituals. It is not "do this" and "do that," or be a sincere and decent person. It is not about registering a decision, whether by praying a "sinner's prayer," or walking a sawdust trail. It is not about you. You and your best efforts are not "the way." Jesus says it simply and absolutely, "I am the way" (v. 6). There are no exceptions to the rule. No other substitutes will be accepted. It is Jesus only, full stop.

The Way is a person.

This Savior is foretold through the prophet Isaiah as "the Highway of Holiness" over which "the ransomed of the Lord shall return, and come to Zion with singing" (Isa. 35:8, 10). This highway is the promised Messiah, Jesus Christ the incarnate Son of God. In the New Testament, the same person is described as "the new and living way" by whom we may have "boldness to enter the Holiest"—that is, to be reconciled to God—"by the blood of Jesus" (Heb. 10:19–20). Jesus is the Way, in that his death on the cross opens the way for all who are covered by his atoning sacrifice for sin. Jesus is the Way because it is in him that his followers will come to the Father's house.

This clearly implies that entering into this way of salvation requires a personal exercise of saving faith in Jesus, which implies in turn the experience of an ongoing personal relationship with him.

The Way is of God.

The street you live on has a name. This street did not miraculously materialize when some town planner's blueprint was approved in the town council room. It had to be laid out and constructed according to plans already hatched. Likewise, Jesus is not the "Way" merely by decree. As the Way—the road to God and eternal life—he had to be, as it were, "constructed." He had to minister to that end in his person and work.

The question then is, "How does Jesus become the Way?" The first answer is that Jesus is able to become the Way because he is already the truth. That is to say, Jesus is God revealed to us. He is, as Philip Henry quaintly puts it, "our acquaintance with the Father."[1] Jesus is "the image of the invisible God" (Col. 1:15). He is "the brightness of [the Father's] glory and the express image of His person" (Heb. 1:3). He is the "Word became flesh," who "dwelt among us, and we beheld His glory, the glory as of the only begotten of the Father, full of grace and truth" (John 1:14). This also is deeply personal in each believer, as Paul notes, "For it is the God who commanded light to shine out of darkness, who has shone in our hearts to give the light of the knowledge of the glory of God in the face of Jesus Christ" (2 Cor. 4:6). Jesus is the Way because he is the truth of God, the truth that sets his people free (John 8:32).

Second, Jesus is able to be the Way because, as God in the flesh, he is also the life. First John 5:20 says, "We know that the Son of God has come and has given us an understanding, that we may know Him who is true; and we are in Him who is true, in His Son Jesus Christ. This is the true God and eternal life." Jesus explains, "For as the Father has life in Himself, so he has granted the Son to have life in Himself...because He is the Son of Man" (John 5:26ff.). Notice how personal this is. Jesus confers and communicates life (eternal) to the believer's heart and soul. He is "the Word of life" (1 John 1:1). And there is the rub, for "He who has the Son has life," whereas "he who does not have the Son of God does not have life" (1 John 5:12).

The simplest test of this for each one of us is not directed to our feelings, but to our heart-commitment to practical obedience: "Now by this we know that we know Him, if we keep His commandments" (1 John 2:3). How about you? Do you actually keep Jesus's commandments?

Jesus Is the Only Way

Jesus's follow-up expresses the full force of the doctrine of his first word: "No one comes to the Father except through Me" (John 14:6). In Philip Henry's words, we are being told "that the Lord Jesus Christ is our only way to the Father, and besides Him there is no other way."[2] This, of course, has very far-reaching consequences—consequences that are as searching as they are unpalatable to those who are determined to go their own way and forge their own "salvation" by their own best efforts.

Saying "I believe in God" is not a confession of saving faith.

> "Fallen man must come to God as Judge," notes Matthew Henry, but cannot come to him as a Father, otherwise than by Christ as Mediator. We cannot perform the duty of coming to God, by repentance and the acts of worship, without the Spirit and grace of Christ, nor obtain the happiness of coming to God as our Father

> without his [Christ's] merit and righteousness; he is the "high priest of our profession", our advocate. (Heb. 3:1; 1 John 2:1)

Remember that "devils also believe" that there is a "God," and the God of the Bible at that (Jas. 2:19). Anyone who says he believes in "God" and has no more than that general sense of a monotheistic Being cannot be a believer and is not (yet) saved. "I believe in God" does not cut it. No Jesus Christ means no saving faith (1 John 4:2–3; 2 John 1:7). "No one" comes to the Father except through Jesus.

Personal saving faith in Christ as Mediator is of the essence.

"Except through Me" is absolutely and utterly exclusive. How so? How is Jesus alone the Way? Paul opens this up as he teaches the Ephesians about Jesus and the gospel:

* Ephesians 1:5—Jesus is the one alone in whom we have *adoption* as God's children, "having predestined us to adoption as sons by Jesus Christ to Himself."
* Ephesians 1:6—Jesus is the one and only *acceptance* we may have with God.
* Ephesians 2:13—Jesus is the one and only *atonement* for our sins, "But now in Christ Jesus you who once were far off have been brought near by the blood of Jesus" (compare with 1 John 1:7).
* Ephesians 2:18—Jesus is the one and only *access* to the Father, "for through Him we…have access by one Spirit to the Father."

It is Jesus the Son of Man and God the Son who is the "one Mediator between God and men" (1 Tim. 2:5). Jesus the Messiah, by his death of the cross, his subsequent resurrection, and his perfect righteousness in his life is the one and only road to redemption and reconciliation to God. "He is our Joshua" writes Philip Henry, "both conquering the promised land for us, and dividing it to us, leading us over the Jordan of death."[3]

Drawing These Threads Together

Notice that the idea of a "way"—the Greek *hodos* just means a path, or a track, or a road—cuts both ways; you can be on the right path or any number of wrong ones. And you are making the choices and will bear the responsibility for the outcomes.

Negatively, if you are not in Christ, you are on the wrong track: "There is a way that seems right to a man, but its end is the way of death" (Prov. 14:12; 16:25). What track(s) are you on in your life? Where are you headed?

Positively, if you have received Christ, you are called to walk with him all your days and forever in glory: "He who says he abides in Him ought himself also to walk just as He walked" (1 John 2:6). Are you actually and seriously following Jesus?

Crucially, if you are listening, then you know that Jesus is calling you, and with precious promises and assurances: "Behold I set before you the way of life and the way of death" (Jer. 21:8). Jesus is calling you for a commitment to take the right track. Early in his earthly ministry he taught people to "enter by the narrow gate; for wide is the gate and broad is the way that leads to destruction, and there are many who go in by it. Because narrow is the gate and difficult is the way which leads to life, and there are few who find it" (Matt. 7:13–14). Jesus is calling you, "I am the way, the truth, and the life."

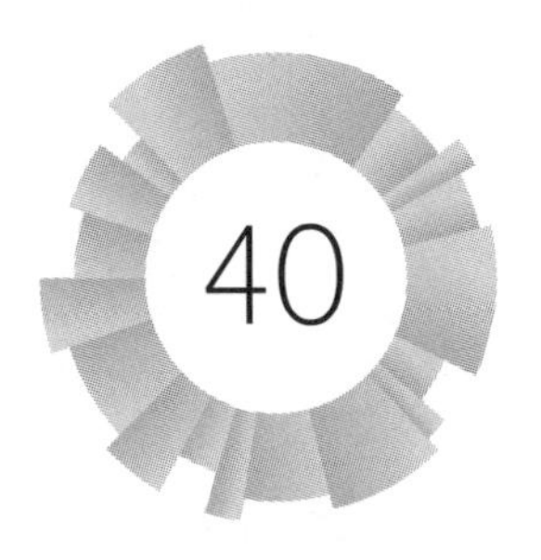

Jesus Is Our

Word

In the beginning was the Word, and the Word was with God,
and the Word was God.... And the Word became flesh and dwelt among us, and we beheld His glory, the glory as of the only begotten of the Father, full of grace and truth.
—John 1:1, 14

READ JOHN 1:1–18

In a magisterial way, Jesus is proclaimed in John 1 to be the eternal Word of God, who is God—the Creator of the world—and the Life and Light of men (vv. 1–5). Furthermore, as "the Word," he was "made flesh, and dwelt among us" (v. 14). He is not only the eternal *Logos*, or Word, who is co-equal with God the Father; he is also truly "God with us" (v. 1; 1 John 1:1; Rev. 19:13 Matt. 1:23). The central thread in all of this is captured in the idea that Jesus is the Word of God. This says that Jesus is God speaking to us about what is necessary for our salvation. We must ask then in what sense—or senses—Jesus is and must be our Word.

There is, however, something of a paradox here, because for all the clarity of John's Gospel as an introduction to Jesus and his message of free grace and eternal life, it begins with the most profound, and even mysterious, truths. It may be clear, but it is not easy. In fact, we are being thrown in at the deep end, theologically, by being taken to eternity before the creation of the world and given a vision-in-words of the pre-incarnate glory of the Son of God. The first doctrine of John's Gospel is that Jesus is God.

Jesus Is the Eternal Word

The Word was "in the beginning" (v. 1).

The parallel with Genesis is deliberate and unmistakable. The Word is uncreated and eternal. "Genesis 1 described God's first creation," observes Leon Morris, "John's theme is God's new creation...brought about through the agency of the Logos, the very Word of God."[1] He is deity himself. Jesus is the eternal Word of God. Amid all the scholarly debates as to what this means, two incontrovertible facts stand out. The first is that Jesus is the eternal wisdom and will of God. The second is that he is, as the writer to the Hebrews puts it, "the express image of His [God's] person" (Heb. 1:3).

This means that Jesus is divine wisdom and he *communicates* something of that wisdom to the human race in virtue of his being the Son of God who came and lived amongst us.

Both the prophecies of the Old Testament and the revelations of the New Testament confirm this with irrefutable clarity (Prov. 8:15–30; Micah 5:2; 1 Cor. 1:24; Heb. 1:3). Jesus was and still is the Word because he eternally reflects the mind of God and reveals that mind to humankind in time and history. He is both *ratio* (thought) and *oratio* (speech). He is the person in whom the wisdom of God is pre-eminently revealed.

The Word was "with God" (v. 1).

Not only did the Word—Jesus-before-he-was-Jesus—have a personal existence as eternal as God the Father, but he bore a precise and intimate relationship with or toward God (*pros ton theon*). "He existed in the closest possible connection with the Father."[2] He was *with* the

Father, but was a distinct personality from the Father. John enlarges on this in his first letter:

> That which was from the beginning, which we have heard, which we have seen with our eyes, which we have looked upon, and our hands have handled, concerning the Word of life—the life was manifested, and we have seen, and bear witness, and declare to you that eternal life which was with the Father and was manifested to us. (1 John 1:1–2)

The Word is co-eternal with God the Father.

Jesus Is the Divine Word

The Word is co-equal with God (v. 1).

The apostle is emphatic: "the Word was God." This means that Jesus is not to be explained away as merely a good man gifted with some measure of the divine. He is divinity in himself.[3] That is to say, not only was Jesus the eternal Word and, therefore, coexistent "with God," but he is himself a divine person. This is the consistent teaching of Scripture, in which Jesus is variously called "the true God," "God over all, blessed forever," and just simply "God" (1 John 5:20; Rom. 9:5 ESV; Heb. 1:8). There is no basis in the text for denying the full deity of Jesus Christ.

The Word was "in the beginning with God" (v. 2).

John repeats himself to leave us in no doubt as to his meaning. Jesus is the eternal Word who was with God—and is God. This ought to have dispelled the kind of prevarications by which Jesus is viewed as no more than a personification of great wisdom (but is not the divine wisdom himself), or is merely a good man and a marvelous teacher (as opposed to the light of the world), or is someone we think of as divine and inspiring to us subjectively (but is not actually God). We are surely taken here to the heart of the gospel, and against all skeptical evasions must confess with John Calvin, "I am unwilling to carry the abstruseness of philosophy beyond the measure of my faith."[4] Why? Because a Jesus who is to live and die and rise again for sinners in order objectively and definitively to remove their guilt and sin and give them new life must be, and can only be, the Son of God incarnate.

The best moral example in the world, or the most inspiring teacher, could not actually save himself, never mind a world of lost sinners. We needed real atonement that cancels real sins, not good advice, moral influence, or myths that make us feel good. John is establishing the qualifications of Jesus the man to be the Redeemer of other men.

Jesus Is the Creator-Word

What did the eternal uncreated Son of God do "in the beginning?" The answer is that "all things were made through Him, and without Him nothing was made that was made" (John 1:3). Reference to the Genesis account of creation is unmistakable: "In the beginning God created the heavens and the earth" (Gen. 1:1). Just as the divine Logos/Word is the wisdom of God and the eternal communicator of that wisdom for God, so also was he active in the creative process that brought all things into existence. Before he was born a son of man, the Son of God was the divine Logos who created all things.

The Word spoke the word.

The Bible's account of creation is a series of events in which God speaks and creative acts follow: "God said, 'Let there be light'; and there was light" (Gen. 1:3). In each instance, God's word is both the marker and the occasion of the accomplishment of the creative act pronounced in his words. He says, and it happens. Just like that! Now whereas to this point God's people had always correctly understood that God created all things out of nothing, now it is made clear that the eternal

Son of God—the Word in John 1:3—was active with the Father as his co-worker in this creation.

Co-creator with the Father.

It is "through Him"—Jesus before he is born and named Jesus—that "all things were made" (John 1:3). The precise nature of this co-operation is explained by the apostle Paul when he writes, " there is one God, the Father, of whom are all things, and we for Him; and one Lord Jesus Christ, through whom are all things, and through whom we live" (1 Cor. 8:6). All that exists has its ultimate source in God the Father, "of whom" (Greek *ex ou*) it came into being. This happened, however, with the co-ordinate creative act of the Son "by [or through] whom" (Greek *di ou*) it was created. Together, they made all things (creation) and to this day they uphold all things (providence), for, says Jesus, "My Father has been working until now, and I have been working…for whatever He does, the Son also does in like manner" (John 5:17, 19; Heb. 1:3).

Creator of all things.

John further emphasizes that Jesus as the eternal Son actually created "all things" by adding "without Him nothing was made that was made." He had a hand in everything:

> For by Him all things were created that are in heaven and that are on earth, visible and invisible, whether thrones or dominions or principalities or powers. All things were created through Him and for Him. And He is before all things, and in Him all things consist. (Col. 1:16–17 ESV)

The Bible is abundantly clear that Jesus the man from Nazareth—so contemptuously dismissed by some as "the carpenter, the son of Mary" (Mark 6:3)—is the creator and upholder of the universe (Ps. 119:73; Isa. 51:12–13; Rom. 4:17; 2 Cor. 4:6; Eph. 2:10; Heb. 1:2).

Why are we told this? Surely it is to impress upon us that what is at stake is Jesus's qualification to be a real Savior. Jesus is the Savior who alone is able to save real people from real sins. He saves his people from the real anger of the only real God who is the real Judge of the living and the dead. For the promised Messiah to be the effective Mediator between God and man (1 Tim. 2:5), he must be powerful enough to secure redemption for otherwise eternally lost people. The fact that Jesus was a good man, a profound teacher, and a courageous exemplar of faithfulness to death does not prove that he could save anyone, including even himself. But his deity and his resurrection do afford the evidence we need to see that his claims are more than stirring words, personal nobility, and an inspiring example of moral behavior.

John here provides the first part of the story. Jesus did not begin his life in Bethlehem. He was first the divine eternal Son who created the world into which he came in the fullness of divine timing to be born of a woman, born under the law, to redeem those that were under the law (Gal. 4:4–5). Hence, says Matthew Henry, "he is appointed the author of our bliss who was the author of our being."[5] He who came to make us new people is able to do so because he made us all in the first place and can make us new creations in the future: "Therefore, if anyone is in Christ, he is a new creation; old things have passed away; behold, all things have become new" (2 Cor. 5:17).

Jesus Is the Life-giving Word

If Jesus as the incarnate Creator is qualified to make people into new creations, the next question is, "Given that the Creator can renew dead souls, what is it in him that effects such transformations?" This will later come to the fore in Jesus's encounter with Nicodemus and his teaching on the doctrine of regeneration by the Holy Spirit (John 3:1–8). In the meantime, John simply asserts: "In Him was life" (1:4). These words signify that Jesus is the source of all that is alive, physically or spiritually. The logic of the text is that the Creator of life must be in himself the very essence and definition of life. He is the eternally self-existent life prior to, and creative of, our finite created existence. Later, Jesus will tell his followers, "For as the Father has life in Himself, so has He given to the Son to have life in Himself, and has given Him authority to execute judgment also, because He is the Son of Man" (John 5:26–27). Life resides in the uncreated mystery of God—Father, Son, and Holy Spirit. This puts our life in proper perspective.

Our life is *derived*. It is created, finite, and transient in nature. Human life was made in order to image the uncreated life of God himself. The Lord is the source of all that we know as our life.

Our life is also *sustained* in its continuing existence, by "the word of His power" (Heb. 1:3). It is not self-existent. This is what Paul means when he says to the Athenian philosophers, in words of their own poets, that in God "we live and move and have our being" and "are also His offspring" (Acts 17:28). The Lord is the *sustainer* of all that we know as our life.

The inner life of the soul needs to be *regenerated* through a spiritual re-birth effected by the Holy Spirit in connection with the hearing of the gospel. When regeneration occurs, life that is fallen into spiritual deadness in sin is redeemed to become new life through faith in Christ as Savior and Lord. With him, we will enjoy glorious fellowship with the Living God now and forever. The Lord is the *regenerator* of the hearts of all those he will save, "a great multitude which no one can number" (Rev. 7:9). These will turn to him in repentance and faith, for with him, "is the fountain of life" (Ps. 36:9; see also John 1:12–13; 3:3, 7–8; Titus 3:5).

Jesus Is the Light-bearing Word

People are endlessly looking for answers. We often say we want "light on the subject," on everything from the trivial to the very meaning of life. And light and life are inseparable from one another—and more profoundly, are inseparable from God, as the psalmist testifies, "For with You is the fountain of life; in Your light we see light" (Ps. 36:9). It is what all who "walk in darkness" need to see and ought to desire most devoutly (compare with Isa. 9:2).

Jesus is the Light.

John says of Jesus, "In Him was life, and the life was the light of men" (John 1:4). Light is just life made manifest. Jesus says it right out, "I am the light of the world. He who follows Me shall not walk in darkness, but have the light of life" (John 8:12; compare with 9:5 and 12:46).

Scripture teaches that Jesus is "the light of men." This is true of both the general *sensus deitatis* (sense of God) that is in all human beings by nature as those created in God's image, and the particular experience of believers who have gospel light through faith in Christ. For this reason, whatever "light" that the unregenerate have is neither recognized nor accepted for what it is, because, as Jesus explains, when "the light has come into the world, and men loved darkness rather than light because their deeds were evil" (John 3:19). Only in the conscious embracing of Christ by a living, saving faith does the sinner see the light that is Christ for what it really is (Matt. 4:16; compare with Ps. 27:1; 36:9; and 119:130).

Jesus dispels darkness.

Jesus's action as the Light is to invade the darkness of this fallen world; "And the light shines in the darkness, and the darkness did not comprehend it" (John 1:5). He illumines "every man" in the sense that he brings his "Light" to bear upon the minds and consciences of lost people (v. 9). The verb *phainei* is in the present tense and denotes his ever-present shining in the world. Meanwhile, the darkness resists and does not "comprehend" it. This can be read in two ways, which are not mutually exclusive:

The failure to "comprehend" means that man, in spiritual darkness, simply cannot understand the light. He draws a blank on the truth that is under his nose (see 1 Cor. 2:14).

Another possibility, however, is that this should be read "overcome"—as in the NIV, "the darkness did not overcome it." This is the thought in Romans 1:18: "For the wrath of God is revealed from heaven against all ungodliness and unrighteousness of men, who suppress the truth in unrighteousness." The idea then is that human darkness fails to *suppress* or *extinguish* the light, as hard as we sinners may try: not at the Fall, when sin came into the world; not at Calvary, when Christ bore the sin of his people; and not at the great day, when man's rebellion against God will utter its last gasp under the final judgement of the returning Jesus.

The practical thrust of the revelation that Jesus is God, Creator, Life, and Light, is that he is offered so as to be received as the Savior of lost and endarkened sinners. He is the good Word in whom is embodied all the goodness of the good news of the gospel.

Jesus Is the Incarnate Word

At the center of the gospel of Christ is the incarnation. Even the efficacy of the cross depends upon this as an historical reality. If a mere man, no different from any of us, died at Calvary, then Christians are deceiving themselves and lying to the world about Christ, the gospel, and salvation. Paul makes the parallel point when he says that if there is no resurrection of Christ: "then our preaching is in vain…your faith is futile and you are still in your sins" (1 Cor. 15:14, 17 ESV). But because the enfleshed God died on that cross and rose again from the dead, it is death itself that died. Jesus was able, in Hugh Martin's pellucid phrase, to "die death dead" precisely because he was the Son of God, with our human nature, but without our sin.

The Word became flesh.

John's simplicity is breathtaking: "And the Word became flesh…" (1:14). Jesus is, says Paul, "the seed of David according to the flesh"

(Rom. 1:3). The Son of God was made "in the likeness of sinful flesh" to be an offering for sin (Rom. 8:3). He was "born of a woman" (Gal. 4:4); came "in the likeness of men" (Phil. 2:7); "was manifested in the flesh" (1 Tim. 3:16); and "shared in [flesh and blood], that through death He might destroy him who had the power of death" (Heb. 2:14). That is why, as John Murray has put it, "the Son of God was sent in that very nature which in every other instance is sinful."[6] This "flesh" is not just the body, but encompasses the whole of human nature. Christ took human nature, both body and soul.

And dwelt among us.

Everyone at the time knew that Jesus had lived and died in Palestine. John says he literally "tented among us" (John 1:14). This language would have caught the attention of Jewish readers and taken their minds to the tabernacle in the wilderness and the presence of God among his people (Ex. 40:34ff.). This would say to them that all those earlier times when God was present with his people for particular periods of time were now fulfilled in the Word becoming flesh. Jesus is Immanuel—God with us. God thereby identifies with humanity in the most personal way possible: "For God so loved the world that He gave His only begotten Son, that whoever believes in Him should not perish but have everlasting life" (John 3:16).

We beheld his glory.

What John goes on to say flows naturally from the truth that Jesus is the God-man who pitched his tent among us. We "beheld His glory" (John 1:14), meaning his "brightness" or "radiance" as it speaks of the majesty and dignity of God. Jesus's glory is a self-evidencing glory, which "we"—John and the other eyewitnesses—saw, both with the eyes and in the calm reflection of careful minds. They saw this glory in two ways.

The only begotten of the Father.

First of all, what the apostles witnessed in Jesus was "the glory as of the only begotten of the Father" (v. 14). Jesus's glory was intimately, inseparably, and uniquely connected with his eternal Sonship as the second person of the triune God. That is what John is saying. This does not mean that they usually saw a visible corona of glory emanating from Jesus—the so-called "exception that proves the rule" being the transfiguration (Matt. 17:1–13). What they did see was a progressive unfolding of Jesus's prophetic self-revelation. All that he said and did flowed from his being the Son of God.

Jesus is the "only begotten" Son of God. The Greek term *monogenes* carries the idea of complete uniqueness, in his case from all eternity. Jesus is the "one and only" Son. This rules out spiritualizing the term to make it say he is merely a son begotten in the way any and all Christians become children of God. Jesus is one of a kind and this reveals the glory of God. The expression "of the Father" is something of a theme in John's gospel. Because Jesus is "of [or "from"] the Father," he is the bread of life, the promised Messiah, and the victorious Mediator (John 6:46; 7:29; 16:27). When he performs miracles like feeding the five thousand, healing the blind beggar, or walking on the water, everything points to the glory of his divine sonship. Jesus is infinitely more than a great teacher and a good man. He is God with us.

Full of grace and truth.

A second way in which Jesus's glory was witnessed is in the transparent perfection of his untainted righteousness. He is "full of grace and truth" (John 1:14). This describes the way he carried himself—what his behavior conveyed to a watching world—in other words, his character. He is the "impress" (Greek, *charakter*) of God's nature (Heb. 1:3). His personal character, writes Charles Simeon, is "wholly without spot or blemish; he was 'full of truth'; and 'in him was no sin', 'no guile' whatever."[7] To say that he was "full" of grace and truth is to say that the "grace" of God that seeks the good of lost people flowed from his innermost being. Like the Father, the Son was "abounding in goodness and truth" (Ex. 34:6). With respect to his ministry toward that gracious goal, he declared the "truth" of God with absolute accuracy and perfection. In this, of course, Jesus is the very Word of God speaking to our hearts and consciences and calling us to newness of life.

The connective "and" is also significant, because grace and truth are two sides of one coin. There is no grace without truth and no truth without grace. Yet we ourselves are not infrequently the one without the other—either being self-righteous ("righteous" at the expense of grace), or latitudinarian ("gracious" at the expense of truth). It is not truly gracious to be nice without principles; nor is it graciously truthful to be right without a loving spirit. In Christ, the two are perfectly conjoined.

Is Jesus Your Word?

It is a curious side effect of the English alphabet that these studies of the Bible's visions-in-words of the Lord Jesus Christ begin with the last figurative characterization of the Lord in all of Scripture—the "Alpha and Omega" of Revelation 22:13—and now conclude with the first such characterization in the fourth Gospel, namely Jesus as "the Word." This is most appropriate, both theologically and experientially, since it draws creation and new creation together by and through the person and work of the Son of God.

No portion of the Scriptures is used more frequently to introduce people to the Christian faith than John's Gospel. His Gospel distills the essence of the good news about Jesus Christ and presents it in a clear, concise, and compelling way. John says as much toward the end of his account, when he tells us "these are written, that you may believe that Jesus is the Christ, the Son of God, and that believing you may have life in His name" (John 20:31). Using the very words of God, the apostle tells a world of ordinary people what they need to know about Jesus, who is the very Word in himself, that in believing they would receive new life through his name.

What John wants us to grasp is that the man Jesus is the Lord from heaven sent to save, and able to save, because, as Octavius Winslow so beautifully expresses it, "the love of Jesus runs parallel with his being… from all eternity to all eternity."[8]

"Therefore I said to you," says Jesus to the skeptics, "that you will die in your sins: for if you do not believe that I am He, you will die in your sins" (John 8:24). Our Lord leaves us no room for maneuvering. It is life through saving faith in him, the Word made flesh, or it is death through ourselves remaining in our unbelief, unrepentant to the last.

Those who deny Jesus as the divine Word and incarnate Christ must reject him as a liar and a fraud, if only to justify to themselves their refusal to believe. They will have no excuse on the day they fly away to eternity. But while we live and hear the voice of Jesus calling in the gospel, the way to life is open for the repentant and believing: "Believe on the Lord Jesus Christ, and you will be saved, you and your household" (Acts 16:31).

Notes

Preface

1. Patrick Fairbairn, *The Typology of Scripture* (Grand Rapids: Baker, 1975 [1845–47]), Book I, p. 1. The same concern was raised by Fairbairn in the nineteenth century with respect to the related issue of "types" in the Bible. What Fairbairn says in his landmark exposition of biblical typology has its echoes today in the neglect of the application of biblical figures of speech in general and types in particular. Peter Masters, in his Foreword to the 1989 publication of Fairbairn's *Typology*, observes,

   > The recent drift toward a highly technical and less theological method of interpretation is chiefly a reaction against the whimsical and extravagant "spiritualization" of biblical passages heard in so many pulpits. However, this reaction often goes too far, creating a hermeneutical strait-jacket that greatly reduces the pastoral scope of the text and inhibits the applied expository approach laid down by Paul [Romans 4:23–24; 15:4; 1 Corinthians 10:1–14; 1 Timothy 3:16–17]. Indeed the new drift seems to want to treat the Bible as a human rather than a divine book.

   The same sentiments have been expressed more recently by David Murray in *Christ on Every Page* (Nashville: Thomas Nelson, 2013), pp. 136–152.

2. E. W. Bullinger, *Figures of Speech Used in the Bible* (Grand Rapids: Baker, 2005 [1898]).
3. Henry Law, *Christ is All* (Stoke-on-Trent: Tentmaker Publications, 2005).
4. Ralph Robinson, *Christ All and in All* (London: 1660). Reprint by Soli Deo Gloria (Ligonier, 1992).
5. Philip Henry, *Christ All in All* (Swengel, PA: Reiner Publications, 1970). Originally written in 1691, this was not published until 1830 as an appendix to *The Miscellaneous Works of the Rev. Matthew Henry, V.D.M.*, and has been recently reprinted by Reformation Heritage Books (2016).
6. Ambrose Serle, *Horæ solitariæ: or, essays upon some remarkable names and titles of Jesus Christ, occurring in the Old Testament, and Declarative of His Essential Divinity and Gracious Offices in the Redemption of Men...* (London, J. W. Pasham: 1776).
7. C. H. Spurgeon, *Types and Emblems* (Pasadena, TX: Pilgrim Publications, 1970). It is also worth mentioning the work of another Baptist, Benjamin Keach, whose massive Tropologia contains one chapter on types and metaphors of Christ. (First published in 1682, and reprinted by Kregel as Preaching from the Types and Metaphors of the Bible, Grand Rapids, 1972).
8. Italics added in both quotations. See also John 4:23; 5:26, 28; 16:2; 17:1.
9. It is a *synecdoche*, the figure of speech in which the part represents the whole, in this instance the "hour" representing a much larger period of time (cf. E. W. Bullinger, *op. cit.*, p. 640).
10. Milton S. Terry, *Biblical Hermeneutics* (Eugene, OR: Wipf & Stock, 1999 [1890]), p. 244.
11. E. W. Bullinger, *op. cit.*, p. 768.
12. Alexander Stewart, *The Tree of Promise—The Mosaic Economy a Dispensation of the Covenant of Grace* (Glasgow: Free Presbyterian Publications, 2009 [1864]), p. 309.
13. Milton S. Terry, *op. cit.*, p. 246.
14. For a careful explanation of the hermeneutical principles to be applied in identifying and interpreting types, see Milton S. Terry, *Biblical Hermeneutics*, pp. 244–256. For a clear and careful exposition of biblical types, see William McEwen, *Grace and Truth: or the Glory and Fullness of the Redeemer displayed in an attempt to explain, illustrate, and enforce the most remarkable types, figures, and allegories of the Old Testament* (Philadelphia: Johnston and Justice, 1792) (see https://archive.org/details/gracetruthorglor00mcew).
15. David Murray, *Jesus on Every Page* (Nashville: Thomas Nelson, 2013, p. 137).

Chapter 1: Alpha & Omega

1. The four instances of this title are to be found in Revelation 1:8, 11; 21:6; 22:13.
2. William Hendriksen, *More than Conquerors* (Grand Rapids: Baker, 1997), p. 53. Hendriksen says this "refers to the Holy Spirit in the fullness of His operations and influences in the world and in the Church."
3. Geoffrey B. Wilson, *Revelation* (Darlington: Evangelical Press, 1985), p. 20.
4. "Alpha & Omega" says William Jay, "regards His Nature and the duration of it; it never began and it will never end." William Jay, *Evening Exercises for Every Day in the Year* (Hinton, Virginia: Sprinkle Publications, [1832] 1999), p. 359. See Psalm 90:2: "From everlasting to everlasting you are God."
5. See James Durham, *Lectures on Revelation*, p. 32.
6. Colossians 1:17: "And He is before all things, and in Him all things consist."
7. *Shorter Catechism* Question 4: "What is God? A. God is a Spirit, infinite, eternal, and unchangeable, in his being, wisdom, power, holiness, justice, goodness, and truth."
8. "I and the Father are One" (John 10:30).
9. Wilson, *Revelation*, p. 17.
10. This has Old Testament roots. See Isaiah 55:4: "Indeed I have given him as a witness to the people, A leader and commander for the people." (See also Wilson, *Revelation*, pp. 18ff.)
11. See Don Fortner, *Discovering Christ in Revelation* (Darlington: Evangelical Press, 2002), pp. 24–25.

Chapter 2: Altar

1. Charles Simeon, *Expository Outlines on the Whole Bible* (Grand Rapids: Baker, 1988 [first published as *Horae Homileticae* in 1847]), 19:524.
2. Simeon, *Expository Outlines on the Whole Bible*, 19:530.

Chapter 3: Apostle

1. *Friberg Lexicon*, "Apostello" (Bible Works 7 electronic edition, *in loco*).
2. Wilhelmus à Brakel summarizes this eternal Covenant as follows:

   > The Father thus gave the elect to His Son as Surety, and the Son accepted them, recorded their names in His book, became Surety for all of them—none

> excepted—and for them alone, and promised to accomplish His Father's good pleasure in bringing them to salvation. (*The Christian's Reasonable Service* [Grand Rapids: Reformation Heritage Books, 2011 (1700)], 1:253)

3. See John 5:46–47: "For if you believed Moses, you would believe Me; for he wrote about Me. But if you do not believe his writings, how will you believe My words?" For a helpful overview of Moses as a type of Christ, see Richard C. Gamble, *The Whole Counsel of God* (Phillipsburg, NJ: P&R, 2009), 1:370–372.
4. Italics added. There are several striking similarities between the Greek translation (Septuagint) of this passage and Hebrews 3:3–6, suggesting that the author had the Covenant with David in view.
5. John Brown, *Hebrews* (Edinburgh: Banner of Truth, 1972 [1862]), p. 157.
6. Hywel R. Jones, *Let's Study Hebrews* (Edinburgh: Banner of Truth, 2002), p. 31.

Chapter 4: Banner

1. James IV and much of his nobility and army perished on Flodden Field, in the worst of Scotland's many military reverses in the wars with England. This is commemorated in the most haunting of Scottish laments, "The Floo'ers o' the Forest (are a' wede awa')."
2. In his famous hymn, "Praise to the Holiest in the height."
3. Edward J. Young, *The Book of Isaiah* (Grand Rapids: Eerdmans, 1972), 1:393ff.
4. Peoples as opposed to political entities.
5. Edward J. Young, *The Book of Isaiah*, 1:393, footnote 22.
6. *Shekinah* derives from the Hebrew *shakan*, which means to settle or rest upon. It refers to the visible presence of God—the glory cloud in the Sinai wanderings of Israel and between the cherubim over the ark of the covenant in the tabernacle.

Chapter 5: Bronze Serpent

1. See James Philip, *Repentance: Its Meaning and Implications* (London: The Tyndale Press, 1963), p. 9.
2. Jennifer S. Holland, "The Bite that Heals," in *National Geographic Magazine*, February 2013 (ngm.nationalgeographic.com/2013/02/125-venom/holland-text [accessed 12.27.14]).
3. *Westminster Shorter Catechism* Question and Answer 19. The Puritan Henry Ainsworth summarizes this point well:

> Here also there was a remembrance of the first sin that came into mankind by the serpent and the death that followed thereupon, Gen.3; for as the venom of the serpents killeth the body, so the venom of Satan, which is sin, killeth both body and soul: and as the serpent biting one part, the venom and contagion spreadeth over all the body and killeth the whole man, so the poison of sin, which entered by one man, hath infected and killed all the lump of mankind, Rom. 5:15–18...and as no salve or medicine could heal the bodies of those that were bitten, so can no work of man cure the biting of that old serpent or sting of sin.

Annotations on the Pentateuch and Psalms (Soli Deo Gloria, 1991 [1612]), 1:86–87. See also Thomas Watson, "Fiery Serpents" in *A Plea for the Godly and other Sermons* (Pittsburgh, PA: Soli Deo Gloria, 1993), pp. 378–399.

4. It is interesting to note that this emblem of the serpent on a pole still exists as a symbol of healing today—emblazoned on ambulances and paramedic uniforms, for instance. It is, however, disputed whether the symbol in this context has a biblical or pagan origin.
5. Charles Hodge, *Princeton Sermons* (London: Banner of Truth, 1958), p. 38.
6. See Hodge, *ibid.*, p. 40
7. The danger of visualizing Christ on a crucifix as a substitute for true faith in the crucified Christ is a lesson taught by the sobering sequel mentioned in 2 Kings 18:4: "[Hezekiah] removed the high places and broke the sacred pillars, cut down the wooden image and *broke in pieces the bronze serpent that Moses had made; for until those days the children of Israel burned incense to it, and called it Nehushtan*" (italics added).

   In a similar way, in the twenty centuries following the crucifixion, the cross itself has become an object of idolatry and superstition; witness the idolatry of the Roman Catholic Church, which ironically uses Numbers 21:4–9 as a proof text for its veneration of images (*Catechism of the Catholic Church* [Vatican City: Libreria Editrice Vaticana, 1992], p. 2130)!

Chapter 6: Captain of Our Salvation

1. See Hywel R. Jones, *Let's Study Hebrews* (Edinburgh: Banner of Truth, 2002), pp. 23–25.
2. *Friberg Lexicon* (Bible Works 7 electronic edition, *in loco*).
3. Here we have a glimpse of the eternal Covenant of Redemption. In eternity past, the Father commissioned the Son to redeem his elect people. Jesus speaks of it in his high priestly prayer in John 17:4–5: "I have glorified You on the earth. I have finished the work which You have given Me to do. And now, O Father, glorify Me together with

Yourself, with the glory which I had with You before the world began." It is this same "glory" that Jesus "brings many sons to" as captain of salvation! (See also John 17:22, 24: "And the glory which You gave Me I have given them…Father, I desire that they also…may be with Me where I am, that they may behold My glory which You have given Me.")

4. *Friberg Lexicon* (Bible Works 7 electronic edition, *in loco*).
5. David Dickson, *A Short Explanation of the Epistle of Paul to the Hebrews* (Edinburgh: Banner of Truth, 1978 [1635]), p. 13.
6. Herman Witsius, *The Economy of the Covenants Between God and Man* (Kingsburg, CA: den Dulk Foundation, 1990 [1677]), 1:191.
7. See also Hebrews 10:10: "we have been sanctified through the offering of the body of Jesus Christ once for all."
8. Note that our English translations suggest various interpretations of this phrase: e.g., compare the ESV ("they have the same source") and NIV ("they are of the same family"). For a helpful discussion of the options, see Leon Morris, *Hebrews* in Expositors' Bible Commentary (Grand Rapids: Zondervan, 1981), 12:27.
9. At this point in Hebrews 2:12–13, it should be noted that the author rallies two messianic passages from the Old Testament to prove Jesus's family connection with his brothers. In Psalm 22:22 the Savior, fresh from his victory on the cross, declares the gospel to those who he may *now* count his brothers by virtue of his sacrifice; his sufferings have made God *their* Father as well as his. Likewise, Isaiah 8:17–18 expresses the Savior's trust in his Father to deliver him from death, and, as a result, the Father's elect children are brought to glory.
10. William Shakespeare, *Henry V*, Act IV, Scene 3.
11. L. Krieger, K. Neill, and S. Jantzen, *World History: Perspectives on the Past*, 4th ed. (Lexington, MA: DC Heath, 1994), p. 144.
12. For a most helpful discussion of this subject, see John Brown, *Hebrews* (Banner of Truth, 1972), pp. 126ff.
13. John Owen, *The Death of Death in The Death of Christ* in *The Works of John Owen* (Edinburgh: Banner of Truth, 1967 [repr. 1647]), 10:139ff.

Chapter 7: Chosen Stone

1. See *Nelson's New Illustrated Bible Dictionary* (Nashville, TN: Thomas Nelson, 1995), p. 304.
2. *Apodokimadzo*, *Friberg* and *Liddell-Scott* Lexicons (Bible Works 7, electronic editions).

3. For a thoughtful development of this theme, see Maurice Roberts, "Our Unpopular Lord Jesus," in *The Thought of Him* (Edinburgh: Banner of Truth, 1995), pp. 86–91.
4. Ralph Robinson, *Christ All and in All* (Ligonier, PA: Soli Deo Gloria, 1992 [1660]), p. 237.
5. Robinson, *op. cit.*, p. 233 (author's italics).
6. en.wikipedia.org/wiki/Golden_Jubilee_Diamond (accessed 9.1.14).
7. Cited in Faith Cook, *Grace in Winter: Samuel Rutherford in Verse* (Banner of Truth, 1989), p. 26.
8. http://www.diamonds.net/news/NewsItem.aspx?ArticleID=9219 (accessed 9.1.14).

Chapter 8: Consolation

1. John Calvin comments,

   > [They] appeared the most wretched people on earth...Not only were they burdened by bitter slavery, they were friendless, in danger of being swallowed up, and so disliked that to hate them was the surest way of earning men's applause...So Jesus Christ is said to be their consolation, signifying that although the world may hate and detest us, although we may be poor simpletons whom others rob, devour and gobble up, although men may abuse and revile us, Christ alone is sufficient to console us.

   John Calvin, *Songs of the Nativity: Selected Sermons on Luke 1 & 2* (Edinburgh: Banner of Truth, 2008 [1562]), p. 161.
2. John Boys, *The Works of John Boys* (Morgan, PA: Soli Deo Gloria: 1997 [1629]), p. 126.
3. Ralph Robinson, *Christ All and in All* (Ligonier, PA: Soli Deo Gloria, 1992 [1660]), pp. 294–295.
4. Only by receiving Christ our consolation can we expect to receive the Holy Spirit our Comforter: "The third person had never been our Comforter, if the second person had not been our Redeemer. There is nothing that can be thought on which hath any causality or efficiency in our consolation but it is of Christ's procurement" (Ralph Robinson, *op. cit.*, p. 291).
5. See *Westminster Shorter Catechism* Question 88: "What are the outward means whereby Christ communicateth to us the benefits of redemption? Answer: The outward and ordinary means whereby Christ communicateth to us the benefits of redemption, are his ordinances, especially the word, sacraments, and prayer; all which are made effectual to the elect for salvation."

Chapter 9: Covenant

1. Wilhelmus à Brakel (1635–1711) explains the covenant of redemption this way:

    > The Father thus gave the elect to His Son as Surety, and the Son accepted them, recorded their names in His book, became Surety for all of them—none excepted—and for them alone, and promised to accomplish His Father's good pleasure in bringing them to salvation.

    Wilhelmus à Brakel, *The Christian's Reasonable Service* (Grand Rapids: Reformation Heritage Books, 2011 [1700]), 1:252–253.

2. J. I. Packer, *Concise Theology* (Wheaton, IL: Tyndale House, 1993), p. 87.
3. E. J. Young, *Isaiah* (Grand Rapids: Eerdmans, 1972, 3:120). E. W. Hengstenberg adds, "The Servant of God is called the personal and embodied Covenant, because in his appearance the Covenant made with Israel is to find its full truth; and everything implied in the very idea of a covenant, all the promises flowing from the idea are to be in Him, Yea and Amen." *Christology of the Old Testament* (Edinburgh: T&T Clark, 1851), 2:220.
4. Ralph Robinson, *Christ All and in All* (Ligonier, PA: Soli Deo Gloria, 1992), p. 473. Robinson's sermon on this text is superb.
5. en.wikipedia.org/wiki/Operation_Jericho (accessed 4.9.14).

Chapter 10: Door

1. George Hutcheson (1618–74), *An Exposition of the Gospel according to John* (Grand Rapids: Baker, 1971), p. 205.
2. *Westminster Shorter Catechism* Question 88 describes the nature and impact of the means of grace: "What are the outward means whereby Christ communicateth to us the benefits of redemption? A. The outward and ordinary means whereby Christ communicateth to us the benefits of redemption, are his ordinances, especially the word, sacraments, and prayer; all which are made effectual to the elect for salvation."
3. Philip Henry, *Christ All in All* (Swengel, PA, Reiner: 1970 [1691]), p. 199.

Chapter 11: Food

1. Christ is the "last" or second Adam (1 Cor. 15:45).
2. Philip Henry, *Christ All in All* (Swengel, PA, Reiner Publications: 1970 [1691]), p. 14.

3. Charles Simeon, *Expository Outlines on the Whole Bible* (Grand Rapids, Baker, 1988 [1847]), 13:396.
4. *Shorter Catechism* Question and Answer 1.

Chapter 12: Foundation

1. Grace Reformed Presbyterian Church in State College, Pennsylvania, where this writer was pastor from 1986–2004.
2. Charles Simeon, *Expository Outlines on the Whole Bible* (Grand Rapids, Baker, 1988 [1847]), 16:10.
3. From which we borrowed our English words, "elect," "eclectic," and so on.
4. George Heriot's School, Lauriston Place, Edinburgh, Scotland (this school was the inspiration, by the way, for "Hogwarts" in J. K. Rowling's Harry Potter books, which were first conceived and written in The Elephant House, just round the corner in George IV Bridge).
5. Edward Mote, "The Solid Rock" (c. 1834).

Chapter 13: Fountain

1. The Word of God—Matthew 9:2–6; 2 Corinthians 5:18–21; 1 Peter 1:25.
   Baptism—Matthew 28:19; Acts 2:38–22:16; Titus 3:5–6; 1 Peter 3:21.
   The Lord's Supper—Matthew 26:27ff.
2. Jesus's words to Nicodemus, "You must be born again" (John 3:3, 7), are not a command, but a statement of fact and necessity. Regeneration has to happen before anyone will be converted to Christ—and I cannot regenerate myself. God must do it. And he does it when he *effectually* calls the lost sinner. The regeneration of the sinner's hitherto dead soul inevitably and even instantaneously breaks into his consciousness and brings him to a conscious conviction of sin and the need of Christ, and to "repentance toward God and faith in the Lord Jesus Christ" (Acts 20:21).
3. An allusion to the experience of Naaman in 2 Kings 5:10–14.
4. Philip Henry, *Christ All in All* (Swengel, PA: Reiner Publications, 1970 [1691]), p. 154. In the last sentence, Henry adds a note to himself, "allude to Gen.xxi, 19"—a reference to Hagar in her despair in the desert opening her eyes and beholding a well.

Chapter 14: Great High Priest

1. See F. F. Bruce, *The Epistle to the Hebrews* (Grand Rapids: Eerdmans, 1990), p. 119.

2. William Symington, *The Atonement and Intercession of Jesus Christ* (Grand Rapids: Reformation Heritage Books, 2006 [1863]), pp. 256–257.
3. Paul Miller, *A Praying Life* (Colorado Springs: NavPress, 2009), p. 135.

Chapter 15: Hope

1. Ralph Robinson, *Christ All and in All* (Ligonier, PA: Soli Deo Gloria, 1992 [1660]), pp. 480–481.
2. See http://en.wikipedia.org/wiki/Barack_Obama_%22Hope%22_poster (accessed 2.1.14).
3. Robinson, *op. cit.*, p. 482.

Chapter 16: Horn

1. The volume of Rory Mor's horn seems to have been limited to about two pints, no doubt so that erstwhile chiefs are not likely to fail the test and forfeit their inheritance.
2. John Calvin, *Harmony of the Evangelists*, Pringle ed. (Grand Rapids: Baker, 1979), 1:67.
3. Calvin, *Harmony of the Evangelists*, 1:70.
4. The same word in the Hebrew Scriptures (*qeren*) covers what we call horns and antlers. Our English word for the substance that horns and hair are made of (*keratin*) comes from this root.
5. Calvin, *Harmony of the Evangelists*, Pringle ed. (Grand Rapids: Baker), 1:72.
6. Philip Henry, *Christ All and in All* (Swengel, PA: Reiner Publications, 1970 [1690]), p. 247.
7. Calvin, *Harmony of the Evangelists*, Pringle ed. (Grand Rapids: Baker, 1979), 1:73.
8. Calvin, *Harmony of the Evangelists*, p. 74.
9. Calvin, *Harmony of the Evangelists*, p. 74.

Chapter 17: King

1. Cited in C. H. Spurgeon, *The Treasury of David* (Peabody, MA: Hendrickson, 1988), 1:15.

2. For a helpful discussion of the twofold nature of Christ's kingship, see chapter 24 of A. A. Hodge, *Outlines of Theology* (Edinburgh: Banner of Truth, 1972) and William Symington, *Messiah the Prince: The Mediatorial Dominion of Jesus Christ* (Pittsburgh: Crown & Covenant Publications, 2012).

Chapter 18: Lamb

1. Revelation 5:6, 8, 12, 13; 6:1, 16; 7:10, 14, 17; 12:11; 13:8, 11; 14:1, 4 (two times), 10; 15:3; 17:14 (two times); 19:7, 9; 21:14, 22–23; 22:1, 3).
2. Charles Hodge, *A Commentary of I and II Corinthians* (Edinburgh: Banner of Truth, 1988 [1857/59]), p. 88.
3. Philip Henry, *Christ in All* (Swengel, PA: Reiner, nd [1691]), p. 112.

Chapter 19: Life

1. Thomas Brooks, "Christ is the Life of Believers," *The Complete Works of Thomas Brooks* (Edinburgh: James Nichol, 1867), 6:318. A masterly and exhaustive exposition of the doctrine of Colossians 3:4.
2. The standard example of metonymy given in "Bouncer" Stott's English class in my youth was "A fleet of fifty sail," where "sail" denoted a warship in Nelson's navy.
3. John Davenant, *An Exposition of the Epistle of St. Paul to the Colossians* (Edinburgh: Banner of Truth, 2005 [1627/1831]), 2:16.
4. Philip Henry, *Christ in All* (Swengel, PA: Reiner, nd [1691]), p. 99.
5. Henry, *Christ in All*, p. 95.

Chapter 20: Light

1. This is the test of all the confidence we might have that our convictions, views, feelings, hopes, plans, etc. have any validity: "To the law and to the testimony! If they do not speak according to this word, it is because there is no light in them" (Isa. 8:20).
2. Little has changed in the position of Judaism to this day—with the notable exception of "Messianic Judaism," which affirms that Yeshua is the Messiah.
3. John Brown, *Discourses and Sayings of our Lord* (Edinburgh: Banner of Truth, 1967 [1850]), 2:29.

Chapter 21: Lion

1. See the earlier chapter in this book on Christ our Banner from Isaiah 11:10, which also refers to the victorious Messiah saving his people and ruling in glory.
2. Richard Brooks, *The Lamb is all the Glory* (Welwyn: Evangelical Press, 1986), p. 65.
3. It was an arrogation to man of what belongs solely to Christ for the Emperors of Ethiopia to style themselves "Conquering Lion of the tribe of Judah," something that is still aspired to by the current claimant to the vacant throne of the so-called Solomonic Dynasty.
4. C. S. Lewis, in his *Chronicles of Narnia*, clearly models the character of Aslan the lion (Aslan is Turkish for lion) upon Christ. Aslan dies to save another character, Edmund, and rises again to continue his mission.
5. Graeme Goldsworthy, *The Gospel in Revelation* (Exeter: Paternoster Press, 1988), p. 140.
6. Goldsworthy, *The Gospel in Revelation*, p. 140.

Chapter 22: Master of the House

1. The title appears twelve times in the New Testament, each from Jesus's lips, and on at least seven of these occasions our Lord applies the title to himself.
2. See oikodespotēs [οἰκοδεσπότης] in Johannes Louw & Eugene Nida, *Greek-English Lexicon of the New Testament* (Bible Works 7 electronic edition).
3. See Kenneth Bailey, *Jesus Through Middle Eastern Eyes* (Downers' Grove, IL: IVP Academic, 2008), p. 315.
4. This is precisely what Jesus had warned them in the previous chapter:

   > There will be weeping and gnashing of teeth, when you see Abraham and Isaac and Jacob and all the prophets in the kingdom of God, and yourselves thrust out. They will come from the east and the west, from the north and the south, and sit down in the kingdom of God. And indeed there are last who will be first, and there are first who will be last. (Luke 13:28–30)

5. That is why throughout Scripture, dining with God is a picture of an intimate saving relationship with him. See e.g., Exodus 24:9, 11: "Then Moses went up [the mountain]...and seventy of the elders of Israel, and they saw the God of Israel...and they ate and drank." Deuteronomy 12:7: "And there you shall eat before the LORD your God, and you shall rejoice in all to which you have put your hand, you and

your households." The sacrament of the Lord's Supper continues this important theme in the New Testament.

Chapter 23: Peace

1. Tacitus, *Agricola*, p. 30. The author puts these words into the mouth of the Caledonian chieftain, Calgacus, as he addresses his army on the eve of their defeat at the hands of the Romans in the battle of Mons Graupius in the Scottish Highlands in AD 83. The full quotation is *"Auferre trucidare rapere falsis nominibus imperium, atque ubi solitudinem faciunt, pacem appellant."* (To ravage, to slaughter, to usurp under false titles, they call empire; and where they make a desert, they call it peace.)
2. Charles Hodge, *Commentary on the Epistle to the Ephesians* (Old Tappan, NJ: Fleming H. Revell, nd), p. 133.
3. When Jesus says, "Do not think that I came to bring peace on earth. I did not come to bring peace but a sword" (Matt. 10:34), he is referring to the fact that there is bound to be division in response to the "gospel of peace" (Rom. 10:15; Eph. 6:15). The Word of God is "living and powerful, and sharper than any two-edged sword, piercing even to the division of soul and spirit, and of joints and marrow, and is a discerner of the thoughts and intents of the heart" (Heb. 4:12). Christ preaches peace, but many fight against him. "'There is no peace,' says the LORD, 'for the wicked'" (Isa. 48:22).
4. D. Martyn Lloyd-Jones, *God's Way of Reconciliation* (Grand Rapids: Baker, 1972), pp. 245–246.
5. Ezekiel Hopkins, *The Works of Ezekiel Hopkins*, 2:585.

Chapter 24: Physician

1. See Thomas Cahill, *How the Irish Saved Civilization* (New York: Doubleday, 1995), pp. 25ff., for an interesting description of the unfortunate class of the *curiales*.
2. See Alfred Edersheim, *The Life and Times of Jesus the Messiah* (New York: Herrick & Co., 1887), 1:515–525.
3. See *Westminster Shorter Catechism* Question and Answer 31: "Effectual calling is the work of God's Spirit, whereby, convincing us of our sin and misery, enlightening our minds in the knowledge of Christ, and renewing our wills, he doth persuade and enable us to embrace Jesus Christ, freely offered to us in the gospel."
4. See e.g., N. R. Needham, *2000 Years of Christ's Power, Part Two: The Middle Ages* (London: Grace Publications, 2000), p. 328.

5. A placebo is a prescription that contains no medicine, but is given for psychological effect; the patient believes he's receiving treatment when none is actually being administered.

Chapter 25: Prophet

1. Doug Pagitt, cited in Gary Johnson & Ronald Gleason (eds.), *Reforming or Conforming? Post-Conservative Evangelicals and the Emerging Church* (Wheaton: Crossway, 2008), p. 236.
2. John Calvin, *Commentary on the Four Last Books of Moses* (Grand Rapids: Baker, 1999), 1:449.
3. Article in *The Indianapolis Star*, October 8, 2009.
4. The word translated "declared" is *exegeomai.* Jesus has *exegeted* God: i.e., he has explained, showed, and declared him to us.
5. See Keith A. Mathison, *Given for You* (Phillipsburg, NJ: P&R, 2002), p. 7.

Chapter 26: Propitiation

1. Rev. 14:6; 1 John 2:2.

Chapter 27: Rain

1. bbc.co.uk/news/world-us-canada-19187115 (accessed 8.10.12).
2. C. H. Spurgeon comments, "It is the Prayer of David, but the Psalm of Solomon" (*Treasury of David*, Hendriksen, 1988, 2 (i): 226). Andrew Bonar posits that it was composed at the time when David transferred his kingly power to his son (whose name, "Solomon," can be loosely translated, *Prince of Peace*), and as such, he prays for the prosperity of Solomon's kingdom (*Christ and His Church in the Book of Psalms* (Grand Rapids: Kregel, 1978 [1866]), pp. 214–215).
3. The psalm's references to a visit from the monarch of Sheba and the peace that marked his reign in contrast to David's are indicators that the reign of Solomon is within the purview of the psalm's prophetic message.
4. See Henry Ainsworth, *Annotations on the Pentateuch and Psalms* (Ligonier, PA: Soli Deo Gloria, 1991 [1612]), 2:557.
5. "Thrones, principalities, powers, and dominions, angels, however distinguished, were all made by Christ; he is their head, and they are given to Christ by His Father, as He is Mediator, to be His servants in the mediatory office." Thomas Manton,

Works (Birmingham, AL: Solid Ground Christian Books, 2008), 16:221. The seminal work on this doctrine is William Symington's 1881 book, *Messiah the Prince* (Pittsburgh: Crown and Covenant, 2012).

6. George Horne, *A Commentary upon the Psalms* (Audubon, NJ: Old Paths Publications, 1997 [1771]), p. 298.
7. *Westminster Shorter Catechism*, Question and Answer 88.
8. Psalm 63B, *The Books of Psalms for Worship* (Pittsburgh: Crown & Covenant Publications, 2009).
9. Adam Clarke, *Commentary* (New York: Abingdon, nd), 3:446.
10. See en.wikipedia.org/wiki/Eskimo_words_for_snow (accessed 8.11.12).

Chapter 28: Refiner

1. Henry Law, *Christ is All* (Stoke-on-Trent: Tentmaker Publications, 2005 [1855]), p. 578.
2. Matthew Henry, *Commentary*, 4:1490.
3. R. M. McCheyne, *Sermons* (New York: Robert Carter, 1863), p. 263 (Sermon XLV, "The Heart Deceitful" from Jer. 17:9–10).
4. T. V. Moore, *Haggai & Malachi* (London: Banner of Truth, 1960 [1856]), p. 142.
5. John Calvin, *Commentaries*, 15:566.
6. Calvin, *Commentaries*, 15:567
7. Anthony Selvaggio, *The Prophets Speak of Him* (Darlington: Evangelical Press, 2006), p. 179.
8. Some commentators understand the "temple" reference to be wider than Jesus's actual connections with the Jerusalem Temple and apply it to the people of God as a whole—the church as "the temple of God" (1 Cor. 3:16). Over against that it should be noted that Jesus's coming(s) to the Jerusalem Temple involve his perfect keeping of the law and demonstrate that it is indeed "his" temple, in terms of his authority and his Messianic office. The element of Jesus's sudden and unexpected coming to his temple is hardly well served by the notion that he comes to believers as his temple, wherever they are. It is the impact of his public ministry, especially in the Temple, that is so shocking to the church leadership who are determined to do away with him.
9. Charles Simeon, *Expository Outlines on the Whole Bible*, 10:606.
10. Thomas Manton, *Works* (Worthington, PA: Maranatha Publications, 1975), 3:376.

11. Charles Simeon, *Expository Outlines on the Whole Bible*, 10:606.
12. T. V. Moore, *Haggai & Malachi*, p. 151.
13. Henry Law, *Christ is All* (Stoke-on-Trent: Tentmaker Publications, 2005), p. 580.
14. Matthew Henry, *Commentary on the Whole Bible* (Iowa Falls, IA: World Bible Publishers, nd), 4:270.
15. Henry, *Commentary on the Whole Bible*, 4:270.
16. John Calvin, *Commentaries on the Twelve Minor Prophets: Zechariah and Malachi* (in Calvin's *Commentaries*, Grand Rapids: Baker, 1979, vol. 15), p. 573.
17. Laetsch, *Commentary on the Minor Prophets* (St. Louis, MO: Concordia Publishing House, 1956), p. 536.
18. *Idem.*

Chapter 29: Resurrection

1. See *The Life and Sermons of Edward D. Griffin* (Edinburgh: Banner of Truth, 1987), 2:103–104.
2. George Hutcheson, *John* (Edinburgh: Banner of Truth, 1986), p. 227.
3. See *Westminster Shorter Catechism* Question and Answers 8–9, 11.
4. John Owen, *The Death of Death in the Death of Christ* (Edinburgh: Banner of Truth, 1989).

Chapter 30: Righteousness

1. See David Murray, *Jesus on Every Page* (Nashville, TN: Thomas Nelson 2013), p. 47.
2. See John Colquhoun, *Sermons on Important Doctrines* (Orlando, FL: Northampton Press, 2007 [1886]), p. 79.
3. Caroline Glick, writing for *Real Clear Politics*, April 22, 2008, realclearpolitics.com/articles/2008/04/obama_the_savior.html (Accessed 3.12.15).
4. James Ussher, *A Body of Divinity* (Birmingham, AL: Solid Ground Christian Books, 2007 [1645]), p. 174.

Chapter 31: Servant

1. See E. J. Young, *The Book of Isaiah* (Grand Rapids, MI: Eerdmans, 1972), 3:295–296.

2. Isaiah is using two examples from Israel's civil law to illustrate the nation's predicament: divorce and bankruptcy. According to Deuteronomy 24, a divorce had to be formalized in writing, and in the case of bankruptcy, a man's children could even be sold into servitude to pay off his creditors (compare with Neh. 5:1–5).
3. E. W. Hengstenberg, *Christology of the Old Testament* (Edinburgh: T&T Clark, 1861), 2:250.
4. C. H. Spurgeon, *Christ in the Old Testament* (Chattanooga, TN: AMG Publishers, 1994), p. 568.
5. *Westminster Shorter Catechism* Question and Answer 27.
6. The "passion" of Christ and his "passive obedience" are derived from the Latin word *passus* (suffer).
7. Compare with *Westminster Shorter Catechism* Question and Answer 28: "Christ's exaltation consisteth in his rising again from the dead on the third day, in ascending up into heaven, in sitting at the right hand of God the Father, and in coming to judge the world at the last day."

Chapter 32: Shelter

1. Unfortunately, the ESV loses this significant reference to the Passover; the NIV helpfully goes out of its way to punctuate it: "he will 'pass over' it and will rescue it."
2. Yohanan Aharoni (ed.), *The MacMillan Bible Atlas, 3rd Edition* (New York: MacMillan, 1993), p. 118.
3. It may be objected that the Book of Chronicles recounts Hezekiah's reforms as *predating* the Assyrian invasion, "After all that Hezekiah had so faithfully done, Sennacherib king of Assyria came and invaded Judah" (2 Chron. 32:1). However, it is *subsequent* to the unsuccessful Assyrian invasion that we are told,

   > So the Lord saved Hezekiah and the people of Jerusalem from the hand of Sennacherib king of Assyria and from the hand of all others. He took care of them on every side. Many brought offerings to Jerusalem for the Lord and valuable gifts for Hezekiah king of Judah. From then on he was highly regarded by all the nations. (2 Chron. 32:22–23)

4. This is E. J. Young's translation; see his *Isaiah* (Grand Rapids: Eerdmans, 1972), 2:385.
5. See Ralph Robinson, *Christ All and In All* (Ligonier, PA: Soli Deo Gloria, 1992), p. 51, and Albert Barnes, *Notes on Isaiah* (London: Routledge, 1852), 2:162.
6. E. J. Young: "For our part, we are impressed by the fact that the picture of righteous

government herein presented is a result of the great judgment and visitation of punishment described in the preceding chapter" (*Op. cit.*, 2:385).

7. Thomas Boston, *Works* (Wheaton, IL: Richard Owen Roberts, 1980 [1853]), 9:220.
8. Edward D. Griffin, *The Life and Letters of Edward D. Griffin* (Edinburgh: Banner of Truth, 1987), 2:69.
9. See *Westminster Shorter Catechism* Question 91: "How do the sacraments become effectual means of salvation? A: The sacraments become effectual means of salvation, not from any virtue in them, or in him that doth administer them; but only by the blessing of Christ, and the working of his Spirit in them that by faith receive them."

Chapter 34: Strength

1. Later, in Zechariah 12–14, he turns to the burden with reference to Israel, which prophesies concerning his dealings with his people in the age of the Messiah.
2. Philip Henry, *Christ All in All* (Swengel, PA: Reiner Publications, 1976 [1691]), p. 230.
3. Brownlow North, *A Great Gulf Fixed* (Edinburgh: Banner of Truth, 1999 [1869]), p. 106.
4. J. C. Ryle, *Are You Asleep?*, a tract published in Brownlow North, *A Great Gulf Fixed*, pp. 117–125.
5. T. V. Moore, *Zechariah* (Edinburgh: Banner of Truth, 1968 [1856]), p. 161.
6. That is, in the Maccabean revolt and revival of 167 BC, and ultimately in the New Testament promise, as articulated by Paul in Romans 11:26, that "all Israel shall be saved" (where the apostle goes on to cite Isa. 59:20; 27:9).
7. As in the Robert Burns' love song, "O whistle an' I'll come tae ye, my lad."
8. From regeneration ("the washing of regeneration," Titus 3:5), to conversion ("repentance toward God and faith toward the Lord Jesus Christ," Acts 20:21) and subsequent growth in grace ("sanctification by the Spirit," 1 Pet. 1:2).
9. Matthew Henry, *Commentary on the Whole Bible*, 3:388.

Chapter 35: Sun

1. Charles Simeon, *Expository Outlines on the Whole Bible* (Grand Rapids: Baker, 1988 [1847]), 10:626.

Chapter 36: Temple

1. John Martin (1789–1854) specialized in apocalyptic biblical themes. "The Plains of Heaven" is in the Tate Gallery, London, along with his more famous painting of the Last Judgment, "The Great Day of His Wrath."
2. Michael Wilcock, *I Saw Heaven Opened* (Leicester: IVP, 1975), p. 207.
3. See Isaiah 44:28, where God calls the pagan Emperor Cyrus "my shepherd" and uses him to restore the Jewish exiles to Jerusalem.
4. The "oath" is Psalm 110:4, which was given later than the Sinai law: "The LORD has sworn and will not relent, 'You are a priest forever according to the order of Melchizedek.'"
5. *The Book of Psalms for Worship* (Pittsburgh: Crown & Covenant Publications, 2009), 65A [Ps. 65:4].

Chapter 37: Truth

1. The United States' *Declaration of Independence* declares, "We hold these truths to be self-evident, that all men are created equal, that they are endowed by their Creator with certain unalienable Rights, that among these are Life, Liberty and the pursuit of Happiness." In the language of the *Declaration*, the "truths" asserted are presented in abstraction from the Word of the God who is described, also in abstract terms, as the "Creator." What is sidestepped is the inextricably related question as to the objective standard that defines what the truth is and also even who the "Creator" is.

   It is true that the God of the Bible reveals enough of himself in his creation, including our very make-up as his creatures, to leave us without excuse (Rom. 1:20), but this self-evidence is routinely denied by human beings and in any case is entirely insufficient to renew a heart and save a soul. Hence the need for *the* truth as it is in Jesus (Eph. 4:21).
2. The seminal distinction is laid out in Galatians 4:21–31, between "the children of the bondwoman" (Hagar/Ishmael) and the "children of the promise" (Sarah/Isaac) who are "free."
3. It is worth pointing out that our English Bibles frontload the interpretation of John 8:38 by capitalizing Jesus's reference to his father as "My Father." It is true he is speaking of God the Father, but in the context of the conversation the words "my father" and "your father" at that moment could only convey a certain ambiguity as to what fathers he is referring to. It is very doubtful that anyone would have concluded from this utterance that God the Father was in view, even though this is made clear a few sentences later.

The only point that is unmistakable in Jesus's words, as spoken and heard at verse 38, is that he and they do not have the same "father" even if they both can claim to be the children of Abraham. What they appear to have taken from it is that Jesus is saying Abraham is his father, but not theirs—which, of course, is true even if it is not the whole story.

Chapter 38: Vine

1. This is the last of the seven "I am" sayings of Jesus recorded in John's Gospel: Bread (6:35); Light (8:12); Gate (10:9); Good Shepherd (10:11); Resurrection and Life (11:25); Way, Truth, and Life (14:6); Vine (15:1).

2. Bruce Milne, *The Message of John* (Downer's Grove, IL: IVP, 1995), p. 220, suggests (against almost all the commentators) that we should "beware of interpretations of this passage which concentrate solely on our inward relationship with the Lord," and asserts that "its real thrust is the renewal of the mission of Israel through Jesus the Messiah and the disciple community." In other words, Milne views the "fruit" that the disciples are to "bear much" as principally consisting in the "objective and missionary" gathering of new converts and planting of new churches, as distinct from the "fruit of the Spirit" in the subjective life of believers.

   To this it must be said that, while it goes without saying that Jesus is preparing the disciples for their future mission to the world, it seems rather clear that the experiential thrust of the Farewell Discourses (John 14–16) is Jesus's preparation of the disciples for the imminent crisis of his crucifixion and their subsequent scattering. *Their* union with Christ is the great thread that ties Jesus's teaching together and links it to the future outpouring of the Holy Spirit and the glory of God in the gospel.

   Likewise, the application to believers for all time is principally to do with their spiritual fruitfulness in their walk with the Lord and only secondarily and derivatively to the fruitfulness of the church as the appointed evangelizer of the world. Far from needing to "beware" such a perspective, we need to grasp from this passage of Scripture the vital necessity of experiential union with Christ, so that we may indeed have the blessing of fruit, both subjective and objective, as we live in and witness to a lost world.

3. See chapter 11, Christ Our Food.

4. Matthew Henry, *Commentary on the Whole Bible* (Iowa Falls, IA: World Bible Publishers, nd), 5:1123.

5. Herman Ridderbos, *The Gospel of John: A Theological Commentary* (Grand Rapids: Eerdmans, 1997), p. 517.

6. Philip Henry, *Christ All in All* (Swengel, PA: Reiner Publ., 1970 [1691]), p. 26.

7. William Hendriksen, *A Commentary on the Gospel of John* (London: Banner of Truth, 1964), 2:302 (this edition has the two volumes in one).

Chapter 39: Way

1. Philip Henry, *Christ All in All* (Swengel, PA: Reiner Publications, 1970 [1691]), p. 166.
2. Henry, *Christ All in All*, p. 165.
3. Henry, *Christ All in All*, p. 168.

Chapter 40: Word

1. Leon Morris, *The Gospel according to John* (Grand Rapids: Eerdmans, 1971), p. 73.
2. Morris, *The Gospel according to John*, p. 76.
3. Jesus is not "*a* god," as the spurious New World Translation of the Jehovah's Witnesses has it. The Greek text has no article; it reads "and God, was the Word" (*kai theos en ho logos*). The absence of an article—definite or indefinite—with "God," observes W. G. T. Shedd, "converts the word into the abstract, denoting the species 'deity' " (Shedd, *Dogmatic Theology*, 1:315).
4. John Calvin, *Commentary on the Gospel according to John* (Grand Rapids: Baker, 1979), 1:26.
5. Matthew Henry, *A Commentary on the Whole Bible* (Iowa Falls, IA: nd), 6:849.
6. John Murray, *Collected Writings* (Edinburgh: Banner of Truth, 1977), 2:133.
7. Charles Simeon, *Expository Outlines*, 13:204.
8. Octavius Winslow, *The Glory of the Redeemer* (New York, 1868), p. 35.

About the Authors

GORDON J. KEDDIE is the author of many commentaries on Bible books and themes (also translated into seven languages, which include Korean, French, Polish, Russian, Czech, Spanish and German), as well as numerous articles. Born in Edinburgh, Scotland, near the close of World War II, he later studied zoology at the Universities of Aberdeen and Edinburgh (and subsequently taught high school biology for some years). He then prepared to enter the ministry by attending Westminster Theological Seminary in Philadelphia and the Reformed Presbyterian Theological Seminary in Pittsburgh.

Over more than forty years he pastored four Reformed Presbyterian churches: North Hills (western Pennsylvania), Wishaw (Scotland), State College (central Pennsylvania), and Southside Indianapolis (Indiana). He retired from active ministry in 2014. Gordon currently lives in Indianapolis with his wife, Jane. Together they have three adult sons and three beloved grandchildren.

DAVID G. WHITLA is professor of church history and director of the Theological Foundations for Youth program at the Reformed Presbyterian Theological Seminary in Pittsburgh. Born in Scotland and raised in Northern Ireland, he emigrated to the United States in 2000. He taught high school world history and Bible before entering gospel ministry, serving as pastor of the Reformed Presbyterian Church of Southside Indianapolis. He received a history PhD from Queens University Belfast in 2019 and is the author of numerous essays, articles, and reviews, both popular and academic. He is married to June, and they have five children.

Portraits of Christ was typeset in Stempel Garamond LT Std set in 11/14 point. Headers are Seravek. It is printed on 55# natural offset paper by Versa Press, Inc., of East Peoria, IL. Bound in Sierra lilac cloth. Interior layout and design by Shelley Davenport Davis. Cover and interior art by Ryan Davis.